Maida Heatter's
Cookies

Maida Heatter's
Cookies

Illustrations by
Melanie Marder Parks

CADER BOOKS • NEW YORK

**Andrews McMeel
Publishing**

Kansas City

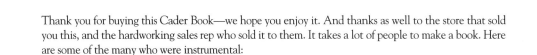

Thank you for buying this Cader Book—we hope you enjoy it. And thanks as well to the store that sold you this, and the hardworking sales rep who sold it to them. It takes a lot of people to make a book. Here are some of the many who were instrumental:

Editorial: Verity Liljedahl, Jake Morrissey, Nora Donaghy, Dorothy O'Brien
Design: Charles Kreloff
Copyediting/Proofing: Nadine Kolowrat, Margaret Madigan
Production: Polly Blair, Carol Coe
Legal: Renee Schwartz, Esq.

If you would like to share any thoughts about this book, or are interested in other books by us, please write to:
Cader Books, 38 E. 29 Street, New York, New York 10016
Or visit our web site: http://www.caderbooks.com

Printed in the United States of America.

Library of Congress Cataloging-in-Publication Data

Heatter, Maida.
    Maida Heatter's cookies / illustrations by Melanie Marder Parks. —1st ed.
       p.   cm.
    Includes index.
    ISBN 0-8362-3733-1
    1. Cookies.   I. Title.
  TX772.H4124 1997
  641.8'654—dc21   97-31043
                                                                                     CIP

October 1997

First Edition

10 9 8 7 6 5 4 3 2 1

ATTENTION: SCHOOLS AND BUSINESSES
Andrews McMeel Publishing books are available at quantity discounts with bulk purchase for educational, business, or sales promotional use. For information, please write to: Special Sales Department, Andrews McMeel Publishing, 4520 Main Street, Kansas City, MO 64111.

Contents

Foreword ix
Bake Cookies! xi

Cookie Basics

Ingredients 2
Equipment 5
Techniques 11

Chocolate Drop Cookies

Chocolate Whoppers 16
Marjorie Kinnan Rawlings's
    Chocolate Cookies 17
Chocolate Hermits 19
Big Sur Chocolate-Chip Cookies . . . 20
Savannah Chocolate Chewies 22
Chocolate Gingersnaps 23
David's Cookies 24
Extra-Bittersweet Chocolate Chunk
    Monster Cookies. 26
Brownie Cookies 27
Cookie Kisses. 28
Chocolate Peanut Butter Cookies . . 30
Candy Cookies 31
Chocolate Miracles 32
Chocolate-Chip Chocolate Oatmeal
    Cookies. 33
Down East Chocolate Cookies 35
Chocolate Fudge-Candy Cookies . . . 36
Chocolate Chocolate-Chip Cookies 37
Santa Fe Chocolate Wafers 38
"Chocolate Street" Cookies 39
Big Old-Fashioned Chocolate
    Cookies. 40
Key West Chocolate Treasures 41

Chocolate Banana Cookies. 42
Chocolate Applesaucers 43
Coconut Grove Cookies 44
Chocolate Raisin Cookies 46
Chocolate and Peanut-Butter
    Ripples 47
Chocolate Peanut Cookies 48

More Drop Cookies

Mrs. L.B.J.'s Moonrocks. 52
Old-Fashioned Spiced Pecan
    Cookies 53
Giant Oatmeal Spice Cookies. 54
Crisp Oatmeal Wafers 55
Coconut Oatmeal Cookies 56
Raisin-Nut Cookies 57
Tea Cakes. 58
My Mother's Gingersnaps 60
100-Percent Whole-Wheat Ginger
    Cookies 61
Granny's Old-Fashioned
    Sugar Cookies. 63
Half-Moon-Shaped Cookies 65
Savannah Crisps 65

Sycamore Cookies 67
Raisin Pillows 68
Whole-Wheat and Honey Hermits . . 70
Connecticut Nutmeg Hermits 71
Giant Ginger Cookies 71
Mountain-Honey Gingersnaps 73
Sour-Cream Ginger Cookies 74
Sunflower Coconut Cookies 75
Date-Nut Wafers 76
Praline Wafers 77
Lemon Walnut Wafers 78
Old-Fashioned Jumbo
    Lemon Wafers 79
Toasted Pine-Nut Cookies 80
Route 7 Raisin-Nut Cookies 81
The Farmer's Wife's Pecan Cookies . . 81
Nut-Tree Walnut Jumbles 82
24-Karat Cookies 83
Indian Figlets 84
Hawaiian Pineapple Cookies 85
Pumpkin Rocks 86
Date-Nut Rocks 87
Banana Rocks 88
Blind Date Cookies 89
Norman Rockwell's
    Oatmeal Wafers 90
Oatmeal Snickerdoodles 91
Oatmeal Molasses Cookies 92
Raisin Oatmeal Cookies 93
German Oatmeal Cookies 94
Poppy-Seed Wafers
    (Mohn Cookies) 95
Tijuana Fiesta Cookies 96
Butterscotch Molasses Cookies 97
Vanilla Butter Wafers 98

Bar Cookies

Pecan Squares Americana 100
Fig Bars 102
Lebkuchen 104
Anise Seed Cookies 106
Pennsylvania Squares 107
Charleston Cheesecake Bars 109
California Fruit Bars 110
World War II Raisin Squares 112
Sour Lemon Squares 113
Johnny Appleseed Squares 115
Palm Beach Brownies 116
Christmas Brownies 118
Petites Trianons 119
All-American Brownies 120
Denver Brownies 121
Greenwich Village Brownies 123
Cream-Cheese Brownies 124
Fudge Brownies 125
Chocolate Mint Sticks 126
Dutch Chocolate Bars 128
Supremes 129
Viennese Chocolate-
    Walnut Bars 130
Dark Rocky Roads 132
Light Rocky Roads 134
Butterscotch Brownies 135
Florida Cream-Cheese Squares 136
Florida Lemon Squares 137
Palm Beach Pineapple Squares 138
Christmas Fruitcake Bars 139
Hermit Bars 140
Brittle Peanut Bars 141
Hungarian Walnut Bars 142
Butterscotch Walnut Bars 144
Cinnamon Almond Cookies 145
Georgia Pecan Bars 147
Pecan Festival Bars 148
Pecan Chews 149
Texas Cowboy Bars 150
Aspen Oatmeal Bars 151
Honey Date-Nut Bars 152
Aspen Date-Nut Fingers 153

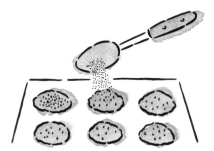

Viennese Linzer Cookies 154
Polish Wedding Cakes. 155
Viennese Marzipan Bars 157

Icebox Cookies

Peanut Butter Icebox Cookies. 160
8-Layer Cookies. 161
New Mexican Chocolate
    Icebox Cooies 163
Black-and-White Coconut Slices . . 164
Wienerstube Cookies. 166
Maxines 167
Cobblestones 168
Neapolitans 170
Fruitcake Icebox Cookies 172
Butterscotch Thins 173
Pecan Butterscotch
    Icebox Cookies 174
Oatmeal Icebox Cookies 175
Peanut-Butter Pillows 176
Whole-Wheat Peanut-Butter
    Cookies 177
Icebox Nut Cookies. 178
Sesame Fingers. 179
Caraway Crisps 180
Almond Spicebox Cookies 181
Anise Icebox Cookies 182
Cardamom Cookies from
    Copenhagen 183
Pinwheels. 184

Rolled Cookies

Rugelach (Walnut Horns) 188
Joe Froggers 189
Coconut Cookies. 191
Almond Sugar Cookies 192
Les Petites 194
Swedish Rye Wafers. 195

Whole-Wheat Squares 196
Whole-Wheat Honey Wafers 198
Wild-Honey and Ginger Cookies . . 199
Honey Graham Crackers. 200
Swedish Honey Cookies 201
Swedish Ginger Cookies 202
Viennese Almond Wafers 205
Ischler Cookies 206
Viennese Chocolate Cookies 208
Tropical Sour-Cream Cookies 209
Caraway Sour-Cream Cookies. 210
Rum-Raisin Shortbread. 212
Hot Butter Wafers 213
Caraway Hardtack 214
Arrowroot Wafers from Bermuda . . 215
Uppåkra Cookies. 216
Ginger Shortbread Cookies. 217
Dione Lucas's Sablés 218
Cornell Sugar Cookies. 220
Plain Old-Fashioned
    Sugar Cookies 221
Chocolate-Chip Pillows 222
Prune Pillows. 223
Hamantaschen. 224
Danish Coffeehouse Slices 226
Big Newtons 228

Hand-Formed Cookies

Kansas Cookies 232
Bow Ties 234
Fudge Mallows 235
Chocolate Pepper Pretzels 237
Chocolate Aggies. 239
Chocolate Oatmeal Crispies 240
Chocolate and Peanut-Butter
    Crecents 241
Señoritas 242
Carrot and Honey Oatmeal
    Cookies 243
Whole-Wheat Cinnamon-Nutmeg
    Cookies. 245

French Filbert Macaroons 246
Danish Butter Sandwiches 248
Coconut Washboards 249
Coconut Pennies 251
Cracker-Barrel Raisin Cookies 252
Austrian Walnut Crescents 253
Sour Cream and Pecan Dreams 254
Charlie Brown's Peanut Cookies . . . 255
English Gingersnaps #1 257
English Gingersnaps #2 258
Italian Sesame Sticks 258

And More

Craig Claiborne's Chocolate
     Macaroons 262
Almond Macaroons 263
Fudge Délices 264
Chocolate Meringue Ladyfingers . . 266
Chocolate Tartlets 267
Almond Tartlets 269
Connecticut Date Slices 270
Connecticut Strippers 272

French Sugar Fans 273
Swedish Fried Twists 274
Basler Brunsli 276
Hazelnut Rusks 277
Black-and-White Rusks 279
Macadamia and Milk Chocolate
     Biscotti 280

Crackers and Extras

Corn Melba 284
Ralph's Corn Melba 286
Cheese Pennies 287
Swedish Hardtack 288
Knäckbröd 290
Black Pepper Crackers 291
Marshmallows 293
Everybody's Favorite Fudge 294
Fantastic Vanilla Ice Cream 296
Devil's Food Chocolate Sauce 297

Index 298
Metric Conversion Table 307

Foreword

Maida Heatter is the fairy godmother of anything sweet, spicy, crunchy, chewy, or fluffy that you could possibly imagine baking. In Greek mythology, Maida, with her elegant halo of silver hair, would have been known as the goddess Alphito, the symbol of flour and lady guardian of the mill. In any culture her art form is pure ambrosia. She is irrefutably an American culinary icon. Most importantly for us (and for anyone who has had the immense pleasure of knowing her and being the recipient of her tasty offerings), she is a delicious and terrific friend.

Now, Maida is not a cream puff. No, she could be more likened to one of her intriguing cookies: a crisp ginger snap seasoned with pepper and mustard, offering a complexity of textures and flavors in a single meaningful bite. Maida will always tell you forthrightly what's on her mind—that is, if she likes you enough. If not, she won't waste her time. She'd rather be baking!

We first met Maida in 1979, when she agreed to teach a class at Ma Cuisine, the cooking school affiliated with Ma Maison, in Los Angeles. Judy Gethers, the school director, was willing to provide all the tools, but Maida drove from Miami to L.A. with every baking utensil she could possibly need packed into the trunk of her car. Measuring cups, spoons, cake rings, spatulas, and sifters appeared—even her own Sunbeam mixer! It became immediately clear that she was a perfectionist. What we were about to find out was that she was also a real trouper. It was summer—a very hot summer—and the facility was a small cramped room with 60 students, a hot oven, and no air conditioning. Maida measured flour and sugar, melted chocolate, and mixed and arranged everything meticulously. The chocolate started to melt when it should have been setting up—the students began to melt as well. We brought in a large portable fan, turned it on and whoosh . . . chocolate, sugar, flour flew everywhere—including on Maida. She simply began again. When the desserts were completed they were absolutely perfect and absolutely scrumptious. Maida never flinched and was always prepared—a veritable "Girl Scout of baking." She didn't have time to complain—because she'd rather be baking!

There have been many unforgettable moments with Maida, many involving food! Her cloudlike chocolate soufflés presented as breakfast in bed. A birthday party where Maida arrived with her gargantuan suitcase filled with hundreds upon hundreds of cookies individually wrapped in her precise signature style: almond chocolate biscotti, intricate black-and-white checkerboard cookies, rich chocolate brownies, gingersnaps, chocolate crescent-shaped cookies with hidden peanut butter fillings—guests were actually hoarding them and taking them home in their pockets and purses. And then, of course, there was the time we went to cook at the 1983 Economic Summit in Williamsburg, Virginia, for all of the heads of state. The highlight was when Maida found out that the Secret Service men had dropped all of her key lime pies.

Maida often says she could not imagine a life of greater well being than baking. It gives the morning purpose and joyous reason and provides happiness to so many other people as well. Who else can seduce a cadre of body-conscious trainers in the gym where she works out—of course, what they're lusting for are her extraordinary brownies. She has presidents, CEOs, magazine and book editors desperately fantasizing over their next care package of cookies. Not only is she well loved for her exuberant approach to life, she is deeply admired by the countless legions of bakers such as Nancy Silverton and Mary Bergin, who themselves have gone on to touch others' lives by spreading Maida's pastry gospel.

Maida is a symbol and conduit of creativity and precision. Her vast talent envelopes both the traditional and the uninhibited experimentation. She is the grande dame of an art form that truly satisfies all of our senses. She is forever motivated, stimulated, and exhilarated with the process of discovery, creation, and execution. It is a testimony to her indefatigable spirit and her dedication to her craft that she not only "keeps on truckin' on" but "keeps on bakin' on" as well. For, with rare exception, she'd rather be baking. Unless of course there's a wonderfully aromatic and beautifully prepared culinary creation in front of her—then unquestionably, she'd rather be eating!

WOLFGANG PUCK AND BARBARA LAZAROFF

Bake Cookies!

A few days ago I heard a doctor talking on television about the dangers of stress. It can kill you. It can cause a heart attack or a stroke. The doctor listed ways of coping with stress. Exercise. Diet. Yoga. Take a walk. I yelled, "Bake cookies." I often talk to the television. I yelled it again and again. The doctor went on with his list of 12 ways to reduce stress . . . and he never once mentioned my sure-fire treatment.

Baking cookies is a great escape. It's fun. It's happiness. It's creative. It's good for your health. It reduces stress.

If you are reading this book, chances are you know what I mean. You have probably baked cookies. You could probably tell me a thing or two about what fun it is. But if you have not baked cookies, then let me tell you. Bake cookies! Happiness is baking cookies.

Maida Heatter

The recipes in this book
were originally published in
Maida Heatter's Book of Great Cookies (1977)
and
Maida Heatter's New Book of Great Desserts (1982)
and
Maida Heatter's Book of Great American Desserts (1985).

Cookie Basics

Ingredients

Butter

Use sweet, unsalted butter.

Coffee as a Flavoring

Often people ask about the instruction "use powdered, not granular, coffee." If a recipe specifies powdered, it is because the granular would stay in granules and would not dissolve. Spice Islands brand, generally available in specialty food stores, makes powdered instant espresso and also a powdered instant coffee. And Medaglia D'Oro instant espresso, which is powdered, is generally available in Italian grocery stores.

Eggs

SIZE
Unless the recipe specifies otherwise, use eggs graded "large."

TO OPEN EGGS
If directions call for adding whole eggs one at a time, they may all be opened ahead of time into one container and then poured into the other ingredients approximately one at a time. Do not open eggs directly into the other ingredients—you would not know if a piece of shell had been included.

TO SEPARATE EGGS
Eggs separate more safely—there is less chance of the yolk breaking—when they are cold. Therefore, if a recipe calls for separated eggs, it is usually the first thing I do when organizing the ingredients so they are cold from the refrigerator.

    The safest way to separate eggs is as follows: Place three small cups or bowls in front of you (or use shallow drinking glasses; glasses generally have a sharper edge and therefore crack the shell more cleanly). One container is for the whites and one for the yolks. The third might not be needed, but if you should break the yolk when opening an egg, just drop the whole thing in the third bowl and save it for some other use.

    Tap the side of the egg firmly (but not too hard or you might break the yolk) on the edge of the bowl or glass to crack the shell, with luck, in a rather straight, even

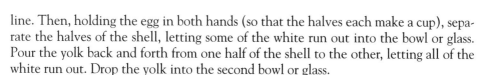

line. Then, holding the egg in both hands (so that the halves each make a cup), separate the halves of the shell, letting some of the white run out into the bowl or glass. Pour the yolk back and forth from one half of the shell to the other, letting all of the white run out. Drop the yolk into the second bowl or glass.

Many professional cooks simply open the egg into the palm of one hand, then hold their fingers, slightly separated, over a bowl. They let the white run through their open fingers and then slide the left-behind yolk into the second bowl.

As each egg is separated, the white should be transferred to another container (that is, in addition to the three—it could be another bowl or glass or it might be the mixing bowl you will beat them in), because if you place all of the whites in one container there is a chance that the last egg white might have some yolk in it, which could spoil all of the whites. Generally, a tiny bit of yolk or shell can be removed from the whites with an empty half shell. Or try a piece of paper towel dipped in cold water.

Flavorings

Naturally, for better flavor buy those labeled "pure extract" instead of "imitation." And make sure that the tops are always tightly closed. Flavorings contain both alcohol and water—the alcohol evaporates rapidly and then of course the water follows, taking some of the essential oils along with it.

Flour

Most of these recipes call for all-purpose flour. It may be either bleached or unbleached. Do not substitute cake flour. However, if you must, use 1 cup plus 2 tablespoons of cake flour for every 1 cup of all-purpose flour that is called for.

Fruit

Dried currants, raisins, dates, and figs must be soft and fresh; baking will not soften them. Currants and raisins may be softened by boiling in water for a few minutes; drain them in a strainer and dry between layers of paper towels.

All of the candied fruits called for in this book are available (in large pieces—the way I like them) from A. L. Bazzini, (800) 228-0172.

Nuts

Nuts can turn rancid rather quickly—walnuts and pecans more so than almonds. Always store all nuts airtight in the freezer or refrigerator. In the refrigerator nuts will last well for 9 months; in the freezer at 0° they will last for 2 years. Bring them to room temperature before using; smell and taste them before you use them (preferably as soon as you buy them)—you will know quickly if they are rancid. If you even suspect that they might be, do not use them; they would ruin a recipe.

In most of the recipes that call for pecans, walnuts can be successfully substituted. However, if the recipe calls for that special pecan taste—as in Praline Wafers (page 77) or the various pecan bars (see Bar Cookies, pages 99 to 158)—it is best to use pecans.

To Toast Pecans

Pecans occasionally become limp after they are frozen, so I toast them. Toasted pecans are so great that now I toast all pecans (those that have been frozen and those that have not) before using them, as follows. Place them in a shallow pan in the middle of a preheated 350° oven for 12 to 15 minutes, stirring them occasionally, until they are very hot but not until they become darker in color.

Oatmeal

All cookie recipes that call for oatmeal mean uncooked. There are many varieties of oatmeal (oats) and they give different qualities to the cookies. Instant oatmeal should not be used in cookies; it is too fine, too absorbent, and does not give any of the crunchy quality you want. Oatmeal that cooks in 1 minute is passable but the kind that takes 3 to 5 minutes to cook is better. There are also rolled oats with cooking directions that call for a few minutes of boiling and then leaving them covered to stand for 12 to 15 minutes. These are fine for cookies; they will remain very crunchy. But, since they are less absorbent than the quicker-cooking ones, drop cookies made with them will spread out more in baking. Steel-cut oats (cooking directions are generally to simmer for 20 to 25 minutes) may be used for cookies, but the oats will remain rather hard and will give an even crunchier texture.

Sugar

All sugars should be measured in the graded measuring cups that are made for measuring dry ingredients. Brown sugar and confectioners sugar should be strained. Hard lumps in brown sugar will not disappear in mixing or baking. (For how to strain sugar, see page 12.)

Brown Sugars

Most brown sugars are made of white granulated sugar to which a dark syrup has been added. Dark brown sugar has a mild molasses, and light brown sugar has a milder, lighter syrup (which may also be molasses). Dark brown has a slightly stronger flavor, but they may be used interchangeably. The label on Grandma's Molasses says, "You can easily make your own brown sugar as you need it by blending together ½ cup of granulated sugar with 2 tablespoons of unsulphured molasses. The yield is equivalent to ½ cup of brown sugar."

Brown sugar is moist; if it dries out it will harden. It should be stored airtight at room temperature. If it has small lumps in it, they should be strained out. With your fingertips press the sugar through a large strainer set over a large bowl. The Savannah Sugar Refinery is now printing the following directions on their boxes of brown sugar: "If your brown sugar has been left open and becomes hard, place a dampened (not wet) paper towel inside the resealable poly bag and close the package tightly for 12 hours or more. A slice of apple can be used in place of the dampened towel or you can process it in a food processor."

CONFECTIONERS SUGAR

Confectioners sugar and powdered sugar are exactly the same. They are both granulated sugar that has been pulverized very fine and has had about 3 percent cornstarch added to keep it in a powdery condition. Of these, 4-x is the least fine and 10-x is the finest. They may be used interchangeably. Confectioners sugar should be strained; you can do several pounds at a time if you wish. (It does not have to be done immediately before using as flour does.) Store it airtight.

CRYSTAL SUGAR

Crystal sugar, also called pearl sugar, or *hagelsucker* in German, is generally used to sprinkle over certain European cookies and pastries before baking. It is coarser than granulated sugar and is very attractive on certain cookies. It can be bought from Sweet Celebrations (formerly Maid of Scandinavia) in Minneapolis, MN, (800) 480-2505. It comes in 1-pound bags and is labeled "Medium Grain."

Equipment

Cellophane

I like to wrap bar cookies in clear cellophane (as you will see in reading the recipes). It keeps them fresh, easy to handle, and adds an attractive, professional look. It's also the best way to pack for the freezer, lunch box, or picnic basket—quick and easy to slip a few of them into a little bag or a basket as a gift.

But clear cellophane is hard to find. It is available from Party Bazaar in Yonkers, NY, (914) 965-1465. It comes in a box with a cutter edge, and is 20 inches wide and 100 feet long.

It is easier to cut cellophane with a knife than with scissors. Cut off a long piece, fold it in half, cut through the fold with a long knife, fold again and cut again, and continue to fold and cut until you have the right-size pieces. Wrap one cookie as a sample to be sure. If the size is close but a bit too large in one direction, do not cut the pieces individually (it takes too long). Instead, place the whole pile in front of you, fold one side of the entire pile to the size you want, and hold the folded portion with one hand while, with the other hand, you cut through the fold with the knife.

Then, if you have room, spread out as many pieces of cellophane as you will need, or as you have room for. Place a cookie in the center of each piece of cellophane (1). Bring the two long sides together up over the top (2). Fold over twice so that the second fold brings the cellophane tight against the cookie (3, 4). Now, instead of just tucking the ends underneath, fold in the corners of each end, making triangular points (5), and then fold the triangles down under the cookie (6).

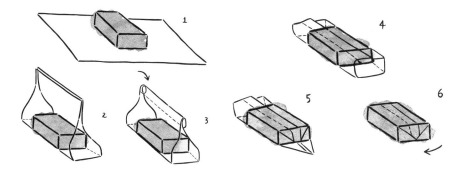

Cookie Cutters

Obviously it is not necessary to use exactly the same size or shape cutter that the recipe calls for; that is just a guide. Cutters should be sharp with no rough edges. If the cutter sticks to the dough, dip it into flour. Always start cutting at the edge of the dough and work toward the center, cutting the cookies as close to each other as possible.

Cookie Sheets

A cookie sheet should be flat, with only one raised side (that's for handling the sheet). The other three sides should not have a raised edge. Shiny, bright aluminum sheets are best. Cookie sheets should be at least 2 inches narrower and shorter than the oven so the heat will circulate around them and the cookies will bake evenly. Generally 12 x 15½ inches is the most practical size.

Cooling Racks

You should have several cooling racks. Almost all cookies should be removed from the cookie sheet immediately after baking (unless the recipe specifies otherwise) and cooled with air circulating around them. Many racks are not raised enough for air to circulate underneath, which causes the bottoms of the cookies to be damp or soggy instead of dry and crisp (there should be ½ inch for thin, crisp wafers; 2 inches for large cookies). To raise the racks (especially if the cookies are large and/or thick), simply place the rack on a right-side-up cake pan or bowl.

Double Boiler

A double boiler is important, especially for melting chocolate, which should never come into direct contact with high heat or it will burn. (For melting chocolate with no other ingredients, make absolutely sure that the top of the double boiler is bone dry.) The thing to look for is one in which the upper section is not too deep (shallow is better) and is smooth (no ridges). I like Revere Ware; it comes in two sizes, and I use both. If necessary, you can create your own double boiler by placing a heatproof bowl over a saucepan of shallow hot water. The bowl should be wide enough at the top so its rim rests on the rim of the saucepan, keeping the bowl suspended over (not touching) the water.

Electric Mixer

An electric mixer is a time and labor saver, but almost all cookies may be made by creaming (or beating until soft) the butter in a bowl using a wooden spoon or rubber spatula, and then stirring in the remaining ingredients. I use an electric mixer on a stand, the type that comes with two different-size bowls. But I have made many cookies for which I creamed the butter with my bare hands and then, with my hands, worked in the remaining ingredients.

Flour Sifter

With very few exceptions these recipes call for sifted flour. This means that you should sift it immediately before measuring it, even if the flour label says presifted. (If the flour is not sifted, or if it is sifted a long time before it is to be used, it packs down and 1 cup is liable to contain a few more spoonfuls than 1 cup of flour sifted immediately before measuring.)

Sift the flour onto a piece of wax paper. Make sure that there is no flour left in the sifter, and transfer the sifter to another piece of wax paper. Measure the amount you need of the sifted flour, place it in the sifter, add any other ingredients it is to be sifted together with, and sift onto the second piece of wax paper. Again, make sure that there is nothing left in the sifter.

If you don't have a sifter, flour can be sifted through a fine-mesh strainer.

Grater

A few of these recipes call for grated lemon or orange rind. It is best to grate the fruit on a grater that has different-size and -shape openings. Use the side that has small, round openings, rather than the diamond-shaped ones. And do not grate deeply. What you want is only the thinnest outer layer—the white part of the rind is bitter.

Measuring Cups

Glass or plastic measuring cups with the measurements marked on the sides and the 1-cup line below the top are only for measuring liquids. With the cup at eye level, fill carefully to measure exactly the amount needed.

To measure dry ingredients, use the metal cups that come in sets of four: ¼ cup, ⅓ cup, ½ cup, and 1 cup. Fill to overflowing (if you are measuring flour do not pack it down) and then scrape off the extra with a metal spatula, a dough scraper, or the straight edge of a knife.

Measuring Spoons

Standard measuring spoons must be used for correct measurements. They come in sets of four: ¼ teaspoon, ½ teaspoon, 1 teaspoon, and 1 tablespoon. When measuring dry ingredients, fill the spoon to overflowing and then scrape off the excess with a small metal spatula or the straight edge of a knife.

Nut Grinder

When recipes call for ground nuts, that means they must be ground to a fine powder. A food processor or a blender does a good job but be careful that you do not overdo it and make nut butter. A nut grinder gives excellent results. I recommend the kind that screws onto the side of a table. The nuts go into the top and come out through the side when the handle is turned. They come in three sizes; I recommend the medium size.

Nutmeg Grater

Nutmeg is sold either ground (grated) or whole. Like peppercorns, it has better flavor if it is freshly grated. Nutmeg graters are available in specialty kitchen-equipment stores. Or you may use a regular four-sided grater. Use the smallest holes, either the round ones or the diamond-shaped; try both and see which you like best. Whole nutmegs are generally available in small jars in the spice section of food markets.

Pastry Bag

A few of these cookies are shaped with a pastry bag. The best ones are made of soft canvas and are coated on the inside only with plastic. The small opening generally has to be cut a bit larger to allow a metal tube to fit into the bag. It is easier to work with a bag that is too large rather than one that is too small.

And it is easier to work with a pastry bag if you work on something at table height instead of at kitchen-counter height. The table is lower, so you have better control of your work.

After using, the bag should be washed thoroughly in hot soapy water, rinsed well, and hung up or spread out on a towel to dry.

Pastry Brush

Use a good one or the bristles will come out while you are using it. Sometimes I use a good-quality artist's watercolor brush in a large size; it is softer and does a very good job.

Pastry Cloth

A pastry cloth is most important for preventing cookie dough from sticking when you roll it out. Buy the largest and heaviest cloth you can find. Always wash it after using. The butter in the dough soaks into the cloth and unless it is kept very clean it will smell rancid. It may be ironed or not. I've tried it both ways and it worked the same.

Rolling Pin

A long, narrow heavy rolling pin is better than one that is short, small, and lightweight, because the extra length and weight give better and faster results. A French-type rolling pin, long and thin with tapered ends and no handles, works very well for cookies. Whichever you use, roll the dough evenly, being especially careful not to make it thinner on the edges.

Use a ruler for measuring the thickness of the rolled dough.

Rubber Spatulas

Rubber spatulas are almost indispensable (I prefer rubber to plastic). They are especially useful for scraping the bowl of an electric mixer while adding ingredients in order to keep everything well mixed. And for scraping all of the dough out of the bowl. And for folding, stirring, mixing, etc. I suggest that you have several. They are made in three sizes; medium is the one that you will have the most use for.

Ruler

If you are baking a variety of cookies, a ruler is an essential kitchen tool. Not only for measuring the thickness of rolled dough and the thickness of icebox cookie slices (place the ruler on top of the bar or roll of cookies, make small scoring lines with the top of a knife, then remove the ruler and cut the cookies), but for measuring the diameter of cookie cutters, the size of cake pans, and especially for marking bar cookies in order to cut them evenly (measure with the ruler and mark by inserting a toothpick).

Stockinette Cover for a Rolling Pin

These are often sold with pastry cloths. You might like them or you might prefer to work without them. Often they are too small. But try one and decide.

Thermometers

One of the most important and often most overlooked requirements for good results in baking is correct oven temperature. The wrong temperature can cause a cake to fall; it can ruin a soufflé; and it can turn cookies that should be wonderfully crisp into pale, limp, soggy messes.

No matter how new or how good your oven is, *please* double-check the temperature every time you bake. Use a small, portable oven thermometer from the hardware store or kitchen shop. Buy the mercury kind—it is best. Turn on your oven at least 20 minutes ahead of time and place the thermometer in the middle of the oven. Give the oven plenty of time to heat and cycle and reheat before you read the thermometer; read it (and all thermometers) at eye level. If it does not register the heat you want, adjust the thermostat up or down until the mercury thermometer registers the correct heat—no matter what the oven setting says.

When you put unbaked cookies in the oven they reduce the oven temperature more than you would expect. If you check the temperature on a portable oven thermometer during about the first 10 minutes of baking don't think that your oven suddenly got sick; give it time to reheat.

CANDY THERMOMETER

For some of the recipes in this book you will need a thermometer labeled a "candy-jelly-frosting thermometer." This thermometer clips on to the side of a saucepan; bend down and read it at eye level in order to get a correct reading. And make sure the stem is deep enough in the liquid being cooked to give an accurate reading.

Techniques

Chopping and Cutting Nuts

All of the recipes that call for chopped, cut, or broken nuts specify a size: "Coarsely cut," "finely cut," or "cut into medium-size pieces." In most cases the size does not have to be exact and it may be a matter of your own taste.

However, "coarsely cut" means that each half of a walnut or pecan, or each whole almond, should be cut into two or three pieces depending on the size of the nuts. "Finely cut" does not mean ground or powdered—it means small pieces about the size of dried split peas or currants. "Medium" is somewhere between coarse and fine, or about the size of raisins.

For medium or finely cut nuts, I place them on a chopping board and cut them all together with a long, heavy chef's knife. For coarse, I either break them, one at a time, with my fingers, or I cut them, one at a time, with a small paring knife.

TO GRIND NUTS IN A FOOD PROCESSOR

Add about ¼ cup (or more) of the sugar or flour called for in the recipe; that will prevent the nuts from becoming oily. And process for 50 to 60 seconds even though you will think it is done sooner—the finer the nuts are, the better.

About Measuring

Meticulously precise measurements are essential for good results in baking.

Glass or plastic measuring cups with the measurements marked on the side and the 1-cup line below the top are only for measuring liquids. Do not use them for flour or sugar. With the cup at eye level fill carefully to exactly the line indicated.

Measuring cups that come in graded sets of four (¼ cup, ⅓ cup, ½ cup, and 1 cup) are for measuring flour, sugar, and other dry ingredients—and for thick sour cream. Fill the cup to overflowing and then scrape off the excess with a dough scraper, a metal spatula, or the flat side of a knife.

Standard measuring spoons must be used for correct measurements. They come in sets of four: ¼ teaspoon, ½ teaspoon, 1 teaspoon, and 1 tablespoon. For dry ingredients, fill the spoon to overflowing and then scrape off the excess with a small metal spatula or the flat side of a knife.

How to Prepare a Pastry Cloth and/or a Stockinette Cover

Spread out the cloth, and slide the cover on the rolling pin. Then sprinkle flour generously over the cloth and the stockinette cover and, with your hand, rub it into the cloth and the cover very thoroughly. The fabric should hold as much flour as you can rub into it and there should be as little excess as possible. Keep additional flour handy for reflouring as necessary.

If you do not use the stockinette cover, just rub flour onto the rolling pin as necessary.

Straining Sugar

BROWN SUGAR
Most of the recipes that call for brown sugar specify that it should be strained. The only reason for straining it is to get rid of any hard lumps in the sugar. It is difficult (almost impossible) to force it through a fine strainer—use a coarse strainer (the larger the better) placed over a large bowl. Place the sugar in the strainer and, with your fingertips, press the sugar through the strainer.

I strain several pounds at a time and it seems to last forever. I mean it does not get lumpy again no matter how long I keep it.

As for measuring the sugar, straining does not affect the measurement (as it does flour), since the sugar should always be pressed firmly (with your fingertips) into the measuring cup. And, of course, the cup should not be a glass cup meant for measuring liquids—it should be a metal cup, the same as you would use for flour.

After pressing the sugar into the cup, use your fingers to wipe off any excess sugar over the top of the cup and make a level measure. If the sugar has gotten really rock hard you can pulverize it back into usable condition in a food processor.

CONFECTIONERS SUGAR
Confectioners sugar is strained for two purposes: For eliminating lumps and for accuracy of measurement; it packs down on standing and the amount of sugar in a measuring cup will vary if the sugar has or has not been strained. But it is not necessary to

strain confectioners sugar immediately before measuring as you do flour.

When using confectioners sugar for an icing or a glaze, the lumps might not show at first—however, when the sugar is mixed with a liquid, the resulting frosting will not be as smooth as if the sugar had been strained. Therefore, if you do much cooking, I suggest that you strain a pound (or several) at a time. This also does not seem to get lumpy again if it stands after being strained.

When measuring confectioners sugar, use the same metal cups as you use for measuring flour. Fill the cup lightly as though you were measuring flour—do not pack confectioners sugar firmly into the cup as you do brown sugar—and then cut excess sugar off the top of the cup.

If you plan to strain both brown sugar and confectioners sugar, do the confectioners first—then it will not be necessary to wash the strainer before doing the brown.

Timing

It is important to time cookies carefully. Set a timer for a few minutes less than the recipe specifies, and check the cookies to be sure you aren't overbaking them.

When directions say to reverse the position of cookie sheets during baking, wait until the baking is at least half or three-quarters finished. Then work quickly—do not keep the oven door open any longer than necessary.

When you bake only one sheet at a time instead of two, cookies bake in a little less time.

About Storing Cookies

With few exceptions these cookies are best when fresh. Even the ones that will last for weeks are best when fresh. So, unless I know that there will be people around to eat them, I freeze almost all cookies in plastic freezer boxes (after reserving at least a few for unexpected company and for my husband's usual daily cookie party). And even in the freezer they do not stay fresh forever—a few weeks, a month or two, but after that they lose their extra-special goodness. Although most charts say that cookies may be frozen for up to 12 months, as far as I'm concerned that only means that they will not spoil. I don't believe that they taste as good after many months in the freezer. (Thaw frozen cookies before removing them from their containers or they might sweat and become soggy or wet. Usually an hour or so at room temperature will do it, but it depends on the size of the container.)

For short-time storage at room temperature, do not mix soft cookies with crisp cookies in the same container or the crisp ones will soon become soft.

To add moisture to soft cookies that have begun to dry out (or that you might have baked too long), place half an apple, skin side down, or a whole lemon or orange, depending on the flavor you want, on top of the cookies in an airtight container (you may use a plastic bag). Let stand for a day or two and then remove the fruit.

A Final Word

But I'm putting the cart before the horse. Enough of what to do with the cookies once they're baked. Before baking, check on your equipment and ingredients, then go to it.

Chocolate Drop Cookies

Chocolate Whoppers

We were at the Soho Charcuterie, one of my favorite restaurants in New York City. They brought us a dish of huge, gorgeous, dark chocolate cookies that we had not ordered. They smiled secretively and knowingly, and watched me. I tasted one; it was wonderful. I was just about to ask for the recipe when they said, "These are yours." I soon learned that they meant it both ways: The cookies were mine to eat or take with me, and also, the recipe was from my first book. They had increased the size of the cookies and made a few other little changes and they called them Chocolate Gobs. They told me that they couldn't make them fast enough. This recipe is based on their adaptation.

At Sonrisa bakery, in beautiful Rancho Santa Fe in southern California, these are called Charlie's Cookies, in memory of a friend of ours who was a great World War II naval pilot. His name was Charles Stimpson, and he shot down 17 Japanese planes. These were Charlie's favorites.

Adjust two racks to divide the oven into thirds and preheat oven to 350°. If you are baking only one sheet, adjust a rack to the middle of the oven. Line cookie sheets with parchment paper or foil.

Place the unsweetened chocolate, semisweet chocolate, and butter in the top of a small double boiler over hot water on moderate heat. Cook, covered, for a few minutes. Then stir occasionally until melted and smooth. Remove the top of the double boiler and set aside, uncovered, to cool slightly.

Sift together the flour, baking powder, and salt, and set aside.

In the small bowl of an electric mixer, beat the eggs, sugar, coffee or espresso, and vanilla at high speed for a minute or two.

Beat in the melted chocolates and butter (which may still be quite warm) on low speed just to mix. Add the sifted dry ingredients and again beat on low speed just to mix, scraping the sides of the bowl as necessary with a rubber spatula to incorporate the ingredients. Remove from the mixer and transfer to a larger bowl.

Stir in the chocolate morsels, the walnuts, and the pecans.

Use a ⅓-cup metal measuring cup to measure the amount of batter for each cookie. Put five cookies on each cookie sheet, one in the middle and one toward each cor-

2 ounces (2 squares)
  unsweetened chocolate
6 ounces semisweet chocolate
3 ounces (¾ stick) unsalted
  butter
¼ cup sifted all-purpose flour
¼ teaspoon baking powder
½ teaspoon salt
2 eggs
¾ cup granulated sugar
2 teaspoons powdered (not
  granular) instant coffee or
  espresso
2 teaspoons vanilla extract
6 ounces (1 cup) semisweet
  chocolate morsels (see
  Note)
4 ounces (generous 1 cup)
  walnuts, broken into large
  pieces
4 ounces (generous 1 cup)
  toasted pecans (see To
  Toast Pecans, page 4),
  broken into large pieces

15 TREMENDOUS COOKIES

ner. Use a rubber spatula to push the mixture into the measuring cup and then to scoop it out onto the lined sheet (the dough is gooey). Do not flatten the tops.

Bake two sheets at a time, reversing the sheets top to bottom and front to back once during baking to ensure even baking. Bake for 16 to 17 minutes—no longer. The surface of the cookies will be dry but the insides will still be soft. There is really no way to test these; just use a portable oven thermometer before baking to be sure your oven is right, and then watch the clock.

If the sheets have four rims the cookies and papers or foil will have to wait on the sheets until cool. If you have used cookie sheets with only one or two raised rims, you can slide the papers off the sheets and let stand until the cookies are cool. (It is not necessary to let the sheet cool before sliding it under another paper with unbaked cookies on it.)

When the cookies have cooled, use a wide metal spatula to release them and turn them over to air the bottoms a bit.

I wrap these individually in clear cellophane, and I know of a few bakeries that do the same and charge up to $4.00 or $5.00 for each cookie.

NOTE: If you wish, in place of semisweet morsels, use 6 ounces of Tobler Tradition, Lindt Excellence, or any similar chocolate, cut into ½-inch chunks.

Marjorie Kinnan Rawlings's Chocolate Cookies

Shortly after I finished work on my chocolate book, we were driving through central Florida and stopped for gas in the town of Cross Creek. I was delighted to see a little sign in the garage office that announced "Homemade Brownies 4 Sale." The garage man told me his wife baked them fresh every day and the delivery for that day was expected in an hour. We paid for a dozen brownies and told him we would be back. After an hour of driving around in circles, we returned just as the brownies were being delivered. They were drop cookies, not bar cookies. They were unusually good, and certainly worth waiting for. When I asked for the recipe I was told that his wife would not part with it, but his mother-in-law had worked for Marjorie Kinnan Rawlings and this had been Mrs. Rawlings's recipe. I couldn't wait to get home to see if it was in Cross Creek Cookery (Mrs. Rawlings's cookbook). It was. The garage man's wife had made a change (she added the chocolate morsels), and I added the coffee and omitted the baking powder.

They taste like brownies should: chewy, chocolatey, wonderful. Best of all, they are quick and easy to make, and keep well too.

Adjust two racks to divide the oven into thirds and preheat oven to 350°. Cut baking parchment to fit cookie sheets. Sift together the flour and salt and set aside.

In a small saucepan, dissolve the coffee in the water, add the chocolate, place over low heat, and stir with a rubber spatula until smooth; it will be a thick mixture. Set aside.

In the large bowl of an electric mixer, beat the butter until it is soft. Add the vanilla and then the sugar and beat until mixed. Add the chocolate mixture (which may still be warm) and beat until smooth and thoroughly mixed. Then add the eggs one at a time, beating well after each addition. On low speed add the sifted dry ingredients, scraping the bowl with a rubber spatula and beating only until mixed. Remove from the mixer.

Stir in the raisins, nuts, and morsels.

Use a heaping teaspoonful of the mixture for each cookie. Place them on the parchment, 2 inches apart; 8 cookies will fit on a 12 x 15½-inch sheet. Slide a cookie sheet under the parchment.

Bake for 13 to 15 minutes, reversing the sheets top to bottom and front to back once during baking to ensure even baking. The cookies are done if they just barely spring back (but just barely—do not overbake) when lightly pressed with a fingertip.

If you bake only one sheet at a time, bake on the higher rack.

With a wide metal spatula, carefully transfer the cookies to racks to cool.

1 cup sifted all-purpose flour
¼ teaspoon salt
Scant 2 teaspoons instant coffee
¼ cup boiling water
2 ounces (2 squares) unsweetened chocolate, coarsely chopped
3 ounces (¾ stick) unsalted butter
½ teaspoon vanilla extract
1 cup granulated sugar
2 eggs
2½ ounces (½ cup) raisins
8 ounces (2 cups) walnuts, cut or broken into large pieces
6 ounces (1 cup) semisweet chocolate morsels

25 LARGE COOKIES

Chocolate Hermits

Hermits are very old-fashioned cookies that usually have raisins, nuts, and spices. Some were made in a shallow, oblong pan and cut into squares; some were drop cookies. This yummy chocolate version is a drop cookie. They are large, thick, semisoft, dark, not too sweet, slightly spicy, full of raisins and nuts, and topped with a white sugar glaze. They keep well; they are great for a lunch box or a picnic, or for wrapping as a gift. Or for just having around.

Adjust two racks to divide the oven into thirds and preheat oven to 350°. Line two cookie sheets with baking parchment.

Place the chocolate in the top of a small double boiler over hot water on moderate heat. Cover until partly melted. Uncover and stir until completely melted. Remove the top of the double boiler and set aside to cool slightly.

Sift together the flour, baking powder, salt, cocoa, cinnamon, and coffee, and set aside.

In the large bowl of an electric mixer, cream the butter. Add the vanilla and then the sugar and beat to mix well. Then add the egg and the melted chocolate (which may still be slightly warm) and beat well. Beat in the milk. Then, on low speed, add the sifted dry ingredients, scraping the bowl as necessary with a rubber spatula, and beating only until mixed. Remove from the mixer and stir in the raisins and nuts.

Use a well-rounded tablespoonful of the dough for each cookie (make these large). Place the mounds at least 1 inch apart (place 12 mounds on a 12 x 15½-inch cookie sheet); they spread only slightly.

Bake for 18 to 20 minutes, reversing the sheets top to bottom and front to back once during baking to ensure even baking. The cookies are done if they feel slightly firm to the touch, and just barely spring back when they are lightly pressed with a fingertip. Do not overbake.

While the cookies are baking, prepare the following glaze.

3 ounces (3 squares) unsweetened chocolate
1¼ cups sifted all-purpose flour
2 teaspoons baking powder
¼ teaspoon salt
1 tablespoon unsweetened cocoa powder (preferably Dutch-process)
1 teaspoon cinnamon
1 teaspoon powder (not granular) instant coffee
4 ounces (1 stick) unsalted butter
1 teaspoon vanilla extract
1 cup granulated sugar
1 egg
⅓ cup milk
5 ounces (1 cup) raisins
4 ounces (generous 1 cup) walnut or pecan halves or pieces

24 LARGE COOKIES

Glaze

In a small bowl, stir all the ingredients to mix well. The mixture must be smooth. It should be about the consistency of thin and runny mayonnaise; adjust it with more sugar or milk. Cover the glaze airtight until you are ready to use it.

Just as soon as you take the cookie sheet out of the oven, spoon or brush some of the glaze over the tops of the hot cookies. Do not attempt to cover all over the tops—just spread it on the middle and let it run down the sides a bit. Then, with a wide metal spatula, transfer the cookies to racks to cool.

When the glaze has dried and is no longer sticky, the cookies should be stored airtight. If you package them in a box, put wax paper between the layers. I wrap them, two to a package, bottoms together, in clear cellophane.

¾ cup sifted or strained confectioners sugar
1 tablespoon unsalted butter, melted
½ teaspoon vanilla extract
1 tablespoon milk or light cream
Pinch of salt

Big Sur Chocolate-Chip Cookies

These California cookies are 6 inches in diameter—they are the largest homemade chocolate chip cookies I know (nothing succeeds like excess). They are crisp, crunchy, buttery, delicious. Too good. Irresistible. But because of their size, don't make them for a fancy tea party. Do make them for a barbecue or a picnic, or for any casual affair.

Adjust two racks to divide the oven into thirds and preheat oven to 350°. Line cookie sheets with parchment or foil. Sift together the flour, salt, baking soda, and cinnamon, and set aside.

In the large bowl of an electric mixer, cream the butter. Add the vanilla and lemon juice and then both of the sugars, and beat to mix. Beat in the eggs one at a time. On low speed, add the sifted dry ingredients and then the rolled oats, scraping the bowl as necessary with a rubber spatula and beating only until mixed.

Remove from the mixer and stir in the nuts and morsels.

Now work next to the sink or have a large bowl of water handy so you can wet your hands while shaping the cookies. Spread out a piece of wax paper or foil. Use a ¼-cup measuring cup to measure the amount of dough for each cookie. Form 12 to 15 mounds of the dough, and place them any which way on the wax paper or foil. Wet your hands with cold water, shake the water off but do not dry your hands; pick up a mound of dough, roll it into a ball, flatten it to about ½-inch thickness, and place it on the prepared foil. Do not place more than 4 cookies on a 12 x 15½-inch cookie sheet. These spread to gigantic proportions.

Bake two sheets at a time for 16 to 18 minutes, reversing the sheets top to bottom and front to back as necessary to ensure even browning. If you bake only one sheet at a time, bake it on the higher rack. Bake until the cookies are well colored; they must not be too pale. Watch these carefully; before you know it they might become too dark.

When you remove these from the oven, let them stand for about a minute until they are firm enough to be moved. With a wide metal spatula, transfer them to racks to cool. If the racks are not raised at least ½ inch from the work surface, place them on a bowl or cake pan to allow more air to circulate underneath.

When cool, wrap them, bottoms together, two to a package, in cellophane or wax paper or in plastic sandwich bags. If you do not plan to serve these soon, freeze them. Place all of the packages in a freezer, in a freezer box, or in one large freezer bag. If you do not plan to serve these soon, freeze them.

1½ cups sifted all-purpose
  flour
½ teaspoon salt
1 teaspoon baking soda
½ teaspoon cinnamon
6 ounces (1½ sticks) unsalted
  butter
1½ teaspoons vanilla extract
1 teaspoon lemon juice
⅔ cup light brown sugar,
  firmly packed
⅓ cup granulated sugar
2 eggs
¼ cup quick-cooking (not
  instant) rolled oats
6 ounces (1½ cups) walnuts,
  cut or broken into medium-
  size pieces
6 ounces (1 cup) semisweet
  chocolate morsels

12 TO 15 VERY LARGE
COOKIES

Savannah Chocolate Chewies

In Savannah, Georgia, we went to one of America's great bookstores, E. Shaver. As soon as I introduced myself, the lovely ladies who run the store—and love to cook—screamed and giggled and swooned (just thinking about chocolate). They asked me if I knew how to make Chocolate Chewies, a Savannah specialty, and a deep dark secret. I was told they are made at Gottlieb's, a 100-year-old local bakery. When they phoned Isser Gottlieb at the bakery, he rushed right over, picked us up, drove us to the bakery, showed us the kitchen, fed us tastes of everything, and gave me this recipe. Talk about Southern hospitality!

The cookies are large, very dark, very chewy, and since they have egg whites and no yolks (and no butter) they are a sort of meringue; a decidedly chocolate meringue.

Adjust a rack to the middle of the oven and preheat oven to 350°. Line cookie sheets with parchment paper or with aluminum foil shiny side up.

The pecans should be chopped rather finely. If you do it in a food processor fitted with the metal chopping blade, process on/off 10 quick times (10 seconds), or chop the nuts on a board using a long chef's knife. Some pieces will be larger than others, but none should be larger than a green pea, and some will be smaller. Set aside.

Place the sugar, cocoa, coffee or espresso, flour, salt, egg whites, and vanilla in the small bowl of an electric mixer. Beat slowly at first until the dry ingredients are moistened, and then beat at high speed for 1 minute. Remove the bowl from the mixer and stir in the nuts.

It is important now to spoon out the cookies as soon as possible. Once they are spooned out they can wait before baking, but if they remain in the mixing bowl for any length of time, they will not be beautifully shiny when baked. Use a tablespoon for spooning out the cookies (not a measuring spoon)—make each cookie one rounded tablespoonful of the dough—and use another spoon for pushing off the mounds of dough. Place the cookies at least 1 inch apart on the prepared sheets.

I think these bake best if you bake only one sheet at a time. Bake for 15 minutes, reversing the sheet front to back once during baking to ensure even baking. When done, the cookies should be dry and crisp on the outside, wet and chewy inside.

If you have used parchment paper the cookies may be removed from the paper with a wide metal spatula as soon as they are done and transferred to a rack to cool. If you have used foil, the cookies will have to stand on the foil until they can then be lifted easily with your fingers (or, if you have trouble, peel the foil away from the backs of the cookies).

8 ounces (generous 2 cups) pecans
3 cups confectioners sugar
⅔ cup unsifted, unsweetened cocoa powder (preferably Dutch-process)
1 teaspoon powdered (not granular) instant coffee or espresso
2 tablespoons unsifted all-purpose flour
Pinch of salt
3 egg whites (they may be whites that were frozen and thawed)
½ teaspoon vanilla extract

12 LARGE COOKIES

Store these airtight.

At Gottlieb's they told me that if these are not served the day they are made, they should be frozen or they will dry out. I packed them in a freezer bag and let them stand on the counter overnight (just to test) and they were still moist and delicious. I also let some stand uncovered overnight (just to test) and they were still just as wonderful. (Maybe there's something in the air.)

Incidentally, this is Gottlieb's number one best-selling cookie.

Chocolate Gingersnaps

Crisp, dark, and gingery, made with three kinds of ginger—ground, fresh, and candied. Gingerful!

Adjust two racks to divide the oven into thirds and preheat oven to 350°. Line cookie sheets with parchment paper or aluminum foil shiny side up, and set aside.

Grate the fresh ginger and set it aside.

Sift together the flour, cocoa, cinnamon, salt, ground ginger, and the baking soda, and set aside.

In the large bowl of an electric mixer, beat the butter until soft. Add the grated fresh ginger and the sugar and beat to mix. Then beat in the egg and molasses. When mixed, gradually add the sifted dry ingredients on low speed, scraping the sides of the bowl as necessary with a rubber spatula, and beating only until incorporated. Remove the bowl from the mixer and stir in the diced candied ginger.

Cover an additional cookie sheet or a jelly-roll pan with aluminum foil shiny side up. Using a barely rounded teaspoonful of the dough for each cookie, form mounds close together on the foil. Transfer to the freezer for about 10 minutes, or longer in the refrigerator, until the mounds are not sticky.

Roll the mounds between your hands into marble-size balls. Place them about 1½ inches apart on the prepared cookie sheets.

1 ounce (a piece about 2 inches long and 1 inch thick) fresh ginger
2 cups sifted all-purpose flour
¼ cup unsweetened cocoa powder (preferably Dutch-process)
½ teaspoon cinnamon
½ teaspoon salt
½ teaspoon powdered ginger
1½ teaspoons baking soda
6 ounces (1½ sticks) unsalted butter
1 cup dark brown sugar, firmly packed
1 egg
¼ cup dark molasses
¼ cup candied ginger, finely diced

ABOUT 50 COOKIES

Bake two sheets at a time for about 15 minutes, reversing the sheets top to bottom and front to back once during baking. Bake until the cookies just barely feel springy if they are pressed gently with a fingertip. If you bake one sheet at a time, bake it on the lower of the two racks; one sheet will bake in about 13 minutes.

Immediately transfer the cookies with a wide metal spatula to racks to cool. Store airtight.

David's Cookies

These are the famous chocolate chunk cookies that took New York City and its suburbs by storm in the mid-'80s. David's trademark is that his cookies are made with coarsely chopped semisweet chocolate bars instead of with morsels. As far as I know, this recipe has been and still is a closely guarded secret—but here it is.

It is best to bake these on parchment. If you line the sheets with foil, or if you butter them, the cookies spread out too much and the edges become too thin and brittle. If you butter and flour the sheets, the cookies tend to burn.

Adjust two racks to divide the oven into thirds and preheat oven to 400°. Line cookie sheets with parchment. Place the chocolate on a cutting board and with a long, heavy, sharp knife cut the chocolate first in one direction and then in the opposite direction, making uneven ¼- to ½-inch (or larger) pieces. Set aside.

In the large bowl of an electric mixer beat the butter until soft. Beat in the salt and vanilla, then the sugar, until well mixed. Add the egg and beat, scraping the bowl with a rubber spatula, until mixed. Then, on low speed, add the flour and beat until incorporated. Remove from the mixer.

With a heavy wooden spoon, stir in the chopped chocolate and the optional nuts. The mixture will be thick and sticky. Use two teaspoons to shape the cookies, one for picking up dough and one for pushing it off. Use a rounded teaspoonful of dough for each cookie. Do not make these too large. Place the cookies 2 inches apart on the lined sheets.

Bake two sheets at a time for 8 to 10 minutes, reversing the sheets top to bottom and front to back as necessary to ensure even browning. Bake only until the edges of the cookies start to brown (see Note). If some are done before others, remove them as they become ready, and bake the rest as necessary. If they are too soft to handle, let them wait on the sheet for a few seconds and they will become firmer. With a wide metal spatula transfer the cookies to racks to cool.

NOTE: To make these like David's, do not overbake. Actually, David underbakes them (6 to 8 minutes baking time), but I like 8 to 10 minutes or even longer if necessary. David's are very soft; mine are slightly crisper.

VARIATION: I have often made these huge, and they are wonderful. I make only 9 or 10 cookies with the full amount of dough. Here's how:

Preheat the oven to only 350° (instead of the 400° used for the smaller-size cookies).

Place a large piece of aluminum foil on the counter next to the sink. Use ¼ cup of the dough for each cookie (measure with a ¼-cup metal measuring cup) and place the mounds any which way on the foil. Wet your hands with cold water, shake the water off but do not dry your hands, roll a mound of the dough between your cold, wet hands to form a ball, and then flatten the ball to about ½-inch thickness. Place only 3 cookies on each lined cookie sheet.

Bake the cookies for 20 to 22 minutes, reversing the sheets top to bottom and front to back as necessary to ensure even browning, until the cookies are lightly colored and just barely spring back when pressed lightly with a fingertip.

Let the cookies cool briefly on the paper until they are firm enough to be moved, and then use a wide metal spatula to transfer them to racks to cool.

8 ounces semisweet or bittersweet chocolate (David uses Lindt. Tobler is equally good. Poulain and Callebaut are wonderful. Use the best you can get.)
8 ounces (2 sticks) unsalted butter
½ teaspoon salt
½ teaspoon vanilla extract
1 cup light or dark brown sugar, firmly packed
1 egg
2 cups sifted all-purpose flour
Optional: 4 ounces (generous 1 cup) pecans or walnuts, broken into large pieces

40 TO 50 SMALL COOKIES

Extra-Bittersweet Chocolate Chunk Monster Cookies

These are huge shortbreads with an inconceivable amount of unusually large chunks of extra-bittersweet chocolate and large pieces of walnuts and barely enough dough to hold them together. Rich, buttery, and crisp/crunchy. A far cry from chocolate chip cookies, yet related—distantly. The recipe can be multiplied by any number, and any semisweet chocolate can be used in place of the extra-bittersweet.

Adjust two racks to divide the oven into thirds and preheat oven to 350°. Line three cookie sheets with parchment paper or aluminum foil shiny side up, and set aside.

With a large, heavy knife or with a cleaver cut the chocolate into chunks approximately ½ inch square; they may be even a bit larger, but preferably not smaller. Set aside.

Break the walnuts into large pieces; each half may be broken in half, but they shouldn't be smaller. Set aside.

In the large bowl of an electric mixer, beat the butter until just barely soft. Beat in the vanilla and almond extracts, then the sugar and salt, and finally the flour.

Remove from the mixer and with a heavy wooden spoon stir in the nuts and chocolate.

Place a large piece of foil or wax paper next to the sink. Use a ⅓-cup metal measuring cup to measure the amount for each cookie. Place eight ⅓-cup mounds of the dough any which way on the foil or wax paper next to the sink.

Wet your hands with cold water, shake off the water but do not dry your hands (they should be cold and damp); pick up a mound of the dough, roll it between your hands into a ball, and then flatten it a bit between your hands. Place 3 cookies on each of two sheets, and 2 cookies on one sheet. Then, with your fingertips, press the cookies a bit to flatten them to about ½-inch thickness and 3½ inches in width. Keep the shape round.

Bake two sheets at a time, reversing the sheets top to bottom and front to

9 ounces extra-bittersweet chocolate (I use 3-ounce bars of Tobler Extra-Bittersweet)

4 ounces (generous 1 cup) walnuts

4 ounces (1 stick) unsalted butter

¾ teaspoon vanilla extract

¼ teaspoon almond extract

⅓ cup granulated sugar

½ teaspoon salt

1 cup sifted all-purpose flour

8 LARGE COOKIES

back, as necessary, to ensure even browning. Bake for 16 to 18 minutes, until the cookies are a pale golden color, darker on the rims. When these are done the tops will feel too soft (they will become crisp as they cool); time them by their looks (color) rather than by their feel.

Remove from the oven and let stand for about a minute.

Meanwhile, bake the one remaining sheet on the higher of the two racks. One sheet will bake in a minute or two less time than it takes for two sheets.

With a wide metal spatula, transfer the cookies, very carefully and gently, to racks to cool.

Store airtight.

Brownie Cookies

These delicious drop cookies (actually they are dropped, but then rolled into balls between your hands) are made with brownie ingredients. They are semisoft and chewy, very dark, dense, fudgelike, not-too-sweet chocolate. Quick and easy, they are mixed in a saucepan.

Adjust two racks to divide the oven into thirds and preheat oven to 375°. Line two cookie sheets with parchment paper or with aluminum foil shiny side up and set aside.

In a 3-quart heavy saucepan over low heat, melt both of the chocolates and the butter, stirring frequently with a heavy wooden spoon. Remove from the heat. Add the remaining ingredients, in order, stirring briskly after each addition.

Place a long piece of aluminum foil next to the sink. Use two teaspoons, one for picking up the dough and one for pushing it off. Use a heaping teaspoonful of dough for each cookie. Place the mounds any which way on the foil.

Then wet your hands with cold water, shake off the water but do not dry your hands. Pick up a mound of the dough, roll it between your hands into a ball, and place it on one of the lined cookie sheets. Continue to roll the balls

2 ounces (2 squares)
   unsweetened chocolate
4 ounces semisweet chocolate
4 ounces (1 stick) unsalted
   butter
½ teaspoon salt
½ teaspoon vanilla extract
1 cup granulated sugar
2 eggs
1½ cups sifted all-purpose
   flour
6 ounces (generous 1½ cups)
   walnuts, cut or broken into
   medium-size pieces

ABOUT 28 COOKIES

of dough and place them about 1 inch apart. Wet your hands again if dough begins to stick.

With the bottom of a fork, press each ball of dough lightly to flatten it to about ½- or ⅗-inch thickness (no thinner).

Bake for 10 to 12 minutes, reversing the sheets front to back and top to bottom once during baking. Bake only until the tops of the cookies lose their shine and become dull; they should feel dry but soft when pressed gently with a fingertip. The cookies become firmer as they cool.

With a wide metal spatula transfer the cookies to racks to cool.

Store airtight.

Cookie Kisses

Hershey's Milk Chocolate Kisses are about as American as can be. Everybody knows them. These are delicious peanut butter cookies shaped by being rolled between your hands. The kisses are put on top as soon as the baked cookies are taken out of the oven. Fun to make and fun to serve.

This is a variation of an old American recipe that is sometimes called Sombreros (they do look like them), Blossoms, or Silver Tipped Blossoms. (Does that mean that they did not remove the foil from the kisses?)

*A*djust two racks to divide the oven into thirds and preheat oven to 375°. Line cookie sheets with parchment. Remove the wrapping from the kisses and set them aside.

This dough can be prepared in a food processor or in the large bowl of an electric mixer.

In a processor: Place the flour, baking soda, salt, granulated sugar, and brown sugar in the processor bowl fitted with the metal chopping blade and process on/off quickly 2 or 3 times to mix. Place the egg, vanilla, and milk in a 1-cup glass measuring cup and set aside. Cut up the butter and add it and the peanut butter to the bowl of the processor. Turn the machine on and pour the egg mixture through the feed tube. Process until the mixture forms a ball and is thoroughly mixed.

Or in a mixer: Sift together the flour, baking soda, and salt, and set aside. Reserve both sugars. Place the egg, vanilla, and milk in a small cup and reserve. Place the butter and peanut butter in the large bowl of the mixer and beat until soft. Add both sugars and beat to mix. Then add half of the sifted dry ingredients, the egg mixture, and the remaining dry ingredients. Beat until thoroughly mixed.

Place a long piece of wax paper or foil on the work surface. Divide the dough into 48 mounds, each one a rounded teaspoonful. (You can either just pick up the cookie-size mounds and place them on the paper or foil, or roll the dough into a log sausage shape and cut it into 48 even pieces.)

Place additional granulated sugar (about 1 cup) on a wide plate and have it handy. One at a time, roll the mounds of dough between your hands to make balls, roll them around in the granulated sugar to coat the cookies, and then place them on the lined sheets, placing only 12 cookies on each sheet.

Place one sheet in the oven; wait a few minutes before placing the second sheet in the oven so that they do not come out of the oven at the same time. (If you might forget which sheet went into the oven first, roll up a little bean-size piece of foil and place it in a corner on the first sheet.) Reverse the sheets top to bottom once during baking to ensure even browning. Bake for 12 to 13 minutes. The cookies will be only lightly colored and will still feel soft to the touch.

Immediately as you remove a sheet from the oven place a chocolate kiss, point up, in the middle of each cookie, pressing it down firmly. Then, with a wide metal spatula, transfer the cookies to racks to cool.

The chocolate kisses will soften from the heat of the cookies and they will remain soft for quite a while. Therefore, if you are packing these or stacking them, be sure that the kisses have become firm; if necessary, chill the cookies.

48 Hershey's Milk Chocolate Kisses
1¾ cups sifted all-purpose flour
1 teaspoon baking soda
¼ teaspoon salt
½ cup granulated sugar
½ cup light brown sugar, packed
1 egg
1 teaspoon vanilla extract
2 tablespoons milk
4 ounces (1 stick) unsalted butter
½ cup smooth peanut butter
Additional granulated sugar

48 COOKIES

Chocolate Peanut Butter Cookies

This is a chocolate version of plain old-fashioned peanut butter cookies. Easy to make, they keep well, mail well, and they are de-e-e-licious.

It is best to bake these one sheet at a time (or some might burn before others are done); adjust a rack to the middle of the oven and preheat oven to 375°. Line cookie sheets with parchment paper.

Place both kinds of chocolate in the top of a small double boiler over warm water on moderately low heat. Cover with a folded paper towel (to absorb steam) and with the pot cover. Let stand until the chocolate is almost all melted. Then uncover and stir until completely melted and smooth. Remove the top of the double boiler and set aside to cool.

Sift together the flour, baking soda, and salt, and set aside.

Place the butter in the small bowl of an electric mixer and beat until soft. Add the vanilla and both sugars and beat until well mixed. Then add the peanut butter, beat to mix, add the melted chocolate and beat to mix, beat in the egg, and finally add the sifted dry ingredients and beat on low speed until incorporated.

Turn the mixture out onto a piece of wax paper or foil and shape it into an even oblong. Cut it into 48 equal pieces. Roll the pieces one at a time between your hands into balls about 1 inch in diameter and place them 2 inches apart on the prepared sheets.

Press the tops of the cookies gently with the bottom of the tines of a fork, pressing in one direction only, forming a ridged pattern and flattening the cookies to about ½-inch thickness.

Bake one sheet at a time for about 15 minutes, reversing the sheet front to back once during baking to ensure even browning. Watch the cookies carefully to see that none of them becomes too dark. When they are done they will feel dry and semifirm when pressed lightly with a fingertip, but they should not darken much or they will taste burnt. These will harden and become crisp as they cool. With a metal spatula transfer to racks to cool.

2 ounces (2 squares) unsweetened chocolate
1 ounce semisweet chocolate
1½ cups sifted all-purpose flour
¾ teaspoon baking soda
½ teaspoon salt
4 ounces (1 stick) unsalted butter
½ teaspoon vanilla extract
½ cup granulated sugar
½ cup dark or light brown sugar, firmly packed
½ cup smooth peanut butter
1 egg

48 COOKIES

Candy Cookies

The narrow dividing line between candy and cookies becomes even narrower with this dessert. This recipe is a combination of two American favorites, chocolate chip cookies and candy bars. The candy bars (crisp toffee covered with milk chocolate) are coarsely cut up and are used in place of chocolate chips (the candy does not melt during baking). Fabulous!

Adjust two racks to divide the oven into thirds and preheat oven to 375°. Line cookie sheets with parchment paper.

Cut the Heath Bars into four ½-inch pieces and set aside.

In the large bowl of an electric mixer, beat the butter until soft. Add the salt, vanilla, and both sugars, and beat to mix. Then beat in the egg. On low speed add the flour, scraping the bowl as necessary with a rubber spatula and beating only until incorporated.

In a small cup, combine the baking soda and water and beat into the dough. Remove the bowl from the mixer, then add the walnuts and the cut-up Heath Bars and stir with a heavy wooden spoon until evenly mixed.

Use a rounded tablespoon of the dough for each cookie. Place them 2 inches apart on the lined sheets.

Bake two sheets at a time for 13 to 15 minutes, reversing the sheets top to bottom and front to back as necessary to ensure even browning. Bake until the cookies are lightly browned all over.

Let the cookies stand on the sheets for about 5 minutes. Then use a wide metal spatula to transfer the cookies to racks to cool.

Store airtight.

9 ounces Heath Bars
4 ounces (1 stick) unsalted butter
½ teaspoon salt
½ teaspoon vanilla extract
⅓ cup granulated sugar
⅓ cup dark brown sugar, firmly packed
1 egg
1¼ cups unsifted all-purpose flour
½ teaspoon baking soda
½ teaspoon hot water
4 ounces (generous 1 cup) walnuts, broken into large pieces

24 LARGE COOKIES

Chocolate Miracles (a.k.a. Chocolate Fudge Cookies)

This is from Barbara (Mrs. Paul) Leand of Brooklandville, Maryland. The recipe has been in her family for many, many years. Dense, dark, candylike—as black and shiny as wet tar—like a combination of chewy macaroons, Tootsie Rolls, and caramel. The miracle is how easy they are to make.

You will need parchment paper (see Note).

P lace the chocolate in the top of a large double boiler over warm water on moderate heat. Cover for a few minutes with a folded paper towel (to absorb steam) and pot cover, then uncover and cook until the chocolate is melted. Raise the heat to high (the water in the bottom of the double boiler should boil after the chocolate has melted). Add the condensed milk. With a rubber spatula, stir and scrape the bottom and sides of the pan, cooking (over boiling water) for 5 minutes, during which time the mixture will thicken very slightly.

Remove the top of the double boiler; stir the mixture briskly a bit with a wire whisk until very smooth.

Let stand, stirring occasionally with the spatula, for 10 to 15 minutes, during which time the mixture will thicken considerably more.

Meanwhile, adjust two racks to the two top positions in the oven and preheat oven to 350°. Line two cookie sheets with parchment paper.

By now, the chocolate mixture will have thickened still more. Stir in the nuts. Transfer to a small bowl for easier handling.

Use two teaspoons to shape the cookies, one for picking up with and one for pushing off with. Use a rounded teaspoonful of dough for each cookie. Place them 1½ to 2 inches apart on the parchment paper.

Bake for 15 minutes, reversing sheets top to bottom and front to back once during baking to ensure even baking. (During baking the cookies will flatten and spread out only slightly.) They will feel very soft when done but will become more firm as they cool.

With a wide metal spatula transfer the cookies to racks to cool. (If the cookies stick to the spatula, turn the spatula over into the palm of your left hand—onto a folded napkin to protect your hand from the heat—lift away the spatula, and then place the cookie right side up on the rack.)

It would be great if you could serve these immediately, because as soon as they

2 ounces (2 squares) unsweetened chocolate
1 14-ounce can sweetened condensed milk
4 ounces (generous 1 cup) pecans, toasted (see To Toast Pecans, page 4), cut into medium-small pieces

25 COOKIES

cool, and for about 12 hours after that, they are crisp on the outside and soft inside: a divine condition. But after they've been standing for a long time the moisture from the inside of the cookies works its way out and the crispness disappears. If they are wrapped or stored airtight, the moisture is contained and the crispness disappears even sooner. (However, the flavor remains and they are still outstanding.) Therefore, if you plan to serve these either the same day or a day later, do not store them airtight; they may be covered loosely with wax paper. Or, if you must make these way ahead of time, package them airtight and freeze them until a few hours before serving time. Then, thaw before unwrapping.

NOTE: These work like magic on parchment paper. If you use foil instead, they stick. If you butter the sheets, the cookies want to burn.

VARIATION: If you wish, each cookie may be topped with a pecan half. It should be done immediately after shaping each cookie, before the surface of the cookie has time to dry out. Press each pecan half into the cookie dough so that it will not fall off after baking. (These halves may be toasted or not before they are used.)

Chocolate-Chip Chocolate Oatmeal Cookies

These are drop cookies that combine several qualities of America's favorite cookies: (1) chocolate, (2) chocolate chips, (3) oatmeal. Plus, they are quick and easy. The original recipe was worked out by the Gold Medal flour people at General Mills to help introduce unbleached flour, which by now needs no introduction, but at one time the average home-maker had never even seen it.

Incidentally, General Mills celebrated its 100th birthday not long ago. Congratulations.

Adjust two racks to divide the oven into thirds and preheat oven to 350°. Line cookie sheets with parchment paper or aluminum foil and set aside. Sift together the flour, baking soda, salt, and cocoa, and set aside.
 In the large bowl of an electric mixer, beat the butter until it is soft. Add the vanilla and almond extracts and then the sugar, beating until well mixed. Beat in the

egg. Mix the coffee and water and add. Now, on low speed, add the sifted dry ingredients, beating only until incorporated.

Remove from the mixer. With a heavy wooden spoon, stir in the chocolate morsels, the oats, and the nuts.

Spread out a long piece of foil next to the sink.

Use a round tablespoonful of the mixture for each cookie; place any which way on the foil.

Wet your hands with cold water and pick up a mound, roll it into a ball, flatten between your hands to ½-inch thickness, and place 2 inches apart on the foil-lined sheets, six to eight on a sheet.

Bake for 14 to 16 minutes, reversing the sheets top to bottom and front to back once during baking to ensure even baking. Bake until the cookies just barely spring back when they are pressed lightly in the center. They will feel soft when they are removed from the oven, but they will become dry and crisp when they cool.

Let the cookies cool briefly on the sheets; then use a wide metal spatula to transfer them to racks to cool.

Store airtight.

1¼ cups sifted unbleached all-purpose flour
½ teaspoon baking soda
½ teaspoon salt
⅓ cup unsweetened cocoa powder (preferably Dutch-process)
8 ounces (2 sticks) unsalted butter
1 teaspoon vanilla extract
¼ teaspoon almond extract
1½ cups granulated sugar
1 egg
2 teaspoons instant coffee
¼ cup hot water
6 ounces (1 cup) semisweet chocolate morsels
3 cups quick-cooking (not instant) rolled oats
10 ounces (2½ cups) walnuts, broken into medium-size pieces

46 COOKIES

Down East Chocolate Cookies

Thin and crisp, intensely chocolate and almond. No flour. They are brittle and hard until they go into your mouth; then they become chewy and caramel-like. The perfect cookie to nibble on with ice cream or custard, or any other time.

This recipe calls for almond paste. It is available at specialty food stores; the brand I use is Odense, which comes in a 7-ounce package. It is stored on the grocer's shelf and lasts indefinitely.

1½ ounces unsweetened chocolate
3 ounces (¾ stick) unsalted butter
¾ cup granulated sugar
⅛ teaspoon salt
3½ ounces (⅓ cup, tightly packed) almond paste (see Note)
1 egg
½ teaspoon almond extract

28 TO 30 THIN COOKIES

Place the chocolate and butter in the top of a large double boiler, uncovered, over warm water on moderate heat. Stir frequently until melted. Add the sugar and salt and stir to mix. Then add the almond paste. Stir with a wooden spoon or rubber spatula, pressing down on the almond paste until it is completely blended; if necessary, stir with a wire whisk. (If the butter separates, it is okay.)

Remove the top of the double boiler from the heat. Add the egg and the almond extract. Beat with an electric mixer, an eggbeater, or a wire whisk until smooth.

Cool and then place in the freezer for about 30 minutes, stirring a few times, until quite thick.

Before baking, adjust two racks to divide the oven into thirds and preheat oven to 300°. Preferably, use cookie sheets that have only one raised rim (flat on three sides). Or, if you must use the ones with raised rims (or jelly-roll pans), turn the sheets (or pans) over and use the bottoms. Cover the sheets (or pans) with aluminum foil shiny side up. Set aside.

Use two teaspoons, one for picking up with and one for pushing off with, to make drop cookies. Use a slightly rounded teaspoonful of the dough for each cookie; these will spread. Do not make them too large, do not flatten them, and do not place more than 6 cookies on a sheet. Do take your time and shape them carefully in order to have nice round cookies when baked.

Bake for 21 or 22 minutes, no less, reversing the sheets top to bottom and front to back once during baking to ensure even baking. If you bake only one sheet at a time, bake it on the lower of the two racks. The cookies will rise and then settle down very flat during baking.

These must cool completely on the foil. I like to let them cool with the foil still on the cookie sheets. However, if you need the sheets now for baking more cookies, you can slide the foil off the sheets.

When completely cool, peel the foil away from the beautifully smooth and shiny backs of the cookies. (If the cookies were not baked enough they will stick to the foil.

If that should happen, place the foil and cookies in the freezer for a few minutes; then peel the foil away.)

I store these in an airtight jar on the coffee table. They last wonderfully; they seem to get even better after a few days.

NOTE: Leftover almond paste should quickly be wrapped airtight in plastic wrap and then aluminum foil.

Chocolate Fudge-Candy Cookies

*The **most** chocolate! Like dark-chocolate fudge candy, only softer and smoother. Chewy. Heavenly. And about the easiest cookies I have ever made.*

Adjust two racks to divide the oven into thirds and preheat oven to 350°. Line cookie sheets with aluminum foil shiny side up, being careful not to crease the foil.

Place the chocolate and the butter in the top of a large double boiler over warm water on moderate heat. Stir occasionally until melted and smooth.

Remove the top of the double boiler. Stir in the condensed milk and vanilla, then the flour, and then the pecans.

Use a rounded teaspoonful of the mixture for each cookie; pick it up with one teaspoon and push it off with another. Place the cookies 1 to 2 inches apart on the foil.

Bake two sheets at a time, reversing the sheets top to bottom and front to back once during baking. Bake for exactly 7 minutes. The cookies will still feel soft; they will become firmer as they cool.

If you bake only one sheet at a time, bake it in the middle of the oven and reverse it front to back once during baking.

(Before baking, the dough will be as shiny as varnish; after baking it will have changed to the dull look of fudge candy.)

If you have used a cookie sheet with only one raised rim, as you remove it from

12 ounces semisweet chocolate, cut into pieces
2 ounces (½ stick) unsalted butter
1 14-ounce can unsweetened condensed milk
1 teaspoon vanilla extract
1 cup sifted all-purpose flour
8 ounces (2¼ cups) pecans, toasted (see To Toast Pecans, page 4), broken into larger pieces

55 RATHER SMALL COOKIES

the oven, slide the foil off and let stand until the cookies are completely cool. (You can slide the hot cookie sheet under another piece of foil with unbaked cookies on it.) If the cookie sheet has raised rims all around, the foil must stand on the sheet until the cookies are completely cool. When they have cooled, use a wide metal spatula to transfer the cookies to racks and let stand until the bottoms become dry.

Store with wax paper or plastic wrap between the layers.

Chocolate Chocolate-Chip Cookies

These are thin, dark, and brittle-crisp.

Adjust two racks to divide the oven into thirds and preheat oven to 350°. Line cookie sheets with parchment.

Sift together the flour and baking soda and set aside. In the large bowl of an electric mixer cream the butter. Add the vanilla and both sugars and beat to mix well. On low speed add the cocoa and beat to mix. Then mix in the cream and, on low speed, gradually add the sifted dry ingredients, scraping the bowl with a rubber spatula and beating only until mixed.

Remove the bowl from the mixer and, with a wooden spoon, stir in the pecans and the morsels.

Use a rounded (less than heaping) teaspoonful of the dough for each cookie. Place them about 1½ inches apart (the cookies will spread during baking) on the cookie sheets.

Bake for about 12 to 13 minutes, reversing the sheets top to bottom and front to back to ensure even baking. The cookies will still feel soft and not done, but don't overbake them or they will become too hard.

Let the cookies stand for a minute or two. (After baking, the cookies will flatten into thin, bumpy, uneven wafers.) With a wide metal spatula transfer the cookies to racks to cool.

1¾ cups sifted all-purpose flour
¼ teaspoon baking soda
8 ounces (2 sticks) unsalted butter
1 teaspoon vanilla extract
1 cup granulated sugar
½ cup dark brown sugar, firmly packed
⅓ cup unsweetened cocoa powder (preferably Dutch-process)
2 tablespoons light cream
3½ ounces (1 cup) pecans, cut or broken into medium-size pieces
6 ounces (1 cup) semisweet chocolate morsels

54 COOKIES

Santa Fe Chocolate Wafers

These dark, thin, crisp cookies are easily mixed in a saucepan. They are very fragile and not suitable for picnics.

Adjust two racks to divide the oven into thirds and preheat oven to 350°. Line cookie sheets with parchment.

Sift together the flour, baking soda, and salt, and set aside. Cut the butter into ½-inch slices and place in a heavy 2½- to 3-quart saucepan. Add the chocolate, sugar, and corn syrup. Stir over low heat until melted and smooth. If the mixture is not smooth (some morsels do not melt completely) stir and beat it briefly with a small whisk. Remove from the heat and let cool for 5 minutes.

Then stir in the vanilla and the egg. When smooth, add the sifted dry ingredients and stir and mix vigorously until smooth. Transfer to a small bowl for ease in handling.

Use a rounded teaspoonful of dough for each cookie. Place them at least 2 inches apart (these spread) on the sheets, keeping the shapes as round as possible.

Bake for 10 to 15 minutes (see Note), reversing the position of the sheets top to bottom and front to back to ensure even baking. If you bake only one sheet at a time use the higher rack, and with only one sheet in the oven the cookies will take less time to bake. The cookies will puff up in the oven and then flatten; they are not done until they are flattened. These will crisp as they cool and they should be very crisp, but be careful not to overbake or the chocolate will taste burnt.

Let the cookies stand on the sheet for a minute or so to firm and then transfer the cookies with a wide metal spatula to racks to cool. Store airtight.

NOTE: If, after the cookies have cooled, they are not crisp, you may replace them in the oven briefly to bake a little bit longer.

1 cup sifted all-purpose flour
½ teaspoon baking soda
⅛ teaspoon salt
4 ounces (1 stick) unsalted
  butter
6 ounces semisweet chocolate,
  cut into small pieces
⅓ cup granulated sugar
¼ cup light corn syrup
1 teaspoon vanilla extract
1 egg

36 WAFERS

"Chocolate Street" Cookies

Sometimes called Brownie Drops, these are small, rather thin, semisoft and very chocolatey.

Adjust two racks to divide the oven into thirds and preheat oven to 350°. Line cookie sheets with parchment.

Sift together the flour, baking powder, cinnamon, and salt, and set aside.

Break up the chocolate and place it in the top of a small double boiler over hot water. Add the butter, and place over moderate heat. Cover and cook until melted. Stir until smooth. Remove from hot water and set aside to cool.

In the small bowl of an electric mixer beat the eggs at high speed for a minute or two until they are light in color. Gradually add the sugar and continue to beat for 4 or 5 minutes until the mixture is almost white in color and forms a ribbon when beaters are raised. Beat in the vanilla.

Add the cooled, melted chocolate and beat on low speed, scraping the bowl with a rubber spatula and beating only until smooth. Add the sifted dry ingredients and beat only enough to blend. Stir in the nuts. Transfer to a small shallow bowl for ease in handling.

Use a slightly rounded teaspoonful of dough for each cookie and place them 1½ inches apart on the prepared sheets. Keep the shape of the cookies as round and even as possible.

Bake about 12 minutes, reversing the position of the sheets top to bottom and front to back during baking to ensure even baking. When done, the tops of the cookies will be cracked and will feel semifirm when lightly touched with a fingertip. Do not overbake—the centers of these cookies will be moist and chewy.

Let cool on the sheets for about a minute. Then, with a wide metal spatula, transfer to racks to finish cooling.

¼ cup unsifted *all-purpose flour*
¼ teaspoon baking powder
Scant ¼ teaspoon cinnamon
⅛ teaspoon salt
8 ounces semisweet chocolate
1 tablespoon unsalted butter
2 eggs
¾ cup granulated sugar
½ teaspoon vanilla extract
2½ ounces (¾ cup) walnuts, finely chopped

42 COOKIES

Big Old-Fashioned Chocolate Cookies

Dark, thick, and soft, covered with a thin, dark chocolate glaze. These are easily mixed in a saucepan.

Adjust two racks to divide the oven into thirds and preheat oven to 375°. Line cookie sheets with parchment. Sift together the flour, baking soda, and salt, and set aside. Cut the butter into ½ inch slices and place in a heavy 3-quart saucepan. Add the chocolate and cook over low heat until melted. Remove from heat and with a wooden spoon, stir in the sugar. (The mixture will look curdled—it is okay.) Add the egg and the vanilla to the warm chocolate mixture and stir until smooth. Stir in half of the sifted dry ingredients. Then, very gradually, just a few drops at a time, stir in the milk. Add the remaining dry ingredients and stir briskly until completely smooth.

Use a heaping teaspoonful of dough for each cookie. Place them in even mounds 2 to 3 inches apart on the sheets.

Bake for 12 to 15 minutes, reversing sheets top to bottom and front to back to ensure even baking. The cookies are done if the tops spring back firmly when lightly touched with a fingertip.

Let stand for about a minute or so and then, with a wide metal spatula, transfer the cookies to racks to cool. Prepare glaze.

2 cups sifted all-purpose flour
½ teaspoon baking soda
Pinch of salt
4 ounces (1 stick) unsalted butter
2 ounces (2 squares) unsweetened chocolate
1 cup dark brown sugar, firmly packed
1 egg
1 teaspoon vanilla extract
½ cup milk

18 COOKIES

Chocolate Glaze

Over hot water, in the top of a small double boiler, melt the chocolate with the butter on moderate heat. Remove top of double boiler and stir in the 1½ tablespoons of hot water and the heavy cream. Add the confectioners sugar and stir until smooth. If necessary, adjust with a bit more water or sugar to make the consistency similar to a heavy cream sauce.

With a small metal spatula, smooth the glaze over the tops of the cookies, staying about ½ inch away from the edges.

Let stand for a few hours to dry.

1 ounce (1 square) unsweetened chocolate
1 tablespoon unsalted butter
1½ tablespoons hot water
2 tablespoons heavy cream
1 cup strained confectioners sugar

Key West Chocolate Treasures

These are large, semisoft chocolate-coconut cookies with chocolate icing.

Adjust two racks to divide the oven into thirds and preheat oven to 375°. Line cookie sheets with parchment. Sift together the flour, salt, and baking soda, and set aside. Dissolve the instant coffee in the boiling water.

Melt the chocolate with the prepared coffee in the top of a small double boiler over hot water on moderate heat. Stir until smooth. Remove the top of the double boiler and set aside.

In the large bowl of an electric mixer cream the butter. Add the vanilla and sugar, and beat to mix well. Beat in the egg. Add the chocolate mixture (which may still be slightly warm) and beat until smooth. On low speed gradually add half of the sifted dry ingredients, then all of the sour cream, and then the remaining dry ingredients, scraping the bowl with a rubber spatula and beating only until smooth after each addition.

Remove the bowl from the mixer and stir in the coconut.

Use a heaping teaspoonful of dough for each cookie—make these large—and place them 2 inches apart on the sheets.

Bake for 12 to 15 minutes, reversing the sheets top to bottom and front to back once to ensure even baking. The cookies are done if the tops spring back firmly when lightly touched with a fingertip. (If you bake only one sheet at a time use the higher rack.)

With a wide metal spatula transfer the cookies to racks to cool. Prepare the following icing.

2 cups sifted all-purpose flour
¼ teaspoon salt
¼ teaspoon baking soda
1 teaspoon instant coffee
½ cup boiling water
3 ounces (3 squares) unsweetened chocolate
4 ounces (1 stick) unsalted butter
1 teaspoon vanilla extract
1 cup dark brown sugar, firmly packed
1 egg
⅔ cup sour cream
2 ounces (generous ½ cup, firmly packed) shredded coconut

32 LARGE COOKIES

Key West Chocolate Icing

Melt the chocolate with the butter and the sour cream in the top of a small double boiler over hot water on moderate heat. Stir until the mixture is smooth. Remove the top of the double boiler and, off the heat, stir in the vanilla; then, gradually stir in the sugar.

Use the icing quickly, as it thickens while it stands. With a small metal spatula, a table knife, or the back of a teaspoon, spread the icing over the top of each cookie, but

1½ ounces (1½ squares) unsweetened chocolate
1 tablespoon unsalted butter
¼ cup sour cream
½ teaspoon vanilla extract
1½ cups strained confectioners sugar

do not spread it all the way to the edges; leave a small margin. Let the cookies stand for about an hour or more until the icing is firm and dry.

NOTE: If you store these in a box, place wax paper between the layers.

Chocolate Banana Cookies

These are large, thick, and soft.

Adjust two racks to divide the oven into thirds and preheat oven to 400°. Line cookie sheets with parchment. Place the chocolate in the top of a double boiler over hot water on moderate heat. Cover until partially melted. Then uncover and stir until completely melted and smooth. Remove from the heat and set aside to cool.

Sift together the flour, baking powder, baking soda, and salt, and set aside. In the small bowl of an electric mixer beat the bananas at low speed to mash them and to make 1 cup of pulp. Set aside.

In the large bowl of the electric mixer (without washing the beaters) cream the butter. Add the vanilla and the sugar and beat well. Add the eggs one at a time and beat well. On low speed gradually add half the sifted dry ingredients, scraping the bowl with a rubber spatula and beating only until mixed. Add the cooled chocolate and the bananas and beat until smooth. Add the remaining half of the dry ingredients and beat only until smooth. Stir in the nuts.

Use a heaping teaspoonful (make these rather large) of the dough for each cookie. Place them 2 inches apart on the cookie sheets.

Bake the cookies 12 to 14 minutes, reversing the position of the sheets top to bottom and front to back once or twice to ensure even baking. The cookies are done if the tops spring back firmly when lightly pressed with a fingertip.

Let the cookies stand for a moment and then, with your fingers (or spatula if you prefer), transfer the cookies to racks to cool.

6 ounces semisweet chocolate, cut into pieces
2¼ cups sifted all-purpose flour
2 teaspoons baking powder
¼ teaspoon baking soda
Scant ½ teaspoon salt
3 small or 2 large ripe bananas (to make 1 cup mashed)
5⅓ ounces (10⅔ tablespoons) unsalted butter
½ teaspoon vanilla extract
1 cup granulated sugar
2 eggs
6 ounces (generous 1½ cups) walnuts, cut or broken into medium-size pieces

55 LARGE COOKIES

Chocolate Applesaucers

These soft, moist, spicy, extra-large cookies were created and perfected in the kitchen of an apple farm in Pennsylvania.

Adjust two racks to divide the oven into thirds and preheat oven to 350°. Line cookie sheets with parchment.

Sift together the flour, baking soda, salt, cinnamon, and cloves, and set aside. Dissolve the instant coffee in the boiling water and set aside. In the large bowl of an electric mixer cream the butter. Add the sugar and beat well to mix. Add the egg and beat well to mix. On low speed beat in the cocoa, then the prepared coffee, and then the applesauce. (The mixture will look curdled—it is okay). On a low speed add the sifted dry ingredients, scraping the bowl with a rubber spatula and beating only until thoroughly mixed. Stir in the nuts and raisins.

These are very large cookies—use a ¼-cup measuring cup (4 level teaspoons) of the dough for each cookie, and place only 5 mounds on each sheet.

Bake for 25 minutes, reversing the sheets top to bottom and front to back as necessary to ensure even baking. If you bake only one sheet at a time, use the higher rack.

With a wide metal spatula transfer the cookies to racks to cool (see Notes).

While the cookies are cooling prepare the following icing.

2½ cups sifted all-purpose
    flour
1 teaspoon baking soda
½ teaspoon of salt
1½ teaspoons cinnamon
½ teaspoon ground cloves
1 teaspoon instant coffee
2 tablespoons boiling water
4 ounces (1 stick) unsalted
    butter
1 cup granulated sugar
1 egg
¼ cup unsweetened cocoa
    powder (preferably
    Dutch-process)
15 ounces (1½ cups) smooth
    (not chunky) applesauce
5 ounces (1 cup) raisins
½ cup walnuts, cut into
    medium-size pieces

22 EXTRA-LARGE COOKIES

Chocolate Icing

Place the sugar, cocoa, and salt in a small bowl of an electric mixer. Melt the butter and pour the hot butter and 3 tablespoons of boiling water into the bowl. Beat until smooth. The icing should be semifluid, but not thin enough to run off the cookies. It might be necessary to add a little more hot water, but add it gradually and only a few drops at a time. Or, if the icing is too thin, add a little more sugar. Transfer to a small shallow bowl for ease in handling.

With a teaspoon, spoon the icing onto a cookie and

1½ cups strained
    confectioners sugar
½ cup unsweetened cocoa
    powder
Pinch of salt
2⅔ ounces (5⅓ tablespoons)
    unsalted butter
About 3 tablespoons boiling
    water

then with the back of a spoon, spread it over the center of the cookie, keeping it ½ to ¾ inch away from the edges. Ice all of the cookies and then let them stand for a few hours to set.

NOTES: Since these are very large cookies, the cooling racks should be raised sufficiently from the counter top for air to circulate under the cookies; place the racks on right-side up cake pans or bowls.

These do not freeze well after they are iced; the icing may become sticky when thawed.

Coconut Grove Cookies

These are chocolate cookies with hidden chunks of chocolate and a baked-on coconut meringue topping.

Chocolate Dough

Adjust two racks to divide the oven into thirds and preheat oven to 375°. Line cookie sheets with parchment.

Sift together the flour, baking powder, and salt, and set aside. Place 4 ounces (reserve remaining 4) of the chocolate in the top of a small double boiler over hot water on moderate heat. Stir occasionally until melted and smooth, then remove from heat and set aside to cool.

To cut the remaining 4 ounces of chocolate, use a heavy knife, work on a cutting board, and cut the chocolate into pieces measuring ¼ to ½ inch across. Set aside.

In the large bowl of an electric mixer cream the butter. Add the vanilla and the instant coffee and then both sugars, and beat well. Beat in the egg yolks, scraping the bowl with a rubber spatula. Beat in the melted chocolate. On low speed gradually add half of the sifted dry ingredients, continuing to scrape the bowl with the spatula. Now gradually add the milk and the remaining dry ingredients and beat only until

2½ cups sifted cake flour (see Note)
1½ teaspoons baking powder
¼ teaspoon salt
8 ounces semisweet chocolate
4 ounces (1 stick) unsalted butter
1 teaspoon vanilla extract
2 teaspoons instant coffee
½ cup granulated sugar
¼ cup dark brown sugar, firmly packed
2 egg yolks (reserve the whites for the meringue topping)
⅓ cup milk

44 COOKIES

smooth. Remove the bowl from the mixer and stir in the cut chocolate pieces. Set the chocolate dough aside at room temperature and prepare the meringue topping.

Meringue Topping

In the small bowl of an electric mixer, with clean beaters, beat the egg whites together with the salt until the whites hold soft peaks. Gradually add the sugar, 1 to 2 spoonfuls at a time, and then beat at high speed until the meringue is very stiff. Toward the end of the beating, beat in the almond extract.

2 egg whites
Pinch of salt
½ cup granulated sugar
Scant ¼ teaspoon almond extract
2 tablespoons sifted cake flour (See Note)
7 ounces (2 cups, packed) finely shredded coconut

Remove the bowl from the mixer and fold in the flour and then the coconut.

To form the cookies: Use a rounded teaspoonful of the chocolate dough for each cookie and place them 2 inches apart on the cookie sheets. Then top each cookie with a slightly rounded teaspoonful of the meringue topping. In order to wind up even, use a tiny bit less of the meringue topping than you use of the chocolate dough for each cookie. Try to place the topping carefully so that it won't run off the chocolate cookie while it is baking. A little of it will run off the side of the cookie no matter what, but that's okay; it looks nice anyhow.

Bake 12 to 13 minutes, until the topping is lightly browned. Reverse the cookie sheets top to bottom and front to back once during baking to ensure even browning.

With a wide metal spatula transfer the cookies to racks to cool.

NOTE: Cake flour (not cake mix and not self-rising) is more finely ground than all-purpose flour and comes in a box. One cup sifted cake flour equals 1 cup minus 2 tablespoons sifted all-purpose flour, so in the dough recipe you could substitute 2¼ cups minus 1 tablespoon all-purpose flour, if cake flour is unobtainable.

Chocolate Raisin Cookies

These are large, rather thin cookies that are both soft-chewy and crisp-crunchy. They are old-fashioned cookie-jar cookies from Rhode Island.

Adjust two racks to divide the oven into thirds and preheat oven to 375°. Line cookie sheets with parchment.

Sift together the flour, baking powder, baking soda, and salt, and set aside. In the top of a small double boiler over hot water on moderate heat, melt the chocolate. Remove the top of the double boiler and set aside to cool slightly.

Pour boiling water over the raisins to cover, let stand 5 to 10 minutes, and then drain in a strainer.

In the large bowl of an electric mixer, cream the butter. Add the vanilla and the sugar and beat well. Add the egg and beat well again. Beat in the chocolate, and then add the sour cream and beat to mix. On low speed, gradually add the sifted dry ingredients, scraping the bowl with a rubber spatula and beating only until mixed. Stir in the raisins.

Transfer to a small bowl for ease of handling.

Use a heaping teaspoonful of dough for each cookie. Place them 2 to 3 inches apart on the sheets. (These spread.)

Bake for 18 to 20 minutes, reversing the sheets top to bottom and front to back once to ensure even baking. These are done if the tops spring back when lightly pressed with a fingertip. Do not overbake—these cookies should remain soft and chewy in the centers (with crisp edges). Overbaking will make them too hard.

If you are baking only one sheet at a time, bake it on the upper rack and be extra-careful not to overbake.

With a wide metal spatula transfer to racks to cool.

VARIATION: To make Chocolate Rum-Raisin Cookies, follow above directions with the following change. Prepare the raisins ahead of time as follows: Place them in a small saucepan and over them pour ½ cup dark rum. Place over moderate heat and bring to a low boil. Remove from the heat, cover, and let stand for several hours or overnight. Drain the raisins in a strainer set over a bowl and use any leftover rum for something else. I pour it (and a little more) into a glass of Coca-Cola.

1¾ cups sifted all-purpose flour
1 teaspoon baking powder
½ teaspoon baking soda
¼ teaspoon salt
2 ounces (2 squares) unsweetened chocolate
5 ounces (1 cup) raisins
Boiling water
5⅓ ounces (10⅔ tablespoons) unsalted butter
1 teaspoon vanilla extract
1⅔ cups granulated sugar
1 egg
½ cup sour cream

42 COOKIES

Chocolate and Peanut-Butter Ripples

A chocolate dough and a peanut-butter dough, baked together, make this a rather thin, crisp, candylike cookie.

Chocolate Dough

Adjust two racks to divide the oven into thirds and preheat oven to 325°. Line cookie sheets with parchment.

Melt the chocolate in the top of a double boiler over hot water on moderate heat. Remove the top of the double boiler and set aside.

In the large bowl of an electric mixer cream the butter. Add the vanilla, salt, and sugar, and beat well. Beat in the egg and then the melted chocolate, scraping the bowl as necessary with a rubber spatula. On low speed gradually add the flour and mix only until smooth.

Transfer the dough to a small shallow bowl for ease in handling. Set it aside and prepare the peanut-butter dough.

2 ounces (2 squares) unsweetened chocolate
4 ounces (1 stick) unsalted butter
1 teaspoon vanilla extract
¼ teaspoon salt
¾ cup granulated sugar
1 egg
1 cup sifted all-purpose flour

ABOUT 30 COOKIES

Peanut-Butter Dough

In the small bowl of the electric mixer cream the butter with the peanut butter. Beat in the sugar until well mixed. Add the flour and beat to mix.

Transfer to a small shallow bowl for ease in handling.

To shape the cookies: Divide the chocolate dough in half and set one-half aside. By level or barely rounded tea-spoonfuls, drop the remaining half on the cookie sheets, placing the mounds 2 inches apart. You will need 2 to 3 cookie sheets and will end up with 30 mounds of the dough.

2 tablespoons unsalted butter
¼ cup smooth (not chunky) peanut butter
½ cup light brown sugar, firmly packed
2 tablespoons sifted all-purpose flour

Top each mound with a scant teaspoon of peanut-butter dough. And then top each cookie with another teaspoonful of the set-aside chocolate dough. Don't worry about the doughs being exactly on top of each other.

Flatten the cookies slightly with a fork, dipping the fork in granulated sugar as necessary to keep it from sticking.

Bake for 15 minutes, reversing the cookie sheets top to bottom and front to back once to ensure even baking. If you bake only one sheet at a time, use the higher rack. Do not overbake. These cookies will become crisp as they cool.

Let the cookies cool briefly on the sheets only until they are firm enough to transfer with a wide metal spatula to racks. When cool, handle with care—these are fragile.

Chocolate Peanut Cookies

These dark-chocolate cookies have whole salted peanuts throughout and a chocolate glaze. They are dense, rich, and candylike.

Adjust two racks to divide the oven into thirds and preheat oven to 350°. Line cookie sheets with parchment.

In a small, heavy saucepan over low heat, or in the top of a small double boiler over hot water on moderate heat, melt the chocolate together with the butter. Then transfer it to the large bowl of an electric mixer and let stand 2 to 3 minutes to cool briefly. Beat in the sugar and then the eggs, one at a time. On low speed add the flour, scraping the bowl with a rubber spatula and beating only until thoroughly mixed. Stir in the peanuts. Transfer to a small bowl for ease in handling.

Place the dough by well-rounded teaspoonfuls 1 inch apart on the cookie sheets.

Bake for about 15 minutes, reversing the cookie sheets top to bottom and front to back once to ensure even baking. The cookies are done if the tops barely spring back when lightly touched with a fingertip.

With a wide metal spatula transfer the cookies to racks to cool.

3 ounces (3 squares) unsweetened chocolate
4 ounces (1 stick) unsalted butter
1½ cups granulated sugar
3 eggs
1½ cups sifted all-purpose flour
4 ounces (1 cup) whole salted peanuts (preferably dry roasted)

45 COOKIES

Chocolate Glaze

Place the milk, butter, chocolate, and salt in a heavy saucepan over low heat, or in the top of a double boiler over hot water on moderate heat. Stir frequently until the butter and chocolate are melted and the mixture is smooth (if it appears curdled, don't worry). Remove from the heat and stir in the vanilla and 2½ cups of the sugar—if necessary transfer the mixture to a larger bowl in order to have room to stir well. If it is not completely smooth, stir it vigorously with a wire whisk.

¼ cup milk
2 ounces (4 tablespoons) unsalted butter
2 ounces (2 squares) unsweetened chocolate
Pinch of salt
1 teaspoon vanilla extract
2½ cups plus about 1 tablespoon strained confectioners sugar (see page 12)

The glaze should be thick enough so that it does not run off the cookies, but it should be thin enough that it will spread out by itself to form a smooth layer about ⅛ inch thick. It might be necessary to add about 1 tablespoon more of the sugar.

Transfer the glaze to a small bowl for easier handling. Work quickly—the glaze thickens as it stands. If it becomes too thick add a bit of hot water, but be careful and only add a drop at a time.

Place about a teaspoonful of the glaze on top of each cookie, flattening it slightly with the back of the spoon, but do not spread it. As noted above, if it is the right consistency, it will run slightly by itself and almost cover the tops of the cookies. If just a bit runs off the top in places, it is to be expected.

Place the glazed cookies on racks set over wax paper and let them stand for a few hours until the glaze is set.

More
Drop Cookies

Mrs. L.B.J.'s Moonrocks

These are large and thick spice cookies with crisp, chewy edges and semisoft centers—real old-fashioned "down home" cookie-jar-fillers. In our home, and surrounding territory, everyone loves them. While they are baking, they perfume the house with an irresistible sweet-and-spicy aroma.

Adjust two racks to divide the oven into thirds and preheat oven to 350°. Line cookie sheets with parchment paper.

Sift together the flour, baking soda, salt, cloves, cinnamon, allspice, and nutmeg, and set aside.

In the large bowl of an electric mixer, beat the butter until it is soft. Beat in the sugar. Then add the eggs one at a time, beating until incorporated after each addition. Beat in the corn syrup. On low speed, add the sifted dry ingredients and beat until incorporated.

Remove from the mixer and with a large, heavy wooden spoon or rubber spatula stir in the coconut, raisins, dates, and nuts.

Use a well-rounded tablespoon of the dough for each cookie. Place the mounds of dough 2 inches apart on the sheets.

Bake two sheets at a time, reversing the sheets top to bottom and front to back as necessary to ensure even browning. Bake for 18 to 20 minutes, until the cookies are golden all over.

With a wide metal spatula transfer the cookies to racks to cool.

Store airtight.

4 cups sifted all-purpose flour
1 teaspoon baking soda
⅛ teaspoon salt
1 teaspoon ground cloves
1 teaspoon cinnamon
1 teaspoon allspice
1 teaspoon nutmeg
8 ounces (2 sticks) unsalted butter
1½ cups granulated sugar
3 eggs
½ cup dark corn syrup
3½ ounces (1 cup, packed) shredded coconut (sweetened or unsweetened)
5 ounces (1 cup) raisins (dark, light, or half of each)
8 ounces (1 cup, packed) dates (each date cut into about 4 pieces)
7 ounces (2 cups) walnuts, broken into large pieces

48 LARGE COOKIES

Old-Fashioned Spiced Pecan Cookies

These are dark, thick, and semisoft, sharply spiced, gingery, peppery, and wheaty. They are wonderful for a cookie jar, lunch box, or a satisfying snack at any time, although somehow I think of these as winter rather than summer cookies.

The dough must be well chilled before it is shaped (rolled into balls between your hands) and baked.

Stir the optional coffee into the boiling water and set aside to cool; if you do not use the coffee, simply measure ¼ cup of room-temperature water and set aside. Sift together the all-purpose flour, baking soda, cinnamon, ginger, cloves, salt, pepper, and nutmeg, and set aside.

In the large bowl of an electric mixer, beat the butter until soft. Beat in the sugar. Add the eggs one at a time, and beat to mix after each addition. Beat in the molasses and coffee or water. (The mixture will appear curdled—it is okay.) On low speed, beat in the sifted flour mixture and then the whole-wheat flour, and beat until incorporated.

Remove from the mixer and stir in the 1½ cups of pecans.

Transfer to a smaller bowl (or leave it in the mixer bowl, if you wish), cover airtight, and refrigerate until firm enough to handle, preferably overnight.

Before baking, adjust two racks to divide the oven into thirds and preheat oven to 350°. Line cookie sheets with parchment paper.

Place one long piece of foil on the counter next to the sink. With a tablespoon, spoon out about 10 or 12 mounds of the dough, each one a well-rounded tablespoonful (they may be placed right next to one another). Return the remaining dough to the refrigerator.

Wet your hands with cold water; shake them off, but do not dry them (they should be damp and cold). Pick up a mound of dough, roll it between your hands into a ball, and place it on a lined sheet. Continue to shape the balls and place them 2½ to 3 inches apart (7 balls on a 15½ x 12-inch cookie sheet).

Optional: 2 teaspoons instant coffee
¼ cup boiling water
1 cup sifted all-purpose flour
1 teaspoon baking soda
1 teaspoon cinnamon
1½ teaspoons powdered ginger
¾ teaspoon ground cloves
½ teaspoon salt
1 teaspoon finely ground white pepper
½ teaspoon nutmeg
4 ounces (1 stick) unsalted butter
1 cup dark brown sugar, firmly packed
2 eggs
¼ cup dark molasses
1½ cups sifted all-purpose whole-wheat flour
6 ounces (1½ cups) pecans, toasted (see To Toast Pecans, page 4), cut or broken into medium-size pieces
32 to 36 additional pecan halves, toasted (as above)

32 TO 36 RATHER LARGE COOKIES

Place a pecan half on top of each cookie and press it down slightly to flatten the cookie only a little bit (the cookies should remain rather thick).

Bake two sheets at a time for about 15 minutes, reversing the sheets front to back and top to bottom once during baking to ensure even browning. To test for doneness, press the top of a cookie gently with your fingertip; when the cookies just barely spring back, they are done.

With a wide metal spatula transfer the cookies to racks to cool.

Giant Oatmeal Spice Cookies

Very large, crisp, and crunchy, with a marvelous blend of spices. You will love them. Once shaped, these cookies should stand for two hours before baking; it will make them bake with a better shape.

Cut aluminum foil or parchment to fit cookie sheets. Sift together the flour, cinnamon, allspice, cloves, ginger, salt, black pepper, and baking soda, and set aside.

In the large bowl of an electric mixer, cream the butter. Add the vanilla and then both sugars and beat to mix well. Add the eggs and beat to mix. On low speed beat in the sifted dry ingredients. Remove from the mixer. With a wooden spoon stir in the oats.

Work next to the sink or have a bowl of water nearby so you can wet your hands while you shape the cookies. Spread out a large piece of wax paper or foil.

Use a ¼-cup measuring cup to measure the dough for each cookie. Form 20 mounds of the dough, and place them any which way on the parchment or foil.

Wet your hands with cold water, shake off the water, but do not dry your hands. Pick up a mound of the dough, roll it between your hands into a ball, flatten it between your hands until it is about ½ inch thick, and then place the cookies on the prepared foil or parchment, placing only 4 of them on a 12 x 15½-inch piece of foil or parchment. (They need a lot of room to spread.)

1½ cups sifted all-purpose flour
2 teaspoons cinnamon
2 teaspoons allspice
1½ teaspoons ground cloves
1½ teaspoons powdered ginger
½ teaspoon salt
½ teaspoon finely ground
  black pepper
½ teaspoon baking soda
8 ounces (2 sticks) unsalted
  butter
1 teaspoon vanilla extract
1 cup granulated sugar
1 cup light brown sugar,
  firmly packed
2 eggs
3 cups quick-cooking (not
  instant) rolled oats

20 VERY LARGE COOKIES

Let stand for 2 hours before baking.

When you are ready to bake, adjust two racks to divide the oven into thirds and preheat oven to 375°.

Slide the cookie sheets under the foil or parchment and bake for 12 to 13 minutes (no longer), reversing the sheets top to bottom and front to back as necessary to ensure even baking. Bake only until the cookies are nicely browned—be careful that they do not become too dark on the edges. If it looks as though they might, reduce the temperature by 10° or 15° for the last few minutes of baking. If you bake only one sheet at a time, bake it on the upper rack.

Let the baked cookies stand for a minute or so until they are firm enough to be moved. Then, with a wide metal spatula, transfer them to racks to cool.

Wrap the cookies two to a package (bottoms together) in clear cellophane or wax paper, or in plastic sandwich bags. Then place them all in a box or a larger plastic bag.

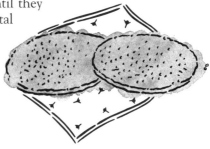

Crisp Oatmeal Wafers

These are the most amazingly and deliciously crisp and crunchy of any cookies I know. Even in my kitchen in humid Florida, they remain that way for weeks in an airtight cookie jar (the glass jars that have a ground-glass rim on the cover are airtight; those that do not have the ground-glass rim are not airtight).

These cookies are wonderful because they are so plain. They are easy-to-mix drop cookies made without flour. Somehow the flavor reminds me of popcorn and peanut brittle. These are especially appropriate when you want something crisp and crunchy to serve with ice cream, custard, or fruit.

Adjust two racks to divide the oven into thirds and preheat oven to 350°. Cut aluminum foil to fit cookie sheets. These must be baked on foil, even if you use a nonstick pan.

In the small bowl of an electric mixer, beat the eggs until foamy. Beat in the cinnamon, vanilla, salt, and sugar, and beat for 2 to 3 minutes until pale and thick. Add the melted butter and beat only to mix. Then add the baking powder (if it is lumpy it should be strained) and beat only for a moment or so to mix. Remove from the mixer, transfer to a larger bowl, and stir in the oats.

Use a rounded teaspoonful of the batter for each cookie, placing them about 2 inches apart, or only 6 on a 12 x 15½-inch piece of foil. Stir occasionally; the liquid settles.

Slide a cookie sheet under the foil. Bake two sheets at a time, reversing them top to bottom and front to back once during baking to ensure even browning. Bake for about 10 minutes. The cookies will rise and then settle down during baking. When they are thin (they will be almost lace cookies) and lightly colored—darker on the rim and lighter in the centers—they are done. You will have to be careful not to bake these either too little or too much; after the first sheet you will know when they are done.

Slide the foil off the sheet. Let stand until the cookies are cool. Slide the cookie sheet under another piece of foil with unbaked cookies on it (it is okay if the cookie sheet is warm).

When the cookies have cooled completely it will be easy to peel the foil away from the backs of the cookies. (If it is not easy it means that the cookies were not baked enough.)

These must be stored airtight or they will not remain crisp.

NOTE: Old-Fashioned Quaker Oats, which cook in 5 minutes, work very well for this recipe. Coarser oats that take longer cooking might not hold together in baking.

3 eggs
1 teaspoon cinnamon
1 teaspoon vanilla extract
½ teaspoon salt
1½ cups granulated sugar
2 tablespoons unsalted butter, melted and cooled
4 teaspoons baking powder
3½ cups quick-cooking (not instant) oatmeal (see Note)

48 COOKIES

Coconut Oatmeal Cookies

This is an old-fashioned, homey, plain and crisp, buttery cookie-jar cookie. They are quick and easy drop cookies that are especially good. The recipe was sent to me as a gift from a bakery in Jacksonville, Florida, where they are baked in huge quantities (700 cookies at a time) and are so popular that the bakery runs out of them every day. If you want to go into the cookie business, this is a good one to start with.

djust two racks to divide the oven into thirds and preheat oven to 350°. Line cookie sheets with aluminum foil or parchment.

Sift together the flour, baking powder, baking soda, salt, and cinnamon, and set aside.

In the large bowl of an electric mixer, cream the butter. Beat in the vanilla and both sugars and beat to mix well. Beat in the eggs, then on low speed beat in the sifted dry ingredients. Remove from the mixer.

With a wooden spoon, stir in the rolled oats and then the coconut.

Use a rounded teaspoonful of the dough for each cookie. Place them 2 to 3 inches apart on the foil-lined cookie sheets (I place only 8 on a 12 x 15½-inch sheet; these spread). Do not flatten the tops—they flatten themselves.

Bake for about 14 to 15 minutes, reversing the sheets top to bottom and front to back once during baking to ensure even browning. These will rise and then fall during baking. Bake only until the cookies are a rich golden brown all over; they will still feel soft to the touch, but do not bake any longer. These become crisp as they cool. When they are cool they should be crisp on the edges but slightly chewy in the middle.

Let the baked cookies stand on the sheet for a few seconds to firm up slightly before you remove them. Then, with a wide metal spatula, transfer the cookies to racks to cool.

2½ cups sifted all-purpose flour
1 teaspoon baking powder
1 teaspoon baking soda
¼ teaspoon salt
½ teaspoon cinnamon
8 ounces (2 sticks) unsalted butter
½ teaspoon vanilla extract
1 cup light or dark brown sugar, firmly packed
½ cup granulated sugar
2 eggs
1 cup quick-cooking (not instant) rolled oats
1 cup shredded coconut, firmly packed (it may be sweetened or unsweetened)

48 COOKIES

Raisin-Nut Cookies

These are especially wonderful, large, semisoft drop cookies full of raisins and nuts, and mildly flavored with a few spices. It is an old recipe from Boston, Massachusetts.

djust two racks to divide the oven into thirds and preheat oven to 375°. Line cookie sheets with parchment. Place the raisins in a small saucepan, pour the boiling water over them, place over moderate heat, bring to a boil, and boil for 3 minutes. Remove from the heat, and set aside to cool. (Do not drain.)

Sift together the flour, baking powder, baking soda, salt, cinnamon, and nutmeg, and set aside.

In the large bowl of an electric mixer, cream the butter. Beat in the vanilla and then the sugar. Beat to mix. Add the eggs and beat well. Then, on low speed, mix in the raisins and their liquid. On low speed, gradually add the sifted dry ingredients and beat, scraping the bowl with a rubber spatula, until thoroughly incorporated. Remove from mixer and stir in the nuts.

Use a rounded tablespoonful (make these large) of the dough for each cookie. Shape the mounds neatly, and place them 2 inches apart on the sheets.

Bake two sheets at a time, reversing the sheets top to bottom and front to back to ensure even browning. Bake for about 18 minutes until the cookies are golden brown and spring back when they are lightly pressed with a fingertip.

With a wide metal spatula, transfer the cookies to racks to cool.

It is best to wrap these individually in clear cellophane or in wax paper (not plastic wrap, because that is too much trouble). Or, if you package them in layers in a box or other container, they must have wax paper between the layers (if these are exposed to humidity they might stick together).

10 ounces (2 cups) raisins
1 cup boiling water
3½ cups sifted all-purpose flour
1 teaspoon baking powder
1 teaspoon baking soda
1 teaspoon salt
1 teaspoon cinnamon
½ teaspoon nutmeg
8 ounces (2 sticks) unsalted butter
1 teaspoon vanilla extract
1¾ cups granulated sugar
2 eggs
4 ounces (generous 1 cup) walnuts and 4 ounces (generous 1 cup) pecans or 8 ounces (2 cups) of either one, cut or broken into medium-size pieces

40 LARGE COOKIES

Tea Cakes

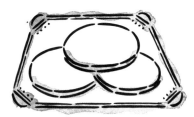

Scotty was about 16 years old, although she looked more like 12, when she knocked on our door looking for domestic work. She was scared stiff. She had absolutely no experience. She told me, in a whisper, that her parents worked as a live-in domestic couple for friends of ours. When Scotty lived with them she was never allowed into the kitchen or the main part of the house. When her grandmother was still alive, she occasionally visited her in Georgia. Scotty looked so sad and pleading that I had to say, "Okay, let's try it." She was bright and learned quickly. But she did not get over being afraid. I thought if I could teach her to cook some-

thing, she might relax and gain a little confidence; she had never cooked a thing. I asked her what she would like to make and she answered Tea Cakes, like her grandmother used to.

I had no idea what Tea Cakes were. We played Twenty Questions until I found out that they were very old-fashioned, extremely plain Southern cookies. I looked through old Southern recipes and picked one that sounded close to what Scotty had described. I made them, and they were wonderful. Scotty could not believe it—she said they were her grandma's Tea Cakes. Then I taught her to make them, and she was thrilled beyond words.

Incidentally, they became our favorite plain cookies and we were seldom without them.

Once Scotty started cooking she couldn't stop. She was a wonderful cook, and I had as much fun teaching her as she did learning. She stayed with us for several years.

(These have no salt or flavoring—typical of many very old recipes—but they are neither tasteless nor too bland.)

The dough must be refrigerated overnight before it is rolled out with a rolling pin, cut with a round cutter, and baked.

S ift together the baking soda with 1 cup of the flour (reserve the remaining 4¼ cups of flour) and set aside. In the large bowl of an electric mixer beat the butter until soft. Gradually add the sugar and beat for about a minute. Scrape the bowl as necessary with a rubber spatula all during the mixing. Add the eggs one at a time, beating until incorporated after each addition.

On low speed beat in the 1 cup of flour that has been sifted with the baking soda. Then add the remaining 4¼ cups of flour in five additions, alternating with the cream in four additions. Beat only until smooth after each addition.

Divide the dough roughly in quarters and wrap them individually in aluminum foil. Refrigerate overnight or longer.

½ teaspoon baking soda
5¼ cups sifted all-purpose flour
8 ounces (2 sticks) unsalted butter
3 cups granulated sugar
3 eggs
1 cup whipping cream

36 VERY LARGE COOKIES

Before baking, adjust two racks to divide the oven into thirds, preheat oven to 400°, and line cookie sheets with parchment paper.

Work with one quarter of the dough at a time, keeping the rest refrigerated. On a floured pastry cloth with a floured rolling pin, roll out the dough until it is ¼ to ⅓ inch thick. Work quickly before the dough softens.

Cut out the cookies with a 3½-inch (or larger or smaller) round cutter, dipping the cutter into flour as necessary to prevent sticking.

With a wide metal spatula, transfer the cookies to the sheets, placing them about 2 inches apart.

Bake for 13 to 15 minutes, reversing the sheets top to bottom and front to back once during baking to ensure even browning; bake until the cookies are slightly colored.

With a wide metal spatula, transfer the cookies to racks to cool.

If you bake only one sheet at a time, bake it on the upper rack.

Leftover pieces of the dough should be pressed together, wrapped, and rechilled before rolling.

My Mother's Gingersnaps

These are the cookies that my mother and I made together probably more often than any other. They may seem like a Christmas cookie, but we had jars and boxes of them around the house all year. For 30-odd years my father did his radio news broadcasts from home; that meant that people were coming and going all day and often late into the night. With plenty of these gingersnaps, we were always prepared, and many famous people left the house carrying a box or a bag.

Crisp, chewy, large and thin, spicy and peppery but mellow. The dough should be refrigerated overnight before rolling, cutting, and baking.

Cut the ginger into pieces ¼ inch or less and set aside. Sift together the all-purpose flour, baking soda, salt, pepper, and ground ginger, and set aside.

In the large bowl of an electric mixer, beat the butter until it is soft. Add the sugar and beat to mix. Beat in the molasses, egg, and vinegar (it might look curdled; it is okay). Then beat in the cut candied ginger. Add the sifted dry ingredients and the whole-wheat flour and beat on low speed until incorporated.

Spread out three lengths of wax paper or foil. Place one-third of the dough on each paper. Wrap and refrigerate overnight. (If you can't wait, freeze the packages for about an hour.)

Before baking, adjust two racks to divide the oven into thirds and preheat to 350°. Line cookie sheets with parchment paper.

To roll the dough, generously flour a pastry cloth and rolling pin. Place one piece of the chilled dough on the cloth, and press down on it a few times with the rolling pin. Turn the dough over to flour both sides; roll out the dough until it is ¼ inch thin. Work quickly. Do not leave the dough unattended; it becomes sticky and gooey if it is allowed to reach room temperature (which seems to happen quickly). Reflour the cloth and the pin as necessary.

With a round cookie cutter measuring 3⅛ inches in diameter (or any other size) cut out the cookies; start cutting at the outside edge of the dough and cut the cookies just barely touching each other. Reserve the scraps and press them together (the dough will be too sticky for you to press the scraps together with your hands—it is best to put the scraps in a bowl and mix them together with a spatula), wrap, and rechill.

3½ ounces (½ cup) candied ginger, loosely packed

2 cups unsifted all-purpose flour

1½ teaspoons baking soda

¾ teaspoon salt

¾ teaspoon finely ground black pepper (preferably fresh ground)

1½ teaspoons powdered ginger

8 ounces (2 sticks) unsalted butter

1 cup granulated sugar

¾ cup dark molasses

1 egg

1¼ teaspoons cider vinegar (see Note)

1 cup unsifted all-purpose whole-wheat flour

35 COOKIES

With a wide metal spatula, quickly transfer the cookies to the foil-lined sheets, placing them 2 inches apart (if the cookies are 3⅛ inches wide, I place only 5 cookies on a 15½ x 12-inch sheet—they spread).

Bake two sheets at a time, reversing the sheets top to bottom and front to back once during baking to ensure even baking. As they bake, the cookies will rise and then settle down into thin waferlike cookies. They will take about 15 minutes to bake; if you bake only one sheet, use a rack in the middle of the oven—one sheet might bake in slightly less time.

When the cookies are done, remove the sheets from the oven and let stand until they are just barely cool.

Then transfer the cookies with a wide metal spatula (if the backs of the cookies stick to the parchment paper the cookies were not baked long enough—return them to the oven).

Place on racks to finish cooling or just turn them over to allow the bottoms to dry. Store airtight.

NOTE: It is best to pour some vinegar into a cup and spoon out the amount you need. If you pour it into a spoon held over the mixing bowl, there is a very good chance you might pour more than you need.

100-*Percent* Whole-Wheat Ginger Cookies

*Thick, semisoft, wholesome, wheaty, and spicy. Made with a huge amount of fresh ginger; they are irresistible. Don't even **think** about these without a cup of hot coffee or a glass of cold milk.*

The dough must be well chilled before baking. This recipe is written for a food processor.

Grate the fresh ginger—do not remove it from the processor bowl. Cut the cold butter in half lengthwise and then cut it crosswise into ½-inch pieces. With the motor going, add the pieces one at a time, pausing briefly between additions. Process until the butter is soft and thoroughly mixed with the ginger. Adding and processing the butter should take about 30 seconds.

Remove the cover of the machine, add the vanilla, salt, cloves, cinnamon, and egg yolks, and process on/off just to mix. Remove the cover again, add the sugar and about half of the flour, and process to mix. Then add the remaining flour and process until the mixture is smooth; it might be necessary to stop the machine and stir the ingredients once or twice with a rubber spatula to help the mixing.

Remove the mixture from the processor to a piece of wax paper, wrap in the paper, and refrigerate for several hours (or overnight if you wish), or freeze for about 1 hour, until firm enough to be rolled out.

Before baking, adjust two racks to divide the oven into thirds and preheat oven to 350°. Line two cookie sheets with parchment paper or aluminum foil shiny side up.

Lightly flour a pastry cloth and rolling pin. Place the chilled dough on the floured cloth, roll it a bit, then turn the dough over to flour the other side. Roll out the dough until it is ⅜ inch thick (it will be an oval or oblong about 12 x 9 inches).

With a 2-inch round cookie cutter, cut out cookies starting at the outside edge of the rolled-out dough and cutting the cookies so they just touch each other.

Place the cookies about 1 inch apart on the lined sheets. (I do not flour the cutter when cutting these cookies because it does not seem to make any difference with this dough, but you might like to try it.)

Chill, reroll, and cut the scraps in the same manner.

Bake these plain—as they are—or with the following optional topping. (The cookies are equally good with or without the topping, but sesame seeds, known as benne seeds in the South, are supposed to bring good luck.)

2½ ounces (a piece about 2½ inches long and about 1½ inches thick—to make ½ cup grated) fresh ginger

4 ounces (1 stick) unsalted butter, cold

½ teaspoon vanilla extract

¼ teaspoon salt

½ teaspoon ground cloves

1 teaspoon cinnamon

2 egg yolks

1 cup dark brown sugar, firmly packed

2 cups sifted all-purpose whole-wheat flour (preferably stone ground from a health food store); see Notes

24 COOKIES

Optional Topping

To bring out the flavor of the seeds they must be toasted before they are used. (I don't understand why they don't become toasted on top of the cookies in the oven while the cookies are baking, but they don't.) Place them in a small, heavy frying pan over moderate heat. Shake the pan frequently for the first few minutes and then constantly as the seeds start to color. It should take about 5 to 7 minutes for the seeds to toast to a nice golden color (some will be darker than others).

Brush the cookies with milk and, while they are still wet, sprinkle them gener-

About 2 tablespoons sesame seeds (bleached or natural)

Milk

ously with the toasted seeds.

Bake for about 25 to 28 minutes, reversing the sheets top to bottom and front to back once during baking to ensure even browning. The cookies should become only slightly darker and almost (but not completely) firm to the touch.

With a wide metal spatula transfer the cookies to racks to cool. Store airtight.

NOTES: Any flour that is too coarse to go through the sifter should be stirred into the part that did go through.

You will probably see fibers of ginger on the edges of the cookies, both before and after baking. Think of it as seeds of a vanilla bean in ice cream; you know it's the real thing.

Granny's Old-Fashioned Sugar Cookies

These are crisp, large, thin, plain cookies with a divine lemon-and-cinnamon flavor. Everyone raves about them and asks for the recipe.

It is best to refrigerate this dough overnight before rolling it out and cutting it with a cookie cutter.

Sift together the flour, baking powder, and salt, and set aside. In the large bowl of an electric mixer, beat the butter until it is soft. Beat in the lemon rind and juice and then add the sugar. Beat in the egg and the whipping cream. Then, on low speed, gradually add the sifted dry ingredients and beat until smoothly mixed. Remove from the mixer.

Turn the dough out onto a length of wax paper or plastic wrap, wrap it, and refrigerate overnight. (In a hurry, I have used the freezer instead of the refrigerator—only until the dough was cold and firm but not frozen.)

When you are ready to bake, adjust two racks to divide the oven into thirds and preheat oven to 375°. Line cookie sheets with parchment paper or with foil shiny side up. Set aside.

Spread out a pastry cloth, flour it well, and flour a rolling pin. Unwrap the dough, cut it into thirds, and place one piece on the floured cloth. If it was refrigerated

overnight, it will be too stiff to roll out; pound it firmly with
the floured rolling pin, turning the dough over occasionally
until it is soft enough to be rolled. Roll it out until it is
quite thin, about ⅛ to 3/16 inch thick.

Use a large round cookie cutter about 3½ inches in diameter (more or less). Start to cut the cookies at the outside
edge of the dough and cut them so close to each other that
they are touching. With a wide metal spatula transfer the
cookies to the lined sheets, placing them ½ inch apart.

It is best not to reroll the scraps if possible because they
would absorb additional flour and would become a bit
tougher than otherwise. Here's a hint: Do not press the
scraps together but, with smaller cutters, cut out as many
smaller cookies as you can. Or use a knife and cut squares or
triangles. There will still be some leftover scraps, but much
less than otherwise. Reserve the scraps. Roll and cut the remaining dough. Then
press all the scraps together, refrigerate if necessary (it will not be), roll it out, and cut
with a knife or with cutters.

1¾ cups unsifted all-purpose
  flour
2 teaspoons baking powder
¼ teaspoon salt
4 ounces (1 stick) unsalted
  butter
Finely grated rind of 2 lemons
1 tablespoon lemon juice
1 cup granulated sugar
1 egg
2 tablespoons whipping cream

18 TO 24 LARGE COOKIES

Cinnamon-Sugar

Mix the ingredients and, with your fingertips, sprinkle over
the cookies.

Bake for 10 to 13 minutes, reversing the sheets top to
bottom and front to back as necessary to ensure even
browning. When done, the cookies will be only sandy colored, slightly darker on the rims.

With a wide metal spatula transfer the cookies to racks to cool.

Store airtight. These last well if you stay away from them.

1 tablespoon granulated sugar
⅓ teaspoons cinnamon
Pinch of nutmeg

Half-Moon-Shaped Cookies

Here is an easy way to cut cookies into an attractive shape and have only a minimum of leftover scraps. (This procedure may be used for any recipe that calls for a cookie cutter. I am placing it here because I have often made the preceding Granny's Old-Fashioned Sugar Cookies this way.)

After rolling out the dough, use a round cookie cutter to cut away a small (about 1-inch) section at the edge of the dough; that piece will be a scrap. Now move the cutter away from you and place it on the dough, forming a wide—or narrow—half moon. Cut the cookie and move the cutter again to cut the next cookie. In this way, the outside curve of each cookie becomes the inside curve of the next cookie, and there are no scraps—except along the edge of the rolled-out dough.

Savannah Crisps

On a recent trip to Savannah, I heard raves about a cookie—a sweet cracker—called Brittle Bread; paper thin . . . golden brown . . . crisp and crunchy . . . mildly sweetened . . . its thinness is unusual and hard to believe, its flavor is buttery and delicious. Do you know lavosh? This is somewhat like a sweet lavosh, but more tender.

It saves time when making these if you have many cookie sheets. The dough is quickly and easily mixed in a food processor, or it can be made without a processor.

These keep well, they stay dry and crisp for weeks in our house, but handle with care; they are fragile.

It is best to bake these on large cookie sheets, doubled (one placed on top of another); have the cookie sheets ready, unbuttered. Adjust as many racks to the middle area of the oven as you have double cookie sheets. Preheat oven to 350°.

Cut the butter into quarters lengthwise, and then across into ½-inch widths, and refrigerate.

To make this in a processor: Place the flour, sugar, salt, and baking soda in the processor bowl fitted with the metal chopping blade. Process on/off a few times to mix. Add the butter and process for about 5 seconds until the mixture resembles coarse crumbs. Then uncover, add the yogurt, and process for 10 to 15 seconds until the mixture holds together and clears the sides of the bowl.

To make this without a processor: Sift the dry ingredients into a mixing bowl. Add the butter and with a pastry blender cut it in until the mixture resembles coarse crumbs. Add the yogurt and stir well until thoroughly mixed.

Turn the mixture out onto a lightly floured surface and knead briefly for a few seconds. With your hands, form the mixture into an even, sausage-like roll, 10 inches long. With a long-bladed knife cut the roll in half the long way. Then cut each half into 10 1-inch pieces. Cover the pieces with plastic wrap to prevent drying out.

One at a time, with your hands, roll each piece into a ball and then, on a lightly floured board with a lightly floured rolling pin, roll out the ball until it is paper thin, turning it over as necessary to keep both sides floured enough not to stick. Reflour the board and rolling pin as necessary. The rolled-out circle of dough should be about 7 inches in diameter. Do not worry about making the circle perfect.

Place the rounds of dough close to each other on an unbuttered cookie sheet. Two or three crackers will fit on each sheet, depending on its size.

Sprinkle the tops of the crackers with the crystal sugar or granulated sugar, using about a teaspoonful for each cracker.

To press the sugar into the crackers, it is best to press down on it firmly with the heel of your hand and/or your fingertips until you are sure that the sugar is there to stay.

Bake the crackers until they are honey-colored, reversing the sheets front to back (and also top to bottom if you are baking on more than one rack) as necessary to ensure even browning. Do not underbake; adequate baking not only assures crisp cookies, but it also improves the flavor. If you bake on only one rack at a time, the crackers might be done in about 10 to 12 minutes; if you bake on two or three racks at the same time, the crackers might take 14 to 16 minutes or longer.

Cool completely on the cookie sheets. Then store airtight in plastic freezer boxes or plastic bags.

VARIATION: There is a less sweet variation of this that is made with a bit of coarse salt sprinkled on top instead of sugar. Make 1 or 2 as samples, using very little salt until you are sure of how much (or how little) to use. Serve this salted cracker plain or with soft cheese.

4 ounces (1 stick) unsalted butter, cold
2¾ cups unsifted all-purpose flour
¼ cup granulated sugar
½ teaspoon salt
½ teaspoon baking soda
8 ounces unflavored yogurt (I use Dannon low-fat)
Crystal sugar (see page 5) or additional granulated sugar

20 6- TO 7-INCH WAFERS

Sycamore Cookies

This is an old recipe from deep in the heart of peanut country, Sycamore, Georgia, from a friend of my husband's who is a peanut farmer and a marvelous cook.

The cookies are quick and easy to make. They are thin, crisp, buttery, irresistible brown-sugar peanut cookies. Serve them with tea or coffee, or alongside vanilla ice cream.

Adjust a rack to the middle of the oven and preheat oven to 325°. Butter a 10½ x 15½-inch jelly-roll pan and place it in the freezer. (It will be easier to spread the very thin layer of dough in a frozen pan.)

Chop the peanuts finely (do not grind them or powder them); to do this in a food processor place them in the processor bowl fitted with the metal chopping blade and process on/off as briefly as possible 10 times (it should take less than 10 seconds); set aside.

Sift together the flour, baking soda, and cinnamon, and set aside. In the small bowl of an electric mixer, beat the butter until soft. Add the vanilla and sugar and beat to mix. Then mix in 2 tablespoons of the egg (save the remaining beaten egg to use below), the sifted dry ingredients, and half of the chopped peanuts (reserve the remaining chopped peanuts).

Place the batter by large spoonfuls all over the frozen pan and with the bottom of a spoon spread it to cover the pan as well as you can. It will be a very thin layer and it might have a few bare spots.

Drizzle the remaining beaten egg over the top and with a brush spread it all over. Sprinkle the remaining peanuts over the top.

Bake for 25 minutes, reversing the pan once front to back after about 15 minutes. The top will be nicely (but lightly) browned and will feel soft to the touch; it will become crisp when cool.

Let stand for about 5 minutes, only until just firm enough to cut. With a small, sharp knife cut into 16 large oblongs and immediately, while they are warm, remove the cookies from the pan with a wide metal spatula. Either place them on a rack to cool or, if you want smaller cookies, place them on a board and cut the oblongs in half; then place on a rack to cool.

Store airtight.

1 cup salted peanuts
1 cup sifted all-purpose flour
¼ teaspoon baking soda
½ teaspoon cinnamon
4 ounces (1 stick) unsalted butter
1 teaspoon vanilla extract
½ cup dark brown sugar, firmly packed
1 egg, beaten

16 LARGE OR 32 SMALL COOKIES

Raisin Pillows

This is an old-fashioned, early American cookie that I have updated and simplified a bit by using a food processor. You will make a thick and chewy raisin filling (see Notes) and a deliciously buttery, crisp-but-tender dough somewhat like sugar cookies. After the filling and the dough are both chilled for an hour or so, the dough is rolled out, cut into rounds, sandwiched together with the raisin filling, and baked. Making these will keep you busy for a few hours; it is fun, gratifying, and the cookies are something special.

Raisin Filling

With a vegetable parer remove the thin orange-colored rind from the orange. Place the sugar and the pared rind in the bowl of a food processor fitted with the metal chopping blade. Process for a few minutes until the rind is cut into small pieces. Add the raisins and without waiting, with the machine running, add the juice (or juice and water) through the feed tube and—now be very careful—process for only 5 to 10 seconds, just until the raisins are chopped coarsely; they should not be in too-small pieces and should definitely not be processed until ground. If the mixture looks like large-egg caviar, it is just right.

1 large deep-colored orange
½ cup granulated sugar
10 ounces (2 cups) dark raisins
⅔ cup orange juice (or part juice and part water)
1 tablespoon plus 1 teaspoon lemon juice
Optional: 2 tablespoons dark rum
1 tablespoon unsalted butter

In a 2½- to 3-quart saucepan stir the raisin mixture frequently over high heat until the sugar melts and the mixture comes to a boil. Then adjust the heat to allow the mixture to boil slowly and stir occasionally for about 15 minutes until the mixture thickens, but do not overcook. The mixture will thicken more as it cools. Add the lemon juice and the optional rum, boil for about 3 more minutes, remove from the heat, add the butter, stir to melt, cool to room temperature, and then chill in the refrigerator or freezer.

Cookie Dough

Sift together the flour, baking powder, and salt, and set aside. In the large bowl of an electric mixer, beat the butter until soft. Beat in the vanilla and the sugar. Add the egg and then, on low speed, gradually add the milk and the sifted dry ingredients, scraping the bowl as necessary with a rubber spatula until thoroughly mixed.

The dough will be soft and sticky. Transfer it to a large piece of wax paper or foil. Fold over the ends of the paper or foil to enclose the dough, or cover it with another long piece of wax paper or foil. Press down on the dough to flatten until it is about 1 inch thick. Slide a cookie sheet under the package of dough and transfer it to the freezer for 30 to 60 minutes, or to the refrigerator for a longer time; it must be chilled enough so you can peel away the wax paper without it sticking to the dough.

Before baking, adjust two racks to divide the oven into thirds and preheat oven to 350°. Line cookie sheets with parchment paper or aluminum foil shiny side up.

Generously flour a pastry cloth and a rolling pin.

Cut off about one-third of the dough and replace the remainder in the freezer or refrigerator. On the floured cloth, turn the piece of dough over to flour both sides, pound it lightly with the rolling pin to soften it a bit, and then roll it out to ⅛-inch thickness. It must not be any thinner; a little thicker will not hurt, but if it is thinner the cookies will not hold together.

With a round cookie cutter measuring about 2⅜ inches in diameter, cut out cookies; start cutting at the outside edges of the dough, flour the cutter as necessary, and cut the cookies as close to one another as possible.

Arrange half of the cookies 2 inches apart (these spread) on the lined sheets. (Leftover scraps may be pressed together and rechilled before rolling—so be sure to chill this thoroughly or the dough will absorb too much flour and will not be as tender.)

Place a scant teaspoonful (more or less depending on the diameter of the cookies) of the raisin filling in the center of each cookie; keep the filling away from the edges. Then top each cookie with another round of the dough (it is best to use a small metal spatula to transfer the dough). With your fingertips gently press the edges of the cookies together; the top cookie will not reach out to the rim of the bottom cookie—it is okay, they will blend together when baked and the filling will not run out of the sides.

Now, dip the prongs of the fork in flour and with the back of the prongs press down gently (not too hard) all around the rims, to seal the tops and bottoms together and to make a slightly ridged design around the rim.

Repeat directions to shape all the cookies.

Bake two sheets at a time for about 20 minutes, reversing the sheets top to bottom and front to back as necessary to ensure even browning. Bake until the cookies are an attractive golden color. Do not underbake; these should not be too pale. (If they bake until golden brown, the flavor of the browned butter is delicious.)

With a wide metal spatula transfer to a rack to cool.

NOTES: To make these without a processor, grate the orange rind on a grater, chop the raisins on a board with a long, heavy, sharp knife, and then just mix the rind, sugar, raisins, and orange juice.

Leftover Raisin Filling makes a delicious spread with toast and butter.

3 cups sifted all-purpose flour
1 tablespoon baking powder
¼ teaspoon salt
8 ounces (2 sticks) unsalted butter
2 teaspoons vanilla extract
1 cup granulated sugar
1 egg
⅓ cup milk

24 TO 36 COOKIES

Whole-Wheat and Honey Hermits

Recipes for Hermits go back hundreds of years. Some were made as Bar cookies. See page 140. But they all have fruit, nuts, and spices.

Adjust two racks to divide the oven into thirds and preheat oven to 400°. Line cookie sheets with parchment. Strain together (see Note) the flour, baking soda, cinnamon, allspice, nutmeg, and salt, and set aside. In the large bowl of an electric mixer cream the butter. Add the sugar and beat well. Beat in the honey, then the eggs and then the milk. On low speed gradually add the strained dry ingredients, scraping the bowl with a rubber spatula and beating only until mixed. Stir in the raisins, currants, dates, and nuts.

Use a heaping teaspoonful of the dough for each cookie. Place them 2 inches apart on the cookie sheets.

Bake for 12 to 15 minutes, until cookies barely spring back when lightly touched with a fingertip. Reverse the cookie sheets top to bottom and front to back once to ensure even baking.

With a wide metal spatula transfer the cookies to racks to cool.

NOTE: Since whole-wheat flour is generally too coarse to be sifted, it is better to strain it. With your fingertips, press it through a large strainer set over a large bowl. Any pieces that are too coarse to go through a strainer should be stirred into the strained flour.

2½ cups strained all-purpose whole-wheat flour (see Note)
1 teaspoon baking soda
1 teaspoon cinnamon
½ teaspoon allspice
¼ teaspoon nutmeg
¼ teaspoon salt
4 ounces (1 stick) unsalted butter
½ cup raw sugar, light or dark, firmly packed
1 cup honey
2 eggs
3 tablespoons milk
5 ounces (1 cup) raisins
5 ounces (1 cup) currants
8 ounces (1 cup) pitted dates, coarsely cut into 3 or 4 pieces
8 ounces (2¼ cups) walnuts, cut or broken into medium-size pieces

48 TO 60 COOKIES

Connecticut Nutmeg Hermits

djust two racks to divide the oven into thirds and preheat oven to 375°. Line cookie sheets with parchment. Sift together the flour, baking soda, salt, and nutmeg, and set aside. In the large bowl of an electric mixer cream the butter. Add the sugar and beat well, then the eggs one at a time, beating well after each addition. On low speed, gradually add the sifted dry ingredients, scraping the bowl with a rubber spatula and beating only until thoroughly blended. Mix in the water and then the raisins and nuts.

Use a rounded teaspoonful of the dough for each cookie, and place them 2 inches apart on the cookie sheets.

Bake for 12 to 15 minutes, until the cookies are well browned and semifirm to the touch. Reverse the sheets top to bottom and front to back as necessary to ensure even browning. If you are baking one sheet at a time, use the higher rack.

With a wide metal spatula transfer the cookies to racks to cool.

2 cups sifted all-purpose flour
½ teaspoon baking soda
¼ teaspoon salt
¾ teaspoon nutmeg
4 ounces (1 stick) unsalted
   butter
1 cup light brown sugar,
   firmly packed
2 eggs
2 tablespoons water
5 ounces (1 cup) raisins
2½ ounces (¾ cup) walnuts,
   cut or broken into medium-
   size pieces

36 COOKIES

Giant Ginger Cookies

These won first prize in a New England county fair. They are huge, soft, and spicy—and enough for filling a large cookie jar (or two).

djust two racks to divide the oven into thirds and preheat oven to 350°. Line cookie sheets with parchment. Sift together the flour, baking soda, salt, cinnamon, ginger, cloves, and mustard, and set aside. In the large bowl of an electric mixer cream the butter. Add the instant coffee and beat well. Then beat in the sugar. Add the molasses and beat until smooth. Add the egg and beat well; the mixture will look curdled—it's okay. On low speed add the sifted dry ingredients in three additions alternately with the milk in two additions, scraping the bowl as necessary with a rubber spatula and beating only until smooth after each addition. Stir in the currants.

Use a heaping tablespoonful of the dough for each cookie. Make these extra-large—use as much dough as you can reasonably pile on the spoon. Place the cookies 2½ to 3 inches apart, keeping the cookies as round and as even as possible.

Bake for 20 to 22 minutes, reversing the sheets top to bottom and front to back a few times to insure even baking. Be careful that the bottoms of the cookies on the lower sheet do not burn; if the bottoms of the cookies seem to be turning too dark, change the position of the lower sheets often, or raise the rack, or slide an extra cookie sheet under the lower one. If you bake only one sheet at a time, use the higher rack. Bake until the tops of the cookies spring back sharply when lightly pressed with a fingertip.

With a wide metal spatula transfer the cookies to racks to cool. Because these are such large cookies they will form steam as they cool and the steam will make the bottoms moist. To prevent that, raise the cooling racks by placing them on right-side-up cake pans or mixing bowls.

4¾ cups sifted all-purpose flour
3 teaspoons baking soda
½ teaspoon salt
2 teaspoons cinnamon
2 teaspoons powdered ginger
1 teaspoon ground cloves
1 teaspoon mustard powder
8 ounces (2 sticks) unsalted butter
1 tablespoon instant coffee
1 cup granulated sugar
1 cup molasses
1 extra-large or jumbo egg
¾ cup milk
6¼ ounces (1¼ cups) currants (see Note)

28 EXTRA-LARGE COOKIES

NOTE: If the currants are not especially soft and fresh they should be softened before using. Do this before starting with the rest of the recipe. Cover the currants with boiling water, let stand for a few minutes, and drain them in a strainer. Or, steam them for a few minutes in a vegetable steamer. Then spread them out on several layers of paper towels, and pat the tops with paper towels. Let the currants stand on the paper until you are ready for them. Or steam them for a few minutes in a vegetable steamer.

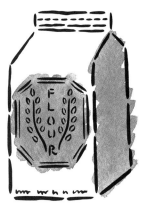

Mountain-Honey Gingersnaps

These come from Chamonix in the French Alps. They are crisp, crunchy, chewy, and mildly spiced.

Adjust two racks to divide the oven into thirds and preheat oven to 350°. Line cookie sheets with parchment. Sift together the flour, baking soda, salt, ginger, cinnamon, and cloves, and set aside. In the large bowl of an electric mixer cream the butter. Beat in the sugar to mix. Beat in the egg and then the honey. On low speed gradually add the sifted dry ingredients, scraping the bowl with a rubber spatula and beating only until thoroughly mixed. Transfer the mixture to a small bowl for ease in handling.

Place the dough by well-rounded teaspoonfuls on the sheets. Shape the cookies carefully in even mounds and place them 3 to 4 inches apart (these spread; place only 6 to 8 cookies on a 12 x 15½-inch cookie sheet).

Place a pecan half on the top of each cookie, pressing it slightly off to one side.

Bake for 13 to 15 minutes, until the cookies are richly browned all over. Reverse the cookie sheets top to bottom and front to back as necessary during baking to ensure even browning. The cookies will still feel soft to the touch but they will harden as they cool—do not overbake. These cookies will rise during baking and then flatten while cooling.

With a wide metal spatula transfer the cookies to racks to cool.

These must be stored airtight or they become soft and limp. (This has to do with the humidity. In the French Alps they stay crisp, but in Miami they do not.) They may be recrisped by placing them on cookie sheets in a moderate oven for a few minutes until they are very hot. Then cool again on racks.

2¼ cups sifted all-purpose flour
1½ teaspoons baking soda
½ teaspoon salt
1 teaspoon powdered ginger
½ teaspoon cinnamon
¼ teaspoon ground cloves
6 ounces (1½ sticks) unsalted butter
1 cup light brown sugar, firmly packed
1 egg
¼ cup honey
36 pecan halves

36 LARGE COOKIES

Sour-Cream Ginger Cookies

These are light-colored cookies—thick, soft, and gingery—with a thin, dry, white glaze.

Adjust two racks to divide the oven into thirds and preheat oven to 375°. Line cookie sheets with parchment. Sift together the flour, baking soda, salt, ginger, and cinnamon, and set aside. In the large bowl of an electric mixer cream the butter. Add the sugar and beat well. Beat in the molasses. Add the egg and beat well. On low speed add the dry ingredients in three additions, alternating with the sour cream in two additions. Scrape the bowl with a rubber spatula and beat only until smooth.

Use a rounded teaspoonful of the dough for each cookie. Shape the mounds carefully and place them 1½ to 2 inches apart.

Bake for 12 to 14 minutes, reversing the sheets top to bottom and front to back once during baking to ensure even browning. When the tops of the cookies are lightly pressed with a fingertip and spring back, the cookies are done.

With a wide metal spatula transfer the cookies to racks to cool.

Prepare the following glaze.

2½ cups sifted all-purpose
   flour
½ teaspoon baking soda
⅛ teaspoon salt
2 teaspoons powdered ginger
1 teaspoon cinnamon
6 ounces (1½ sticks) unsalted
   butter
1 cup light brown sugar,
   firmly packed
2 tablespoons light molasses
1 egg
½ cup sour cream

42 COOKIES

White Glaze

In the small bowl of an electric mixer beat the egg white briefly only until it is foamy. Add the sugar, salt, butter, and vanilla, and beat well for 2 or 3 minutes. The mixture should be runny enough to make a smooth glaze, but not so thin that much of it runs off the sides (a little bit will)—if necessary add more sugar. Transfer to a small bowl for ease in handling.

Place the racks of cookies over wax paper.

With a pastry brush, brush the glaze over the cookies and then let stand on the racks until the glaze is completely hard and dry.

1 egg white
1½ cups strained
   confectioners sugar
⅛ teaspoon salt
1 tablespoon unsalted butter,
   melted
1 teaspoon vanilla extract

Sunflower Coconut Cookies

Adjust two racks to divide the oven into thirds and preheat oven to 375°. Line cookie sheets with parchment.

Sift together the flour, baking powder, baking soda, and salt, and set aside. In the large bowl of an electric mixer cream the butter. Beat in the brown sugar, then the honey, egg, and orange juice. On low speed gradually add half of the sifted dry ingredients, then the sour cream, and then the remaining dry ingredients, scraping the bowl with a rubber spatula and beating only until thoroughly mixed.

Remove the bowl from the mixer. Add the orange and lemon rinds and stir to mix well. Then stir in the oatmeal, coconut, raisins, and the sunflower kernels.

Use a heaping teaspoon or a rounded tablespoon of the dough for each cookie—make them rather large. Place the mounds evenly 2½ to 3 inches apart on the sheets.

If you wish, sprinkle the tops of the cookies with the optional coconut or chopped nuts.

Bake the cookies for 18 to 20 minutes, until the tops spring back when lightly pressed with a fingertip and the cookies are golden brown. Reverse the position of the sheets top to bottom and front to back as necessary to ensure even browning. These cookies have a tendency to burn on the bottom, so be prepared to slide extra cookie sheets under the sheets holding the cookies—at least under the one on the lower rack. If you bake only one sheet at a time, use the higher rack.

With a wide metal spatula transfer the cookies to racks to cool.

NOTE: Do not use toasted or salted sunflower kernels (seeds). Use the raw, natural, unprocessed ones that are available at health-food stores.

2½ cups sifted all-purpose flour
1 teaspoon baking powder
½ teaspoon baking soda
½ teaspoon salt
6 ounces (1½ sticks) unsalted butter
1 cup light brown sugar, firmly packed
½ cup honey
1 egg
1 tablespoon orange juice (grate and reserve the rind before squeezing the juice)
¾ cup sour cream
Finely grated rind of 1 large orange
Finely grated rind of 1 large lemon
1 cup old-fashioned or quick-cooking (not instant) oatmeal
3½ ounces (1 cup, packed) shredded coconut
5 ounces (1 cup) raisins
4 ounces (1 cup) sunflower kernels (see Note)
Optional: additional shredded coconut or coarsely chopped walnuts or pecans (for topping the cookies)

36 LARGE COOKIES

Date-Nut Wafers

These are large, thin, crisp-chewy, old-fashioned wafers.

Adjust two racks to divide the oven into thirds and preheat oven to 350°. Line cookie sheets with parchment.

Place the cut dates in a medium-size mixing bowl. Add about 2 tablespoons of the sifted flour. With your fingers, toss the dates to separate them thoroughly and coat each piece with flour. Set aside.

Sift together the remaining flour, baking soda, cream of tartar, and cinnamon, and set aside. In the large bowl of an electric mixer cream the butter. Beat in the vanilla and then add both sugars and beat well. Add the eggs one at a time, beating well after each addition. On low speed gradually add the sifted dry ingredients, scraping the bowl with a rubber spatula and beating only until thoroughly mixed.

Remove the bowl from the mixer. With a rubber spatula or wooden spoon, stir in the dates, (including any left-over flour), and the nuts.

Use a heaping teaspoonful of the dough for each cookie—make these rather large. Place the mounds of dough 3 inches apart, placing only 5 on each sheet (these spread during baking). With the back of the spoon, flatten the cookies slightly in order to distribute the dates and nuts and keep them from piling up in the center of the cookies.

8 ounces (1 cup, firmly packed) pitted dates, cut into medium-size pieces (each date should be cut into 4 or 5 pieces)
2 cups sifted all-purpose flour
1 teaspoon baking soda
1 teaspoon cream of tartar
½ teaspoon cinnamon
8 ounces (2 sticks) unsalted butter
1 teaspoon vanilla extract
½ cup granulated sugar
1 cup dark brown sugar, firmly packed
2 eggs
3½ ounces (1 cup) walnuts, cut or broken into medium-size pieces

35 LARGE WAFERS

Bake for about 15 minutes, until the cookies are well browned all over, including the centers. Do not underbake. Reverse the sheets top to bottom and front to back as necessary to ensure even browning. When done, the cookies will flatten into thin, bumpy wafers. (If you bake only one sheet at a time, use the upper rack.)

Let stand for a few seconds until the cookies are firm enough to be moved (no longer). Then, with a wide metal spatula, transfer the cookies to racks to cool.

As soon as the cookies have cooled they should be placed in an airtight container in order to keep the edges crisp and crunchy.

Praline Wafers

This is an old recipe from New Orleans. They are fragile wafers similar to praline candy—made without a mixer.

Adjust two racks to divide the oven into thirds and preheat oven to 350°. Line cookie sheets with aluminum foil shiny side up.

Melt the butter in a 1½- to 2-quart saucepan. Remove from the heat and stir in the sugar. Add the vanilla and the egg and stir until smooth. Then stir in the flour and finally the nuts.

Place well-rounded teaspoonfuls of the dough 2½ to 3 inches apart (no closer, these spread) on the cut aluminum foil. With the back of a spoon move the nuts around gently so they are spread out all over the cookie and not piled on top of each other. Slide cookie sheets under the foil.

Bake for 7 to 10 minutes, reversing the cookie sheets top to bottom and front to back as necessary to ensure even browning. The cookies are done when they are completely colored, including the centers—the nuts will remain light. If you bake only one sheet at a time, place the rack in the center of the oven.

Let the cookies stand on the foil until they are completely cool and the foil may be easily (but gently) peeled away. If the foil does not peel away easily, the cookies have not baked long enough.

As soon as these are removed from the foil they must be stored airtight in order to remain crisp. If they are not to be served soon, they may be frozen.

1½ ounces (3 tablespoons) unsalted butter
1 cup light brown sugar, firmly packed
1 tablespoon vanilla extract
1 egg
2 tablespoons (must be exact) sifted all-purpose flour
3½ ounces (1 cup) pecans, cut medium fine (see page 11)

28 WAFERS

Lemon Walnut Wafers

Theses are semisoft with a tart lemon flavor—an old-fashioned cookie from Florida.

Adjust two racks to divide the oven into thirds and preheat oven to 350°. Line cookie sheets with parchment. Sift together the flour, baking powder, salt, and ginger, and set aside. In a small cup mix the lemon rind and juice and set aside. In the small bowl of an electric mixer cream the butter. Add the sugar and beat well. Add the egg and the yolks, scraping the bowl with a rubber spatula and beating until the mixture is light and fluffy. On low speed gradually add the sifted dry ingredients, scraping the bowl with the spatula and beating only until the mixture is smooth.

Remove the bowl from the mixer and stir in the lemon rind and juice and then the nuts.

Use a well-rounded teaspoonful of the dough for each cookie. Place them 2 inches apart on the cookie sheets.

Bake for 18 to 20 minutes, reversing the sheets top to bottom and front to back once to ensure even baking. These cookies will not brown on the tops, but there will be a thin brown edge. They are done if the tops spring back when lightly pressed with a fingertip. (If you bake one sheet at a time, use the upper rack.)

With a wide metal spatula transfer the cookies to racks to cool.

1½ cups sifted all-purpose flour
½ teaspoon baking powder
¼ teaspoon salt
Generous pinch of powdered ginger
Finely grated rind of 1 large lemon
3 tablespoons lemon juice
4 ounces (1 stick) unsalted butter
1 cup granulated sugar
1 egg plus 2 egg yolks
2 ounces (generous ½ cup) walnuts, cut or broken into medium-size pieces

36 COOKIES

Old-Fashioned Jumbo Lemon Wafers

This is a very old recipe from Connecticut for old-fashioned drop cookies. They are wide, flat, semisoft, crisp, and brown on the edges, and they have a gorgeous lemon/mace flavor. Because these are so large and fragile, do not choose them to make for mailing or packing as a gift.

Adjust two racks to divide the oven into thirds and preheat oven to 350°. Line cookie sheets with parchment or foil shiny side up.

Sift together the flour, salt, baking powder, and mace, and set aside. In the large bowl of an electric mixer, beat the butter until it is soft. Add the lemon extract and then the sugar and beat well for 2 to 3 minutes. Add the egg and the yolk and beat for 2 or 3 minutes more. Then, on low speed, add the sifted dry ingredients, scraping the bowl with a rubber spatula and beating only until incorporated. Remove from the mixer and stir in the rind.

Transfer the mixture to a small bowl for easy handling.

Make these very large; use a heaping teaspoonful or a rounded tablespoonful of the dough for each cookie. They will spread considerably in baking; do not place more than 5 cookies on a 12 x 15½-inch sheet—one near each corner and one in the center. However, I suggest that you try a sample sheet first with only 3 or 4 cookies so you know just what to expect. (If you bake only one sheet at a time, adjust a rack to the center of the oven.)

Wet a teaspoon in cold water. Press down gently on each cookie with the back of the wet spoon to flatten the cookies to about ¾-inch thickness. Then, with the wet spoon, smooth the edges of each cookie to round it.

Sprinkle the tops generously with crystal sugar or with granulated sugar.

Bake for about 10 minutes, reversing the sheets top to bottom and front to back once during baking to ensure even browning. When the cookies are done they will have brown rims and the tops will feel semifirm to the touch. Do not underbake.

With a wide metal spatula transfer the cookies to racks to cool.

Store the cookies airtight, preferably in a plastic freezer box, placing two cookies at a time, bottoms together, with wax paper between the layers.

1¼ cups sifted all-purpose flour
¼ teaspoon salt
½ teaspoon baking powder
½ teaspoon mace
6 ounces (1½ sticks) unsalted butter
½ teaspoon lemon extract
¾ cup granulated sugar
1 egg plus 1 egg yolk
Finely grated rind of 2 or 3 lemons
Crystal sugar (see page 5) or additional granulated sugar (to sprinkle on the tops)

14 4½-INCH COOKIES

Toasted Pine-Nut Cookies

This is an easy recipe that makes a small number of dainty butter cookies. They are crisp and crunchy, flavored with rum and toasted pine nuts—delicious. Make them to serve with tea or coffee; or with ice cream, custard, or fruit; or to package as a gift.

3 ounces (½ cup) pine nuts
   (pignoli)
4 ounces (1 stick) unsalted
   butter
2 tablespoons honey
2 tablespoons granulated
   sugar
Pinch of salt
2 tablespoons dark rum,
   brandy, or whiskey
1 cup sifted all-purpose flour

24 SMALL COOKIES

Adjust two racks to divide the oven into thirds and preheat oven to 375°. Line cookie sheets with parchment or foil shiny side up.

Toast the nuts by placing them in a wide frying pan over moderate heat (the pan should be dry—the nuts release oil as they become warm). Shake the pan frequently to move the nuts around. Watch carefully; after they become hot and start to color it doesn't take long before they burn. When they are golden brown, remove the pan from the heat and set aside for the nuts to cool. Then chill them in the freezer or refrigerator.

In the large bowl of an electric mixer, beat all the remaining ingredients, adding them in the order listed. Remove from the mixer and stir in the chilled nuts.

Place a large piece of wax paper or foil on a tray or shallow pan. Using two teaspoons (one for picking up and one for pushing off), divide the mixture into 24 equal mounds, placing them any which way on the wax paper or foil. Place in the freezer for about 5 minutes or in the refrigerator for a little while longer, until they are not too sticky to be handled.

Then, between your hands, roll the mounds into balls, flatten them very slightly, and place them about 1 inch apart on the cookie sheets. Now, to flatten the cookies still more and to decorate them, dip a fork into cold water and, with the backs of the wet tines, flatten the cookies (pressing in one direction only) until the cookies are about ½ inch thick. Wet the fork before pressing it on each cookie.

Bake for 12 to 15 minutes, reversing the sheets top to bottom and front to back once during baking to ensure even baking. Bake until the cookies are lightly colored; do not underbake—they must be crisp.

With a wide metal spatula transfer the cookies to racks to cool.

Store airtight.

Route 7 Raisin-Nut Cookies

This recipe comes from New England. The cookies are thick and crunchy, a traditional cookie-jar cookie.

Adjust two racks to divide the oven into thirds and preheat oven to 400°. Line cookie sheets with parchment.

Sift together the flour, salt, baking soda, baking powder, cinnamon, nutmeg, and cloves, and set aside.

In the large bowl of an electric mixer cream the butter. Add the vanilla and sugar and beat well. Add the eggs one at a time and beat until smooth. On the lowest speed gradually add the sifted dry ingredients and beat only until they are thoroughly incorporated. Stir in the raisins and nuts.

Place well-rounded teaspoonfuls of the dough 2 inches apart on the cookie sheets.

Bake for 12 to 15 minutes, reversing the cookie sheets top to bottom and front to back as necessary to ensure even browning. The cookies are done when they are browned and spring back if lightly pressed with a fingertip. If you bake only one sheet at a time use the higher rack.

With a wide metal spatula transfer the cookies to racks for cooling.

1¾ cups sifted all-purpose flour
½ teaspoon salt
½ teaspoon baking soda
1 teaspoon baking powder
1 teaspoon cinnamon
1 teaspoon nutmeg
¼ teaspoon ground cloves
4 ounces (1 stick) unsalted butter
1 teaspoon vanilla extract
1 cup granulated sugar
2 eggs
5 ounces (1 cup) raisins
6 ounces (generous 1½ cups) walnuts, cut or broken into medium-size pieces

36 LARGE COOKIES

The Farmer's Wife's Pecan Cookies

An old Southern recipe, mixed in a saucepan, for thin cookies that are both crisp and chewy.

Adjust two racks to divide the oven into thirds and preheat oven to 350°. Line cookie sheets with parchment. Sift together the flour, baking soda, and salt, and set aside. Cut the butter into 1-inch pieces and place in a heavy 2- to 3-quart saucepan. Melt slowly over low heat, stirring occasionally. Remove from the heat, and with a heavy wooden spoon stir in the sugar, then the vanilla and the egg. Add the sifted dry ingredients, stirring until smooth. Mix in the cut pecans. Transfer to a small bowl for ease in handling.

Use a rounded teaspoon of dough for each cookie. Place them 2 inches apart on the sheets. Place a pecan half on each cookie, pressing it gently and lightly into the dough.

Bake for 12 to 14 minutes, reversing the position of the sheets top to bottom and front to back to ensure even browning. When baking only one sheet at a time use the higher rack.

These will rise during baking and then will settle down. They should be medium brown—do not underbake.

With a wide metal spatula, transfer the cookies to racks to cool.

1¼ cups sifted all-purpose
flour
¼ teaspoon baking soda
⅛ teaspoon salt
4 ounces (1 stick) unsalted
butter
1¼ cups light brown sugar,
firmly packed
½ teaspoon vanilla extract
1 egg
2¼ ounces (⅔ cups) pecans,
cut medium fine (see page
11)
36 pecan halves

36 THREE-INCH COOKIES

Nut-Tree Walnut Jumbles

These are large, semisoft, sour-cream cookies.

Adjust two racks to divide the oven into thirds and preheat oven to 375°. Line cookie sheets with parchment.

Sift together the flour, baking soda, and salt, and set aside. In the large bowl of an electric mixer cream the butter. Add the vanilla and sugar and beat well. Add the egg and beat well. On the lowest speed gradually add half of the sifted dry ingredients, then all of the sour cream, and finally the remaining dry ingredients, scraping the bowl with a rubber spatula and beating only until thoroughly mixed. Stir in the cut or broken walnuts.

Use a rounded tablespoonful (make these large) of the dough for each cookie. Place them 2 inches apart on the sheets. Top each cookie with a walnut half.

Bake for 12 to 13 minutes, reversing the cookie sheets

1¾ cups sifted all-purpose flour
¾ teaspoon baking soda
Scant ½ teaspoon salt
4 ounces (1 stick) unsalted
butter
1 teaspoon vanilla extract
1 cup dark brown sugar,
firmly packed
1 egg
½ cup sour cream
4 ounces (generous 1 cup)
walnuts, cut or broken into
medium-size pieces
24 walnut halves

24 LARGE COOKIES

top to bottom and front to back as necessary during baking to ensure even browning. The cookies are done if they spring back when lightly pressed with a fingertip.

   With a wide spatula transfer the cookies to racks to cool.

24-Karat Cookies

These are made with grated raw carrots. Probably no one will recognize the taste, but the carrots will keep the cookies soft and moist.

Adjust two racks to divide the oven into thirds and preheat oven to 350°. Line cookie sheets with parchment.

   Sift together the flour, baking soda, baking powder, and salt, and set aside. In the large bowl of an electric mixer cream the butter. Add the egg and beat to mix. Beat in the honey and the carrots. On the lowest speed gradually add the sifted dry ingredients, and then the oatmeal, scraping the bowl with a rubber spatula and beating only until thoroughly mixed. Stir in the raisins and the walnuts.

   Place the dough by rounded teaspoonfuls about 2 inches apart on the cookie sheets.

   Bake for 15 minutes, reversing the cookie sheets top to bottom and front to back as necessary during baking to ensure even browning. The cookies are done if they are golden colored and spring back when lightly pressed with a fingertip.

   With a wide spatula transfer the cookies to racks to cool.

1 cup sifted all-purpose flour
1 teaspoon baking soda
1 teaspoon baking powder
¼ teaspoon salt
4 ounces (1 stick) unsalted butter
1 egg
½ cup honey
¾ cup grated raw carrots, firmly packed (see Note)
½ cup old-fashioned or quick-cooking (not instant) oatmeal
½ cup raisins
2½ ounces (¾ cup) walnuts, cut or broken into medium-size pieces

32 COOKIES

NOTE: It is not necessary to peel the carrots, just clean them with a brush under running water. Grate them on the medium-fine side of a grater. Two medium-large carrots will make ¾ cup when grated.

Indian Figlets

The inspiration for this recipe came to me from an Indian woman in Taos, New Mexico, in exchange for some Florida seashells. The cookies are soft, plain, not too sweet.

Adjust two racks to divide the oven into thirds and preheat oven to 375°. Line cookie sheets with parchment.

Remove the hard stems from the figs and cut the figs into medium-small pieces (see page 102). Place them in a small saucepan with the water. Bring to a boil over moderate heat. Cook, stirring occasionally, for about 5 minutes until the water is absorbed. Set aside to cool.

Sift together the flour, baking soda, salt, cinnamon, ginger, and nutmeg, and set aside. In the large bowl of an electric mixer cream the butter. Add the sugar and beat well. Beat in the corn syrup and then the vanilla and the egg. On low speed gradually add the sifted dry ingredients, scraping the bowl with a rubber spatula and beating only until mixed. Remove the bowl from the mixer and stir in the lemon rind and then the cooled figs.

Use a rounded teaspoonful of the dough for each cookie. Place them 2 inches apart on the cookie sheets.

Bake for 12 to 15 minutes, reversing the cookie sheets top to bottom and front to back as necessary during baking to ensure even browning. The cookies are done if they spring back when lightly pressed with a fingertip.

With a wide metal spatula transfer the cookies to racks to cool.

8 ounces (1 cup, packed) dried brown figs
½ cup water
2½ cups sifted all-purpose flour
1 teaspoon baking soda
½ teaspoon salt
1 teaspoon cinnamon
¼ teaspoon powdered ginger
¼ teaspoon nutmeg
5⅓ ounces (10⅔ tablespoons) unsalted butter
½ cup light brown sugar, firmly packed
½ cup dark corn syrup
1 teaspoon vanilla extract
1 egg
Finely grated rind of 2 lemons

44 COOKIES

Hawaiian Pineapple Cookies

Adjust two racks to divide the oven into thirds and preheat oven to 375°. Line cookie sheets with parchment.

Drain the pineapple in a strainer set over a bowl. Press gently on the pineapple to extract most of the juice, but do not squeeze it so hard that the pineapple actually becomes dry. Set aside both the pineapple (you should have ⅔ cup) and the juice.

Sift together the flour, baking soda, baking powder, and salt, and set aside. In the large bowl of an electric mixer cream the butter. Add both sugars and beat well, scraping the bowl as necessary with a rubber spatula. Add the egg and beat well. Beat in 1 tablespoon of the reserved pineapple, and the cup of cut pecans. On the lowest speed gradually add the sifted dry ingredients, continuing to scrape the bowl with the rubber spatula, and beating only until thoroughly incorporated. Remove the bowl from the mixer and stir in the lemon rind.

Use a rounded tablespoonful (make these large) of the dough for each cookie. Place them 2 inches apart on the sheets. Place a pecan half, rounded side up, on each cookie and press it down very slightly.

Bake for 15 to 17 minutes, reversing the cookie sheets top to bottom and front to back as necessary during baking to ensure even browning. The cookies are done if they are golden brown and spring back when lightly pressed with a fingertip. If you bake only one sheet at a time use the higher rack.

With a wide metal spatula transfer the cookies to racks to cool.

1 8-ounce can crushed
   pineapple
2 cups sifted all-purpose flour
½ teaspoon baking soda
1 teaspoon baking powder
¼ teaspoon salt
4 ounces (1 stick) unsalted
   butter
½ cup granulated sugar
½ cup dark brown sugar,
   firmly packed
1 egg
4 ounces (generous 1 cup)
   pecans, cut or broken into
   medium-size pieces
Finely grated rind of 2 lemons
30 pecan halves

30 COOKIES

Pumpkin Rocks

Many old cookie recipes are called "rocks," not because they're hard as rocks, but because of their shape. These are thick, soft, spicy, and old-fashioned.

Adjust two racks to divide the oven into thirds and preheat oven to 375°. Line cookie sheets with parchment.

Sift together the flour, baking soda, baking powder, salt, cinnamon, nutmeg, ginger, cloves, and allspice, and set aside. In the large bowl of an electric mixer cream the butter. Beat in both sugars. Add the eggs one at a time and beat well, then beat in the pumpkin. (The mixture might look curdled—it's okay.) On low speed gradually add the sifted dry ingredients, scraping the bowl with a rubber spatula and beating only until thoroughly mixed. Stir in the raisins and walnuts.

Use a rounded tablespoonful (make these large) of the dough for each cookie. Place them 1 to 1½ inches apart (these do not run or change shape during baking) on the cookie sheets. Bake for about 18 minutes, reversing the cookie sheets top to bottom and front to back as necessary during baking to ensure even browning. The cookies are done if they are lightly browned and spring back when lightly pressed with a fingertip. While the cookies are baking, prepare the following glaze.

2½ cups sifted all-purpose flour
½ teaspoon baking soda
2 teaspoons baking powder
½ teaspoon salt
1 teaspoon cinnamon
¾ teaspoon nutmeg
½ teaspoon powdered ginger
¼ teaspoon ground cloves
¼ teaspoon allspice
4 ounces (1 stick) unsalted butter
1 cup granulated sugar
½ cup dark brown sugar, firmly packed
2 eggs
1 pound (about 1¾ cups) canned pumpkin (not pumpkin pie filling)
5 ounces (1 cup) raisins
7 ounces (2 cups) walnuts, cut or broken into medium-size pieces

Glaze

Place all of the glaze ingredients in the small bowl of an electric mixer and beat until completely smooth. The mixture should have the consistency of soft whipped cream—it might be necessary to add more liquid (either lemon juice or milk) or more sugar. Cover the glaze airtight when you are not using it.

As you remove the baked cookies from the oven, immediately, while the cookies are very hot, brush the glaze generously over the tops. It should be a rather heavy coating, which should run unevenly down the sides.

With a wide metal spatula, transfer the cookies to racks to cool. The glaze will dry completely.

2 tablespoons soft unsalted butter
1½ cups confectioners sugar
Pinch of salt
2 tablespoons lemon juice
1 tablespoon milk

48 LARGE COOKIES

Date-Nut Rocks

These are large, thick, and soft—cookie-jar or lunch-box cookies. In the western part of the country these are called Billy Goats.

Adjust two racks to divide the oven into thirds and preheat oven to 375°. Line cookie sheets with parchment. Sift together the flour, baking soda, baking powder, salt, and allspice, and set aside. In the large bowl of an electric mixer cream the butter. Beat in the vanilla and then add the sugar and beat well. Add the eggs one at a time, beating well after each addition. On low speed add half of the sifted dry ingredients, then the sour cream, and finally the remaining dry ingredients, scraping the bowl with a rubber spatula and beating only until mixed.

Remove from the mixer. Add the dates and, with a rubber spatula or wooden spoon, stir until they are evenly distributed through the dough. Then stir in the nuts.

Use a heaping teaspoonful (make these rather large) of the dough for each cookie. Place them 2 to 2½ inches apart on the cookie sheets.

Bake for 18 to 20 minutes, reversing the cookie sheets top to bottom and front to back as necessary during baking to ensure even browning. The cookies are done if they are lightly colored all over and the tops spring back when lightly pressed with a fingertip—do not overbake. If you bake only one sheet at a time, use the upper rack. With a wide spatula transfer the cookies to racks to cool.

2 cups sifted all-purpose flour
½ teaspoon baking soda
2 teaspoons baking powder
Pinch of salt
1 teaspoon allspice
4 ounces (1 stick) unsalted butter
1 teaspoon vanilla extract
1 cup light brown sugar, firmly packed
2 eggs
½ cup sour cream
1 pound (2 cups, firmly packed) pitted dates, coarsely cut into 3 or 4 pieces
7 ounces (2 cups) pecans or walnuts, coarsely cut or broken (see page 11)

36 LARGE COOKIES

Banana Rocks

These thick, soft oatmeal cookies contain raisins, dates, prunes, nuts, and bananas.

Adjust two racks to divide the oven into thirds and preheat oven to 375°. Line cookie sheets with parchment. Sift together the flour, baking soda, salt, cinnamon, nutmeg, and ginger, and set aside.

Place the raisins, dates, and prunes in a medium-size mixing bowl. Add a large spoonful of the sifted dry ingredients and, with your fingertips, toss the fruit until the pieces are all separated and coated with the dry ingredients. Add the nuts, toss again, and set aside.

In the large bowl of an electric mixer cream the butter. Add the sugar and beat well, then beat in the egg. Add the mashed banana and beat, scraping the bowl with a rubber spatula, until well mixed. Beat in the oatmeal, then on the lowest speed add the sifted dry ingredients, scraping the bowl with the rubber spatula and beating only until incorporated.

Remove the bowl from the mixer. With a large wooden spoon stir in the lemon rind and then the floured fruit-nut mixture.

Use a heaping teaspoonful (make these rather large) of the dough for each cookie. Place them 1½ to 2 inches apart on the sheets, mounding the dough high. Do not flatten.

Bake for 17 to 18 minutes, reversing the cookie sheets top to bottom and front to back as necessary during baking to ensure even browning. The cookies are done if they are lightly browned and spring back when lightly pressed with a fingertip. Do not overbake—these should remain soft.

While the cookies are baking prepare the following glaze.

1½ cups sifted all-purpose flour
½ teaspoon baking soda
½ teaspoon salt
1 teaspoon cinnamon
¼ teaspoon nutmeg
¼ teaspoon powdered ginger
3½ ounces (¾ cup) raisins
6 ounces (¾ cup) pitted dates, coarsely cut (see Note)
6 ounces (¾ cup) pitted prunes (not stewed), coarsely cut (see Note)
6 ounces (1½ cups) walnuts, cut or broken into medium-size pieces
6 ounces (1½ sticks) unsalted butter
1 cup dark brown sugar, firmly packed
1 egg
3 small or 2 large ripe bananas (to make 1 cup, mashed)
1¾ cups old-fashioned or quick-cooking (not instant) oatmeal
Finely grated rind of 2 lemons

48 LARGE COOKIES

Glaze

In the small bowl of the electric mixer beat all of the glaze ingredients together until the mixture is completely smooth. The mixture should have the consistency of very heavy cream sauce; if necessary add a bit more milk or sugar—do not make the glaze too thin.

3 tablespoons soft unsalted butter
1½ cups confectioners sugar
Pinch of salt
3 tablespoons milk

As you remove the baked cookies from the oven, immediately, while the cookies are very hot, use a pastry brush and brush the glaze over the tops of the cookies. Work quickly—the heat of the cookies will melt the glaze and it will run down the sides unevenly. With a wide metal spatula transfer the cookies to racks to cool and let the glaze dry completely.

NOTE: The dates and the prunes should not be cut into very small pieces—cutting them into thirds or quarters is about right.

Blind Date Cookies

Although these came to me from a friend in New York, I am told that the recipe originated over 100 years ago with a famous pastry shop in Milwaukee. They are semisoft drop cookies with a surprise date and nut hidden inside. Technically these cookies are dropped onto the cookie sheet but, since each cookie contains a stuffed date, the procedure is slightly different from that of the usual drop cookie.

Adjust a rack to the top position of the oven and preheat oven to 400°. Line cookie sheets with parchment. Slit one long side of each date, stuff with one walnut half or a few pieces of walnut, close the dates around the nuts, and set aside.

Sift together the flour, salt, baking powder, and baking soda, and set aside. In the small bowl of an electric mixer cream the butter. Add the vanilla and the sugar and beat to mix well. Add the egg and beat thoroughly. On the lowest speed gradually add half of the sifted dry ingredients, then all of the sour cream and then the remaining half of the dry ingredients, scraping the bowl with a rubber spatula and beating only until smooth after each addition. Remove the dough from the mixer and transfer it to a shallow bowl for easy handling.

Using two forks, drop each stuffed date into the dough and roll it around until the date is completely coated. There will be enough dough to cover each date with a generous

30 large (about 10 ounces) pitted dates
30 large (1¼ ounces) walnut halves, or about ⅓ cup large pieces
1¼ cups sifted all-purpose flour
¼ teaspoon salt
¼ teaspoon baking powder
½ teaspoon baking soda
2 ounces (4 tablespoons) unsalted butter
½ teaspoon vanilla extract
¾ cup light brown sugar, firmly packed
1 egg
½ cup sour cream

30 COOKIES

coating, but don't overdo it or you will not have enough dough to go around. Using the forks, place the dough-coated dates 2 to 3 inches apart on the cookie sheets.

Bake one sheet at a time for about 10 minutes until lightly browned, reversing the position of the sheet once during baking to ensure even browning.

While the first sheet of cookies is baking, prepare the following glaze.

Glaze

Melt the butter and mix it well with the remaining ingredients, using only enough milk to make a mixture the consistency of soft mayonnaise. Keep the glaze covered when you are not using it.

2 ounces (4 tablespoons)
unsalted butter
1 cup confectioners sugar
½ teaspoon vanilla extract
2 to 3 tablespoons milk

Remove the baked cookies from the oven. With a pastry brush, immediately brush the tops of the hot cookies with a generous coating of the glaze. Then, with a wide metal spatula, transfer the cookies to a rack to cool.

Bake and glaze the remaining cookies. Let them stand until the glaze is dry.

Norman Rockwell's Oatmeal Wafers

These are large, thin wafers that are crisp, crunchy, and fragile. They were a favorite of Norman Rockwell, the great illustrator of Americana.

Adjust two racks to divide the oven into thirds and preheat oven to 350°. Line cookie sheets with aluminum foil shiny side up. Sift together the flour, salt, and baking soda, and then set aside.

In the small bowl of an electric mixer cream the butter. Gradually add both sugars and beat for 2 to 3 minutes. Add the vanilla, water, and egg, and beat well. On low speed gradually add the sifted dry ingredients, scraping the bowl with a rubber spatula and beating only until smooth. Stir in the oatmeal and then the nuts.

Use a rounded tablespoonful of dough for each cookie. Place them 3½ to 4 inches apart (these spread a lot) on the cut aluminum foil. With the back of a wet spoon, flatten each cookie until it is ¼ to ⅓ inch thick.

Bake for 13 to 15 minutes, reversing the position of the cookie sheets top to bottom and front to back as necessary during baking to ensure even browning. Bake until the cookies are completely golden brown. These must be timed carefully; if they are underbaked the bottoms will be wet and sticky and it will be difficult to remove the cookies from the aluminum foil; if overbaked they will taste burnt and bitter.

If you bake only one sheet at a time use the higher rack.

Let the baked cookies stand until they are completely cool. Then carefully and gently, peel the parchment away from the backs of the cookies. (If you have any trouble, use a wide metal spatula to move the cookies.) Turn the cookies upside down and let them stand for 5 to 10 minutes on the parchment to allow the bottoms to dry a bit.

These must be stored airtight.

½ cup sifted all-purpose flour
¼ teaspoon salt
¼ teaspoon baking soda
4 ounces (1 stick) unsalted butter
¼ cup granulated sugar
½ cup light brown sugar, firmly packed
½ teaspoon vanilla extract
2 tablespoons water (measure carefully)
1 egg
1 cup old-fashioned or quick-cooking (not instant) oatmeal
2½ ounces (¾ cup) walnuts, cut medium fine (see page 11)

18 LARGE WAFERS

Oatmeal Snickerdoodles

Snickerdoodles are early American; there are many different versions. These from Connecticut are plain old-fashioned—thin, crisp, and crunchy.

Adjust two racks to divide the oven into thirds and preheat oven to 400°. Line cookie sheets with parchment.

Sift together the flour, baking soda, salt, and cinnamon, and set aside. In the large bowl of an electric mixer cream the butter. Add the vanilla and both sugars and beat well. Add the eggs one at a time and beat well. On low speed gradually add the sifted dry ingredients, scraping the bowl with a rubber spatula and beating only until mixed. Stir in the oatmeal.

Place by rounded teaspoonfuls 2 inches apart on the cookie sheets.

2 cups sifted all-purpose flour
1 teaspoon baking soda
½ teaspoon salt
1 teaspoon cinnamon
8 ounces (2 sticks) unsalted butter
1 teaspoon vanilla extract
¾ cup granulated sugar
¾ cup light brown sugar, firmly packed
2 eggs
1½ cups old-fashioned or quick-cooking (not instant) oatmeal

54 COOKIES

Topping

Stir the sugar and cinnamon together well and, with a teaspoon, sprinkle it generously over the cookies.

Bake for 10 to 12 minutes, reversing the sheets top to bottom and front to back as necessary to ensure even browning. Bake until the cookies are browned all over, including the centers.

Let the cookies stand on the sheets for a few seconds until they are firm enough to transfer. Then with a wide metal spatula, transfer the cookies to racks to cool. Store airtight.

2 tablespoons granulated
    sugar
2 teaspoons cinnamon

Oatmeal Molasses Cookies

These are crunchy and chewy, with a molasses flavor.

Adjust two racks to divide the oven into thirds and preheat oven to 375°. Line cookie sheets with parchment. Sift together the flour, baking soda, and salt, and set aside. In the large bowl of an electric mixer cream the butter. Beat in the vanilla and then add the sugar and beat well. Add the molasses and beat to mix. Add the eggs one at a time, scraping the bowl with a rubber spatula and beating well after each addition. On low speed gradually add the sifted dry ingredients, continuing to scrape the bowl and beating only until mixed. Then add the oatmeal, coconut, and nuts, stirring only until mixed.

Use a well-rounded (but not heaping) teaspoonful of the dough for each cookie. Place them 2 inches apart on the cookie sheets.

Bake for about 15 minutes, reversing the cookie sheets top to bottom and front to back as necessary during baking until the cookies are lightly colored. The cookies will still feel slightly soft and underdone, but do not overbake. If you bake only one sheet at a time, use the upper rack (it will

3 cups sifted all-purpose flour
2 teaspoons baking soda
1 teaspoon salt
8 ounces (2 sticks) unsalted
    butter
1½ teaspoons vanilla extract
2 cups granulated sugar
½ cup molasses (see Note)
2 eggs
2 cups old-fashioned or quick-
    cooking (not instant)
    oatmeal
3½ ounces (1 cup, firmly
    packed) shredded coconut
4 ounces (generous 1 cup)
    walnuts or pecans, cut or
    broken into medium-size
    pieces

take less time to bake than two sheets).

Remove from the oven and let the cookies stand on the sheets for a minute or so and then, with a wide metal spatula, transfer them to racks to cool.

NOTE: You will definitely taste the molasses in these. Unless you love the flavor of strong, dark molasses, use a light mild-flavored kind.

Raisin Oatmeal Cookies

These are rather thin, very chewy, and crunchy.

Adjust two racks to divide the oven into thirds and preheat oven to 350°. Line cookie sheets with parchment.

Sift together the flour, baking soda, and salt, and set aside. In the small bowl of an electric mixer cream the butter together with the oil. Add the sugar, honey, egg, and the water, and beat until smooth, scraping the bowl with a rubber spatula. Remove from the mixer. With a wooden spoon stir in the oatmeal and then the currants and raisins.

Use a heaping teaspoonful of the dough for each cookie. Place them 2 to 2½ inches apart. These will spread and flatten in baking.

Bake for 17 to 20 minutes, reversing the cookie sheets top to bottom and front to back as necessary during baking to ensure even browning. The cookies are done if they are lightly colored and spring back when lightly pressed with a fingertip. If you bake only one sheet at a time use the higher rack.

The cookies will still feel soft when they are done, but they will crisp as they cool. With a wide metal spatula transfer the cookies to racks to cool.

½ cup unsifted *all-purpose flour*
¼ teaspoon baking soda
¼ teaspoon salt
2 tablespoons unsalted butter
1 tablespoon vegetable oil (not olive oil)
½ cup dark brown sugar, firmly packed
¼ cup honey
1 egg
1 tablespoon water
1½ cups old-fashioned or quick-cooking (not instant) oatmeal
2½ ounces (½ cup) currants
2½ ounces (½ cup) raisins

24 LARGE COOKIES

German Oatmeal Cookies

These are thick, soft cookies full of fruit, nuts, and chocolate bits. They are real old-fashioned cookie-jar cookies.

Adjust two racks to divide the oven into thirds and preheat oven to 400°. Line cookie sheets with parchment. Place the raisins in a small saucepan. Cover with boiling water and let simmer for 5 minutes. Then drain the raisins in a strainer set over a small bowl (reserve ⅓ cup of the water). Sift together the flour, salt, baking soda, cinnamon, cloves, and allspice, and set aside.

In the large bowl of an electric mixer cream the butter. Add the sugar and beat well. Add the eggs one at a time and beat until smooth after each addition. Add the dates and drained raisins and beat just to mix. Beat in the oatmeal. Gradually beat in the reserved ⅓ cup water that the raisins cooked in. Then, on the low speed, slowly add the sifted dry ingredients, scraping the bowl with a rubber spatula and beating only until mixed. Stir in the cut pecans and the chocolate morsels.

Place the dough by heaping teaspoonfuls (make these rather large) 2 inches apart on the cookie sheets. Place an optional pecan half on each cookie.

Bake for 12 to 14 minutes, reversing the cookie sheets top to bottom and front to back as necessary during baking to ensure even browning. (If you bake only one sheet at a time use the higher rack.) Bake until the cookies are golden brown and the tops spring back when lightly pressed with a fingertip. With a wide metal spatula transfer the cookies to racks to cool.

5 ounces (1 cup) raisins
Boiling water
2 cups sifted all-purpose flour
½ teaspoon salt
½ teaspoon baking soda
1 teaspoon cinnamon
½ teaspoon ground cloves
½ teaspoon allspice
8 ounces (2 sticks) unsalted
 butter
1 cup granulated sugar
3 eggs
4 ounces (½ cup) pitted dates,
 coarsely cut into 3 or 4
 pieces
2 cups old-fashioned or quick-
 cooking (not instant)
 oatmeal
⅓ cup water (in which the
 raisins were boiled)
4 ounces (generous 1 cup)
 pecans, coarsely cut or
 broken (see page 11)
6 ounces (1 cup) semisweet
 chocolate morsels
Optional: 48 pecan halves

48 COOKIES

Poppy-Seed Wafers (Mohn Cookies)

These Hungarian cookies are thin, crisp, and crunchy. The poppy seeds have a mild nutlike flavor. Incidentally, poppy seeds do come from a poppy plant (so does opium). The seeds are usually slate blue and they are so tiny that it is said there are more than 900,000 to the pound.

Adjust two racks to divide the oven into thirds and preheat oven to 350°. Line cookie sheets with parchment.

In a small saucepan heat the milk until it is very hot but not boiling. Stir in the poppy seeds and set aside.

Sift together the flour, baking powder, salt, and nutmeg, and set aside.

Place the raisins on a board. With a long, heavy knife chop them into medium-size pieces and set aside.

In the small bowl of an electric mixer cream the butter. Add the almond extract and sugar and beat well. On the low speed gradually add the sifted dry ingredients, scraping the bowl with a rubber spatula and beating only until incorporated. Mix in the raisins and the poppy-seed-and-milk mixture.

Using a slightly rounded teaspoonful of the dough for each cookie, place them 2 inches apart on the cookie sheets.

Bake for 18 to 20 minutes, reversing the cookie sheets top to bottom and front to back once during baking to ensure even browning. The cookies are done when they are lightly browned on the rims and semifirm to the touch in the centers. They will crisp as they cool.

With a wide spatula, transfer the cookies to racks to cool.

½ cup milk
5 ounces (1 cup) poppy seeds
  (see Notes)
1 cup sifted all-purpose flour
1 teaspoon baking powder
Pinch of salt
¼ teaspoon nutmeg
2½ ounces (½ cup) raisins
  (see Notes)
4 ounces (1 stick) unsalted
  butter
½ teaspoon almond extract
½ cup granulated sugar

42 COOKIES

NOTES: Always store poppy seeds in the freezer.

The raisins have to be chopped. If they are frozen when you chop them they will be less sticky and easier to cut.

Tijuana Fiesta Cookies

These are from Mexico. They are soft cookies with an exotic flavor and white vanilla icing.

Adjust two racks to divide the oven into thirds and preheat oven to 350°. Line cookie sheets with parchment. Sift together the flour, baking soda, ginger, cinnamon, cloves, and salt, and set aside. Dissolve the instant coffee in the boiling water and set aside.

In the large bowl of an electric mixer cream the butter. Beat in the sugar and then the egg. Gradually beat in the molasses, scraping the bowl as necessary with a rubber spatula. On the lowest speed gradually add half of the sifted dry ingredients, continuing to scrape the bowl and beating only until mixed. Beat in the prepared coffee and then the remaining dry ingredients, beating only until smooth. Stir in the anise seed and coriander seeds.

Place heaping teaspoonfuls of the dough 2 inches apart on the cookie sheets.

Bake for 12 to 13 minutes, reversing the cookie sheets top to bottom and front to back as necessary during baking to ensure even browning. (If you bake only one sheet at a time, place the rack in the center of the oven.) The cookies are done if the tops spring back when lightly pressed with a fingertip. Prepare the icing while the cookies are baking.

2¼ cups sifted all-purpose
   flour
2 teaspoons baking soda
2 teaspoons powdered ginger
1 teaspoon cinnamon
¼ teaspoon ground cloves
¼ teaspoon salt
2 teaspoons instant coffee
⅓ cup boiling water
4 ounces (1 stick) unsalted
   butter
½ cup granulated sugar
1 egg
½ cup molasses
1 tablespoon whole anise seed
1 teaspoon coriander seeds,
   crushed (see Note)

36 COOKIES

Icing

In a small bowl, with a rubber spatula, mix the sugar, vanilla, and milk. Stir well until smooth. The icing should be about the consistency of soft mayonnaise. Add more sugar or milk as necessary to make it soft enough to form a smooth layer. It should not be so thin that it will run off the sides.

Place a teaspoonful of icing on top of a hot cookie and spread it with the back of the spoon, leaving a ½- to ¾- inch un-iced margin. Place a pecan half on top of each cookie and transfer the cookies to racks until the icing is set.

3 cups strained confectioners
   sugar (see page 5)
1½ teaspoons vanilla extract
About 5 tablespoons milk
36 pecan halves

NOTE: The coriander seeds may be crushed in a blender or with a mortar and pestle—they do not have to be powdered.

Butterscotch Molasses Cookies

These are crisp and chewy cookie-jar cookies, easily mixed in a saucepan.

Melt the butter in a heavy 3-quart saucepan over moderate heat. Still on heat, add the sugar and molasses and stir until the sugar is melted. Bring the mixture to a rolling boil and then remove it from the heat and set it aside to cool to room temperature.

Adjust two racks to divide the oven into thirds and preheat oven to 375°. Line cookie sheets with parchment.

Sift together the flour, baking soda, mace, and salt, and set aside.

Add the egg and the vanilla to the cooled butter mixture and beat with a wooden spoon until smooth. Gradually add the sifted dry ingredients and beat with a wooden spoon until smooth. Transfer to a small bowl for ease in handling.

Using a rounded teaspoonful of dough for each cookie, place the mounds 1 to 1½ inches apart on the cookie sheets. Slide cookie sheets.

Bake for 10 minutes, reversing the cookie sheets top to bottom and front to back as necessary during baking to ensure even baking. The cookies will still feel slightly soft, or barely set, but they will crisp as they cool. (If you bake only one sheet at a time use the higher rack.)

With a wide spatula transfer the cookies to racks to cool.

5 ounces (1½ sticks) unsalted butter
1 cup light brown sugar, firmly packed
¼ cup molasses
2½ cups sifted all-purpose flour
1 teaspoon baking soda
¼ teaspoon mace
⅛ teaspoon salt
1 egg
½ teaspoon vanilla extract

36 COOKIES

Vanilla Butter Wafers

These thin, buttery rounds will be brown and crisp on the edges, light and slightly soft on the tops. They are simple, easy cookies to make, but are extremely delicate and fragile. This recipe makes only 24—double it if you wish.

Adjust two racks to divide the oven into thirds and preheat oven to 350°. Line cookie sheets with parchment.

In the small bowl of an electric mixer cream the butter. Add the vanilla and the sugar and beat very well for 2 to 3 minutes. Add the egg and beat well again for 2 to 3 minutes more. On low speed add the flour, scraping the bowl with a rubber spatula and beating only until smooth.

Transfer the dough to a shallow bowl for ease in handling.

Use a slightly rounded teaspoonful of the dough for each cookie (keep these small). If you place the dough neatly and carefully, the cookies will bake into perfect rounds, which is the way they should be. Place the mounds of dough 3 inches apart on the cookie sheets.

Bake for 12 to 15 minutes, until the edges are well browned. Reverse the sheets top to bottom and front to back once to ensure even browning.

With a wide metal spatula transfer the cookies to racks to cool.

NOTE: If these are too large or too close to each other they will run together.

4 ounces (1 stick) unsalted butter
1 teaspoon vanilla extract
⅓ cup granulated sugar
1 egg
⅓ cup sifted all-purpose flour

24 SMALL COOKIES

Bar Cookies

Pecan Squares Americana

Many years ago a Miami newspaper published a letter to the food editor from the wife of Governor Collins of Florida. She raved about the pecan cookies she had eaten at the Americana Hotel in Miami Beach. She went on to say that she had requested the recipe from the hotel, that they had given it to her, but it did not work for her. The letter included the recipe as she had received it. I ran to the kitchen to try it. The recipe did not work for me either. I called the hotel and asked to speak to the pastry chef. His name was Jacques Kranzlin; he could not have been more gracious or charming, and he invited me to his kitchen to watch him work. It was a treat.

*When I got home I was able to make the Pecan Squares. I made them again and again and again. I wrote the recipe. I taught it in my dessert classes. It was unanimously **the best**! I included the recipe in my first dessert book. And when I taught classes around the country, it was one of my favorite recipes to teach because I knew how people would rave about them.*

During a class in Ohio, as I started to make the recipe, I explained that there was one hitch: The filling sometimes ran through the bottom crust and stuck to the pan, making it difficult to remove the cookies. A nice lady in the class said, "Since you use so much foil to line so many pans, why not line this one?"

I had not thought of it. I tried it right then and it was great! It was terrific! The cookies simply cannot stick to the pan this way. I have always worried about the people who are making this without the foil. Here's the way I do it now.

Pastry Shell

Butter a 15½ x 10 ½ x 1-inch jelly-roll pan and then line it with aluminum foil as follows: Turn the pan upside down. Center a piece of foil 18 to 19 inches long (and 12 inches wide) shiny side down over the pan; check the long sides to be sure there is the same amount of overhang on each side. Fold down the sides and the corners to shape the foil. Remove the foil, turn the pan right side up, place the shaped foil in the pan, and press it carefully into place. Do not butter the foil. Place the prepared pan in the freezer (it is easier to spread this dough on a cold pan—the coldness will make the dough cling to the pan).

In the large bowl of an electric mixer, beat the butter until it is softened, add the sugar, and beat to mix well. Beat in the egg, salt, and lemon rind. Gradually add the flour and beat, scraping the bowl with a rubber spatula, until the mixture holds together.

8 ounces (2 sticks) unsalted butter
½ cup granulated sugar
1 egg
¼ teaspoon salt
Finely grated rind of 1 large lemon
3 cups sifted all-purpose flour

32 TO 48 (OR MORE) SQUARES

Now you are going to line the pan with the dough; it is important that you have enough dough on the sides of the pan to reach generously to the top of the pan. It will work best and be easiest if you place the dough, one rounded teaspoonful at a time, around the sides of the pan, just pressing against the raised sides. (I don't actually use teaspoons for this. It is easiest to lift a generous mound of the dough, hold it in your left hand, and use the fingers of your right hand to break off teaspoon-size pieces.) Place the pieces about ½ to 1 inch apart. Then place the remaining dough the same way all over the rest of the bottom of the pan. Flour your fingertips (if necessary) and start to press the mounds of dough, working up the sides first and then on the bottom, until you have formed a smooth layer all over the sides and bottom. There must not be any thin spots on the bottom or any low spots on the sides (it is best if it comes slightly above the top). Take your time; it is important for this shell to be right. PATIENCE is the name of the game.

With a fork, carefully prick the bottom at about ½-inch intervals. Chill in the refrigerator for about 15 minutes.

Adjust a rack one-third up from the bottom of the oven and preheat oven to 375°.

Bake for 20 minutes. Watch it constantly. If the dough on the sides starts to slip down a bit, reach into the oven and press it with your fingertips or the back of a spoon to put it back into place (although this does not seem to happen since I stopped buttering the foil). If the dough starts to puff up, prick it gently with a cake tester to release trapped air and flatten the dough. (There have been times when it insisted on puffing up, and it was a question of which one of us would win. I did. Here's how: Place one or more pot holders on the puffed-up part for a few minutes. The puffed-up dough will get the message and will know you mean business, and it will lie down flat.) After 20 minutes, the edges of the dough will be lightly colored; the bottom will be pale but dry. Remove from the oven but do not turn off the heat. Prepare the topping.

Pecan Topping

In a heavy 3-quart saucepan over moderately high heat, cook the butter and honey, stirring occasionally, until the butter is melted. Add both sugars, stir to dissolve, bring to a boil, and let boil without stirring for exactly 2 minutes.

Without waiting, remove from the heat, stir in the heavy cream and then the pecans. (Although the original recipe says to do the next step immediately, I have recently decided it is better to wait a bit.) Wait 5 minutes. Then, with a large slotted spoon, place most of the pecans evenly over the crust. Then drizzle the remaining mixture over the pecans so it is distributed evenly—watch the corners. Use a

8 ounces (2 sticks) unsalted butter
½ cup honey
¼ cup granulated sugar
1 cup plus 2 tablespoons dark brown sugar, firmly packed
¼ cup heavy cream
20 ounces (5 cups) pecan halves or large pieces

fork or a spoon to move around any nuts that are piled too high and place them in any empty or thin spots. (It will look like there is not enough of the thin syrupy mixture, but it is okay.)

Bake at 375° with the rack one-third up from the bottom for 25 minutes. (Now you will see that syrupy mixture has spread out and boiled up and filled in any hollows.)

Cool to room temperature—do not chill.

Cover with a large rack or a cookie sheet, hold them firmly together, turn the pan and rack or sheet over, and remove the pan and the foil. If the bottom of the dough looks very buttery, you may pat it with a paper towel if you wish, but it is not really necessary, the dough absorbs it as it stands. Cover with a rack or sheet and turn over again, leaving the cake right side up. It is easiest to cut the cake into neat pieces if it is chilled first; chill it briefly in the refrigerator. Then transfer it to a large cutting board. Use a ruler and toothpicks to mark the cake into quarters. Use a long and heavy, sharp knife, and cut straight down (not back and forth). These are very rich, and although most people like them cut into 48 bars, I know several caterers who make them almost as small as lump sugar. And I have made them larger because I wrap them individually in clear cellophane and it is more fun to wrap cookies that are not too small.

Fig Bars

A pastry chef on a cruise ship that sails from the port of Miami and cruises through the Caribbean gave me this recipe. He makes it frequently for the passengers to have with tea in the afternoon. These cookies are almost solid figs, a few nuts, and just barely enough batter to hold them together—delicious on land or sea. They are homey, old-fashioned cookies— moist, chewy, yummy, not too sweet. Great for a picnic or lunch box, wonderful to mail.

Adjust a rack to the center of the oven and preheat oven to 350°. Prepare a shallow 9-inch square cake pan as follows: Turn the pan upside down, cover it with a 12-inch square of foil shiny side down, fold down the sides and the corners of the foil, then remove the foil, turn the pan right side up, and place the foil in the pan. To butter the foil, place a piece of butter in the pan and place the pan in the oven to melt the butter. Then, with a pastry brush, brush the butter over the bottom and the sides of the pan, and set the pan aside.

With a small, sharp knife, cut off and discard the tough stems on the figs. The figs should now be cut into ¼- to ½-inch pieces; they should not be finely chopped or ground. It can be done with a small, sharp knife or with scissors (I use scissors). Set the prepared figs aside.

Sift together the flour, baking powder, and salt, and set aside.

In a mixing bowl, beat or whisk the eggs just to mix well. Beat in the sugar and vanilla. Add the sifted dry ingredients and beat or whisk until smooth (if necessary, use a mixer). Then stir in the figs and nuts.

Turn into the prepared pan and smooth the top.

Bake for 35 minutes. Cool in the pan until tepid.

Cover with a rack, turn the pan and rack over, remove the pan, peel off the foil, cover with a fresh square of foil or wax paper (these might stick to the rack) and another rack, and turn over again, leaving the cake right side up (on the foil or wax paper) on a rack.

When cool, place in the freezer for about an hour (it is much easier to cut these when they are almost frozen). Transfer to a cutting board and, with a long, sharp, heavy knife, cut into 4 strips. Then cut each strip into 6 bars.

To sugar the cookies, place them on wax paper. Place confectioners sugar in a strainer and sugar them generously. Then turn them over and sugar the other side.

Wrap these individually in clear cellophane or wax paper, or package them in an airtight container.

1 pound (2 generous packed cups) dried brown figs (although they are called "dried," they should be soft and moist)

½ cup sifted all-purpose flour

½ teaspoon baking powder

½ teaspoon salt

2 eggs

½ cup light brown sugar, firmly packed

1 teaspoon vanilla extract

6 ounces (1½ cups) walnuts, cut or broken into medium-size pieces

Confectioners sugar (to be used after the cookies are baked)

24 BARS

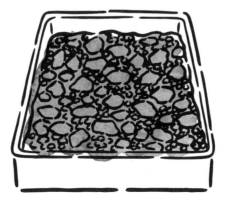

Lebkuchen

Lebkuchen are traditional German cookies baked at Christmas time. They are usually the first cookies baked for the holiday season because they not only keep well for weeks, but they get better as they age. There are many varieties, although most contain honey, spices, and candied fruits. And most, like these, stand overnight after they are shaped, before they are baked. These are rolled out with a rolling pin and cut with a knife into oblongs. As soon as they are baked they are brushed with a white sugar glaze. They are very firm and chewy, mildly spiced, and just as delicious in the summer as in the winter.

These take longer to prepare than most cookies do, but they are worth it.

The almonds must be ground to a fine powder; this can be done in a food processor (see To Grind Nuts in a Food Processor, page 11) or a nut grinder. Set the ground almonds aside.

In the small bowl of an electric mixer, beat the eggs for several minutes until they are slightly thickened. Then, while beating, add the baking powder, salt, cinnamon, cloves, and gradually add the sugar. Continue to beat for a few minutes until the mixture is pale and forms a ribbon when the beaters are raised. Transfer to the large bowl of the mixer. On low speed add the almonds, brandy, honey, and then the diced fruit. Gradually add about 3 cups of the flour, scraping the bowl with a rubber spatula and beating only until incorporated. Remove from the mixer. With a large wooden spoon stir in the remaining flour—it will be a very stiff mixture. (However, if the mixture is too wet or too sticky to be rolled out, add a bit more flour, but not unless you are sure you need it. It is best to first flour a pastry cloth and rolling pin and try to roll about one-third of the dough. If it needs more flour return it to the bowl and work in as much as you need.) Let stand while you prepare the cookie sheets.

These cookies will stick to plain aluminum foil. Therefore it is necessary either to butter and flour the foil, or to use parchment. Nonstick cookie sheets will not stick either, but since these stand overnight on the paper or cookie sheets, you might not have enough nonstick sheets. Prepare the foil or paper (cut the foil or paper to fit the sheets, butter and flour the foil), or have the nonstick sheets ready.

Turn the dough out onto a well-floured pastry cloth, flour your hands, form the dough into a heavy cylinder, cut it into thirds, and work with one piece at a time. Form it into an oblong, flour it on all sides, and roll it on the floured pastry cloth with

6 ounces (scant 1¼ cups) blanched almonds

2 eggs

½ teaspoon baking powder

¼ teaspoon salt

½ teaspoon cinnamon

½ teaspoon powdered cloves

1 cup granulated sugar

1 tablespoon plus 1½ teaspoons brandy

⅓ cup honey

¾ cup (generous ¼ pound) mixed candied citron, lemon rind, and orange rind, finely diced

About 3½ cups sifted cake flour (use a triple sifter, or sift the flour three times before measuring)

28 LARGE COOKIES

a floured rolling pin. Turn it over as necessary to keep both the top and bottom floured. Roll into an oblong shape ¼ inch thick.

It is easiest to cut the cookies with a large and heavy knife. The blade will become sticky after almost every cut unless you keep it wet. Either wipe it with a damp cloth, or hold it under running water, or dip it in a deep pitcher of water. Cut the cookies into 2 x 4-inch oblongs.

To transfer the cookies, use a wide metal spatula. (If the cookies lose their shape slightly while being transferred, just straighten them with the edge of the spatula.) Place the cookies, as you cut them, on the foil, paper, or nonstick sheets, about ½ inch apart.

Press the scraps together and reroll them.

Cover the cookies loosely with plastic wrap and let stand overnight.

To bake, adjust two racks to divide the oven into thirds and preheat oven to 325°.

Place one sheet of cookies in the oven, and wait 5 minutes before starting the second sheet, so they do not all finish baking at once. Bake the cookies for 20 minutes, reversing the sheets top to bottom and front to back once during baking to ensure even baking. Bake until the cookies are lightly colored all over.

While the cookies are baking, prepare the following glaze.

Glaze

Stir the ingredients together in a small bowl. The glaze should be thick but fluid; as thick as molasses. If necessary, adjust with more sugar or liquid.

1½ cups strained or sifted confectioners sugar
Scant 1 tablespoon fresh lemon juice
Scant 1 tablespoon boiling water

When the cookies are baked, with a wide metal spatula transfer them to racks set over foil, wax paper, or a brown paper bag.

Immediately, with a pastry brush, brush the glaze on the hot cookies. The heat will melt the glaze and make it almost transparent. Let stand to dry.

Store airtight. I wrap these individually in clear cellophane. They will be very crisp, but they will soften, as they should, after a few days.

NOTE: When I bake these, I double the recipe. But it takes hours, and it spreads out of the kitchen into the living room and dining room.

Anise Seed Cookies

This is an old Shaker recipe from Ohio; it makes beautiful and delicious cookies that are traditional at Christmas time. They are hard and crunchy with just a hint of anise. They keep well, and should ripen for a few days before they are served. They are perfect cookies for a cookie jar, and they make a wonderful gift.

They are rolled out with a rolling pin, and are cut with a small, round cookie cutter.

The dough should be chilled for half an hour or longer before it is rolled out, cut, and baked.

P lace the skinned almonds in a small shallow pan in a moderate oven. Shake or stir occasionally until the nuts are just lightly colored.

Crush the anise seeds in a mortar and pestle. Or place them on a board, cover with a towel to keep them from flying around, and whack them with the back of a wide cleaver. They do not have to be fine or powdered or strained. Set them aside.

In the large bowl of an electric mixer, beat the butter until it is soft and smooth. Add the vanilla and then the sugar and beat until well mixed. Add the salt and then the eggs, one at a time, beating after each addition until incorporated. Add the anise seeds and, on low speed, gradually add the flour, scraping the bowl with a rubber spatula and beating only until mixed.

The dough will be soft and sticky. Chill it (in the mixing bowl if you wish, or transfer to foil or wax paper) in the freezer for about half an hour, or longer in the refrigerator, until it is firm enough to be rolled.

Before baking, adjust two racks to divide the oven into thirds and preheat oven to 350°. (Or you can bake only one sheet at a time, in which case the rack should be in the center.) Line two cookie sheets with parchment or foil.

Flour a pastry cloth and a rolling pin. Work with only half of the dough at a time; keep the rest cold. Work quickly before the dough becomes sticky. First flour your hands and knead the dough briefly until it is smooth. Then form it into a ball, flour it lightly, flatten it slightly between your hands, and then roll it on a floured pastry cloth with a floured rolling pin until it is ½ inch thick.

Have flour handy to dip the cutter into. Flour a 1½-inch round cutter and cut rounds of the dough, starting at the outside edge of the dough and cutting the rounds as close to each other as possible. Place them 1 inch apart (no closer) on the lined cookie sheets.

50 to 60 (scant ½ cup) whole blanched almonds
1 teaspoon anise seeds (not ground; see Note)
4 ounces (1 stick) unsalted butter
1 teaspoon vanilla extract
1½ cups granulated sugar
¼ teaspoon salt
3 eggs
3 cups sifted all-purpose flour
1 egg white
A bit of pearl or crystal sugar (see page 5) or additional granulated sugar (to be sprinkled over the tops)

50 TO 60 COOKIES

Press the scraps of dough together, rechill, and reroll them.

Beat the egg white until it is foamy. With a pastry brush, brush it over the tops of the cookies. Then press an almond on its flat side gently into the top of each cookie. Brush over the almond and the top of the cookie again with the beaten egg white. (It will have separated and should be beaten again.)

Sprinkle the tops generously with the pearl or crystal sugar, or with granulated sugar.

Bake for about 20 to 22 minutes, reversing the sheets top to bottom and front to back as necessary to ensure even browning. The cookies will be slightly colored and will feel semifirm to the touch. Do not overbake or they will become too hard.

With a wide metal spatula transfer the cookies to racks to cool. Then store them airtight at room temperature for a few days before serving. They can be frozen but they keep very well at room temperature if they are stored airtight.

NOTE: Anise seed is a spice, found in the spice department of grocery stores. It has a licorice flavor. The amount called for in this recipe is mild; if you know you like it, it may be increased to 1½ teaspoons.

Pennsylvania Squares

I met a lady who works in the test kitchen at the Hershey company. She spends all her time testing chocolate recipes. I asked if she had a favorite. She didn't hesitate and gave me this recipe. They are very thin, brown sugar cookie squares covered with milk chocolate and chopped walnuts. The result is like a combination of chewy butterscotch and English toffee. Quick, easy, foolproof, wonderfully delicious candylike cookies.

You need rather small (1.45 ounce each) thin bars of Hershey's milk chocolate, although I don't see any reason you couldn't use any other brand of milk chocolate, and if the bars are not the same size, approximately the same size will do.

Adjust a rack one-third up from the bottom of the oven and preheat oven to 350°. Butter a 9 x 13-inch baking pan with butter (additional to that called for) and set aside.

In the large bowl of an electric mixer, beat the butter until soft. Beat in the vanilla, salt, and sugar. Then add the egg yolk and beat well. On low speed, gradually add the flour, scraping the bowl as necessary with a rubber spatula and beating until incorporated. (It might be necessary to finish the beating by hand.)

To make a thin layer of the dough in the buttered pan it will be best if you first place the dough by rounded teaspoonfuls over the bottom of the pan. Cover with a length of wax paper and, with the palm of your hand and your fingertips, press down on the paper to press the mounds of the dough together into a rather smooth layer. Remove the wax paper.

Bake for 23 minutes. (During baking the dough will rise and then settle down.)

Meanwhile, as the cake is baking, unwrap the chocolate bars and set them aside. And, on a large chopping board, with a long, heavy chef's knife, chop the nuts into rather small pieces. Small is better than large for these cookies. Set the nuts aside.

8 ounces (2 sticks) unsalted butter
1 teaspoon vanilla extract
¼ teaspoon salt
1 cup dark brown sugar, firmly packed
1 egg yolk
2 cups sifted all-purpose flour
8 1.45-ounce bars of Hershey's milk chocolate
5 ounces (1¼ cups) walnuts

32 SQUARES

Remove the baked layer from the oven and immediately, without waiting, place the chocolate bars on the hot cake. Keep them about ¼ inch away from the sides of the pan. Break the bars into pieces wherever necessary and fit them together to cover the cake; a few empty areas—uncovered—will be all right.

In about a minute or two, the chocolate will have softened from the heat of the cake. With the bottom of a teaspoon smooth over the chocolate. Then, with your fingertips, sprinkle the nuts all over the chocolate. Cover with a length of plastic wrap or wax paper and, with the palms of your hands and your fingertips, press down gently on the nuts to make sure that they are all embedded in the chocolate. Remove the plastic wrap or wax paper.

With a small, sharp knife cut around the sides of the cake to release. Let stand until cool. Then refrigerate only until the chocolate is set.

With a small, sharp knife cut the cake into 32 rectangles. (Or cut it into 16 rectangles and, after removing them from the pan, cut each one in half.)

To remove the first 1 or 2 cookies from the pan it might be helpful to use a fork to pry the cookie up; then use a metal spatula to remove the remaining cookies.

Wrap the cookies individually in clear cellophane or wax paper or aluminum foil, if you wish, or place them on a tray and cover with plastic wrap until serving time.

Charleston Cheesecake Bars

When we recently visited Charleston, South Carolina, I found a wonderful cookie recipe in The Post and Courier. When we returned home I made the cookies before unpacking the suitcases. They have a crunchy, nutty oatmeal base, a lemon-cream cheese filling, and a layer of the crunchy oatmeal sprinkled over the top. They are unusual and wonderful, fancy enough for a party, but easy to make. These should be stored in the refrigerator.

Oatmeal

Adjust a rack one-third up from the bottom of the oven and preheat oven to 350°. Line an 8-inch square cake pan with foil as follows. Turn the pan over, place a 12-inch square of foil shiny side down over the pan, press down on the sides and corners to shape the foil, remove the foil, turn the pan over again, place the foil in the pan, and press it gently into place. To butter the foil, place a piece of butter in the pan and place it in the oven to melt; then spread it with a pastry brush or with crumpled wax paper. Set the pan aside.

Sift together the flour, salt, and cinnamon, and set aside. In the small bowl of an electric mixer, beat the butter until soft, beat in the sugar, then on low speed add the sifted dry ingredients, the nuts, and the rolled oats. When well mixed, remove and reserve 1 cup of the mixture.

Turn the remaining mixture into the prepared pan. With your fingertips spread it evenly over the bottom of the pan and then press firmly to make a compact layer.

Bake for 15 minutes.

1 cup sifted all-purpose flour
¼ teaspoon salt
½ teaspoon cinnamon
4 ounces (1 stick) unsalted butter
½ cup dark brown sugar, firmly packed
2 ounces (½ cup) pecans, toasted (see To Toast Pecans, page 4), chopped fine
1 cup quick-cooking (not instant) rolled oats

16 SMALL BARS

Cream-Cheese Layer

Combine the rind and juice and set aside.

In the small bowl of an electric mixer beat the cheese until it is soft. Beat in the sugar and then the egg and sour cream. When smooth, remove from the mixer and stir in the rind and juice.

Pour the mixture over the baked bottom crust (which may still be hot). Smooth the top.

Finely grated rind of 1 lemon
1 tablespoon lemon juice
8 ounces Philadelphia brand cream cheese
½ cup granulated sugar
1 egg
2 tablespoons sour cream

Now, with your fingertips, sprinkle the reserved oatmeal mixture as evenly as you can to cover the cheese mixture completely (or almost completely). Then, with your fingertips, press the oatmeal mixture slightly into the cheese mixture so that none of it remains loose, and also to smooth the top.

Bake for 25 minutes.

Set aside to cool completely.

Place the cooled cake in the freezer for about an hour. Then cover the top of the pan with a piece of foil, and fold down the sides. Cover the foil with a board or a cookie sheet, turn the pan and the board or cookie sheet over, remove the pan, peel off the foil lining, cover the cake with a board or cookie sheet, turn over again, and remove the remaining foil (it was put there only to catch any loose bits of topping that might fly around when the pan is turned over).

Now, to cut the cake. Use a strong, sharp knife. If the cheese mixture sticks to the blade, hold the blade under very hot running water before making each cut (cut with the hot, wet blade). If the cheese mixture squashes out even a bit, place the cake in the freezer again for 10 to 20 minutes (or as necessary) until it is firm enough.

Cut into quarters and then cut each quarter into 4 pieces. Cover and refrigerate until serving time. These may be frozen; if so, thaw in the refrigerator for an hour or two, or longer.

California Fruit Bars

We were living in La Jolla in a house right on the beach. It was a spectacular location with a picture-postcard view. But the thing I looked forward to the most each day was food shopping; the fruits and vegetables bowled me over. Even when we didn't need anything, I went just to look. In my favorite market, located in what had been a private home, and staffed by a crew of friendly young people, they sold these fruit bars to customers who arrived early enough; the bars sold out quickly. When I brought them some Chocolate Cheesecake Brownies, they offered me this recipe.

These are butterless, wonderfully chewy, full of nuts and dried fruits, brown-sugar caramel-like, and delicious. They keep well, they travel well, they are good for mailing. As a matter of fact, they are good for everything.

Adjust a rack one-third up from the bottom of the oven and preheat oven to 400°. Line a 10½ x 15½ x 1-inch jelly-roll pan with foil as follows: Turn the pan over. Center a length of foil about 18 inches long, shiny side down, over the pan. With your hands fold down the sides and corners to shape the foil, remove it, turn the pan over again, put the foil in the pan, and press it firmly into place. To butter the foil, place a piece of butter in the pan and put it in the oven to melt. Then, with a pastry brush or crumpled wax paper, spread the melted butter over the foil and set aside.

With scissors, cut the dried fruit (except the raisins) into small pieces.

Then steam all the fruit by placing it in a vegetable steamer over shallow water (not touching the fruit) in a saucepan, covered, on high heat. When the water comes to a boil reduce the heat and let simmer for 15 minutes. Uncover and set aside. The fruit should be very soft and moist.

In a 2½- to 3-quart saucepan, beat the eggs with a beater or a whisk to mix well. Add the sugar and stir with a rubber spatula to mix.

1 cup assorted dried fruits, firmly packed (in La Jolla they use dates, figs, apricots, and raisins—see Variation)
4 eggs
1 1-pound box (2¼ cups, packed) light brown sugar
¼ teaspoon salt
1 teaspoon vanilla extract
2 cups sifted all-purpose flour
7 ounces (2 cups) walnuts halves or large pieces

ABOUT 32 BARS

Place over medium-low heat, stir and scrape the bottom and sides with the rubber spatula for 10 to 15 minutes until the sugar is dissolved; taste to test. Remove from the heat.

Add the salt, vanilla, and the flour 1 cup at a time. Beat briskly with a heavy whisk to incorporate the flour smoothly. Then stir in the fruit and mix well to be sure that the fruit is not lumped together. Now stir in the nuts.

Turn into the prepared pan and spread to distribute the fruit and nuts all over. Smooth the top. It will be a thin layer; be sure it is the same thickness all over (watch the corners).

Bake for 15 to 20 minutes, until the top is a rich golden color and shiny. As it bakes, if the cake is not browning evenly reverse the pan front to back after 10 to 12 minutes.

Let stand until cool. Cover with a cookie sheet, turn the pan and the sheet over, remove the pan, and very gradually peel off the foil. Cover with wax paper and another cookie sheet and turn over again.

Slide the cake and the wax paper off onto a cutting board. With a ruler and toothpicks mark the cake into even sections. Use a long, sharp knife. These are chewy and they might want to stick to the knife (they will stick if you cut them too soon, but not if you wait a while); if you have any trouble, spray Pam on the blade.

I recommend that you wrap these individually in clear cellophane (see page 5) or wax paper or foil; plastic wrap is too hard to handle.

VARIATION: The "1 cup assorted dry fruits" called for is a variable ingredient. I recently made these with 1 cup (8 ounces) dried apricots and 1 cup (8 ounces) dried figs. I cut both the apricots and the figs, with scissors, into slices—some rather coarse. The cookies were yummy. (Because of this larger amount of fruit the cake is thicker and takes a little longer to bake.)

And I made California Pecan Bars: Omit the dried fruits and use 3 cups pecans, toasted (see To Toast Pecans, page 4) in place of the 2 cups walnuts.

World War II Raisin Squares

This old recipe was called Depression Cake when we first used it because it originated during the Great Depression, when people could not afford expensive ingredients. And we made it during the war, when butter and eggs were rationed. We mailed it to men in the service, we ate it at home, we brought it to the local USO, and it was always delicious. It is still delicious, even if you are rich, have a dairy farm, or are in the butter-and-egg business.

It is soft, spicy, moist, cakelike, and easy to make.

Incidentally, in Colorado they call this River Rafting Cake because it travels so well on rafting and camping trips (see Notes).

Adjust a rack one-third up from the bottom of the oven and preheat oven to 375°. Line a 9 x 9 x 1¾-inch pan as follows: Turn the pan over, cover it with a 12-inch square of aluminum foil shiny side down, press down the sides and corners of the foil to shape it, then remove the foil, turn the pan over again, place the foil in the pan, and press it into place. To butter the foil, place a piece of butter in the pan and put it in the oven to melt, then spread it over the bottom and sides with a pastry brush or crumpled wax paper and set aside.

Put the raisins and the water in a 3- to 4-quart heavy saucepan. Bring to a boil, then reduce the heat, allowing the water to boil gently or simmer, and continue to cook, partly covered, for about 15 to 20 minutes.

Pour the raisins and their water into a strainer set over a bowl.

Measure the water; you will want 1 cup of it. If you have less, add warm water; if you have more, discard excess. Pour the water into a large bowl. Stir in the oil, sugar, and baking soda (it will fizz). Set aside briefly.

Sift together both the flours, the cinnamon, allspice, cloves, nutmeg, ginger, salt, cocoa, and coffee.

Add the sifted ingredients to the water (which may still be warm), stir or whisk until smooth, then stir in the lemon rind and drained raisins.

Turn into the prepared pan and smooth the top.

Bake for 30 to 35 minutes, until the top springs back when it is pressed gently with a fingertip.

Cool in the pan for 10 to 15 minutes. Then cover with a rack, turn the pan and rack over, remove the pan, peel off the foil, cover with another rack, and turn over again, leaving the cake to cool right side up.

8 ounces (generous 1½ cups) dark raisins
2½ cups water
⅓ cup plus 1 tablespoon vegetable oil
¾ cup granulated sugar
1 teaspoon baking soda
1 cup sifted all-purpose flour
1 cup sifted all-purpose whole-wheat flour
1 teaspoon cinnamon
1 teaspoon allspice
1 teaspoon ground cloves
½ teaspoon nutmeg
¼ teaspoon powdered ginger
½ teaspoon salt
1 tablespoon unsweetened cocoa powder (preferably Dutch-process)
1 tablespoon powdered (not granular) instant coffee or espresso (see Notes)
Finely grated rind of 1 large lemon

When cool, slide the cake onto a cutting board and cut it into portions.

If you wish, these may be wrapped individually in clear cellophane, wax paper, or aluminum foil. Or arrange them on a serving dish and cover the whole thing with plastic wrap until serving time.

NOTES: My friends in Colorado who make this like to take it right in the pan when they go camping. They do not line the pan with foil; they butter it and leave the cake in it until ready to serve.

If you do not have powdered instant coffee or espresso you can omit it from the recipe or you can use granular (or freeze-dried) coffee; stir it into the measured 1 cup of warm water after the raisins are drained.

Sour Lemon Squares

This recipe comes from a friend in Scottsdale, Arizona. The cookies have a crisp, buttery base and a soft, custardy, sour-lemon topping. They are more delicate than many other cookies and they are fabulous! Make them to serve with tea (especially) or coffee, or serve them as dessert, or along with a fruit or custard dessert. They may be frozen.

Pastry Base

Adjust a rack to the center of the oven and preheat oven to 350°. To line an 8 x 8 x 2-inch square pan with foil, turn the pan upside down. Center a 12-inch square of foil shiny side down over the pan, fold down the sides and corners to shape it, remove the foil, turn the pan right side up, place the foil in the pan, and press it into shape. To butter the foil, put a piece of butter (in addition to what is called for in the recipe) in the pan, place the pan in the oven to melt the butter, and then brush the butter over the bottom and halfway up the sides. Let the pan cool and then place it in the freezer (it is easier to press the bottom crust into place if the pan is cold).

3 ounces (¾ stick) unsalted
    butter
¼ teaspoon salt
¼ cup light brown sugar,
    firmly packed
1 cup sifted all-purpose flour

16 SQUARES

In a small bowl, cream the 3 ounces of butter. Beat in the salt, sugar, and then the flour. (Or you can do this in a food processor: Place the dry ingredients in the bowl with the steel blade, cut the butter into pieces and add, then process until thoroughly mixed.) If the mixture does not hold together, turn it out onto a work surface and knead it until it does.

Place the mixture in mounds (each one about a rounded teaspoonful) over the bottom of the cold pan. Then, with your fingers, press it to make a smooth and firm layer on the bottom only.

Bake for about 18 minutes, until the crust is lightly colored.

Meanwhile, prepare the Lemon Layer.

Lemon Layer

In a small cup mix the rind and juice and set aside.

In the small bowl of an electric mixer, beat the eggs well. Add the sugar, flour, and baking powder, and beat for 1 minute at high speed (see Note). Stir in rind and juice.

Pour the lemon mixture over the hot bottom crust.

Bake for 25 to 30 minutes, until the top is lightly colored and dry to the touch; when it is done it will feel spongy and custardy, not dry or stiff.

Cool completely in the pan and then chill in the freezer for about half an hour. Cover the pan with a rack or a small cookie sheet, turn over the pan and rack or sheet, remove the pan, and slowly and carefully peel off the foil. Cover with a small cutting board and turn over the board and the rack or sheet, leaving the cake right side up. The cake will be only about ½ inch deep.

Use a long, heavy, sharp knife and cut the cake into 16 squares. Wipe the blade after making each cut. Place them on wax paper and strain confectioners sugar generously over the tops.

Package these in a shallow box or arrange them on a tray and cover with plastic wrap.

These may be refrigerated and served cold or they may be served at room temperature. When they are cold, the lemon layer is more firm and wonderful; when they are at room temperature the lemon layer is softer and wonderful.

*Finely grated rind of 2
  medium-size lemons*
*3 tablespoons fresh lemon
  juice*
2 eggs
¾ cup granulated sugar
*2 tablespoons sifted all-
  purpose flour*
¼ teaspoon baking powder
*Confectioners sugar (to be
  used after the cookies are
  baked)*

NOTE: I once made these in a kitchen that did not have an electric mixer or an egg beater. I used a wire whisk, and they were just as good.

Johnny Appleseed Squares

Recently, during a beautiful drive through the Appalachian Mountains and along the spectacular Skyline Drive in Virginia, we picked up some local literature and learned about John Chapman, better known as Johnny Appleseed. During the early 1800s Chapman personally planted a veritable forest of apple trees throughout Pennsylvania, Indiana, and Ohio. He later sold the grown trees to early settlers for a penny each—ah, those were the good old days!

At a local gift shop, we bought some wonderful apple cookies. I had only to ask for the recipe; they had it typed and printed and were so happy I asked.

The recipe consists of a chewy, chunky oatmeal mixture that is spread thinly in a pan, covered with sliced apples, and topped with another layer of the oatmeal mixture. It is unusual for bar cookies to have a layer of juicy apples in the middle. They are extremely, deliciously chewy, and easy and fun to make. They may be frozen.

Adjust a rack to the middle of the oven and preheat oven to 350°. Line a 9 x 1¾-inch square pan as follows: Turn the pan over, center a 12-inch square of foil shiny side down over the pan, fold down the sides and corners to shape the foil, remove the foil, turn the pan over again, place the foil in the pan, and, with a potholder, firmly press the foil into place. Butter the pan by putting a piece of butter in the pan and then placing it in the oven to melt. Spread the butter with a pastry brush or a piece of crumpled wax paper. Place the prepared pan in the freezer (it is easier to spread a thin layer of dough in a frozen pan).

Sift together into a mixing bowl the flour, baking soda, salt, cinnamon, and nutmeg or mace. Stir in the oats and sugar. In a small bowl stir in the butter, egg, and vanilla, and mix into the oat mixture.

With your fingertips press half (1 cup) of the dough into the prepared pan; it will be a very thin layer. Set aside.

Place the remaining dough between two 12-inch lengths of wax paper and with a rolling pin roll over the top piece of paper to roll out the dough into a 9-inch square; it will be very thin. You may remove the top piece of paper, cut off pieces of the rolled-out dough, and place them where you need them, to make the square even. Slide a flat-sided cookie sheet under the dough and the wax paper and transfer it to the freezer for a few minutes.

Meanwhile, peel, quarter, and core the apples, and cut each quarter lengthwise into 5 or 6 slices.

1 cup sifted all-purpose flour
½ teaspoon baking soda
Scant ½ teaspoon salt
1 teaspoon cinnamon
¼ teaspoon nutmeg or mace
1½ cups quick-cooking (not instant) rolled oats
⅔ cup dark or light brown sugar, firmly packed
4 ounces (1 stick) unsalted butter, melted
1 egg
1 teaspoon vanilla extract
2 to 3 firm cooking apples (preferably Granny Smith or Jonathan)
½ cup pecans, toasted (see To Toast Pecans, page 4), cut or broken into medium-size pieces

16 TO 24 SQUARES

Place the apples in rows, each slice slightly overlapping another, to cover the bottom layer of dough. Sprinkle with the nuts.

Remove the rolled-out square of dough from the freezer, peel off the top piece of paper, turn the dough over the apples, remove the remaining paper, and press down on the edges of the dough.

Bake for about 25 to 30 minutes, reversing the pan front to back once during baking to ensure even browning. About 10 minutes before the cake is done, if the top has not started to brown, raise the rack to a higher position to encourage browning.

Cool in the pan. Then cover with a rack or a cookie sheet, turn the pan and rack or sheet over, remove the pan, peel off the foil, cover the cake with a cookie sheet or a cutting board, and turn it over again, leaving the cake right side up.

It is best to chill the cake a bit before cutting it into squares, but this has a good texture and will cut well even if it is not chilled.

Cut into squares or bars.

Palm Beach Brownies

These are the biggest, thickest, gooiest, chewiest, darkest, sweetest, mostest-of-the-most . . . with an almost wet middle and a crisp-crunchy top.

The baked cake should be refrigerated for a few hours or overnight, or frozen for an hour or two before it is cut into bars.

Adjust an oven rack one-third up from the bottom and preheat oven to 425°. Line a 9 x 13 x 2-inch pan as follows: Invert the pan and center a 17-inch length of aluminum foil shiny side down over the pan. (If you are using a Magic Line pan that has straight sides and square corners, use heavy duty foil or the sharp corners will tear the foil.) With your hands press down on the sides and corners of the foil to shape it to the pan. Remove the foil. Turn the pan right side up. Place the foil in the pan and very carefully press the foil into place in the pan. (If you press it with a pot holder or a folded towel there will be less chance of tearing it.) To butter the foil, place a piece of butter (additional to that in the ingredients) in the pan and put the pan in the oven until the butter melts. Then, with a pastry brush or a piece of crumpled wax paper, spread the butter all over the foil. Set the prepared pan aside.

Place the chocolate and the butter in the top of a large double boiler over hot water on moderate heat, or in a 4- to 6-cup heavy saucepan over low heat. Stir occasionally until the chocolate and butter are melted and smooth. Remove from the heat and set aside.

In the large bowl of an electric mixer beat the eggs with the vanilla and almond extracts, salt, espresso, sugar, and flour at high speed for 10 minutes. On low speed add the chocolate mixture (which may still be warm) and beat only until mixed. Remove the bowl from the mixer.

Stir in the nuts.

Turn into the prepared pan and smooth the top.

Bake for 35 minutes, reversing the pan front to back once during baking to insure even baking. At the end of 35 minutes the cake will have a thick, crisp crust on top, but if you insert a toothpick into the middle it will come out wet and covered with chocolate. Nevertheless it is done. Do not bake it any longer.

Remove the pan from the oven and let stand until cool.

Then cover with a rack or a cookie sheet and invert. Remove the pan and the foil lining. Cover with a length of wax paper and another cookie sheet and invert again, leaving the cake right side up.

Refrigerate the cake for a few hours or overnight, or place it in the freezer for an hour or two.

When you are ready to cut the cake use a long, heavy knife with a sharp blade. Try a serrated knife or a straight one and see which cuts best. Cut the cake into quarters. (Actually, I use one knife for cutting the cake into quarters and then a different one for cutting the smaller pieces.) Cut each quarter into half, cutting through the long sides. Finally, cut each piece into 4 bars, cutting through the long sides. (I like these better in narrow bar shapes than in squares.)

Pack in an airtight box or wrap individually in clear cellophane, wax paper, or foil.

NOTE: When you remove the cake from the pan you might see burned edges. (You might not—it depends on which pan you use.) If you do, you can leave them on or cut them off. I have friends who say that the burned edges are the best part. If you do decide to cut them off, it is easiest if you cut the cake into quarters first.

---

8 ounces unsweetened chocolate

8 ounces (2 sticks) unsalted butter

5 eggs

2 teaspoons vanilla extract

½ teaspoon almond extract

¼ teaspoon salt

1 tablespoon plus 1 teaspoon powdered instant espresso (I use Medaglia D'Oro from an Italian grocery store)

3¾ cups granulated sugar

1⅔ cups sifted all-purpose flour

8 ounces (generous 2 cups) walnut halves or large pieces

32 VERY LARGE BROWNIES

Christmas Brownies

*Of course it's silly to limit these or any brownies to Christmas. These have this name because they contain diced candied fruits, which are generally more available during the holiday season. These are extra special, **very chocolatey**, and chewy, even though they are only ½ inch thick. They are crusty on top and wet inside.*

Adjust a rack one-third up from the bottom of the oven and preheat oven to 300°. Prepare a shallow 9-inch square metal cake pan as follows: Turn the pan upside down and cover with a 12-inch square of aluminum foil shiny side down. Fold down the sides and the corners to shape the foil, remove the foil, turn the pan right side up, place the foil in the pan, and carefully press it into place. To butter the foil, place a piece of butter (in addition to that called for in the recipe) in the pan in the oven to melt. Then, with a pastry brush, brush the butter all over the bottom and halfway up on the sides.

Place the chocolate and the butter in the top of a small double boiler over warm water on moderate heat. Cover until melted. Stir until smooth. Remove the top of the double boiler and set aside to cool slightly.

In the large bowl of an electric mixer, beat the eggs only to mix; they should not be foamy. Add the vanilla and sugar, and beat to mix. Beat in the melted chocolate mixture. Then, on low speed, add the flour and beat only until mixed, scraping the bowl as necessary with a rubber spatula.

Remove from the mixer and stir in the diced candied fruit.

Turn into the lined and buttered pan and if necessary tilt the pan to level the batter.

Bake for 35 minutes. A toothpick inserted into the middle of the cake should come out just barely clean, or there may still be a tiny bit of the batter clinging to the toothpick—if necessary, bake for 2 to 3 minutes more.

Remove from the oven and cool in the pan for 5 minutes. Then cover the pan with a rack, turn the pan and the rack over, remove the pan, and carefully peel off the foil. Cover with another rack and carefully turn over again, leaving the cake right side up. This cake has a tendency to stick to the rack now. To prevent that, let it stand right side up for only 5 minutes. Then cover it with another rack and turn the rack and the cake over, cover what was originally the bottom of the cake with a piece of foil or wax paper, cover with a rack again and invert again, leaving the cake right side up on foil. The cake will be about ½ inch thick.

Let stand until completely cool.

2 ounces unsweetened chocolate
2 ounces (½ stick) unsalted butter
2 eggs
1 teaspoon vanilla extract
1 cup granulated sugar
¼ cup unsifted all-purpose flour (stir to aerate before measuring)
⅓ cup finely diced, mixed candied fruits (see Notes)

16 THIN BROWNIES

Then place in the freezer or the refrigerator long enough to chill. This cuts best when it is cold or even almost frozen.

Transfer to a cutting board. With a long, heavy, sharp knife cut into 16 squares (cutting down with the full length of the blade, not just the point). If necessary, clean the blade after making each cut.

Wrap individually in clear cellophane or wax paper (not plastic wrap), or pack in an airtight box with wax paper between the layers.

NOTES: These are especially and wonderfully moist; they must be handled more carefully than most brownies or they will squash.

For the candied fruits, I use citron, lemon, orange, and sometimes a bit of candied ginger. See Note on page 3 for the kind I buy and the source. I cut them on a board with a small, sharp knife.

Petites Trianons

This is a French recipe for small, plain fudge squares, similar to brownies without nuts. These are quick and easy to make; they are mixed in a saucepan.

Adjust a rack one-third up from the bottom of the oven and preheat oven to 350°. Prepare an 8-inch square cake pan as follows: Turn pan upside down. Cut a 12-inch square of aluminum foil. Center it over the inverted pan shiny side down. Fold down the sides and the corners and then remove the foil and turn the pan right side up. Place the foil in the pan. In order not to tear the foil use a pot holder or a folded towel and, pressing gently with the pot holder or towel, smooth the foil into place. Lightly butter the bottom and halfway up the sides, using soft or melted butter and a pastry brush or crumpled wax paper. Set aside.

Place the butter and chocolate in a heavy 2- to 3-quart saucepan over low heat. Stir occasionally with a rubber spatula or wooden spoon until melted and smooth. Set aside to cool for about 3 minutes.

Stir in the sugar and the vanilla and then the eggs, one at a time, stirring until smooth.

4 ounces (1 stick) unsalted butter, cut into 1-inch slices
2 ounces (2 squares) unsweetened chocolate
1 cup granulated sugar
½ teaspoon vanilla extract
2 extra-large or jumbo eggs
1 cup sifted all-purpose flour
Pinch of salt

16 SQUARES OR 12 TO 14 BARS

Pour the mixture into the prepared pan and spread evenly.

Bake for exactly 28 minutes. Do not overbake; this should remain moist in the center. Cool in the pan for 5 minutes.

Cover with a rack and invert. Remove the pan and aluminum foil. The bottom of the cake will be slightly moist in the center. Cover with another rack and invert again to cool right side up. (The cake will be about ¾ inch thick.)

When the cake is cool transfer it to a cutting board. With a long, thin, sharp knife cut the cake into squares or oblongs.

These may be arranged on a tray and covered with plastic wrap until serving time. Or they may be wrapped individually in clear cellophane or wax paper. Either way, do not allow them to dry out. They may be frozen and may be served either at room temperature or about 5 minutes after being removed from the freezer—they're awfully good still frozen.

All-American Brownies

This recipe is almost the same as the Petites Trianons above. There are a few minor changes.

Use only ½ cup sifted all-purpose flour and, at the end, stir in 2 ounces (generous ½ cup) walnuts, cut or broken into medium-size pieces (see page 11).

Bake for 20 to 25 minutes. To test, insert a toothpick into the center of the cake. When it just barely comes out clean but not dry, the brownies are done. Do not overbake. These should be soft and moist to be at their best.

Since this dough is more moist than that of the Petites Trianons (which have more flour), let the brownies cool to room temperature in the pan before inverting and removing.

These may be served frozen, directly from the freezer (delicious), or at room temperature.

Denver Brownies

When my husband and I were on a tour for my chocolate book, I made hot fudge sauce on a Denver TV program. As we left the station, the receptionist handed me a recipe and said, "Since you like chocolate so much, you should have this recipe. When Julia Child was here, one of the men in the station made these for her and she loved them."

They are fancy little bite-size chocolate squares with a layer of white icing that is covered with chocolate icing. They look like elegant candy—make them for a party. They freeze well, but they are not for packing or mailing.

Adjust a rack to the center of the oven and preheat oven to 325°. Prepare a 9-inch square cake pan as follows: Turn the pan over and cover it with a 12-inch square of aluminum foil shiny side down. Fold down the sides and the corners of the foil to shape it, remove the foil, turn the pan right side up, place the foil in the pan, and carefully press it into place. To butter the foil, put a piece of butter in the pan and place it in the oven to melt. Then brush it over the foil. Set the pan aside.

Sift together the flour, baking powder, and salt, and set aside.

Place the honey, water or coffee, butter, and chocolate in a 2- to 3-quart saucepan over moderate heat. Stir until the chocolate and butter are melted. Remove from the heat. With a wooden spoon, stir in the vanilla and then the eggs, one at a time. Mix well. Add the dry ingredients and whisk vigorously with a wire whisk until smooth. Stir in the nuts.

Turn into the prepared pan and smooth the top.

Bake for about 25 minutes until a toothpick inserted into the middle just barely comes out clean—do not over-bake.

Remove from the oven and brush the bourbon, brandy, or rum over the hot cake.

Cool to tepid in the pan.

Cover the pan with a rack, turn over the pan and the rack, remove the pan and the foil, cover with another rack, and turn over again, leaving the cake right side up. Let stand to cool completely and then transfer to a small board. (The cake will be ¾ inch high.)

¾ cup sifted all-purpose flour
¼ teaspoon baking powder
¼ teaspoon salt
⅓ cup honey
2 tablespoons water or black coffee
4 ounces (1 stick) unsalted butter, cut into pieces, at room temperature
6 ounces semisweet chocolate, coarsely chopped
1 teaspoon vanilla extract
2 eggs
6 ounces (generous 1½ cups) walnuts, cut into medium-size pieces
2 tablespoons bourbon, brandy, or rum

64 TINY BROWNIES

White Icing

In the small bowl of an electric mixer, beat the butter until soft. Add the vanilla and then gradually add the sugar, beating well until soft and fluffy.

Spread the white icing over the top of the cake. With a long, narrow metal spatula, smooth the top.

Refrigerate.

4 ounces (1 stick) unsalted butter
1 teaspoon vanilla extract
2 cups sifted confectioners sugar

Chocolate Icing

Place the chocolate, shortening, and butter in the top of a small double boiler over hot water on moderate heat. Cover until partly melted. Then uncover and stir until completely melted and smooth. Remove from the heat.

Pour in a thick ribbon all over the white icing, working quickly before the chilled white icing sets the chocolate. With a long, narrow metal spatula smooth the top.

Refrigerate.

To cut: The chocolate might be so firm that it cracks while you cut it. Either let it stand at room temperature briefly or score the cutting lines gently and carefully with a long serrated knife, and then cut through with a long, thin knife, cutting straight down (not back and forth). First trim the edges slightly. Then cut the cake into eight 1-inch strips. With a small, sharp paring knife, cut each strip into 1-inch squares.

Place the brownies in a single layer in a shallow covered box, or place them on a tray; be sure the chocolate is firm and then cover with plastic wrap.

6 ounces semisweet chocolate, coarsely chopped
1 tablespoon vegetable shortening (Crisco or other)
1 tablespoon unsalted butter

Greenwich Village Brownies

These are a specialty of a New York pastry shop. It is a recipe with a large yield. The brownies are moist, fudgy, and extra-chewy—almost like chocolate caramels.

Adjust a rack one-third up from the bottom of the oven and preheat oven to 350°. Prepare a 15½ x 10½ x 1-inch jelly-roll pan as follows: Turn it upside down and place an 18-inch length of aluminum foil over the inverted pan. Turn down the sides and corners of the foil just to shape it. Remove the foil and turn the pan right side up. Place the foil in the pan. Coat the foil with melted butter, spreading it thin with a pastry brush.

Measure the flour before sifting, then sift it together with the salt and set aside. Melt the chocolate in the top of a small double boiler over hot water on moderate heat. Stir until smooth, remove the top of the double boiler, and set aside.

In the large bowl of an electric mixer cream the butter. Add the vanilla and the granulated and brown sugars. Beat to mix well. Add the corn syrup and beat until smooth. Add the eggs one at a time, beating until smooth after each addition. Beat in the melted chocolate. On low speed, gradually add the flour, scraping the bowl as necessary with a rubber spatula and beating until smoothly mixed. Stir in 2 cups (reserve 1 cup) of the pecans.

Turn the mixture into the prepared pan and spread to make a smooth layer. (The pan will be filled to the top). Sprinkle the reserved 1 cup of pecans over the top.

Bake for 40 to 45 minutes until a toothpick inserted in the center of the cake comes out clean but not dry.

Cool in the pan for 30 minutes. Then cover with a large rack or cookie sheet and invert. Remove the pan and the foil. Cover with a large rack and invert again, leaving the cake right side up to cool completely.

The cake will be easier to cut if it is chilled first; place it in the freezer or refrigerator until it is quite firm.

Slide the cake onto a cutting board. Use a long, thin, sharp knife or a finely serrated one to cut it into bars. (See Note.)

Wrap the brownies individually in clear cellophane or wax paper, or store them in an airtight freezer box.

NOTE: If there are any burnt edges on the cake they may be cut off. Cut the cake into quarters and place the quarter upside down on the board to trim the edges. Then turn the cake right side up again for cutting into bars.

2 cups unsifted *all-purpose flour*
¼ teaspoon salt
6 ounces (6 squares) unsweetened chocolate
8 ounces (2 sticks) unsalted butter
1 teaspoon vanilla extract
2 cups granulated sugar
1 cup light brown sugar, firmly packed
⅔ cup light corn syrup
6 eggs
10 ounces (3 cups) pecan halves or large pieces

32 LARGE BROWNIES

Cream-Cheese Brownies

Part brownies, part cheesecake—layered and marbled together. These must be stored in the refrigerator or frozen. And they may be eaten directly from the freezer or thawed.

Chocolate Mixture

Adjust a rack one-third up from the bottom of the oven and preheat oven to 350°. Prepare a 9-inch square pan as follows: Turn it upside down and place a 12-inch square of aluminium foil shiny side down over the inverted pan. Turn down the sides and corners of the foil just to shape it. Remove the foil and turn the pan right side up. Place the foil in the pan. In order not to tear the foil place a folded towel or a pot holder in the pan and, pressing against the towel or pot holder, press the foil gently into place. Coat the foil with soft or melted butter, spreading it thin with a pastry brush or crumpled wax paper.

Sift together the flour, baking powder, and salt, and set aside. Melt the chocolate and the butter in the top of a small double boiler over hot water on moderate heat. Stir until smooth, remove from heat, and set aside to cool slightly.

In the small bowl of an electric mixer beat the eggs until foamy. Add the sugar and vanilla and beat at high speed for 3 to 4 minutes, until the mixture is slightly lemon-colored and forms a ribbon when beaters are lifted. On low speed beat in the chocolate mixture and then the sifted dry ingredients, scraping the bowl with a rubber spatula and beating only until the dry ingredients are incorporated.

Remove and set aside ¾ cup of the mixture. To the remaining batter add ½ cup of the nuts (reserve ¼ for topping) and stir to mix. Spread the chocolate mixture evenly in the pan; it will be a very thin layer.

½ cup unsifted *all-purpose flour*
½ teaspoon baking powder
¼ teaspoon salt
4 ounces (4 squares) semisweet chocolate
3 tablespoons unsalted butter
2 eggs
¾ cup granulated sugar
1 teaspoon vanilla extract
2½ ounces (¾ cup) walnuts, cut into medium-size pieces (see page 11)

24 BROWNIES

Cheese Mixture

In the small bowl of an electric mixer beat the cream cheese with the butter until soft and smooth. Add the vanilla and sugar, and beat well. Then add the egg and beat again until very smooth.

To cover the chocolate mixture with a thin layer of the

4 ounces cream cheese
2 tablespoons unsalted butter
½ teaspoon vanilla extract
¼ cup granulated sugar
1 egg

cheese mixture, slowly pour the cheese mixture over the chocolate layer, then smooth with the back of a spoon to the edges of a pan. Place the reserved ¾ cup of the chocolate mixture by heaping tablespoonfuls onto the cheese layer, letting the cheese show through between mounds—you should have abut 8 or 9 chocolate mounds. With a small metal spatula or a table knife cut through the chocolate mounds and the cheese layer. It is best if you don't cut down into the bottom layer. Zigzag the knife to marbleize the batters slightly; don't overdo it. Sprinkle with reserved ¼ cup nuts. Bake for 35 minutes.

Let stand at room temperature for a few hours. Then cover the pan with a sheet or board. Turn upside down. Remove the pan and foil. Cover with another sheet or board. Turn upside down again. Cut the cake into quarters. Cut each quarter into 6 bars.

Transfer the bars to a serving plate, cover airtight with plastic wrap, and refrigerate. Or pack them in a freezer box and freeze. Or they may be wrapped individually in clear cellophane or wax paper and then placed in the refrigerator or freezer.

Fudge Brownies

On the theory that there can't be too much of a good thing, here is still another brownie— another fudgy, moist, candylike, dark-chocolate bar cookie.

Adjust a rack one-third up from the bottom of the oven and preheat oven to 350°. Prepare a 9-inch square pan as follows: Turn it upside down and place a 12-inch square of aluminum foil shiny side down over the inverted pan. Turn down the sides and corners of the foil just to shape it. Remove the foil and turn the pan right side up. Place the foil in the pan. In order not to tear the foil place a folded towel or a pot holder in the pan and, pressing against the towel or pot holder, press the foil gently into place. Coat the foil with soft or melted butter, spreading it thin with a pastry brush or crumpled wax paper.

Place the chocolate and the butter in the top of a small double boiler over hot water on moderate heat. Cover and cook until almost melted. Remove the cover and stir until completely melted and smooth. Then remove the top of the double boiler and set it aside to cool slightly.

In the small bowl of an electric mixer beat the eggs at high speed for only about half a minute until foamy and slightly increased in volume.

*4 ounces (4 squares)
   unsweetened chocolate*
*4 ounces (1 stick) unsalted
   butter, cut into large pieces*
3 eggs
1½ cups granulated sugar
1 teaspoon vanilla extract
Pinch of salt
¾ cup sifted all-purpose flour
*Optional: 2½ ounces (¾ cup)
   walnuts, cut or broken into
   medium-size pieces (these
   are equally good with or
   without the nuts)*

24 BROWNIES

On low speed gradually add the sugar and beat for only a few seconds to mix. Add the vanilla, salt, and the chocolate mixture, scraping the bowl with a rubber spatula and beating only until barely mixed. Do not overbeat (see Note). Now add the flour, still scraping the bowl and beating only until mixed.

Remove the bowl from the mixer and, if you are using the walnuts, fold them in.

Turn the mixture into the prepared pan and smooth the top.

Bake for 35 minutes or a few minutes longer until a toothpick inserted in the center of the cake comes out barely clean. The inside should still be soft. Do not overbake.

Remove the pan from the oven, place it on a rack, and let it stand for 45 minutes to 1 hour until the bottom of the pan is only slightly warm.

Cover the cake with a rack and invert, remove the cake pan and foil, cover the cake again with a rack or a small cookie sheet, and invert again.

In order to cut the cake neatly it is best to chill it first in the freezer or refrigerator. If you partially freeze it, it will cut perfectly.

Slide the chilled cake onto a cutting board and with a long, sharp knife or a finely serrated one, cut it into bars. The bars may be placed on a tray and covered airtight with plastic wrap or stored airtight in a plastic freezer box—or, preferably, wrap each bar in clear cellophane or waxed paper.

NOTE: If you overbeat the eggs or the eggs and sugar, it will make the brownies cake-like, spongy, and dry, instead of moist.

Chocolate Mint Sticks

These are similar to brownies, but are covered with a layer of mint-flavored icing and a thin bitter-chocolate glaze.

Adjust a rack one-third up from the bottom of the oven and preheat oven to 350°. Butter a 9-inch square cake pan and dust it all over with fine, dry bread crumbs; invert the pan to shake out excess. (This cake has a tendency to stick to the pan; using the crumbs will prevent that.)

Melt the chocolate and the butter in the top of a small double boiler over hot water on moderate heat. Stir until smooth. Remove the top of the double boiler and set aside to cool slightly.

In the small mixing bowl of an electric mixer beat the eggs until they are foamy. Beat in the salt, vanilla, and sugar. Add the chocolate mixture (which may still be warm) and beat to mix. On low speed add the flour, scraping the bowl with a rubber spatula and beating only until mixed. Stir in the nuts. Pour the mixture into the prepared pan and spread it to make a smooth layer.

Bake for 28 minutes, or until a toothpick inserted in the center of the cake comes out clean.

Remove the cake from the oven and let it stand, in the pan, at room temperature until completely cool.

Prepare the following Mint Icing.

2 ounces (2 squares)
  unsweetened chocolate
4 ounces (1 stick) unsalted
  butter
2 eggs
Pinch of salt
½ teaspoon vanilla extract
1 cup granulated sugar
½ cup sifted all-purpose flour
2 ounces (generous ½ cup)
  walnuts, cut into medium-
  size pieces (see page 11)

32 SMALL BARS

Mint Icing

Place all of the icing ingredients in the small bowl of an electric mixer and beat until smooth. It might be necessary to add a few drops more of the heavy cream, but it should be a thick mixture, not runny.

Spread the icing evenly over the cake still in the pan. It will be a very thin layer. Place the cake in the refrigerator for 5 minutes, no longer.

Prepare the following glaze.

2 tablespoons unsalted butter,
  at room temperature
1 cup strained or sifted
  confectioners sugar
1 tablespoon (or a few drops
  more) heavy cream
½ teaspoon peppermint
  extract

Bitter-Chocolate Glaze

Melt the chocolate and the butter in the top of a small double boiler over hot water on moderate heat. Stir until completely smooth.

1 ounce (1 square)
  unsweetened chocolate
1 tablespoon unsalted butter

Pour the hot glaze onto the chilled icing and quickly tilt the pan in all directions, to cover the icing completely with the glaze. It will be a very, very thin layer of glaze, just barely enough to cover all of the icing. (But if the icing does show through in a few small spots, don't worry.)

Refrigerate the cake for about half an hour, or until the glaze starts to look dull.

With a small, sharp knife cut around the sides of the cake to release it. Wipe the knife blade as necessary to keep it clean, and cut the cake into quarters.

With a wide metal spatula transfer the quarters to a cutting board. With a long, sharp knife cut each quarter in half and then cut each half into four small bars, wiping the knife blade as necessary. Transfer the bars to a tray or cake plate and let stand at room temperature for at least several hours before serving to allow the glaze to dry.

These may be frozen and are very good when served directly from the freezer.

Dutch Chocolate Bars

These have a crisp, crunchy base with a thick, moist, baked-on chocolate topping. They are made without a mixer.

Bottom Layer

Adjust a rack to the center of the oven and preheat oven to 350°.

Into a mixing bowl sift together the flour, baking soda, and salt. Add the sugar and stir to mix thoroughly. Stir in the oatmeal and nuts and then the butter. The mixture will be crumbly and it will not hold together.

Turn the dough into an unbuttered 8-inch square cake pan. With your fingertips, press the dough to form a smooth, compact layer.

Bake for 10 minutes.

Meanwhile, prepare the topping.

⅓ cup sifted all-purpose flour
¼ teaspoon baking soda
⅛ teaspoon salt
½ cup light brown sugar, firmly packed
1 cup old-fashioned or quick-cooking (not instant) oatmeal
2 ounces (generous ½ cup) pecans, finely chopped (see page 11)
2⅔ ounces (5⅓ tablespoons) unsalted butter, melted

Topping

Sift together the flour, baking soda, and salt, and set aside. Melt the chocolate and the butter in the top of a large double boiler over hot water on moderate heat (or in a heavy saucepan over very low heat). Stir the chocolate and butter until smooth and remove from the heat. Mix in the sugar and then the egg, stirring until thoroughly mixed. Stir in the vanilla and milk. Add the sifted dry ingredients and stir until smooth.

Pour the chocolate topping over the hot bottom layer and spread smoothly.

Bake for about 35 minutes, or until a toothpick inserted in the center of the cake barely comes out clean and dry. Do not overbake; the chocolate should remain moist.

Cool the cake completely in the pan.

With a small sharp knife cut the cooled cake into squares or bars.

These are best when very fresh. Wrap them individually in clear cellophane or wax paper or place them on a tray and cover airtight. Or pack them in an airtight freezer box. Just don't let them dry out.

⅔ cup sifted all-purpose flour
¼ teaspoon baking soda
¼ teaspoon salt
1 ounce (1 square) unsweet-ened chocolate
2 ounces (4 tablespoons) butter
¾ cup granulated sugar
1 egg
1 teaspoon vanilla extract
2 tablespoons milk

16 OR 18 BARS

Supremes

These are rich walnut-oatmeal bars with a baked-in sweet chocolate filling. The recipe gives a large yield and the cookies are generally best stored in the refrigerator and served cold.

Adjust a rack one-third up from the bottom of the oven and preheat oven to 350°. Butter a 15½ x 10½ x 1-inch jelly-roll pan.

Sift together the flour, baking soda, and salt, and set aside. In the large bowl of an electric mixer cream the butter. Add the coffee, vanilla, and sugar, and beat well. Add the eggs and beat well. On low speed gradually beat in the sifted dry ingredients and then the oatmeal, scraping the bowl with a rubber spatula as necessary. Finally mix in 1 cup of the walnuts (reserve the remainder for the topping).

Remove and reserve 2 cups of the dough. Place the remainder by large spoonfuls over the bottom of the buttered pan. With well-floured fingertips press all over to make a smooth, even layer. Set aside and prepare the following filling.

2½ cups sifted all-purpose flour
1 teaspoon baking soda
½ teaspoon salt
8 ounces (2 sticks) unsalted butter
1 teaspoon instant coffee
1 teaspoon vanilla extract
2 cups light brown sugar, firmly packed
2 eggs
3 cups old-fashioned or quick-cooking (not instant) oatmeal
7 ounces (2 cups) walnuts, cut or broken into medium-size pieces

Chocolate Filling

Place the condensed milk, chocolate, butter, and salt in the top of a large double boiler over hot water on moderate heat. Stir occasionally until the chocolate and butter are melted and the mixture is smooth.

Remove the top of the double boiler from the heat and stir in the vanilla. Pour the warm chocolate mixture over the bottom oatmeal layer and spread evenly. Place the reserved oatmeal mixture by small spoonfuls over the chocolate, letting the chocolate show through between spoonfuls. Do not spread smooth. Sprinkle the reserved cup of walnuts evenly over the top.

Bake for 25 minutes or until the top is golden brown. Reverse the pan front to back once toward the end of baking to ensure even browning. The top mounds of dough will flatten slightly but they will not run together to cover the chocolate.

Cool completely in the pan at room temperature, not in the refrigerator, for several hours or overnight.

1 14- or 15-ounce can sweetened condensed milk
12 ounces semisweet chocolate cut into small pieces
2 tablespoons unsalted butter
Pinch of salt
1 teaspoon vanilla extract

32 OR 48 LARGE OR 64 SMALL BARS

To cut the cookies: Cut around the sides to release the cake. Then cut the panful into eighths and with a wide metal spatula transfer the sections to a cutting board. Cut each eighth into 4 or 6 pieces. If the cookies are soft and do not cut neatly and evenly (if they squash), chill the pieces on wax paper on a tray or cookie sheet in the freezer or refrigerator only until they are firm enough to cut neatly.

The cookies may be placed on a tray and covered with plastic wrap or packed in a freezer box or wrapped individually in clear cellophane or wax paper.

If the filling is too soft, these should be stored in the refrigerator.

PS: I received a letter from Chad Foreman, a private investigator, requesting a recipe that contained the ingredients that this recipe calls for. I don't know if he bakes and wanted the recipe for himself, or if someone hired him to track it down. (I felt like hiring a detective many times when I couldn't get a particular recipe. (See Corn Melba, page 284.)

Viennese Chocolate-Walnut Bars

These are soft, rich, and fudgy. There is a buttery crust, a walnut filling, and a dark chocolate.

Crust

Adjust a rack one-third up from the bottom of the oven and preheat oven to 375°.

In a small bowl of an electric mixer cream the butter. Beat in the sugar. On low speed gradually add the flour and beat only until the mixture holds together.

Place the dough by large spoonfuls over the bottom of an unbuttered 9-inch square cake pan. With your fingertips press the dough to make a smooth layer over the bottom of the pan.

Bake for 10 minutes.

Meanwhile prepare the filling.

4 ounces (1 stick) unsalted butter
¼ cup dark brown sugar, firmly packed
1¼ cups sifted all-purpose flour

32 SMALL BARS

Chocolate Walnut Filling

In a small bowl stir the preserves just to soften them, and set aside.

    Grind the walnuts to a fine powder in a food processor (see To Grind Nuts in a Food Processor, page 11) or nut grinder and set aside. In the small bowl of an electric mixer beat the eggs at high speed for 2 to 3 minutes until they are slightly thickened. Add the salt and vanilla and then, on low speed, add the sugar and cocoa. Increase the speed to high again and beat for 2 to 3 minutes more. On low speed mix in the ground walnuts, beating only until the nuts are incorporated.

    Spread the preserves over the hot crust, leaving a ½-inch border. It will be a very thin layer but it is really enough.

    Pour the filling over the preserves and tilt the pan to level the filling.

    Bake at 375° for 25 minutes.

    Let the cake cool completely and then prepare the icing.

¼ cup apricot preserves
6 ounces (generous 1½ cups) walnuts
2 eggs
¼ teaspoon salt
½ teaspoon vanilla extract
¾ cup dark brown sugar, firmly packed
2 tablespoons unsweetened cocoa powder (preferably Dutch-process)

Chocolate Icing

In the top of a small double boiler, over hot water on moderate heat, cook the chocolate until it is melted. Add the corn syrup, rum or coffee, and the boiling water, and stir until smooth.

    Spread the icing evenly over the cake. Sprinkle with the nuts and press down gently with a wide metal spatula to press the nuts slightly into the icing.

    Let stand at room temperature until the icing is firm; it will probably take a few hours.

    With a small, sharp knife cut around the sides of the cake to release it and then cut the cake into quarters. With a wide metal spatula transfer the quarters to a cutting board and cut each quarter into small bars.

    Place the bars on a serving dish, cover with plastic wrap, and let stand at room temperature for a few hours (or overnight) before serving.

6 ounces semisweet chocolate cut into small pieces
2 tablespoons light corn syrup
2 teaspoons rum or strong prepared coffee
2 teaspoons boiling water
2 ounces (generous ½ cup) walnuts, cut medium fine (see page 11)

PS: A young lady named Missy Stout wrote to tell me she had won two first place ribbons at county fairs with these Walnut Bars.

Dark Rocky Roads

Made without a mixer, these chocolate, brownielike bars are topped with marshmallows, pecans, and a thick, dark-chocolate glaze. It is best to make these the night before, or early in the day of the night they are to be served, because they must stand before being cut into bars.

Chocolate Layer

Adjust a rack to the center of the oven and preheat oven to 350°. Butter an 11 x 7½ x 1¾-inch baking pan and set aside.

Sift together the flour, baking powder, and salt, and set aside.

Place the chocolate and the butter in a 2- to 3-quart saucepan over moderately low heat. Stir constantly until they are melted. Remove from the heat. Add the vanilla and the sugar and stir to mix well. Add the eggs one at a time, stirring until thoroughly incorporated after each addition. Stir in the sifted dry ingredients until thoroughly mixed, then stir in the nuts.

Pour into the prepared pan and spread into an even layer.

Bake for 23 to 25 minutes, or until a toothpick inserted in the middle of the cake comes out barely dry. Do not overbake.

While the cake is baking, prepare the topping and start to prepare the glaze.

¾ cup sifted all-purpose flour
½ teaspoon baking powder
¼ teaspoon salt
1 ounce (1 square) unsweet- ened chocolate
3 ounces (6 tablespoons) unsalted butter
½ teaspoon vanilla extract
1 cup granulated sugar
2 eggs
2 ounces (generous ½ cup) pecans, coarsely cut or broken (see page 11)

24 BARS

Topping

Cut the marshmallows in half crossways. This may be done with a knife or with scissors (try both and see which you prefer). If the marshmallows stick, dip the knife blade or the scissors into cold water to eliminate this problem. Set the cut marshmallows aside on wax paper, placing them cut side up. Also have the pecans ready.

A few minutes before the chocolate layer is done, start to prepare the glaze.

23 regular-size marshmallows
2½ ounces (¾ cup) pecan halves or large pieces

Glaze

Melt the chocolate and butter in the top of a small double boiler over hot water on moderate heat. Remove from the heat, but do not mix in the remaining ingredients until you are ready to use the glaze.

When the chocolate layer is done, remove it from the oven, but do not turn off the oven heat. Quickly place the cut marshmallow halves in even rows over the top of the cake—cut side down, five in each short row and nine in each long row. They should just touch each other (there will be one half left over).

Immediately return the pan to the oven and bake for exactly 1 minute—no longer; the marshmallows should only soften slightly; they should not bake long enough to melt. Remove the pan from the oven and finish the glaze as follows: Add the sugar, vanilla, and 2 tablespoons of boiling water to the melted chocolate-butter mixture. Stir until smooth. The mixture should be thick, but thin enough to drizzle over the marshmallows. It will probably be necessary to add a bit more water, but add it very gradually and be sure that you do not add too much.

Quickly sprinkle the pecans over the marshmallows and then immediately (while the cake is still hot and before the glaze thickens), drizzle the glaze unevenly over the marshmallows and nuts. Some of the marshmallows should show through in a few spots, but the nuts should all be at least partly covered in order to keep them from falling off.

Let stand uncovered overnight or for at least 5 or 6 hours if possible; if you try to cut these any sooner the marshmallows might be sticky and difficult to handle. (See Note.) Cut around the sides with a small, sharp knife to release the cake. Then cut the cake into eighths. Keep dipping the knife into cold water to prevent it from sticking. Dip a wide metal spatula into cold water (every time) and transfer the eighths to a cutting board. Then, with a wet knife, cut each eighth into three bars.

NOTE: Cutting these into bars is liable to be a little messy and frustrating even after letting them stand. Just be brave and remember that you're the boss. The cookies are well worth a little trouble.

1 ounce (1 square) unsweetened chocolate
1 tablespoon unsalted butter
1 cup strained confectioners sugar
¼ teaspoon vanilla extract
About 2 tablespoons boiling water

Light Rocky Roads

These candylike bars have a thin brown-sugar layer that is topped with marshmallows, nuts, and chocolate.

Adjust a rack one-third up from the bottom of the oven and preheat oven to 350°. Butter an 8-inch square cake pan.

Sift together the flour, baking powder, and salt, and set aside. In a small bowl beat the egg lightly only until it is foamy. Add the brown sugar and vanilla and beat just to mix. Mix in the butter and then the sifted dry ingredients. Stir in the nuts.

Turn the dough into the prepared pan and spread it evenly. It will be a very thin layer.

Bake for 15 minutes or until the top of the cake springs back when lightly pressed with a fingertip.

Meanwhile line up the ingredients for the topping.

¼ cup sifted all-purpose flour
¼ teaspoon baking powder
Pinch of salt
1 egg
⅓ cup dark or light brown sugar, firmly packed
½ teaspoon vanilla extract
1 tablespoon unsalted butter, melted
½ cup walnuts or pecans, finely cut (see page 11)

18 BARS

Rocky Road Topping

Remove the cake from the oven and immediately cover it with a layer of the marshmallows, then with the nuts, and then place the chocolate morsels on top.

Raise the rack to the top position in the oven. Bake the cake for only 2 to 3 minutes, no longer, just until the chocolate is softened but not long enough to melt the marshmallows. Immediately, with the back of a spoon, spread the chocolate lightly and unevenly over the marshmallows and nuts, letting some of the marshmallows show through in a few places.

Cool the cake to room temperature and then chill it briefly to barely set the chocolate.

With a small, sharp knife cut the cake in half in one direction and in thirds in the opposite direction. Cut around the sides to release. With a wide metal spatula transfer the pieces to a cutting board and then cut each piece into three bars.

1 cup miniature marshmallows
2 ounces (½ cup) walnuts or pecans, coarsely cut or broken
6 ounces (1 cup) semisweet chocolate morsels

NOTE: If the chocolate becomes spotty after the cookies have cooled, sprinkle the top with confectioners sugar, pressing the sugar through a fine strainer held over the cookies.

Butterscotch Brownies

All brownies are not chocolate; these are brown-sugar bars with a butterscotch flavor, especially moist and chewy.

*A*djust a rack one-third up from the bottom of the oven and preheat oven to 350°. Prepare a 9-inch square pan as follows: Turn it upside down and place a 12-inch square of aluminum foil shiny side down over the inverted pan. Turn down the sides and corners of the foil just to shape it. Remove the foil and turn the pan right side up. Place the foil in the pan. In order not to tear the foil place a folded towel or a pot holder in the pan and, pressing against the towel or pot holder, press the foil gently into place. Coat the foil with soft or melted butter, spreading it thin with a pastry brush or crumpled wax paper.

4 ounces (1 stick) unsalted butter
1 teaspoon vanilla extract
1 tablespoon light molasses
1¼ cups dark brown sugar, firmly packed
2 eggs
1 cup sifted all-purpose flour
2½ ounces (¾ cup) pecans, coarsely cut or broken

24 BROWNIES

In the large bowl of an electric mixer cream the butter. Beat in the vanilla and molasses. Add the brown sugar and beat well. Add the eggs one at a time, beating well after each addition, and then beat at moderately high speed for a minute or two, scraping the bowl occasionally with a rubber spatula, until the mixture is very smooth and light in color. On low speed add the flour, continuing to scrape the bowl with the spatula, and beating only until thoroughly mixed.

Remove the bowl from the mixer and stir in the nuts.

Transfer the dough to the buttered pan. Spread the top to make it an even layer.

Bake for 32 to 35 minutes, until a toothpick inserted in the center comes out just barely dry.

Let the cake cool in the pan.

Cover the cake with a rack and invert, remove the pan and foil, cover the cake again with a rack or board and invert again. Transfer the cake to a cutting board. Cut the cake into quarters. Cut each quarter in half and then cut each piece into three bars.

The bars may be wrapped individually in clear cellophane or wax paper. Or they may be placed on a tray and covered with plastic wrap, or stored in a covered freezer box. Or, for a picnic, leave the cake in the pan but cut it into 24 bars. Cover the pan with plastic wrap or aluminum foil and take a metal spatula along with you and remove the bars from the pan at the picnic.

Florida Cream-Cheese Squares

These are layered squares with a baked-in cream-cheese filling. They should be refrigerated until serving time.

Adjust a rack one-third up from the bottom of the oven and preheat oven to 350°. Butter an 8-inch square cake pan.

In the small bowl of an electric mixer cream the butter. Add the brown sugar and beat well. On low speed gradually add the flour and then the walnuts, scraping the bowl with a rubber spatula and beating until well mixed. The mixture will be crumbly and won't hold together. Remove and set aside 1 cup of the mixture.

Distribute the remainder evenly over the bottom of the prepared pan. Then, with your fingertips, press it firmly to make a smooth, compact layer.

Bake for 15 minutes.

Meanwhile, mix the lemon rind with the lemon juice and set aside. In the small bowl of an electric mixer cream the cheese. Add the granulated sugar and beat well. Add the vanilla and the egg, and beat to mix well. Remove the bowl from the mixer and stir in the lemon rind and juice mixture.

Pour the cream-cheese mixture over the hot baked crust. Tilt the pan gently to level the filling. Carefully sprinkle the reserved crumb mixture evenly over the filling.

Bake for 25 minutes. Cool the cake in its pan to room temperature. Then refrigerate it for 1 hour or more.

With a small, sharp knife cut around the sides to release. Then cut the cake into quarters. With a wide metal spatula transfer the quarters to a cutting board. If you have trouble releasing the first piece, cut it into quarters and remove the pieces individually. If necessary, use a fork to ease the first few pieces out of the pan. Use a long knife to cut each quarter into four squares, wiping the blade with a damp cloth after each cut.

Place the squares on a tray or serving dish. Cover with plastic wrap and refrigerate until serving time. Or pack the squares in a freezer box and freeze them. These may be served frozen, directly from the freezer.

2⅔ ounces (5⅓ tablespoons) unsalted butter
⅓ cup dark brown sugar, firmly packed
1 cup sifted all-purpose flour
½ cup walnuts, chopped medium fine
Finely grated rind of 1 lemon
1 tablespoon lemon juice
8 ounces Philadelphia brand cream cheese, preferably at room temperature
¼ cup granulated sugar
½ teaspoon vanilla extract
1 egg

16 SQUARES

Florida Lemon Squares

These are rich layered bars with a baked-in tart lemon filling. They should be refrigerated until serving time.

Adjust a rack one-third up from the bottom of the oven and preheat oven to 350°. Butter a 9 x 13 x 2-inch pan.

Sift together the flour, baking powder, and salt, and set aside. Pour the condensed milk into a medium-size mixing bowl. Add the grated lemon rind and then, gradually, add the lemon juice, stirring with a small wire whisk to keep the mixture smooth. (The lemon will thicken the milk.) Set the mixture aside.

In the large bowl of an electric mixer cream the butter. Add the sugar and beat well. On lowest speed gradually add the sifted dry ingredients, scraping the bowl with a rubber spatula and beating only until thoroughly mixed. Mix in the oatmeal. The mixture will be crumbly—it will not hold together.

Sprinkle a bit more than half of the oatmeal mixture (2 generous cups) evenly over the bottom of the prepared pan. Pat the crumbs firmly with your fingertips to make a smooth, compact layer. Drizzle or spoon the lemon mixture evenly over the crumb layer and spread it to make a thin, smooth layer. Sprinkle the remaining crumbly oatmeal mixture evenly over the lemon layer. Pat the crumbs gently with the palm of your hand to smooth them—it is okay if a bit of the lemon layer shows through in small spots.

1½ cups sifted all-purpose flour
1 teaspoon baking powder
½ teaspoon salt
1 14- or 15-ounce can unsweetened condensed milk
Finely grated rind of 1 large lemon
½ cup lemon juice
5⅓ ounces (10⅔ tablespoons) unsalted butter
1 cup dark brown sugar, firmly packed
1 cup old-fashioned or quick-cooking (not instant) oatmeal

24 OR 32 SQUARES

Bake for 30 to 35 minutes, until the cake is lightly colored.

Cool the cake completely in the pan. Then refrigerate it for about 1 hour (or more).

With a small, sharp knife cut around the sides of the cake to release it. Cut it into small squares. With a wide metal spatula remove the squares from the pan; transfer them to a serving plate, cover with plastic wrap, and refrigerate.

OPTIONAL: Just before serving, the squares may be topped with confectioners sugar. Use your fingertips to press the sugar through a fine strainer held over the squares. (It is best to have the squares on wax paper while coating them with sugar.)

Palm Beach Pineapple Squares

These have a soft, cakelike chocolate bottom and a pineapple topping.

Adjust a rack one-third up from the bottom of the oven and preheat oven to 375°. Butter a 13 x 9 x 2-inch pan and then dust it all over lightly with fine, dry bread crumbs; invert the pan to shake out excess.

Sift together the flour, baking powder, and salt, and set aside. Melt the chocolate in the top of a small double boiler over hot water on moderate heat and then set aside to cool.

Place the pineapple in a strainer set over a bowl and let stand to drain.

In the large bowl of an electric mixer cream the butter. Add the vanilla and sugar and beat well. Add the eggs one at a time, beating well after each addition. On low speed add the dry ingredients, scraping the bowl with a rubber spatula and beating only until thoroughly mixed.

Remove 1 cup of the mixture and place it in a medium-size bowl. Stir the lemon rind and the drained pineapple into this cup of batter. Set aside.

Add the melted chocolate to the mixture remaining in the large bowl and beat until thoroughly mixed. Stir in the nuts.

Spread the chocolate mixture in an even layer in the prepared pan. Place the pineapple mixture by small spoonfuls evenly over the chocolate layer. With the back of a small spoon spread the pineapple mixture to make a smooth thin layer—it is all right if a bit of the chocolate shows through in places.

Bake for 40 to 45 minutes, reversing the position of the pan once to ensure even browning. The cake is done if the top springs back when lightly pressed with a fingertip and the cake begins to come away from the sides of the pan.

Let the cake cool in the pan for about 15 minutes. Then cover it with a cookie sheet and invert. Remove the pan and cover the cake with a large rack. Invert again to cool completely right side up.

When completely cool, transfer the cake to a cutting board. With a long, thin, sharp knife cut into squares or bars.

1½ cups sifted all-purpose flour
1½ teaspoons baking powder
¼ teaspoon salt
2 ounces (2 squares) unsweetened chocolate
1 8-ounce can (1 cup) crushed pineapple
6 ounces (1½ sticks) unsalted butter
1 teaspoon vanilla extract
1½ cups granulated sugar
3 eggs
Finely grated rind of 1 lemon
4 ounces (generous 1 cup) walnuts, cut into medium-size pieces

24 TO 36 SQUARES OR BARS

Christmas Fruitcake Bars

These are traditional for the holidays—and they're good for mailing.

Adjust a rack to the center of the oven and preheat oven to 325°. Butter a 10½ x 15½ x 1-inch jelly-roll pan. Place the walnuts, raisins, dates, and candied fruit in a large mixing bowl. Add ¼ cup of the flour (reserve the remaining ¾ cup). With your fingers, toss the fruit and the nuts with the flour to separate and coat all the pieces thoroughly. Set aside.

In the small bowl of an electric mixer beat the eggs just to mix. Add the salt, sugar, and vanilla, and beat just to mix. On low speed add the reserved ¾ cup flour, scraping the bowl with a rubber spatula and beating only until mixed. Remove from the mixer and stir in the orange rind.

The batter will be thin. Pour it over the floured fruit and nuts. Stir to mix thoroughly.

Turn the mixture into the buttered pan and spread evenly.

Bake for 30 to 35 minutes, until the top is golden brown. Reverse the pan front to back once during baking to ensure even browning.

Cool completely in the pan.

With a small, sharp knife cut around the edges to release, and cut the cake into bars—they will be only a scant ½ inch thick.

6 ounces (generous 1½ cups) walnuts, coarsely cut or broken
5 ounces (1 cup) raisins
8 ounces (1 cup, packed) pitted dates, cut in large pieces
8 to 10 ounces (generous 1 cup) candied fruit (see Note)
1 cup sifted all-purpose flour
4 eggs
½ teaspoon salt
1 cup light brown sugar, firmly packed
1 teaspoon vanilla extract
Finely grated rind of 1 large, deep-colored orange
Confectioners sugar

32 BARS

With a wide metal spatula transfer the bars to a large piece of wax paper. Dust the tops generously with confectioners sugar by pressing the sugar with your fingertips through a fine strainer held over the cookies.

These may be wrapped individually in cellophane (clear, red, or green) or wax paper, or they may be stored with wax paper between the layers in an airtight box.

NOTE: The candied fruit may be a mixture of either red and/or green cherries and candied pineapple or cherries alone, or it may be the prepared mixed fruit. The cherries and pineapple should be cut into medium-size pieces (not small); the mixed fruit should be used as is.

Hermit Bars

An early American classic; every woman had her own version—the fruits and spices varied, and some were made as drop cookies. The ladies on Cape Cod packed these for their men who went to sea because they kept well.

Adjust a rack to the center of the oven and preheat oven to 350°. Butter a 13 x 9 x 2-inch baking pan. Sift together the flour, baking soda, baking powder, salt, cinnamon, cloves, nutmeg, mace, and allspice, and set aside.

Place the currants or raisins in a small bowl and pour boiling water over them to cover. Let stand for a few minutes. Drain in a strainer and then spread the fruit out on paper towels to dry slightly.

In the large bowl of an electric mixer cream the butter. Add the sugar and beat well. Add the eggs one at a time and beat until smooth. Beat in the molasses; the mixture will look curdled—it's okay. On low speed gradually add the sifted dry ingredients, scraping the bowl with a rubber spatula and beating only until mixed. Mix in the currants or raisins and the nuts.

Spread the dough smoothly in the buttered pan.

Bake for about 30 minutes, until the top of the cake springs back when lightly pressed with a fingertip.

Remove the pan from the oven and prepare the glaze immediately.

2 cups sifted all-purpose flour
¾ teaspoon baking soda
¾ teaspoon baking powder
½ teaspoon salt
1 teaspoon cinnamon
½ teaspoon powdered cloves
¼ teaspoon nutmeg
¼ teaspoon mace
⅛ teaspoon allspice
5 ounces (1 cup) currants or raisins
Boiling water
4 ounces (1 stick) unsalted butter
½ cup granulated sugar
2 eggs
½ cup molasses
4 ounces (generous 1 cup) pecans, coarsely cut or broken (see page 11)

24 BARS

Glaze

Place the sugar in the small bowl of an electric mixer (see Note). Add the butter and vanilla. Beat on low speed while gradually adding the boiling water. Use only enough water to make a mixture the consistency of medium-thick cream sauce.

Pour the glaze over the hot cake and brush it with a pastry brush to make it cover the cake. Let the cake stand until the glaze is dry.

With a small, sharp knife cut the cake into bars.

The bars may be left in the pan and covered airtight so they remain moist and fresh, or they may be wrapped individually in clear cellophane or wax paper.

1½ cups confectioners sugar
2 tablespoons unsalted butter, melted
½ teaspoon vanilla extract
3 to 4 tablespoons boiling water

NOTE: The glaze may be mixed without the electric mixer: Follow the above directions using a medium-size mixing bowl and stirring well with a rubber spatula. But it must be smooth with no lumps.

Brittle Peanut Bars

These are hard, chewy, and crunchy, like brittle candy.

Adjust a rack to the center of the oven and preheat oven to 375°. In the large bowl of an electric mixer cream the butter. Add the sugar and beat to mix well. On low speed gradually add the flour, scraping the bowl with a rubber spatula and beating only until the dough holds together. Mix in one-half of the nuts (reserving the remaining nuts for topping).

Turn the dough into an unbuttered 15½ x 10½ x 1-inch jelly-roll pan. Dip your fingertips in flour and use them to press the dough into a thin layer. Don't worry about smoothing the layer now, that will come soon.

Sprinkle the reserved nuts evenly over the dough.

Place a large piece of wax paper over the nuts. With a small rolling pin or a glass with straight sides, roll over the paper to press the nuts firmly into the top of the dough and to smooth the dough at the same time.

Remove the wax paper and bake for 23 to 25 minutes until golden brown. Reverse the pan once during baking to insure even browning. The cake will puff up during baking and then sink, leaving the edges higher and the surface slightly wrinkled.

Cool in the pan for about 5 minutes and then, while the cake is still warm, cut into bars. (When cool, it will become too hard and brittle to cut.)

With a wide metal spatula remove the bars from the pan and finish cooling them on racks.

8 ounces (2 sticks) unsalted butter
1 cup granulated sugar
2 cups sifted all-purpose flour
4 ounces (1 cup) salted peanuts, chopped into medium-size pieces

32 BARS

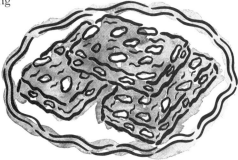

Hungarian Walnut Bars

This is a classic recipe—two layers of rolled-out pastry with a rich, baked-in walnut filling.

Pastry

Adjust a rack one-third up from the bottom of the oven and preheat oven to 375°. Prepare a 9-inch square cake pan as follows: Turn it upside down and place a 12-inch square of aluminum foil over the inverted pan. Turn down the sides and corners of the foil just to shape. Remove the foil and turn the pan right side up. Place the foil in the pan. In order not to tear the foil, place a folded towel or a pot holder in the pan and, pressing against the towel or pot holder, press the foil gently into place. Coat the foil with soft or melted butter, spreading it thin with crumpled wax paper or a pastry brush. Dust the pan thoroughly with fine, dry bread crumbs and then invert to shake out excess.

Sift together into a mixing bowl the flour, baking powder, and salt. Stir in the sugar. With a pastry blender cut in the butter until the particles are fine and mixture resembles coarse meal.

In a small cup stir the egg yolk with the milk just to mix, then stir it into the dry ingredients. Add the lemon rind.

Either in the bowl or on a smooth work surface, work the dough with your hands only until it is smooth and holds together.

Divide the dough into halves. Place each half between two large pieces of wax paper. Roll over the wax paper with a rolling pin, rolling each piece of dough into a 9-inch square. To make perfect squares: Use the baking pan as a pattern and place it on the top of the wax paper. Use the back (or dull side) of a small knife to trace around the pan, pressing just enough to mark the dough without cutting through the wax paper. Then remove the pan and the top layer of paper and cut away excess dough, using it to fill in the corners or wherever needed. Replace the wax paper and with a rolling pin roll very gently only to smooth the top.

Slide a flat-sided cookie sheet under both squares of dough (still in wax paper) and transfer them to the freezer or refrigerator to chill briefly. (At this stage the dough will be sticky and will stick to the wax paper. It should be chilled until it is almost firm and the wax paper comes away neatly.)

1 ½ cups sifted all-purpose
    flour
1 teaspoon baking powder
¼ teaspoon salt
⅓ cup granulated sugar
6 ounces (1 ½ sticks) cold
    unsalted butter, cut into
    ½- to 1-inch slices
1 egg yolk (reserve the white
    for the filling)
1 tablespoon milk
Finely grated rind of 1 large
    lemon

18 BARS

Walnut Filling

Place the walnuts, sugar, and salt in a bowl and stir to mix well.

In a small bowl beat the rum or water with the egg white only until foamy. Then stir it into the nut mixture and set aside.

Remove the dough squares from the freezer or refrigerator and remove the top piece of wax paper from each square. Invert one dough square into the prepared pan and remove the remaining piece of wax paper.

Place the filling by spoonfuls on the dough and spread to make an even layer. Invert the second square of dough over the filling and remove the remaining wax paper.

With a fork pierce the top layer of dough all over at ½-inch intervals.

Bake for 30 minutes. Cover with a rack or a small cookie sheet and invert. Remove the pan and the aluminum foil. Cover with a rack and invert again, leaving the cake right side up to cool.

It will be easier to cut the cake neatly if it is cold; chill it briefly in the freezer or refrigerator. Then transfer it to a cutting board. Cut with a long, thin, sharp knife, cutting with the full length of the blade. To make 18 bars, first cut the cake in one direction into thirds, and then cut each strip into 6 bars.

If you wish, strain confectioners sugar generously over the tops.

With a wide metal spatula transfer the bars to a serving plate and cover with plastic wrap.

NOTE: I place the walnuts on the large cutting board and chop them with a long, heavy chef's knife. They should be cut into small pieces, but if a few larger pieces are left, that's okay.

6 ounces (generous 1½ cups) walnuts, finely chopped (not ground, see Note)
1¼ cups strained or sifted confectioners sugar (see page 12)
Pinch of salt
2 tablespoons rum or water
1 egg white

Butterscotch Walnut Bars

These have a crisp, buttery layer with a chewy, candylike, caramel-nut topping. They are made without a mixer.

Crust

Adjust a rack one-third up from the bottom of the oven and preheat oven to 375°.

Place the flour, salt, and sugar in a mixing bowl and stir to mix well. Add the pieces of butter to the flour mixture, and with a pastry blender cut in the butter until the particles are very fine and the mixture resembles coarse meal. (It will be dry and powdery but will hold together when pressed into the pan.)

Place the mixture in an unbuttered 9 x 13 x 2-inch pan. With your fingertips, distribute it evenly over the bottom of the pan. Then, with your fingertips and the palm of your hand, press firmly to make a smooth, compact layer.

Bake the crust for about 12 minutes until it is lightly browned. Remove it from the oven but do not turn off the oven. Let the crust stand while you prepare the topping.

1½ cups sifted all-purpose flour
Scant ¼ teaspoon salt
¾ cup light brown sugar, firmly packed. (If the sugar is at all lumpy it must be strained. With your fingertips press it through a large strainer set over a large bowl.)
4 ounces (1 stick) unsalted butter, cut into ½- to 1-inch slices

32 BARS

Butterscotch Walnut Topping

Place the corn syrup, butterscotch morsels, salt, butter, and water in the top of a large double boiler over hot water on moderate heat. Stir constantly with a rubber spatula, pressing against the morsels until they are melted and the mixture is smooth. (Having a few tiny pieces of unmelted morsels is okay.)

Now work quickly because the mixture will harden if it is left standing. Stir in the nuts, remove from the heat, and place the mixture by large spoonfuls over the baked crust (which will still be warm). Then, with the back of the spoon, spread the butterscotch around on the crust, leaving a ½- to ¾-inch border. (During baking, the topping will run toward the edges.)

Return to the oven and bake for 10 minutes—no more, no less.

¼ cup light corn syrup
6 ounces (1 cup) butterscotch morsels
Pinch of salt
2 tablespoons unsalted butter
1 tablespoons water
7 ounces (2 cups) walnuts, cut medium fine (see page 11)

Let the cake cool in the pan for 30 to 40 minutes, until it is only slightly warm. Then, with a small, sharp knife, cut around the edges to release and then cut into 16 oblongs. The bars in the center of the pan will appear too soft but they will become firmer as they cool (it might be necessary to wait a little longer before removing them).

With a wide metal spatula transfer the bars to a cutting board. Let them stand until they are completely cool and firm. Then cut each one in half, making small bars.

Place the bars in a covered freezer box, or on a tray and cover with plastic wrap. Or wrap them individually in clear cellophane or wax paper.

Cinnamon Almond Cookies

In a small tearoom near London these are called "toffee." They are served there with tea and also packaged in little brown bags to take out. They are rather thin, buttery, crisp cinnamon cookies with a lemon glaze.

Adjust a rack to the center of the oven and preheat oven to 300°. Butter a 10½ x 15½ x 1-inch jelly-roll pan. The almonds must be crumbled and broken into coarse pieces. If they have been stored in the freezer it is easiest to do this while they are still frozen. It may be done by squeezing the nuts between your hands in a bowl or over paper. Or place the almonds in a plastic bag and squeeze and press on the bag to break the nuts. Set aside.

In the large bowl of an electric mixer cream the butter. Add the cinnamon and sugar and beat to mix well. Beat in the egg yolk (reserve the white) and then on low speed gradually add the flour, scraping the bowl with a rubber spatula and beating only until thoroughly mixed.

Place the dough by large spoonfuls in the buttered pan. With the back of the spoon spread the dough to cover the bottom of the pan. Cover the dough with a large piece of wax paper and press down on the paper with your hands to make a smooth, even layer. Or use a straight-sided glass as a rolling pin and roll over the paper. Remove the wax paper.

In a small bowl beat the egg white only until it is foamy and slightly thickened.

6 ounces (1¾ cups) thinly sliced blanched almonds
8 ounces (2 sticks) unsalted butter
2 teaspoons cinnamon
1 cup granulated sugar
1 egg, separated
2 cups sifted all-purpose flour

32 COOKIES

Pour it over the layer of dough, and with a pastry brush spread it to cover the top of the dough.

With your fingertips sprinkle the crushed almonds evenly over the egg white. Cover again with wax paper. With the straight-sided glass roll over the paper to press the almonds into the dough and then remove the wax paper.

Bake for 45 minutes until golden brown.

A minute or so before removing the pan from the oven prepare the following glaze.

Glaze

Place the sugar, butter, water, and lemon juice in a small bowl and mix with a rubber spatula until completely smooth. The glaze should be the consistency of heavy cream.

When you remove the pan from the oven drizzle the glaze unevenly in a thin stream over the top of the cake. It will form a shiny, transparent glaze.

Let the cake cool in the pan for 10 to 15 minutes; the cake will still be warm. With a small, sharp knife cut around the sides to release and then cut the cake into eighths. With a wide metal spatula transfer each piece to a cutting board and cut each eighth into quarters. Transfer to a rack to finish cooling.

1 cup strained confectioners sugar (see Note)
1 tablespoon unsalted butter, melted
1 tablespoon boiling water
1 tablespoon lemon juice

NOTE: The confectioners sugar should be strained before measuring. With your fingertips press the sugar through a strainer set over a bowl.

Georgia Pecan Bars

The taste and texture of these will remind you of pecan pie.

Crust

Adjust a rack one-third up from the bottom of the oven and preheat oven to 350°. Prepare a 13 x 9 x 2-inch square cake pan as follows: Turn it upside down and place a 17-inch length of aluminum foil shiny side down over the inverted pan. Turn down the sides and corners of the foil just to shape it. Remove the foil and turn the pan right side up. Place the foil in the pan. In order not to tear the foil place a folded towel or a pot holder in the pan and, pressing against the towel or pot holder, press the foil gently into place. Coat the foil with soft or melted butter, spreading it thin with a pastry brush or crumpled wax paper.

Sift the flour and baking powder together into a bowl. Stir in the sugar. Add the pieces of butter to the bowl with the dry ingredients. With a pastry blender cut in the butter until the mixture resembles fine meal.

Turn the crust mixture into the buttered pan. With your fingertips and with the palm of your hand press down on the crust to make a smooth, firm layer. Set aside and prepare the topping.

1⅓ cups sifted all-purpose flour
½ teaspoon baking powder
½ cup dark brown sugar, firmly packed
4 ounces (1 stick) unsalted butter, cut into ½- to 1-inch slices

32 BARS

Topping

In a bowl beat the eggs lightly just to mix. Add the vanilla, sugar, corn syrup, and flour, and beat until smooth.

Pour the topping over the crust and tilt the pan gently to form an even layer. If the pecan halves are large they may be placed evenly, rounded side up, to cover the topping completely. But if the halves are small or if you use pieces, sprinkle them over the topping.

Bake for 35 to 40 minutes, reversing the position of the pan once during baking to ensure even browning. If the cake puffs up during baking pierce it gently with a cake tester or a small, sharp knife to release the trapped air. Bake until the top is golden brown. Do not overbake; the bars should remain slightly soft in the center.

2 eggs
1 teaspoon vanilla extract
¼ cup dark brown sugar, firmly packed
¾ cup dark corn syrup
3 tablespoons sifted all-purpose flour
7 ounces (2 cups) pecan halves or large pieces

Cool the cake in the pan for 15 to 20 minutes. Then cover the cake pan with a cookie sheet and invert. Remove the pan and foil. Cover the cake with a rack and invert again to finish cooling right side up.

When the cake is completely cool transfer it to the freezer for about 20 minutes or to the refrigerator for about an hour until firm enough to cut.

If the cookies are cut with a plain, straight knife they will squash and look messy. Use a serrated bread knife and cut with a back-and-forth, sawing motion—they will cut perfectly. Cut into bars or squares.

These may be placed on a serving tray and covered with plastic wrap or they may be wrapped individually in clear cellophane or wax paper. Or they may be stored in a freezer box.

Pecan Festival Bars

These are thin, crisp brown-sugar wafers topped with chopped pecans. This classic Southern recipe calls for long, slow baking.

Adjust rack one-third up from the bottom of the oven and preheat oven to 250°. Butter a 10½ x 15½ x 1-inch jelly-roll pan.

In the large bowl of an electric mixer cream the butter. Add the vanilla, salt, and sugar, and beat well. Beat in the egg yolk (reserve the white). On low speed gradually add the flour, scraping the bowl with a rubber spatula and beating only until the mixture is smooth and holds together.

Place spoonfuls of the dough all over the bottom of the buttered pan. With the back of the spoon spread the dough as evenly as possible. This will make a very, very thin layer.

In a small bowl beat the egg white until it holds a soft shape, but is not stiff. Pour it over the layer of dough, and with a pastry brush, brush the white so that it covers the dough completely.

With your fingertips sprinkle the nuts evenly over the egg white. Cover with a large piece of wax paper. Press down gently with the palms of your hands to make a smooth, even layer of dough with the nuts pressed well into it. Remove the wax paper.

Bake for 1 hour and 50 minutes, or until golden brown.

8 ounces (2 sticks) unsalted butter
1½ teaspoons vanilla extract
¼ teaspoon salt
1 cup strained light brown sugar, firmly packed
1 egg, separated
2 cups sifted all-purpose flour
6 ounces (generous 1⅔ cups) pecans, cut medium fine (see page 11)

32 COOKIES

These cookies should be cut immediately, in the pan, while they are still hot; they will become crisp and brittle as they cool. Use a small, sharp knife and cut into even bars or squares. Transfer to racks to cool.

Pecan Chews

These are soft, tender, chewy squares from a recipe given to me by a Georgia pecan-grower.

Adjust a rack one-third up from the bottom of the oven and preheat oven to 350°. Prepare a 9-inch square cake pan as follows: Turn it upside down and place a 12-inch square of aluminum foil over the inverted pan. Turn down the sides and corners of the foil just to shape it. Remove the foil and turn the pan right side up. Place the foil in the pan. In order not to tear the foil place a folded towel or a pot holder in the pan and, pressing against the towel or pot holder, press the foil gently into place. Coat the foil with soft or melted butter, spreading it thin with a pastry brush or crumpled wax paper.

Sift together the flour and the baking powder and set aside. In the small bowl of an electric mixer beat the eggs lightly just to mix. Add the vanilla, instant coffee, and sugar, and beat only to mix. Mix in 1 generous cup (reserving remaining ⅔ cup) of the pecans.

Turn the dough into the prepared pan and spread it level. Sprinkle with the remaining ⅔ cup pecans.

Bake for 25 to 28 minutes—the cake will still be slightly soft inside. Remove from the oven and cool in the pan for about 20 minutes. Cover the pan with a cookie sheet and invert. Remove the pan and the aluminum foil. Cover with a rack or another cookie sheet and invert again, leaving the cake right side up to cool.

The cake will be very tender. Before cutting it into squares let it stand for several hours or chill it briefly in the freezer or refrigerator. Then gently transfer it to a cutting board. With a long, sharp knife, using the full length of the blade, cut the cake into squares or bars.

½ cup sifted all-purpose flour
¼ teaspoon baking powder
2 eggs
½ teaspoon vanilla extract
1 teaspoon instant coffee
1 cup dark brown sugar, firmly packed
6 ounces (generous 1⅔ cups) pecans, cut into medium-size pieces

16 SQUARES OR 24 BARS

Texas Cowboy Bars

Rich, he-man oatmeal bars with a baked-in soft date filling.

Filling

Cut the dates into medium-size pieces. Place the dates, water, and sugar in a heavy 2-quart saucepan over moderate heat and bring to a boil, stirring occasionally. Continue to boil, stirring occasionally, for 10 to 12 minutes until the mixture is thick. Watch it carefully toward the end. As it begins to thicken, it will bubble and splash; reduce the heat as necessary. Stir in the grated lemon rind and set aside to cool to lukewarm.

8 ounces (1 cup) pitted dates
1 cup water
1 cup granulated sugar
Finely grated rind of 1 large lemon

24 BARS

Crust

Adjust a rack one-third up from the bottom of the oven and preheat oven to 350°. Prepare a 9-inch square cake pan as follows: Turn the pan upside down and place a 12-inch square of aluminum foil over it. Turn down the sides and corners of the foil just to shape. Lift off the foil and turn the pan right side up. Place the foil in the pan. In order not to tear the foil, place a folded towel or a pot holder in the pan and, pressing against the towel or pot holder, press the foil gently into place. Butter the foil; this is most easily done with melted butter and a pastry brush.

Place the flour, salt, and sugar in a mixing bowl and stir to mix. Mix in the oatmeal and nuts. Add the melted butter and stir well until completely mixed.

1½ cups sifted all-purpose flour
½ teaspoon salt
1 cup dark brown sugar, firmly packed
1½ cups old-fashioned or quick-cooking (not instant) oatmeal
2 ounces (generous ½ cup) walnuts or pecans, cut medium fine (see page 11)
8 ounces (2 sticks) unsalted butter, melted

Remove 1 generous cup of the mixture and set it aside for the topping. Place the remaining crust mixture over the bottom of the prepared pan and press it firmly with your fingertips to make a smooth, even layer.

Cover the crust with the filling mixture and spread evenly. Sprinkle the reserved crust mixture evenly over the filling. Press gently with your fingertips to make a smooth, even layer.

Bake for 45 minutes.

Cool the pan for 45 minutes. Cover with a rack or a cookie sheet and invert. Remove the pan and the aluminum foil. Cover with a rack and very gently invert again—handle with care.

Cool completely and then chill briefly in the freezer or refrigerate until the cake is firm enough to be cut.

Use a long, thin, sharp knife and cut the cake into squares or bars.

Aspen Oatmeal Bars

These are the height of ease and simplicity. Mixed in a saucepan, with no flour, they are chewy and crunchy with a butterscotch flavor.

Adjust a rack to the center of the oven and preheat oven to 350°. Butter an 8-inch cake pan. Place the butter and sugar in a medium-size saucepan. Stir over moderate heat until melted.

Remove the pan from the heat. Through a fine strainer add the baking powder and stir until smooth. Stir in the salt and the oats. It will be a thick mixture.

Turn the dough into the buttered pan. Use your fingertips and the palm of your hand to press the dough into a smooth, compact layer.

Bake for 25 minutes. The cake will still be soft but it will harden as it cools. Do not bake any longer.

While the cake is still warm, cut around the sides to release but then let the cake finish cooling in the pan.

With a small, sharp knife cut the cake into quarters. With a wide metal spatula transfer the quarters to a cutting board. Cut each quarter into 6 bars.

4 ounces (1 stick) unsalted
    butter
1 cup light brown sugar,
    firmly packed
1 teaspoon baking powder
Scant ¼ teaspoon salt
2 cups old-fashioned or quick-
    cooking (not instant)
    oatmeal

24 SMALL BARS

Honey Date-Nut Bars

These are soft and chewy like old-fashioned date-nut bars, but are made with honey instead of sugar.

Adjust a rack to the center of the oven and preheat oven to 350°. Prepare a 15½ x 10½ x 1-inch jelly-roll pan as follows: Turn the pan upside down. Cut a piece of aluminum foil large enough to cover the pan and the sides. Place the foil over the inverted pan and fold down the sides and corners just to shape. Remove the foil. Wet the inside of the pan lightly—do not dry it (the wet pan will hold the foil in place). Place the foil in the pan. With a pot holder or a folded towel (so the foil doesn't tear) press the foil into place in the pan. Spread or brush the foil all over with very soft butter. Set the prepared pan aside.

Sift together the flour, baking powder, and salt, and set aside. In the large bowl of an electric mixer beat the eggs until they are slightly foamy. Beat in the honey and the vanilla. On low speed add the sifted dry ingredients, scraping the bowl with a rubber spatula and beating until thoroughly mixed. Add the dates and the nuts and stir or beat, preferably by hand, to mix well.

Turn the mixture into the prepared pan and spread it as evenly as possible. Bake for about 35 minutes, reversing the position of the pan once during baking, until the cake is golden brown. It is done when the top springs back firmly if it is lightly pressed with a fingertip.

Cool the cake for only a few minutes and then cover it with a large rack or cookie sheet and invert. Let the cake stand until it is completely cool.

Transfer the cake to a cutting board. With a long, thin, sharp knife, using the full length of the blade and pressing down firmly, cut the cake into bars.

Place the bars on a large piece of wax paper and cover them generously with confectioners sugar, pressing the sugar with your fingertips through a strainer held over the bars.

1⅓ cups sifted all-purpose flour
1 teaspoon baking powder
Pinch of salt
3 eggs
1 cup honey
1 teaspoon vanilla extract
1 pound (2 cups) pitted dates, coarsely cut
8 ounces (2¼ cups) walnuts, cut or broken into medium-size pieces
Confectioners sugar (for sprinkling over the baked cookies)

32 BARS

Aspen Date-Nut Fingers

These have whole-wheat flour, wheat germ, oatmeal, and honey. They may be made without a mixer.

Adjust two racks to divide the oven into thirds and preheat oven to 350°. Prepare two 9-inch square cake pans as follows: Turn them upside down and place a 12-inch square of aluminum foil over each pan. Turn down the sides and corners of the foil just to shape it. Remove the foil and turn the pans right side up. Place the foil in the pans. In order not to tear the foil place a folded towel or a pot holder in each pan and, pressing against the towel or pot holder, press the foil gently into place. Coat the foil with soft or melted butter, spreading it thin with a pastry brush or crumpled wax paper.

This batter may be mixed with an electric mixer or a manual egg beater. In a large bowl beat the eggs with the salt only until the eggs are foamy. Beat in the honey. Add the flour, wheat germ, and oatmeal, and beat or stir until smooth. Mix in the dates and nuts.

Divide the mixture between the two prepared pans. Spread to make smooth layers—they will be thin.

Bake for 25 to 30 minutes, reversing the pans top to bottom once during baking to ensure even baking. The cakes are done when they are lightly colored and semifirm to the touch.

Cool the cakes in the pans for about 10 minutes. Then cover each pan with a rack or a cookie sheet and invert. Remove the pans and foil. Cover each cake with a rack and invert again, leaving the cakes right side up. Let stand to cool slightly and then slide the cakes off onto a cutting board.

With a long, sharp knife cut each cake into three strips and then cut each strip into eight fingers.

Place the cookies on a large piece of wax paper. Cover the tops generously with confectioners sugar by pressing the sugar through a fine strainer held over the cookies.

Either wrap the cookies individually in clear cellophane or wax paper, or pack them in an airtight container.

3 eggs
¼ teaspoon salt
1 cup honey
1 cup unsifted all-purpose whole-wheat flour (stir lightly to aerate before measuring)
½ cup natural, untoasted wheat germ (available at health-food stores)
½ cup old-fashioned or quick-cooking (not instant) oatmeal (see Note)
8 ounces (1 cup) pitted dates, coarsely cut
5 ounces (1¼ cups) pecans, cut into medium-size pieces
Confectioners sugar (for sprinkling over the tops)

48 SMALL FINGERS

NOTE: For these cookies I use El Molino Old-Fashioned Hull-less Rolled Oats, which I buy in a health-food store, but you can also use the ones just called "old fashioned" and made by Quaker Oats.

Viennese Linzer Cookies

This is the classic Linzertorte, cut into small bars. It has a bottom crust, a raspberry-preserve filling, and a thin lattice topping of strips of the crust—all baked together. The filling keeps the cookies moist and juicy. These are made without a mixer.

Adjust an oven rack one-third up from the bottom and preheat oven to 375°. Sift together 1½ cups of the flour (reserve the remaining 2 tablespoons), baking powder, cinnamon, cloves, salt, and granulated sugar into a large mixing bowl. Add the brown sugar and stir to mix well.

Slice the butter into ½-inch pieces; then, with a pastry blender, cut it into the dry ingredients until the mixture is fine and crumbly.

Grind the almonds to a fine powder in a nut grinder, (see To Grind Nuts in a Food Processor, page 11) or a food processor. Add the ground almonds to the dry ingredients and butter, and stir to mix well.

In a small bowl stir the egg lightly with a fork just to mix. Add the lemon rind to the egg and stir to mix. Then add the egg to the dough and, with a fork, stir well until the dry ingredients are evenly moistened. Remove and reserve ½ cup of the dough.

Place the remaining dough in an unbuttered 9-inch square pan and set aside.

Replace the reserved ½ cup of dough in the mixing bowl. Add the reserved 2 tablespoons of flour. Stir together until the flour is incorporated. With your hands form the dough into a flattened square and place it between two large pieces of wax paper. With a rolling pin, roll over the wax paper to roll the dough into a square the same size as the bottom of the pan. (Keep the shape as square as you can, but if the sides are not exact don't worry—a few uneven strips will not really matter.) Slide a cookie sheet under the paper and transfer the dough to the freezer for a few minutes. When the dough is rolled out into about a 9-inch square it will be very thin. You will have to be extremely careful handling it when cutting it into strips.

Meanwhile, flour your fingertips and press the dough that is in the pan to even it out on the bottom of the pan.

In a small bowl, stir the preserves slightly just to soften. Spread them evenly over the layer of dough in the pan, keeping the preserves ¼ to ⅓ inch away from the edges.

Now remove the chilled dough from the freezer. Remove and replace one piece of the wax paper just to loosen it. Turn the dough and both pieces of wax paper over.

1½ cups plus 2 tablespoons sifted all-purpose flour
½ teaspoon baking powder
1 teaspoon cinnamon
⅛ teaspoon ground cloves
¼ teaspoon salt
¼ cup granulated sugar
½ cup dark brown sugar, firmly packed
4 ounces (1 stick) unsalted butter
2½ ounces (½ cup) blanched almonds
1 egg
Finely grated rind of 1 large lemon
¾ cup thick red or black raspberry preserves
1 egg yolk—for glazing the tops of the cookies
1 teaspoon water—for glazing the tops of the cookies

24 BARS

Then remove and do not replace the other piece of paper. With a long knife, cut the dough into ½-inch-wide strips; you will have 18 strips, each ½ inch wide and 9 inches long. Place half of the strips over the preserves, placing them ½ inch apart and parallel. Then place the remaining strips crosswise over the first ones, again placing them ½ inch apart, and forming a lattice top. (If the strips become too soft to handle while you are working with them, rechill as necessary.)

To make the glaze, stir the egg yolk and the water together lightly just to mix. With a soft brush, brush the glaze over the top of the lattice and the preserves.

Bake for 30 minutes or until the top is a rich golden brown. If the cake is not dark enough, raise the pan to a higher rack. When the cake is done, you should see the preserves bubbling up in the spaces on top.

Cool the cake completely in the pan. When completely cool, with a small, sharp knife, cut around the cake to release it, then cut it into quarters, cut each quarter in half, and then cut each strip into thirds. With a metal spatula transfer the bars to a tray or serving plate.

Or cut the cake into quarters in the pan and, with a wide metal spatula, transfer the quarters to a cutting board. Then, with a long, heavy knife, cut into small bars.

If you wish, these may be wrapped individually in clear cellophane or wax paper. Or they may be stored in a covered box with plastic wrap or wax paper between the layers.

Polish Wedding Cakes

These are called Mazurka in Polish. There are many versions, all rich and moist. This one has a crunchy crust and tart apricot filling.

Apricot Filling

Bring the apricots and the water to a boil, uncovered, in a small, heavy saucepan with a tight cover over high heat. Reduce the heat to low, cover the pan, and simmer until the apricots are very tender, about half an hour, depending on the apricots. The fruit should be very soft and the water should be partially but not completely absorbed.

Press the apricots with a potato masher or stir and mash vigorously with a fork. The mixture should be very thick.

4 ounces (about 24 halves) dried apricots
½ cup water
2 tablespoons sugar

16 TWO-INCH SQUARES, OR
32 OR 48 SMALL BARS

Add the sugar and stir until it dissolves. Cool to room temperature. (If you wish, this filling may be made ahead of time and refrigerated.)

Polish Pastry

This is not like American pastry. It will resemble a crumb mixture.

Adjust an oven rack one-third up from the bottom and pre-heat oven to 325°.

Place the flour, salt, and sugar in a mixing bowl. With a pastry blender cut in the butter until the mixture resembles coarse meal. Stir in the coconut, oatmeal, and walnuts.

Place half (3 cups) of the mixture in an unbuttered 8-inch square cake pan. Press it evenly with your fingertips. Cover with a piece of wax paper and with the palm of your hand press against the paper to make a smooth, compact layer. Remove the wax paper.

Spread the apricot filling smoothly over the pastry, staying ¼ to ½ inch away from the edges. Sprinkle the remaining pastry evenly over the filling and repeat the directions for covering with wax paper and pressing smooth. Remove the wax paper.

Bake for 60 to 70 minutes until the top is barely semi-firm to the touch.

Cool in the pan for 15 minutes. Cut around the sides of the cake to release it. Cover with a rack or a cookie sheet. Invert, remove the pan, cover with a rack, and invert again so that the cake is right side up. Let cool completely and then refrigerate briefly—the cake cuts best if it is cold. Transfer it to a cutting board.

Use a long, thin, sharp knife or a finely serrated one to cut the cake into squares or fingers.

1¼ cups sifted all-purpose flour
¼ teaspoon salt
1 cup dark brown sugar, firmly packed
6 ounces (1½ sticks) cold unsalted butter, cut into ½-inch pieces
1¾ ounces (½ cup, firmly packed) shredded coconut
¾ cup old-fashioned or quick-cooking (not instant) oatmeal
2 ounces (generous ½ cup) walnuts, cut medium fine (see page 11)

OPTIONAL: These may be topped with confectioners sugar. Press it through a fine strainer held over the cookies to cover the tops generously.

Viennese Marzipan Bars

These fancy little cakes are really petits fours. They have a tender, buttery base, a thin layer of apricot preserves, a ground-almond filling, and a thin dark-chocolate glaze.

Crust

Adjust a rack one-third up from the bottom of the oven and preheat oven to 375°. Butter the bottom and sides of an 8-inch square cake pan.

Sift together the flour and baking powder and set aside. In the small bowl of an electric mixer cream the butter. Add the sugar and beat to mix well. Beat in the egg yolk and the milk. On low speed gradually add the sifted dry ingredients, scraping the bowl with a rubber spatula and beating only until the mixture holds together.

Place the dough in the prepared pan. Press it firmly with floured fingertips to make a smooth layer.

Bake for 12 to 15 minutes, or until barely colored around the edges. The crust will sink slightly when it is removed from the oven.

Meanwhile prepare the following filling.

1 cup sifted all-purpose flour
½ teaspoon baking powder
2⅔ ounces (5⅓ tablespoons) unsalted butter
½ cup granulated sugar
1 egg yolk (reserve the white for the filling)
1 tablespoon milk

24 SMALL BARS

Almond Filling

In a small bowl stir the preserves just to soften, and set aside.

Grind the almonds to a fine powder in a processor (see To Grind Nuts in a Food Processor, page 11) or nut grinder and place them in a bowl. Add the sugar and salt and stir with a rubber spatula to mix. Add the egg, egg white, vanilla and almond extracts, and 2 or 3 drops of food coloring. (Add another drop or two of food coloring if necessary to make a pale pea-green.) Stir to mix thoroughly.

Spread the preserves over the hot crust, leaving a ½-inch border—it will be a thin layer of preserves. Top with the almond filling, and spread it to make an even layer.

Bake at 375° for 25 minutes, or until the top of the cake barely springs back when lightly pressed with a fingertip.

Cool completely and then prepare the following glaze.

¼ cup apricot preserves
4 ounces (generous ¾ cup) blanched almonds
⅔ cup granulated sugar
¼ teaspoon salt
1 egg plus 1 egg white
½ teaspoon vanilla extract
Few drops of green food coloring

Chocolate Glaze

Strain the sugar by pressing it with your fingertips through a strainer set over a bowl. Set aside.

Place the chocolate and the butter in the top of a small double boiler over hot water on moderate heat. Cover until it is melted and then stir until smooth. Stir in the sugar, vanilla, and water, and stir again until completely smooth.

Pour the glaze over the cooled cake and spread evenly. It will be a thin layer.

Let the cake stand in the pan for an hour or longer. Then, with a small, sharp knife, cut around the sides to release. Cut the cake into quarters. With a wide metal spatula transfer the quarters to a cutting board. If it is difficult to move the first quarter, cut it into individual portions—bars or slices. Use a fork to ease out the first few portions and then, with a wide metal spatula, transfer the remaining pieces to a cutting board and cut them into portions.

These little cakes are best after they stand for a few hours. Place them on a serving dish, cover with plastic wrap, and let stand at room temperature.

½ cup confectioners sugar
½ ounce (½ square) unsweetened chocolate
1 tablespoon unsalted butter
½ teaspoon vanilla extract
1 tablespoon boiling water

Icebox Cookies

Peanut Butter Icebox Cookies

Crisp, plain, crunchy, sandy; like a peanut butter shortbread. Divine to serve with ice cream or tea or coffee. A jar of these makes a wonderful gift.
The dough must be well chilled before the cookies are sliced and baked.

Sift together the flour, baking soda, and cinnamon, and set aside. In the large bowl of an electric mixer, beat the butter and peanut butter until soft and smooth. Add the vanilla and almond extracts and both sugars and beat until incorporated. Beat in the egg. Then, on low speed, add the dry ingredients and beat until thoroughly mixed.

Turn the mixture out onto a work surface, knead it a bit, and then "push off" the dough as follows: Form the dough into a ball; start at the far end of the dough and, using the heel of your hand, push off small pieces (the size of about 2 tablespoons) against the work surface and away from you. Continue until all the dough has been pushed off. Re-form the dough and push it off (or "break" it) again; re-form the dough (it will feel like clay).

Form the dough into a long round shape or a long oblong. Either way, the shape should be 10 to 12 inches long and 1¾ to 2 inches in diameter.

Wrap in plastic wrap and refrigerate for several hours until firm, or place the wrapped dough in the freezer for 45 to 60 minutes until firm.

When you are ready to bake, adjust two racks to divide the oven into thirds and preheat oven to 350°. Line cookie sheets with aluminum foil or parchment paper. Slice the firm dough into ¼-inch slices. Place them ½ to 1 inch apart on the lined sheets.

Bake for 18 to 20 minutes until lightly colored (darker on the rims), reversing the sheets top to bottom and front to back once during baking to ensure even browning.

With a wide metal spatula transfer the cookies to racks to cool.

2 cups unsifted all-purpose
   flour
¼ teaspoon baking soda
¼ teaspoon cinnamon
4 ounces (1 stick) unsalted
   butter
⅓ cup smooth peanut butter
1 teaspoon vanilla extract
⅛ teaspoon almond extract
⅓ cup granulated sugar
⅓ cup dark brown sugar,
   firmly packed
1 egg

40 TO 48 COOKIES

8-Layer Cookies

Icebox cookies, thin and crisp, made up of contrasting layers of dark and light doughs. Too pretty to eat. Force yourself—they're delicious. These are the ones to make for a fancy party.

S ift together the flour, cornstarch, baking powder, and salt, and set aside. In the large bowl of an electric mixer, beat the butter completely until soft. Beat in the vanilla and then the sugar, beating until completely mixed. Add the yolks one at a time, beating until incorporated after each addition. On low speed, gradually add the sifted dry ingredients and beat until incorporated (it will be a thick mixture).

Remove and set aside half (1½ cup plus 2 tablespoons) of the dough.

Beat the almond extract into the remaining dough until incorporated. Remove the almond-flavored dough from the mixing bowl, and return the other half of the dough to the bowl. On low speed, gradually add the cocoa and the powdered coffee and beat until incorporated. Remove this chocolate dough from the mixing bowl; if it is not a perfectly even color, knead it with your hands.

With your hands, form each piece of the dough into a 5-inch square, 1 inch thick. Wrap the squares in wax paper or plastic wrap and refrigerate for about 1 hour, or freeze for less time, until barely firm.

Cut each square into quarters, making 2½-inch squares.

Then, on a lightly floured pastry cloth with a lightly floured rolling pin, roll each square of dough out slowly and carefully until it measures 10 x 4 inches. Make the edges as even as possible; you will not be able to make them perfectly even—it is okay, they will be trimmed later. As each piece is rolled, transfer it to a piece of wax paper (as large as the rolled-out dough or slightly larger); the easiest way is to roll them the long way over the rolling pin, and then unroll them onto the wax paper. The pieces of rolled-out dough (each on a piece of wax paper) can be stacked on top of each other. Slide a flat-sided cookie sheet (or anything else flat) under the pile and transfer them all to the freezer for 15 to 20 minutes, until the dough is firm enough to handle but is not brittle. Remove them from the freezer.

Place a piece of the dough in front of you on a work surface. Brush the top lightly with cold tap water. Place a piece of the other color dough on top of the wet one. Press down gently all over the surface of the top dough to seal the pieces together.

2¼ cups sifted all-purpose flour
¾ cup cornstarch, unsifted
½ teaspoon baking powder
½ teaspoon salt
9 ounces (2¼ sticks) unsalted butter
1 teaspoon vanilla extract
1 cup minus 2 tablespoons granulated sugar
4 egg yolks
½ teaspoon almond extract
¼ cup unsweetened cocoa powder (preferably Dutch-process)
½ teaspoon powdered (not granular) instant coffee

40 COOKIES

Brush the top with water again and cover with a contrasting piece, press down, wet, et cetera. Continue to stack the pieces as evenly as possible, alternating the colors.

Wrap the whole pile of 8 layers in plastic wrap and refrigerate for a few hours or overnight. Or freeze briefly until firm enough to slice very neatly; the dough should be refrigerated, but not frozen when it is sliced.

Before baking, adjust two racks to divide the oven into thirds, and preheat oven to 375°. Line cookie sheets with parchment paper or aluminum foil shiny side up.

Unwrap the dough. With a very sharp knife carefully trim one narrow end. (At this stage it seems as though the thing to do is to trim the two long sides also, but actually I have much better results and make neater cookies if I slice them and then trim the uneven ends.) With a ruler and the tip of a small sharp knife mark the dough every ¼ inch. Then, carefully, slice a few cookies, trim the ends individually, and transfer the cookies to the lined sheets, placing them about ½ inch apart. (Reserve all the scraps of dough.)

Bake two sheets at a time for 15 to 20 minutes, reversing the sheets top to bottom and front to back as necessary to ensure even browning. Bake until the cookies are lightly colored on the edges, paler in the centers. Watch them carefully; these are too beautiful to chance overbaking.

With a wide metal spatula, transfer the cookies to racks to cool.

The trimmed edges that you reserved may be pressed together to make attractive marbleized cookies. On a lightly floured pastry cloth with a lightly floured rolling pin, roll out the marbleized dough to ¼-inch thickness, cut out the cookies with a knife or with a cookie cutter, and bake as above.

New Mexican Chocolate Icebox Cookies

These are not solid chocolate but filled with chopped chocolate chips.

P repare a 10 x 5 x 3-inch loaf pan as follows: Cut two long strips of wax paper or aluminum foil, one for the length and one for the width. The pieces should be long enough to fold over the top of the pan and cover the surface completely. Place them carefully in the pan. Set aside.

Sift together the flour, baking soda, salt, and nutmeg, and set aside.

Grind the chocolate in a processor, or chop it fine with a long, heavy knife on a cutting board; it must be fine—any large chunks would make it difficult to slice the cookies. Set aside.

In the large bowl of an electric mixer cream together the butter and the shortening. Beat in the sugar and mix well, then beat in the vanilla and the egg and then the sour cream. On low speed add the sifted dry ingredients, scraping the bowl with a rubber spatula and beating only until thoroughly incorporated. Finally mix in the ground or chopped chocolate and the nuts.

Pack the dough firmly into the prepared pan. Fold the paper over the top and press firmly down to smooth the dough.

Freeze for 6 to 8 hours (or longer if you wish), until the dough is firm all the way through.

Adjust two racks to divide the oven into thirds and preheat oven to 400°. Line cookie sheets with parchment or foil.

Remove the block of dough from the pan. Remove the paper and place the dough on a cutting board. With a long, heavy knife, slice the block of dough in half the long way. Rewrap one piece and return it to the freezer. With a sharp knife, cut the frozen dough into slices a generous ¼ inch thick. Place them about 1½ to 2 inches apart on the cut cookie sheets. (The reserved half of the dough may be sliced now or later, as you wish.)

Bake the cookies about 10 minutes until they are semifirm to the touch. During baking, reverse the sheets top to bottom and front to back to ensure even browning.

3½ cups sifted all-purpose flour
1 teaspoon baking soda
½ teaspoon salt
½ teaspoon nutmeg
6 ounces semisweet chocolate cut into pieces
2⅔ ounces (5⅓ tablespoons) unsalted butter
⅓ cup vegetable shortening (such as Crisco)
2 cups dark brown sugar, firmly packed
1 tablespoon vanilla extract
1 egg
½ cup sour cream
3 ounces (generous ½ cup) pine nuts (pignoli) (see Note)

66 COOKIES

With a wide metal spatula transfer the cookies to racks to cool.

NOTE: Other nuts may be substituted—walnuts, pecans, cashews, or hazelnuts—cut into medium-size pieces. Or you can leave out the nuts if you prefer.

Black-and-White Coconut Slices

Cream-cheese coconut-nut centers wrapped on the outside edges with bittersweet-chocolate cookie dough.

Filling

Place the shredded coconut on a large cutting board and chop it into shorter pieces, using a long, heavy knife, or chop for a few seconds in a food processor. Set aside.

In the small bowl of an electric mixer cream the cheese. Beat in the vanilla and almond extracts and the sugar. On low speed beat in the coconut and the nuts.

Tear off an 18-inch length of wax paper. Spoon the filling down the length of the paper to make a strip almost 14 inches long. Fold the long sides of the paper over the filling and, with your hands, form the filling into an even, compact roll or rectangle 14 inches long.

Wrap the filling in the paper, slide a cookie sheet under the roll, and transfer it to the freezer.

3½ ounces (1 cup, packed) shredded coconut
3 ounces Philadelphia brand cream cheese, preferably at room temperature
½ teaspoon vanilla extract
¼ teaspoon almond extract
⅓ cup granulated sugar
2 ounces (generous ½ cup) pecans, finely chopped (see page 11)

56 COOKIES

Chocolate Dough

Sift together the flour, baking soda, and salt, and set aside. Melt the chocolate in the top of a small double boiler over hot water on moderate heat. Set it aside to cool slightly. In the small bowl of an electric mixer cream the butter. Beat in the vanilla and sugar and mix well. Beat in the egg and then the chocolate. On low speed add the sifted dry ingredients, scraping the bowl with a rubber spatula and beating only until smooth.

Tear off a piece of wax paper about 12 inches long. Place the dough down the length of the paper, forming a strip about 8 inches long. Fold the long sides of the paper up around the dough and, with your hands, form the dough into a fat roll or a rectangle about 8 to 10 inches long. Refrigerate for about half an hour or a little longer.

Tear off two 16-inch pieces of wax paper. Place the chocolate roll on one piece of the paper and cover it with the other piece. With a rolling pin, roll over the wax paper to form the chocolate dough into a 14 x 6-inch rectangle. If necessary, you may remove the top piece of paper, cut off some of the dough, and replace it where needed.

Unwrap the roll of filling and center it on the chocolate dough. Then wrap the chocolate dough firmly around the filling, overlapping the edges slightly and pressing firmly to make a smooth, compact roll.

Wrap the roll in the paper and freeze for a few hours or overnight; it must be firm in order to slice well.

Before baking adjust two racks to divide the oven into thirds and preheat oven to 375°. Line cookie sheets with parchment or aluminum foil.

Loosen the roll of frozen dough from the wax paper but do not remove it; just open the paper and leave the dough on it. With a sharp knife cut the roll into ¼-inch slices. If the dough starts to soften while you are slicing it, rechill the roll until it is firm. Or if the kitchen is warm, cut the dough in half and work with only one-half at a time, keeping the other piece in the freezer. Place the slices 1½ to 2 inches apart on the cookie sheets.

Bake for 10 to 11 minutes, reversing the sheets top to bottom and front to back to ensure even baking. When these are done the filling will feel barely semifirm to the touch; do not overbake or the chocolate will burn before you know it.

Use a wide metal spatula to slip the cookies carefully off the sheets and transfer them to racks to cool.

NOTE: These are not nearly as involved as they sound. Just follow the directions and you will find them really quite easy.

1½ cups sifted all-purpose flour
½ teaspoon baking soda
¼ teaspoon salt
2 ounces (2 squares) unsweetened chocolate
3 ounces (6 tablespoons) unsalted butter
1 teaspoon vanilla extract
1 cup confectioners sugar
1 egg

Wienerstube Cookies

These are Austrian. They are coal-black, chocolate, black-pepper cookies—buttery, crunchy, and spicy.

S ift together the flour, baking powder, salt, cinnamon, allspice, black pepper, cayenne, and cocoa, and set aside. In the large bowl of an electric mixer cream the butter. Add the vanilla and sugar and beat well. Beat in the egg to mix. On low speed gradually add the sifted dry ingredients, scraping the bowl with a rubber spatula and beating only until thoroughly mixed.

Tear off a strip of wax paper about 16 inches long. Place the dough by heaping tablespoonfuls down the length of the paper, forming a heavy strip about 10 inches long. Fold the long sides of the paper up around the dough. Pressing against the paper with your hands, shape the dough into an even oblong about 12 inches long and 2¾ inches thick.

Wrap the dough in the paper. Slide a cookie sheet under the paper and transfer the dough to the freezer or refrigerator for several hours (or longer) until firm.

Adjust two racks to divide the oven into thirds and preheat oven to 375°. Line cookie sheets with parchment.

Unwrap the firm dough. Place it on a cutting board and, with a sharp knife, cut the dough into ¼-inch slices. Place the slices 1 inch apart on the cookie sheets.

Bake for 10 to 12 minutes, reversing the sheets top to bottom and front to back to ensure even baking. The cookies are done when the tops spring back when pressed with a fingertip. Do not overbake.

With a wide metal spatula transfer the cookies to racks to cool.

1½ cups sifted all-purpose flour
1½ teaspoons baking powder
¼ teaspoon salt
¾ teaspoon cinnamon
¼ teaspoon allspice
½ teaspoon finely ground black pepper (preferably freshly ground)
Pinch of cayenne pepper
¾ cup unsweetened cocoa powder (preferably Dutch-process)
6 ounces (1½ sticks) unsalted butter
1½ teaspoons vanilla extract
1 cup granulated sugar
1 egg

48 COOKIES

Maxines

Chewy, fudgy, chocolate-almond slices edged with a buttery, brown-sugar layer.

Chocolate Mixture

Place the chocolate and shortening in the top of a medium-size double boiler over hot water on medium heat, cover, and cook until partially melted. Uncover and stir until completely melted. Remove from heat. Stir in the condensed milk and the vanilla and almond extracts, then the almonds.

Tear off a piece of wax paper about 15 inches long. Place the dough by large spoonfuls the long way down the middle of the paper, forming a heavy strip about 10 inches long. Fold the sides of the paper up against the chocolate mixture. With your hands, press against the paper and shape the mixture into an even round or square roll 12 inches long and 1½ inches in diameter. Wrap in the paper. Slide a cookie sheet under the paper and transfer to the freezer or refrigerator until firm.

Meanwhile, prepare the Brown-Sugar Dough.

6 ounces semisweet chocolate cut into pieces
1 tablespoon vegetable shortening (such as Crisco)
⅓ cup sweetened condensed milk
½ teaspoon vanilla extract
¼ teaspoon almond extract
5 ounces (1 cup) blanched almonds, coarsely cut (each almond should be cut into 3 or 4 pieces)

24 COOKIES

Brown-Sugar Dough

Sift together the flour, baking powder, and salt, and set aside. In the small bowl of an electric mixer, cream the butter. Add the vanilla and sugar, and beat well. Beat in the egg yolk, and then gradually, on low speed, add the sifted dry ingredients. Beat only until thoroughly mixed. The mixture will be crumbly; remove it from the mixer and press it together with your hands until it forms a ball.

Place the ball of dough on a piece of wax paper a little more than 12 inches long. With your hands, shape it into a flattened oblong. Cover with another long piece of wax paper. Roll a rolling pin over the top wax paper; then invert and do the same with bottom wax paper, in order to keep both pieces of paper smooth and unwrinkled.

1 cup sifted all-purpose flour
¼ teaspoon baking powder
¼ teaspoon salt
2 ounces (4 tablespoons) unsalted butter
½ teaspoon vanilla extract
½ cup light brown sugar, firmly packed
1 egg yolk

Remove the top piece of wax paper. Unwrap the chocolate roll and center it on the brown-sugar dough. Using the wax paper, lift one long side of the brown-sugar dough and press it firmly against the chocolate. Then lift the other side so that the sides of dough overlap slightly. (If the dough does not fit perfectly, the excess may be cut off and pressed into place where needed.)

Enclose the roll in the wax paper, then run your hands firmly over the roll to remove any air trapped between the dough and the chocolate mixture.

Rechill the roll only until it is firm enough to slice. (If the dough is frozen firm it will crack when sliced. If this happens, let it stand briefly at room temperature.)

Adjust two racks to divide the oven into thirds and preheat oven to 375°.

Unwrap the roll of dough and place it on a cutting board. With a sharp knife, cut slices ½ inch thick—no thinner! Place the slices flat, 1 inch apart, on unbuttered cookie sheets. Bake about 12 minutes, until cookies are lightly colored. Reverse sheets top to bottom and front to back to ensure even browning.

Let the cookies stand on sheets for a minute or so until firm enough to transfer, then with a wide metal spatula transfer cookies to racks to cool.

Cobblestones

These are thick, semisoft, and full of raisins and nuts. The name describes the shape, not the texture. The directions are for an unusual way of making icebox cookies.

Prepare a 10½ x 15½ x 1-inch jelly-roll pan as follows: Cut a piece of aluminum foil large enough to cover the bottom and sides of the pan. Invert the pan. Place the foil evenly on the pan and fold down the sides and corners to shape the foil. Now remove the foil and rinse the inside of the pan with water but do not dry it—the wet pan will hold the foil in place. Carefully place the foil in the pan and press it into place. Set aside.

Sift together the flour, baking soda, salt, cinnamon, nutmeg, cloves, and ginger, and set aside.

In a bowl or large measuring cup, pour the boiling water over the raisins to cover, and let them stand for about 10 minutes. Then pour into a strainer or a colander to drain. Spread the drained raisins on several thicknesses of paper towels and pat the tops lightly with paper towels.

In the large bowl of an electric mixer cream the butter. Add the coffee, vanilla, and both sugars, and beat to mix well. Beat in the egg. On low speed gradually add about one-third of the sifted dry ingredients, then the sour cream, and finally the remaining dry ingredients, scraping the bowl as necessary with a rubber spatula and beating only until smoothly incorporated. Remove from the mixer.

The dough will be stiff—use a heavy wooden spoon to stir in the raisins and nuts.

Place the dough by large spoonfuls into the lined pan. Cover with a large piece of wax paper. With your hands, press gently on the wax paper to spread the dough evenly. Now, with a small rolling pin or a glass with straight sides, roll over the wax paper to smooth the top of the dough. Do not remove the wax paper.

Chill the pan of dough in the freezer for several hours or more, or in the refrigerator overnight, until the dough is quite firm—the firmer the better.

Adjust two racks to divide the oven into thirds and preheat oven to 400°. Line cookie sheets with parchment.

Lightly flour a section of a large cutting board, spreading the flour to cover a surface a little larger than the jelly-roll pan.

Slowly peel the wax paper off the dough. Invert the pan onto the floured surface. Remove the pan and peel off the foil. Work quickly before the dough softens! With a long, heavy, sharp knife, cutting down firmly with the full length of the blade, cut the dough into 48 bars, each measuring about 1¼ x 2½-inches (cut the cake into quarters, cut each piece across into thirds, and then cut each third into 4 bars). If the blade sticks, wipe it occasionally with a damp cloth.

Place the cookies 2 inches apart on the cookie sheets.

Bake for 12 to 13 minutes, reversing the sheets top to bottom and front to back once to ensure even baking. The cookies are just done when the tops barely spring back when lightly pressed with a fingertip. Do not overbake or they will be hard and dry, instead of semisoft. (These will probably lose their shapes a bit while baking–it is okay!)

Let the cookies stand on the sheets for a few seconds and then, with a wide metal spatula, transfer them to racks to cool.

3½ cups sifted all-purpose flour
1 teaspoon baking soda
½ teaspoon salt
1 teaspoon cinnamon
½ teaspoon nutmeg
¼ teaspoon ground cloves
¼ teaspoon powdered ginger
10 ounces (2 cups) raisins
Boiling water
5⅓ ounces (10⅔ tablespoons) unsalted butter
1 tablespoon instant coffee
1 tablespoon vanilla extract
1 cup light brown sugar, firmly packed
1 cup granulated sugar
1 egg
½ cup sour cream
7 ounces (2 cups) walnuts, cut or broken into medium-size pieces

48 LARGE COOKIES

Neapolitans

These Italian cookies present an interesting way of making icebox cookies. They are dramatic and unusual. You will make two entirely separate recipes for the dough—and it must chill overnight.

Dark Dough

You will need an 11 x 5 x 3-inch loaf pan, or any other loaf pan with an 8- to 9-cup capacity (or use two smaller pans equaling that capacity). To prepare the pan: Cut two strips of aluminum foil, one for the length and one for the width; they should be long enough so that they can be folded over the top of the pan when it is filled and should cover the whole surface. Place them in the pan and set aside.

Sift together the flour, salt, baking soda, cloves, and cinnamon, and set aside. Grind the chocolate in a processor or a blender, or chop fine on a board with a large knife. It must be fine or it will be difficult to slice the cookies), and set aside. In the large bowl of an electric mixer cream the butter. Add the coffee and brown sugar, and beat well. Add the eggs and beat to mix. Beat in the ground chocolate. On low speed gradually add the sifted dry ingredients, scraping the bowl with a rubber spatula and beating only until blended. Beat in the nuts.

Transfer the dough to another bowl, unless you have another large bowl for the electric mixer. Set dough aside at room temperature and prepare the following light dough.

3 cups sifted all-purpose flour
¼ tablespoon salt
1 teaspoon baking soda
½ teaspoon ground cloves
½ teaspoon cinnamon
6 ounces semisweet chocolate cut into pieces
8 ounces (2 sticks) unsalted butter
2 teaspoons instant coffee
1½ cups dark brown sugar, firmly packed
2 eggs
5 ounces (1 cup) nuts, either whole pine nuts (pignoli), green pistachios, walnuts, or pecans, cut into medium-size pieces

80 COOKIES

Light Dough

Sift together the flour, salt, and baking soda, and set aside. In a clean large bowl of the electric mixer, with clean beaters, cream the butter. Add the vanilla and almond extracts, the sugar, and water, and beat well. Add the egg and beat to mix. On low speed gradually add the sifted dry ingredients, scraping the bowl with a rubber spatula and beating only until blended. Mix in the currants, lemon rind, and both kinds of cherries.

To layer the doughs in the prepared pan: Use half (about 2¾ cups) of the dark dough and place it by spoonfuls over the bottom of the pan. Pack the dough firmly into the corners of the pan and spread it as level as possible. With another spoon, spread all of the light dough in a layer over the dark dough—again, as level as possible. Form an even top layer with the remaining dark dough. Cover the top with the foil or wax paper and, with your fingers, press down firmly to make a smooth, compact loaf.

Chill the dough overnight in its pan in the freezer or refrigerator.

To bake the cookies: Adjust two racks to divide the oven into thirds and preheat oven to 400°. Line the cookie sheets with parchment or foil.

To remove the dough from the pan: Use a small, narrow metal spatula or a table knife to release the dough from the corners of the pan. Fold back the foil or parchment from the top of the loaf of dough, invert the pan onto a cutting board, and remove the pan and the foil or parchment.

With a long, heavy, sharp knife cut the dough in half the long way. Wrap one half and return it to the freezer or refrigerator while working with the other half.

With a very sharp knife cut the dough into slices about ¼ inch thick. Place the slices 1 to 1½ inches apart on the cookie sheets.

The second half of the dough may be sliced and baked now or it may be frozen for future use.

Bake for about 10 minutes, reversing the cookie sheets top to bottom and front to back as necessary during baking to insure even browning. Bake until the light dough is lightly colored, but watch them carefully—the dark dough has a tendency to burn.

With a wide metal spatula transfer the cookies to racks to cool.

NOTE: When slicing the cookies, if the dough crumbles and is difficult to slice, it has not chilled enough. It should be wrapped and placed in the freezer for about an hour.

2 cups sifted all-purpose flour
¼ teaspoon salt
¼ teaspoon baking soda
4 ounces (1 stick) unsalted butter
1 teaspoon vanilla extract
½ teaspoon almond extract
¾ cup granulated sugar
2 tablespoons water
1 egg
3½ ounces (¾ cup) currants, unchopped, or raisins, coarsely chopped
Finely grated rind of 1 large lemon
12 candied red cherries, cut into quarters
12 candied green cherries, cut into quarters

Fruitcake Icebox Cookies

Sift together the flour and cream of tartar and set aside. In the large bowl of an electric mixer cream the butter. Add the sugar and beat to mix. Add the egg and beat well. On low speed gradually add the sifted dry ingredients, scraping the bowl with a rubber spatula and beating only until mixed. Remove from mixer.

With a heavy wooden spoon or with your bare hands mix in the fruit and nuts.

Tear off two 15-inch lengths of wax paper. Place one-half of the dough in a heavy strip about 9 inches long down the center of each piece of paper. Fold up the long sides of the paper and with your hands press against the paper to form the dough into rolls or oblongs 2 inches in diameter and 9 to 10 inches long. Squeeze and press firmly to smooth the sides. Wrap in the paper.

Slide a cookie sheet under the rolls and place them in the freezer for several hours or longer, until firm. Adjust two racks to divide the oven into thirds and preheat oven to 375°. Line cookie sheets with parchment or foil.

The dough must be cold and very firm when you slice it. Unwrap one roll at a time, place it on a cutting board, and cut into ¼-inch slices. If the dough crumbles or is difficult to slice it needs more freezing.

Place the cookies ½ to 1 inch apart (these do not spread) on the cookie sheets.

Bake 12 to 14 minutes, reversing sheets top to bottom and front to back during baking to ensure even browning. The tops of the cookies will not color, but the cookies should be baked until the edges and the bottoms are golden brown. Check the color of the bottom before removing them.

With a wide metal spatula transfer cookies to racks to cool.

NOTE: Green pistachio nuts are lovely in these cookies but they might be hard to find. Shelled, unsalted green pistachios are generally available at specialty nut stores or wholesale nut dealers. You may add about 1 cup along with the pecans.

2½ cups sifted all-purpose flour
¼ teaspoon cream of tartar
8 ounces (2 sticks) unsalted butter
1 cup confectioners sugar
1 egg
½ pound (1 cup) candied pineapple, coarsely cut
½ pound (1 cup) candied cherries, left whole
6 ounces (generous 1⅔ cups) pecans, halves or large pieces

72 TO 80 COOKIES

Butterscotch Thins

Sift together the flour and baking soda and set aside. Place the butter and butterscotch morsels in the top of a small double boiler over hot water on moderate heat. Cover and cook for a few minutes until partially melted. Then uncover and stir (on the heat) until completely melted. The mixture will not be amalgamated; the butter will be a layer over the morsels. However, both must be completely melted.

Transfer the butterscotch mixture to the small bowl of an electric mixer and beat until smooth. Add the sugar, egg, and vanilla, and beat again until very smooth. On low speed gradually add the sifted dry ingredients and then the nuts, scraping the bowl with a rubber spatula and beating only until well incorporated.

The dough will be soft. Place it, in the mixing bowl, in the refrigerator only until it is firm enough to shape. It will probably take less than half an hour; do not leave it much longer than that or it will become too stiff.

Tear off a piece of wax paper about 16 inches long. Spoon the dough lengthwise down the center of the paper in a heavy strip about 10 to 11 inches long. Fold the long sides of the paper up against the dough and, with your hands, press against the paper to shape the dough into a long roll or an oblong 12 inches long. Wrap the dough in the wax paper. Slide a cookie sheet under it and transfer to the freezer or refrigerator until very firm (or longer if you wish).

Adjust two racks to divide the oven into thirds and preheat oven to 375°. Line cookie sheets with parchment or foil.

Unwrap the dough and replace it on the wax paper. With a sharp knife cut the dough into very thin slices—⅛ inch, no more. (It is important that these be sliced thin, and as even as possible, or some will burn before the others have baked.) Place the cookies 1½ inches apart on the sheets. Bake the cookies for about 6 to 8 minutes, until they are well browned. Reverse the sheets top to bottom and front to back to ensure even browning. The cookies will rise as they bake and then flatten. The best way to time these is to leave them in the oven until all or almost all of the cookies have flattened. If they are underbaked they will be soft and chewy instead of crisp. But some people prefer them soft and chewy.

Let the cookies stand for about half a minute or a bit longer, and then, with a wide metal spatula, transfer them to racks to cool.

1⅓ cups sifted all-purpose flour
¾ teaspoon baking soda
4 ounces (1 stick) unsalted butter, cut into 4 or 5 pieces
6 ounces (1 cup) butterscotch morsels
⅔ cup light brown sugar, firmly packed
1 egg
¾ teaspoon vanilla extract
⅓ cup pecans, finely cut

96 COOKIES

Pecan Butterscotch Icebox Cookies

An early American recipe from Massachusetts. The recipe originated before baking powder was available; early recipes used baking soda plus cream of tartar. These are thin and crisp.

Sift together the flour, baking soda, cream of tartar, and salt, and set aside. In the large bowl of an electric mixer, cream the butter. Add the vanilla and the sugar and beat well. Add the egg and beat until smooth. Gradually, on low speed, add the sifted dry ingredients and beat until the mixture holds together. Mix in the nuts.

Turn the dough out onto a board, a smooth work surface, or a piece of wax paper. The dough will be firm enough to handle and not sticky. With your hands, shape it into a long rectangle.

Place it lengthwise on a piece of wax paper about 18 inches long. Fold the paper up on the sides and, with your hands, press and smooth over the paper to form a 12- to 14-inch roll about 2 inches in diameter.

Wrap the dough in the wax paper, slide a cookie sheet under it, and transfer to the freezer or refrigerator for several hours or overnight. The dough must be very firm, preferably frozen solid, in order to slice it thin enough.

Adjust two racks to divide oven into thirds and preheat oven to 375°. Line cookie sheets with parchment or foil shiny side up.

Unwrap the dough and place it on a cutting board. With a thin, sharp knife cut into very thin slices—⅛ to ¼ inch thick, or about 6 slices to an inch.

Place the slices 1 inch apart on the cookie sheets.

Bake for about 8 to 10 minutes until the cookies are golden brown all over, reversing the sheets top to bottom and front to back as necessary to ensure even browning.

With a wide metal spatula, transfer to racks to cool.

2 cups sifted all-purpose flour
½ teaspoon baking soda
½ teaspoon cream of tartar
¼ teaspoon salt
4 ounces (1 stick) unsalted butter
½ teaspoon vanilla extract
1 cup light brown sugar, firmly packed
1 egg
4 ounces (generous 1 cup) pecan halves or pieces

70 TO 80 COOKIES

Oatmeal Icebox Cookies

These are thin, crisp, and crunchy.

S ift together the flour, salt, baking soda, and ginger, and set aside. In the large bowl of an electric mixer cream the butter. Add the vanilla and both sugars, and beat well. Add the eggs one at a time and beat to incorporate after each addition. On low speed gradually add the sifted dry ingredients and then the oatmeal, scraping the bowl as necessary with a rubber spatula and beating only until thoroughly mixed. Stir in the nuts.

Spread out two pieces of wax paper, each about 13 to 15 inches long. Place spoonfuls of the dough lengthwise on each piece of paper to make strip about 9 to 10 inches long. Fold the long sides of the paper up against the dough and, pressing against the papers with your hands, shape the dough into oblongs about 10 inches long, 3 inches wide, and 1 to 1½ inches thick. Wrap the dough in the wax paper.

Slide a cookie sheet under the two oblongs of dough and place in the freezer for an hour or two, or in the refrigerator overnight (or longer if you wish), until the dough is firm enough to slice.

Adjust two racks to divide the oven into thirds and preheat oven to 350°. Line cookie sheets with aluminum foil shiny side up.

Unwrap one piece of dough at a time. Place it on a cutting board. With a thin, sharp knife cut the dough into ¼-inch slices and place them on the cut foil 2 inches apart (these will spread).

Bake for 12 to 14 minutes, until the cookies are well browned. Reverse the sheets top to bottom and front to back as necessary to ensure even browning.

Slide the foil off the cookie sheets and let stand for a few minutes until the foil can be easily peeled away from the backs of the cookies. Place the cookies on racks to finish cooling.

These must be stored airtight.

1½ cups sifted all-purpose flour
½ teaspoon salt
1 teaspoon baking soda
1 teaspoon powdered ginger
8 ounces (2 sticks) unsalted butter
1 teaspoon vanilla extract
1 cup granulated sugar
1 cup dark brown sugar, firmly packed
2 eggs
3 cups old-fashioned or quick-cooking (not instant) oatmeal
4 ounces (generous 1 cup) walnuts, cut medium fine (see page 11)

80 COOKIES

Peanut-Butter Pillows

Peanut butter is sandwiched between two peanut-butter icebox cookies and then the cookies are baked. They are crisp; the filling is soft.

S ift together the flour, baking soda, and salt, and set aside. In the small bowl of an electric mixer cream the butter. Add the peanut butter and sugar and beat until thoroughly mixed. Beat in the corn syrup and the milk. On low speed add the sifted dry ingredients, scraping the bowl as necessary with a rubber spatula and beating only until smooth.

Turn the dough out onto a large board or a smooth work surface. Knead it briefly and then, with your hands, form it into an even roll or oblong about 7 inches long and 2¼ to 2½ inches in diameter. Wrap the dough in wax paper. Slide cookie sheets under the paper and transfer the dough to the refrigerator for several hours, or longer if you wish.

Adjust two racks to divide the oven into thirds and pre-heat oven to 350°. Line the cookie sheets with parchment.

With a sharp knife cut half of the roll of dough into slices ⅛ to ¼ inch thick and, as you cut the slices, place them 2 inches apart on the cookie sheets.

Place 1 level measuring teaspoonful of the additional peanut butter in the center of each cookie. Then spread the peanut butter only slightly to flatten it, leaving a ½- to ¾-inch border.

Slice the remaining half of the roll of dough (same thickness) and, as you cut each slice, place it over one of the peanut-butter-topped cookies. Let the cookies stand for 2 to 3 minutes for the dough to soften slightly. Then seal the edges by pressing them lightly with the back of the tines of a fork, dipping the fork in flour as necessary to keep it from sticking. (Don't worry about slight cracks in the tops.)

Bake for 12 to 15 minutes, reversing the position of the cookie sheets top to bottom and front to back to ensure even browning. (If you bake only one sheet at a time bake it high in the oven.) Bake until the cookies are lightly colored.

Let the cookies stand on the sheets for about a minute. Then, with a wide metal spatula, transfer them to racks to cool.

1½ cups sifted all-purpose
  flour
½ teaspoon baking soda
¼ teaspoon salt
4 ounces (1 stick) unsalted
  butter
½ cup smooth (not chunky)
  peanut butter
½ cup granulated sugar
¼ cup light corn syrup
1 tablespoon milk
Additional peanut butter for
  filling (a scant ½ cup)

16 TO 20 FILLED COOKIES

NOTE: This dough may be mixed without a mixer. Simply place the sifted dry ingredients and the sugar in a mixing bowl. With a pastry blender cut in the butter and the peanut butter until the mixture resembles coarse meal. Stir in the syrup and milk. Then, on a board or a smooth work surface, knead the dough briefly with the heel of your hand until it is smooth.

Whole-Wheat Peanut-Butter Cookies

These are extra-crisp and crunchy, with a lovely sandy texture from the raw sugar.

Sift together the flour, baking soda, and salt, and set aside. In the large bowl of an electric mixer cream the butter. Add the peanut butter and beat until smooth. Add the sugar and beat well, then add the egg and beat well again. On low speed gradually add the sifted dry ingredients, scraping the bowl with a rubber spatula and beating only until smooth.

Tear off a piece of wax paper about 16 inches long. Spoon the dough lengthwise down the center of the paper in a heavy strip about 10 to 11 inches long. Fold the long sides of the paper over the dough and, with your hands, shape the dough into a long, round or oblong roll, 12 inches long. Wrap the dough in the wax paper.

Slide a cookie sheet under the dough and transfer it to the freezer or refrigerator until firm (or longer, if you wish).

Adjust two racks to divide the oven into thirds and preheat oven to 350°.

Unwrap the dough and replace it on the wax paper. With a sharp knife cut the dough into slices ¼ inch thick and place them 1 to 1½ inches apart on unbuttered cookie sheets.

Bake for 15 minutes or a little longer, until the cookies are lightly colored and semifirm to the touch. Reverse the sheets top to bottom and front to back to ensure even browning.

With a wide metal spatula transfer the cookies to racks to cool.

1¼ cups unsifted *whole-wheat pastry flour (available at health-food stores)*
1 teaspoon baking soda
¼ teaspoon salt
4 ounces (1 stick) unsalted butter
½ cup smooth (not chunky) peanut butter
1 cup raw sugar
1 egg

48 COOKIES

Icebox Nut Cookies

This simple recipe is a popular tea party specialty of a famous Washington hostess.

In the large bowl of an electric mixer cream the butter. Add the mace or nutmeg and the sugar and beat well. Add the eggs one at a time and beat well after each addition. On a low speed gradually add the flour, scraping the bowl with a rubber spatula and beating only until the mixture is smooth and holds together. Remove the bowl from the mixer and, with a heavy wooden spoon mix in the nuts and the lemon rind.

The cookies may now be shaped in one of two ways. Traditionally, the dough is turned out onto a long piece of wax paper and, with floured hands, shaped into a long roll or oblong (or it may be divided in half and shaped into two rolls or oblongs). Wrap in the wax paper and place in the freezer or refrigerator.

Another way of shaping the dough is to line a 3- to 4-cup ice-cube tray (without dividers) with aluminum foil. Pack the dough into the lined tray. Cover with foil and press down firmly with the palm of your hand to smooth the top. Freeze or refrigerate until the dough is stiff—or longer if you want. Whichever way you shape the dough it must be chilled until it is very firm—it may be sliced when it is frozen solid.

Adjust two racks to divide the oven into thirds and preheat oven to 350°. Line cookie sheets with parchment or aluminum foil shiny side up.

Unwrap the dough and place it on a cutting board. With a thin, sharp knife cut the dough into ¼-inch slices. Place the slices ½ to 1 inch apart on the cookie sheets and bake for 18 to 20 minutes, until the cookies are lightly colored. Reverse the sheets top to bottom and front to back as necessary to ensure even browning. Do not underbake; these should be very crisp when cool.

With a wide metal spatula transfer the cookies to racks to cool.

8 ounces (2 sticks) unsalted butter
1 teaspoon mace or nutmeg
2 cups granulated sugar
2 eggs
3 cups sifted all-purpose flour
8 ounces (2¼ cups) walnut or pecan halves or large pieces
Finely grated rind of 1 large or 2 small lemons

45 TO 50 COOKIES

Sesame Fingers

There is an old saying in the South that sesame seeds, also known as benne seeds, bring good luck. These cookies from Charleston, South Carolina, are hard and dry and full of toasted sesame seeds. The dough should be chilled overnight in the freezer.

Place the sesame seeds in a large, heavy frying pan over medium-low heat. Stir almost constantly and shake the pan frequently until the seeds are toasted to a golden-brown color. (Toasting brings out the sweet, nutty flavor of the seeds.) Be careful not to let them burn. Transfer the toasted seeds to a shallow plate and set aside to cool.

In the large bowl of an electric mixer cream the butter. Add the vanilla, salt, and sugar, and beat to mix well. Add the egg and beat to mix. On low speed gradually add half of the flour, then all of the milk, and finally the remaining flour, scraping the bowl with a rubber spatula and beating only until smooth after each addition. Mix in the cooled toasted sesame seeds.

4 ounces (¾ cup) sesame seeds (see Note)
4 ounces (1 stick) unsalted butter
¾ teaspoon vanilla extract
¼ teaspoon salt
1 cup granulated sugar
1 egg
2 cups sifted all-purpose flour
¼ cup milk

48 COOKIES

If the dough is too soft at this point to form it into a block for icebox cookies, chill it in the mixing bowl, stirring occasionally until it is slightly firm.

Then tear off a piece of wax paper about 18 inches long. Place the dough by large spoonfuls lengthwise down the center of the paper to form a heavy strip about 10 inches long. Fold up the two long sides of the paper. With your hands press against the paper to mold the dough into an oblong 12 inches long, ¾ inch wide, and 1 inch thick.

Slide a cookie sheet under the paper and transfer the dough to the freezer. Let stand overnight.

Adjust two racks to divide the oven into thirds and preheat oven to 375°. Line cookie sheets with parchment or aluminum foil shiny side up.

Lightly flour a section of a cutting board a little larger than the oblong of dough. Unwrap the dough and place it on the floured board.

With a sharp, heavy knife, quickly cut the dough into ¼-inch slices, and place them 1 inch apart on the cookie sheets.

Bake for about 15 minutes, reversing the position of the sheets top to bottom and front to back as necessary to ensure even browning. When done, the cookies will be slightly brown on the edges but still pale on the tops. (If you bake only one sheet at a time, use the higher rack.)

With a wide metal spatula transfer the cookies to racks to cool.

NOTE: Sesame seeds vary in color from so-called white (hulled) to grayish-tan (unhulled). I use the white.

Caraway Crisps

This is a classic Scottish recipe.

Sift together the flour, baking soda, and salt, and set aside. Mix the lemon rind and juice and set aside. In the large bowl of an electric mixer cream the butter. Beat in the sugar and then the egg and the caraway seeds. On low speed gradually add the sifted dry ingredients, scraping the bowl with a rubber spatula and beating only until well mixed. Stir in the lemon rind and juice.

Place the dough on a large board or smooth work surface. Squeeze the dough between your hands and then knead it lightly just until the mixture holds together and is smooth. With your hands form the dough into a roll or an oblong 10 inches long and about 2 inches in diameter.

Wrap the dough in wax paper and slide a cookie sheet under it. Transfer to the freezer or refrigerator until it is firm enough to slice (or longer, if you wish). This dough may be sliced when it is frozen solid.

Adjust two racks to divide the oven into thirds and preheat oven to 400°.

With a sharp knife slice the cookies a scant ¼ inch thick and place them 1 inch apart on unbuttered cookie sheets.

Bake for 10 minutes, reversing the sheets top to bottom and front to back during baking to ensure even browning. The cookies are done when they are lightly browned on the edges and barely sandy-colored in the centers.

With a wide metal spatula transfer cookies to racks to cool.

2⅔ cups sifted all-purpose flour
½ teaspoon baking soda
¼ teaspoon salt
Finely grated rind of 1 large lemon
2 tablespoons lemon juice
4 ounces (1 stick) unsalted butter
1 cup granulated sugar
1 egg
2 teaspoons caraway seeds

50 COOKIES

Almond Spicebox Cookies

Sift together the flour, cinnamon, ginger, salt, and baking soda, and set aside. In the large bowl of an electric mixer cream the butter. Add the coffee, almond extract, and both sugars, and beat well. Add the eggs one at a time, beating until smooth after each addition. On low speed gradually add the sifted dry ingredients, scraping the bowl with a rubber spatula and beating only until smooth. (When most of the dry ingredients have been added the mixture might start to crawl up on the beater; if so, finish stirring it by hand with a wooden spoon; the dough will be stiff.) With a wooden spoon and/or your bare hands, mix in the almonds.

Spread out two pieces of wax paper, each about 16 inches long. Place large spoonfuls of the dough lengthwise on each piece of paper to form heavy strips about 10 to 11 inches long. Fold the long sides of the paper up against the dough and, pressing against the paper with your hands, shape each strip of dough into a smooth oblong 12 inches long, 3 inches wide, and about 1 inch thick. Wrap the dough in the wax paper.

Slide a cookie sheet under both packages of dough and transfer them to the freezer or refrigerator for several hours or overnight (or longer, if you wish). This slices best when it is frozen solid.

Adjust two racks to divide the oven into thirds and preheat oven to 375°.

Unwrap one roll at a time. Place it on a cutting board. With a very sharp knife cut the dough into ¼-inch slices and place them 1 to 1½ inches apart on unbuttered cookie sheets.

Bake the cookies for about 12 minutes, reversing the position of the sheets top to bottom and front to back as necessary to ensure even browning. The cookies are done if they are slightly colored and spring back when lightly pressed with a fingertip.

With a wide metal spatula transfer the cookies to racks to cool.

4 cups sifted all-purpose flour
3 teaspoons cinnamon
1 teaspoon powdered ginger
½ teaspoon salt
1 teaspoon baking soda
8 ounces (2 sticks) unsalted butter
2 teaspoons instant coffee
½ teaspoon almond extract
1 cup granulated sugar
1 cup dark brown sugar, firmly packed
3 eggs
8 to 10 ounces (2⅓ to 3 cups) blanched and thinly sliced almonds

90 COOKIES

Anise Icebox Cookies

Anise is an herb. The seeds, which are used whole in this recipe, have a licorice flavor.

S ift together the flour, salt, and baking powder, and set aside. In the small bowl of an electric mixer cream the butter. Beat in the vanilla extract and the sugar. Add the egg and the anise seed and beat well. On low speed gradually add the sifted dry ingredients, scraping the bowl with a rubber spatula and beating only until thoroughly mixed.

Remove the bowl from the mixer and with a wooden spoon stir in the lemon rind.

Tear off a 15-inch piece of wax paper. Place the dough by large spoonfuls lengthwise down the middle of the paper, forming a heavy strip about 10 inches long.

Fold the paper up on the long sides. With your hands, press against the paper to shape the dough into an even oblong or roll about 11 inches long, 2½ inches wide, and 1 inch thick (or any other size you wish). Wrap the dough in the paper.

Slide a cookie sheet under the dough and transfer it to the freezer until it is firm (or longer, if you wish—the dough may be sliced when frozen solid).

Adjust two racks to divide the oven into thirds and preheat oven to 400°. Line cookie sheets with parchment or foil shiny side up.

Unwrap the frozen dough and place it on a cutting board. With a thin, sharp knife cut the dough into ¼-inch slices. Place the cookies 1 inch apart on the cookie sheets.

Bake for about 10 minutes, reversing the sheets top to bottom and front to back to ensure even browning. These are done when they are golden brown. Do not underbake—these should be very crisp when cool.

With a wide metal spatula transfer the cookies to racks to cool.

1¾ cups sifted all-purpose flour
¼ teaspoon salt
1½ teaspoons baking powder
4 ounces (1 stick) unsalted butter
½ teaspoon vanilla extract
1 cup granulated sugar
1 egg
1¾ teaspoons anise seed
Finely grated rind of 1 large lemon

42 COOKIES

Cardamom Cookies from Copenhagen

This is a classic Danish butter cookie—plain, light, crisp, and dry, with a definite cardamom flavor.

Sift together the flour, baking soda, and cardamom, and set aside. In the large bowl of an electric mixer cream the butter. Beat in the vanilla and then add the sugar and beat well. On low speed alternately add the sifted dry ingredients in three additions with the cream in two additions, scraping the bowl with a rubber spatula and beating only until thoroughly mixed. Remove from the mixer and, with a rubber spatula or wooden spoon, stir in the almonds.

Turn the dough out onto a smooth work surface or a piece of wax paper. Knead it slightly and then, with your hands, form it into a smooth roll or oblong about 2 inches wide and 10 inches long.

Wrap the dough in plastic wrap or wax paper and place in the freezer for several hours or longer, if you wish—this dough slices best when it is frozen solid.

Before baking, adjust two racks to divide the oven into thirds and preheat oven to 350°. Line cookie sheets with parchment or foil.

Unwrap the dough and place it on a cutting board. With a long, heavy, sharp knife cut the dough into ¼-inch slices and place them 1 inch apart on the cookie sheets—these do not spread or change shape during baking.

Bake for about 15 minutes, until the cookies are only slightly sandy-colored on the edges—these barely color, if at all, on the tops. Reverse the position of the sheets top to bottom and front to back as necessary during baking to ensure even browning.

With a metal spatula, transfer the cookies to racks to cool.

2 cups sifted all-purpose flour
¼ teaspoon baking soda
1½ teaspoons ground cardamom
4 ounces (1 stick) unsalted butter
½ teaspoon vanilla extract
½ cup light brown sugar, firmly packed
⅓ cup light cream
2½ ounces (generous ½ cup) slivered almonds (julienne-shape pieces)

40 COOKIES

Pinwheels

This is an attractive, crisp, black-and-white cookie (the two doughs are rolled together like a jelly-roll). They are fancy cookies, but not difficult to make.

Sift together the flour, baking powder, and salt, and set aside. Melt the chocolate in the top of a small double boiler over hot water on moderate heat. Set aside to cool.

In the large bowl of an electric mixer cream the butter. Add the vanilla and then the sugar and beat to mix well. Add the egg and beat well. On low speed gradually add the sifted dry ingredients, scraping the bowl with a rubber spatula and beating only until thoroughly mixed.

Place half (scant 1 cup) of the dough in another mixing bowl. To one-half of the dough add the melted chocolate and the coffee powder, mix thoroughly, and set aside.

To the other half of the dough add the almond extract and the pecans, mix thoroughly, and set aside.

Tear off four pieces of wax paper, each about 17 inches long. On one piece, place one of the doughs. Cover with another piece of paper. Flatten the dough well with your hands. With a rolling pin, roll over the paper to roll the dough into an oblong 14 x 9 inches. (During rolling, check both pieces of wax paper—if the paper wrinkles, peel it off and then replace it to remove the wrinkles.) When the dough is almost the right size, remove the top piece of paper, cut away excess dough (from the sides), and place it where needed (in the corners). Be careful not to have the edges thinner than center or there will be an air space in each end of the roll. Replace wax paper and roll the dough again to smooth it, check the size, then set it aside. Repeat with the remaining piece of dough.

Remove the top piece of wax paper from both of the rolled doughs. Place the white dough in front of you. Now, the chocolate dough must be inverted over the white dough, but you must be careful because you will not be able to move it if it is not placed correctly; the two doughs will stick together. So invert it cautiously over the white dough, lining up the edges as evenly as possible (see Notes). Then remove the piece of wax paper from the top of the chocolate dough. There will still be one piece of paper under the white dough; use that to help roll the doughs, jelly-roll fashion, starting with a long side.

Wrap the roll in the wax paper. Slide a cookie sheet under the roll in order to transfer it to the freezer or refrigerator to chill until firm. (This should be very firm, and may be sliced when frozen.)

Adjust two racks to divide the oven into thirds and preheat oven to 350°. Line

1¾ cups sifted all-purpose flour
½ teaspoon baking powder
¼ teaspoon salt
1 ounce (1 square) unsweetened chocolate
4 ounces (1 stick) unsalted butter
½ teaspoon vanilla extract
¾ cup granulated sugar
1 egg
1 teaspoon powdered instant coffee (see Notes)
¼ teaspoon almond extract
⅓ cup pecans, finely chopped

56 COOKIES

cookie sheets with parchment or foil.

Unwrap the dough and place it on a cutting board. Cut into ¼-inch slices. (If the dough softens while you are slicing it, rewrap and rechill it until firm.) Place the slices 1 inch apart on the cookie sheets.

Bake for about 12 minutes, until the cookies are slightly colored on the edges. Reverse the position of the sheets top to bottom and front to back as necessary to ensure even browning. Do not overbake. (If you bake only one sheet at a time bake it on the higher rack.)

With a wide metal spatula transfer the cookies to racks to cool.

NOTES: Powdered coffee is better than granules for this recipe. I use Medaglia D'Oro instant espresso, generally available in Italian markets. Or the coffee may be left out.

A wonderful trick that makes it easy to place one dough exactly over the other: Slide a cookie sheet beneath each piece of waxed paper under the rolled-out dough. Transfer both doughs to the freezer and leave until they are firm. Then invert the chocolate dough over the white as directed. (Because the dough is firm, if you haven't placed the chocolate layer evenly it will be easy to correct.) Remove the top piece of waxed paper, then let the doughs stand at room temperature until they are completely thawed before rolling them up together.

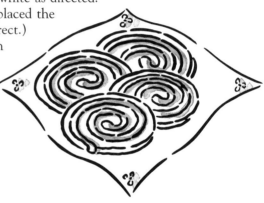

Rolled Cookies

Rugelach (Walnut Horns)

This is a traditional Jewish recipe that my grandmother used to make. Like all pastry, it is best when very fresh. They freeze perfectly. The dough must be refrigerated overnight. This is one of the most popular recipes I ever wrote.

Cream-Cheese Pastry

In the large bowl of an electric mixer cream the butter and cream cheese together until completely blended and smooth. Beat in the salt and on low speed gradually add the flour. While beating in the flour, toward the end, the dough might start to run up on the beaters. If so, the last of it may be stirred in by hand. When the dough is smooth, flour your hands lightly and, with your hands, form it into a short, fat roll. Cut the roll into three equal pieces. Form each piece into a round ball, flatten slightly, and wrap each individually in plastic wrap or wax paper. Refrigerate the balls or dough overnight or for at least 5 or 6 hours.

When you are ready to bake, prepare the following filling and then adjust two racks to divide the oven into thirds. Preheat oven to 350°. Line cookie sheets with parchment.

8 ounces (2 sticks) unsalted butter
½ pound Philadelphia brand cream cheese
½ teaspoon salt
2 cups sifted all-purpose flour

36 COOKIES

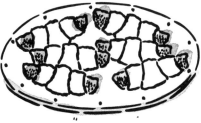

Filling

Stir the sugar and cinnamon together and set aside. (Do not mix the remaining ingredients.)

Place one ball of dough on a floured pastry cloth. With a floured rolling pin pound the dough firmly to soften it slightly. On the floured cloth, with the floured rolling pin, roll out the dough (turning it over occasionally) into a 12-inch circle—don't worry about slightly uneven edges.

With a pastry brush, brush the dough with 1 tablespoon of the melted butter and, quickly, before the cold dough hardens the butter, sprinkle with one-third of the sugar-cinnamon mixture. Then sprinkle with one-third of the currants and the nuts. With the rolling pin, roll over the filling to press the topping

½ cup plus 2 tablespoons granulated sugar
3 teaspoons cinnamon
3 tablespoons unsalted butter, melted
¾ cup currants
5 ounces (1¼ cups) walnuts, finely chopped (see page 11)

slightly into the dough.

With a long, sharp knife, cut into 16 pie-shaped wedges. Roll each wedge jelly-roll fashion, rolling from the outside toward the point. Then place each little roll, with the point down, 1 inch away from the previous roll on the lined sheet.

Repeat with remaining dough and filling. Since some of the filling will fall out while you are rolling up the horns, after preparing each third of the dough it will be necessary to clean the pastry cloth; either shake it out or scrape it with a dough scraper or a wide metal spatula and then reflour it.

Glaze

In a small cup, with a fork, stir the yolk and water just to mix. With a pastry brush, brush the glaze over the tops of the horns. Sprinkle generously with optional sugar.

Bake two sheets at a time for about 30 minutes, until the horns are golden brown. Reverse the sheets top to bottom and front to back once to ensure even browning. If you bake one sheet at a time use the higher rack.

With a wide metal spatula immediately transfer the horns to racks to cool.

1 egg yolk
1 teaspoon water
Optional: crystal sugar (see page 5)

Joe Froggers

Once upon a time—actually, it was over 100 years ago, in Marblehead, Massachusetts—there was an old man who was called Uncle Joe. He lived alongside a frog pond that was known as Uncle Joe's Frog Pond.

Uncle Joe made the biggest and the bestest molasses cookies for miles around. The local fishermen would swap a jug of rum for a batch of the cookies, which came to be known as Joe Froggers, because they were as big and as dark as the frogs in the pond. The fishermen liked them because they never got hard when they took them to sea.

Uncle Joe said the secret of keeping them soft was that he used rum and sea water. But that was all he said. He would not part with the recipe. When he died people said, "That's the end of Joe Froggers."

However, there was a woman named Mammy Cressy who said she was Joe's daughter. She gave the recipe to a fisherman's wife. And soon most of the women in Marblehead were making Joe Froggers. And they were sold at a local bakery. And the recipe traveled. The last I heard about them, a few years ago, they were still being served with a pitcher of cold milk on Sunday nights in the Publick House in the Colonial Village in Sturbridge, Massachusetts.

With their background, it is obvious that these would be a good choice for mailing or traveling.

Originally they were 6 inches in diameter. I use a plain, round cookie cutter that is 5 inches in diameter (that's my largest one). They can be smaller but they are wonderful large.

The dough should be refrigerated overnight before the cookies are rolled, cut, and baked. Allow plenty of time for baking since they are baked only four at a time.

S ift together the flour, baking soda, salt, ginger, cloves, nutmeg, mace, allspice, and optional black pepper. Set aside.

In the large bowl of an electric mixer, beat the butter until it softens. Add the sugar and beat to mix. Beat in the molasses. Then, on low speed, add about half of the dry ingredients, scraping the bowl as necessary with a rubber spatula and beating until mixed. Beat in the water or coffee and rum, and then the remaining dry ingredients.

Cover the bowl with plastic wrap or foil and refrigerate until it is firm enough to be handled. Then divide it in thirds and wrap each piece in plastic wrap. Refrigerate overnight.

When you are ready to bake, adjust a rack to the center of the oven and preheat oven to 375°. Line cookie sheets with parchment or foil.

Flour a pastry cloth and a rolling pin, using more rather than less flour. Unwrap one of the packages of dough and place it on the cloth. Pound it a bit with the rolling pin to soften it slightly. Turn it over to flour both sides. Work very quickly because the dough will become sticky and unmanageable if it softens too much. Roll out in all directions until the dough is ¼ inch thick. Quickly cut with a floured 5-inch round cutter (or what-have-you).

Use a wide metal spatula to transfer the cookies to the sheets. Quickly and carefully place them about 1 inch apart. (I place four on a 12 x 15½-inch sheet.)

Press the scraps together and rechill (the freezer is okay), then reroll and cut.

Bake one sheet at a time for 13 to 15 minutes, reversing the sheet front to back once during baking to ensure even baking. Watch these very carefully. They must not burn even a bit on the bottoms or it will spoil the taste. If they seem to be browning too much on the bottoms be prepared to slide an extra cookie sheet under the one that is

4⅓ cups sifted all-purpose flour
1 teaspoon baking soda
¾ teaspoon salt
2 teaspoons powdered ginger
¾ teaspoon ground cloves
¾ teaspoon nutmeg
¼ teaspoon mace
¼ teaspoon allspice
Optional: 1 teaspoon finely ground black pepper (Uncle Joe did not use the pepper, but I do)
6 ounces (1½ sticks) unsalted butter
¾ cup granulated sugar
1 cup dark or light molasses
⅓ cup water (it needn't be sea water), coffee, and dark rum, mixed (amounts can vary according to your taste; use all of any one, or try 1 tablespoon instant coffee dissolved in 3 tablespoons water, and the rest rum)

16 TO 18 5-INCH COOKIES

baking. Or raise the rack slightly higher in the oven. (But I have found that if I bake these high in the oven, they crack. It is only minor, but it does not happen when they are baked on the middle rack. That is why I bake these only one sheet at a time.)

Be very careful not to overbake these cookies. They will become firmer as they cool, and they should remain a bit soft and chewy in the middle. If you use a smaller cutter the cookies will probably bake in slightly less time.

Remove from the oven and let stand for a few minutes. Use a wide metal spatula or the bottom of a loose-bottomed quiche pan to transfer the cookies to racks to cool. Since these are so large, if the rack is not raised enough (at least ½ inch or more), place the rack on any right-side-up bowl or pan to make more room for air to circulate underneath.

When completely cool, store these airtight. I wrap them, two to a package, bottoms together, in clear cellophane.

Coconut Cookies

These are plain, old-fashioned, thin, extra-crisp, perfectly wonderful refrigerator cookies. The dough must be refrigerated overnight or longer before baking.

This is a homemade version of a famous coconut cookie that used to be sold in Havana. My Cuban friends tell me this is better.

P lace the coconut in a shallow baking pan in the center of a preheated 350° oven. Stir it occasionally until it is toasted to a golden color. Set aside. Sift together the flour, baking powder, and salt, and set aside.

In the large bowl of an electric mixer, cream the butter. Add the vanilla and almond extracts, then the sugar and beat to mix. Add the egg and beat to mix. On low speed, gradually add the sifted dry ingredients, beating only to mix. Remove from the mixer and stir in the coconut.

Place the mixture in the refrigerator for 20 to 30 minutes to chill a bit. Then flour your hands and a work surface. Turn the dough out onto the floured surface, press it together, and shape it into a cylinder about 6 inches long and 2 to 2½ inches in diameter. Wrap in plastic wrap. Refrigerate overnight. (If this is frozen it becomes difficult to slice thin enough without cracking, but it can be refriger-

3½ ounces (1 to 1⅓ cups) shredded coconut
2 cups sifted all-purpose flour
½ teaspoon baking powder
¼ teaspoon salt
6 ounces (1½ sticks) unsalted butter
1 teaspoon vanilla extract
¼ teaspoon almond extract
1 cup light or dark brown sugar, firmly packed
1 egg

ABOUT 36 COOKIES

ated for a few days if you wish.)

When you are ready to bake, adjust two racks high in the oven, or adjust them to divide the oven into thirds. If your oven has enough adjustments, higher is better. Preheat oven to 325°. Line cookie sheets with parchment.

With a very sharp knife, cut extra-thin cookies; they should be less than ¼ inch thick. Place the cookies 1 inch apart on the cookie sheets.

Bake for about 16 minutes, reversing the sheets top to bottom and front to back once during baking to ensure even baking. Watch carefully; if the cookies appear to be browning too much on the bottoms, be prepared to slide an additional cookie sheet under them. Do not underbake. Bake until the cookies are lightly browned. You won't believe how wonderfully crisp these are, but only if they are baked enough. (And then they will only stay that way if they are stored airtight.)

With a wide metal spatula gently transfer the cookies to a rack to cool. As soon as they are cool, package them airtight.

Almond Sugar Cookies

These are Swedish; quick and easy, fancy and elegant. Crisp, rich, crumbly, not too sweet. A plain sugar-and-butter dough made with egg yolks and ground almonds is rolled with a rolling pin, cut with a scalloped cookie cutter, decorated with lines made with a fork, and topped with more almonds and sugar. Although they are a snap to make, they are for a fancy tea party or a swanky dinner. They keep well, they may be frozen, and the recipe may be multiplied to make more if you wish.

Adjust two racks to divide the oven into thirds and preheat oven to 375°. Line cookie sheets with parchment or foil shiny side up.

The almonds must be ground very fine. It can be done in a food processor (see To Grind Nuts in a Food Processor, page 11) or a nut grinder.

Then all of the ingredients may be combined in one of many ways. If you have ground the almonds in a processor, the remaining ingredients may all be added and processed until thoroughly mixed. Or they can all be mixed together in an electric mixer. Or they can be stirred together by hand in a mixing bowl.

2½ ounces (½ cup) blanched almonds
1 cup sifted all-purpose flour
¼ teaspoon salt
2 ounces (½ stick) unsalted butter
¼ cup granulated sugar
2 egg yolks
½ teaspoon vanilla extract
¼ teaspoon almond extract

10 VERY LARGE COOKIES

Then turn the mixture out onto a work surface and "break" the dough as follows. First, form it into a ball. Then, starting at the side of the ball farthest from you and using the heel of your hand, push off small pieces (about the size of 2 tablespoons), pushing against the work surface and away from you. Continue until all the dough has been pushed off. Repeat "breaking" the dough once or twice until it is smooth.

Do not chill the dough before rolling it out.

Form the dough into a ball, flour it lightly, and flatten it slightly. Place it between two pieces of wax paper. With a rolling pin, roll over the top piece of paper until the dough is a scant ¼ inch thick.

Peel off the top piece of paper just to release it and then replace it. Turn the dough over with both pieces of paper. Then peel off the other piece of paper but do not replace it.

Use a scalloped, round cookie cutter 3¼ inches in diameter (or any other size, shape, or design that you prefer). Cut the cookies, starting at the outside edge of the dough and cutting them as close to each other as possible. This dough wants to stick; I find that the best way to transfer the cookies is to lift one carefully with a wide metal spatula, turn it over into the palm of my hand, and then place it, either side up, on the cookie sheets.

Press the scraps of dough together and reroll and cut cookies until it is all used.

Topping

In a small cup stir the yolk and water just to mix. With a pastry brush, brush the mixture generously over the tops of the cookies.

1 egg yolk
1 teaspoon water
About 2 tablespoons coarsely chopped, sliced, or slivered almonds, blanched or unblanched
Additional granulated sugar

Then, to form a plaid design completely covering the tops, hold a four-pronged fork as though you were eating with it. Rest the back of the tines lightly on a cookie and pull it across the cookie from one side to the other side to score the top lightly. Repeat, making additional lines, to cover the top of the cookie completely with lines all going in one direction. Then score again, this time at right angles to the first lines.

Now brush a little more of the egg-yolk mixture on the middle of each cookie. Sprinkle a few of the almonds on the middle of each cookie. Then, with your fingertips, sprinkle sugar over each cookie, sprinkling it heavily in the middle and lightly at the edges.

Bake for about 15 minutes, reversing the sheets top to bottom and front to back as necessary to ensure even browning. The cookies will have a nice golden color and a shine like varnish.

With a wide metal spatula transfer to racks to cool.

Store airtight.

Les Petites

These are dainty, delicate, delicious, fancy little French cookies. There are two cookies sandwiched together with chocolate between them; the top cookie has a hole cut out in the middle for the chocolate to show through. They are nicknamed Black-eyed Susans.

Make these for a wedding reception (there is an old saying that a ring-shaped cookie symbolizes eternal happiness because it has no end), a bridal shower, a tea party, or anything fancy and special.

Adjust two racks to divide the oven into thirds and preheat oven to 350°. Line two cookie sheets with parchment or foil, shiny side up.

The nuts must be ground fine. This can be done in a food processor (see To Grind Nuts in a Food Processor, page 11) or a nut grinder.

The dough can be put together in a mixer or a processor.

In a mixer: Cream the butter, mix in the vanilla, sugar, salt, then the flour and finally the ground nuts, beating until mixed.

In a food processor: After grinding the nuts, do not remove them from the bowl; add the butter, which should be cut into small pieces, and all the other ingredients except the chocolate, and process until the dough holds together.

Do not chill the dough before rolling it; chilling makes it crack when it is rolled.

Flour a pastry cloth and a rolling pin. Use only half of the dough at a time. Form it into a ball and flour it lightly. Flatten it slightly between your hands. Then roll it carefully (flouring the top, the bottom, and the rolling pin as necessary) until it is a scant ¼ inch or a generous ⅛ inch thick.

You will need a round (preferably scalloped) cookie cutter that measures 1½ inches in diameter. Starting at the outside edge of the rolled-out dough, cut rounds and place them about ½ inch apart on the lined sheets. Then, with a round cutter that measures ¾ inch in diameter, cut holes out of the middle of half of the cookies. (Save the cut-out holes and the leftovers and roll them out again to make more cookies.)

Bake for about 10 to 15 minutes or a bit longer (depending on the thickness of the cookies), reversing the sheets top to bottom and front to back as necessary to ensure even browning. Bake until the cookies are sandy colored. Do not underbake.

With a wide metal spatula transfer the cookies to racks to cool.

5 ounces (1 cup) blanched hazelnuts or almonds, or a combination of both
6 ounces (1½ sticks) unsalted butter
½ teaspoon vanilla extract
½ cup granulated sugar
Pinch of salt
1½ cups sifted all-purpose flour
5 ounces semisweet chocolate (to be used for sandwiching the cookies)

46 SMALL SANDWICH COOKIES

Coarsely chop the chocolate and place it in the top of a small double boiler over hot water on low heat. Cover until partly melted, then uncover and stir until completely melted. Transfer to a small shallow cup for easy handling.

Turn the cookies that do not have holes in them upside down. With the tip of a small spoon, place a bit (about ¼ teaspoon) of melted chocolate in a mound in the center of each cookie. Do not spread it out. Then place one of the cookies that has a hole in it over the chocolate with the two undersides together. Press together lightly. The chocolate should not extend out to the edges. Repeat, sandwiching all the cookies.

Let stand until the chocolate is firm. (A few minutes in the refrigerator or freezer will save time, if you wish.)

Store airtight.

Swedish Rye Wafers

These are thin, crisp, buttery, and exotic, with caraway seeds. They may easily be made without a mixer; simply use a wooden spoon or your bare hands for creaming and mixing.

Adjust two racks to divide the oven into thirds and preheat to 350°. Line cookie sheets with parchment or foil. In the large bowl of an electric mixer cream the butter. Beat in the sugar and then on low speed gradually mix in both of the flours, scraping the bowl as necessary with a rubber spatula and beating only until thoroughly mixed.

Dust a pastry cloth and a rolling pin (if you have a stockinette cover for the pin, use it) with either white or rye flour or with untoasted wheat germ (see Notes). Do not use any more flour or wheat germ than is necessary to keep the dough from sticking.

Roll half of the dough at a time, rolling it to ⅛-inch thickness. If the dough is too sticky to roll, form it into a ball, flatten slightly, and let stand on the floured pastry cloth for 30 minutes to 1 hour before rolling out. Cut with a plain, round 2½-inch cookie cutter. Then, with a very small round cutter, about ½ inch in diameter, cut a hole out of each cookie (see Notes). The hole should not be in the center of the cookie; it should be about ¾ inch from the edge. (In place of a very small round

8 ounces (2 sticks) unsalted butter
½ cup granulated sugar
1¼ cups strained rye flour (see Notes)
1¼ cups sifted all-purpose white flour
Milk
Caraway seeds

50 WAFERS

cookie cutter, use either the wide end of a pastry-bag decorating tube or a thimble.) Reserve the scraps and roll and cut them all at one time in order not to use any more flour than necessary.

With a metal spatula transfer the cookies to the cookie sheets, placing them about ½ inch apart.

Using a soft pastry brush, brush milk all over the top of each cookie and then sprinkle it with a moderate number of caraway seeds.

Bake 12 to 14 minutes, reversing the sheets top to bottom and front to back to ensure even browning. Bake until cookies are lightly colored.

With a wide metal spatula transfer cookies to racks to cool.

NOTES: Since rye flour is too coarse to be sifted it must be strained to aerate it. With your fingertips press it through a large strainer set over a large bowl. The part that doesn't go through the strainer should be stirred into the strained part.

Rye flour and untoasted wheat germ are both available at health-food stores.

Traditionally the hole in these cookies is off center. You could cut them out with a doughnut cutter, and have the holes in the middle, but then the cookies would not have their classic and charming look.

Whole-Wheat Squares

These are plain and not too sweet. The taste and texture will remind you of English wheat-meal biscuits. The recipe does not call for salt or flavoring, and does not require a mixer.

Place the flour in a large mixing bowl. Slice the butter into ½- to 1-inch pieces, and with a pastry blender cut it into the flour until the particles are fine and the mixture resembles coarse meal. Stir in the sugar. Through a fine strainer add the cream of tartar and the baking soda. Beat the egg lightly just to mix and stir it in. Stir in the water.

Turn the mixture out onto a large board or smooth work surface and squeeze between your hands until it holds together. Now "break" it by pushing off small pieces of the dough with the heel of your hand. Push against the work surface and smear it away from you. Re-form the dough and "break" it again.

The dough should be chilled before it is rolled. Form it into a flattened oblong with square corners, wrap in wax paper or plastic wrap, and refrigerate for one hour—no longer.

Adjust two racks to divide the oven into thirds and preheat to 350°. Line cookie sheets with parchment or foil.

Cut the dough crossways into three equal pieces. Work with one piece at a time, letting the other pieces stand at room temperature. Place each piece on a floured pastry cloth. With a floured rolling pin roll out the dough. Roll it up around the rolling pin occasionally, reflouring the cloth as necessary, then unroll the dough other side down to keep both sides lightly floured. If the dough cracks while you are rolling it, use a bit from the edge to patch the crack—just put the patch in place and roll over it lightly with the rolling pin. Roll the dough into an even rectangle 9 x 12 inches and ¼ inch thick. (See Note.)

With a very long knife or a pastry wheel, trim the edges. (The scraps may be pressed together and rerolled.) Then cut the dough into 3-inch squares. Now score the cookies once lengthwise down the middle with the dull edge of a knife—the scoring should be deep enough to show, but be careful that it does not cut through the cookie.

Use a wide metal spatula to transfer the cookies to the cookie sheets, placing them ½ to 1 inch apart.

Bake 20 to 30 minutes, until cookies are slightly colored. Reverse the sheets top to bottom and front to back as necessary during baking to ensure even browning. Do not overbake. If the dough has been rolled unevenly the thinner cookies will be done first and should be removed as they are done. If you bake only one sheet at a time use the higher rack.

With a wide metal spatula transfer the cookies to racks to cool.

NOTE: These may be rolled a little thicker or a little thinner. I like them best a bit thick, or no less then ¼ inch. The baking time will depend on the thickness.

---

4 cups unsifted *all-purpose whole-wheat flour* (stir to aerate before measuring)
8 ounces (2 sticks) unsalted butter
1 cup light brown sugar, firmly packed
1 teaspoon cream of tartar
1 teaspoon baking soda
1 egg
½ cup boiling water

36 TO 42 COOKIES

Whole-Wheat Honey Wafers

These are large, thin, crisp, and plain old-fashioned.

Through a large strainer, set over a large bowl, strain together the flour, baking soda, salt, cinnamon, and ginger, pressing the ingredients through the strainer with your fingertips. Set aside.

In the large bowl of an electric mixer cream the butter. Beat in the instant coffee, brown sugar, honey, and egg. On lowest speed gradually add the strained dry ingredients, scraping the bowl as necessary with a rubber spatula and beating only until thoroughly mixed.

Divide the dough in half and wrap each half in a large piece of wax paper or aluminum foil. Refrigerate for a few hours (or longer if you wish) until the dough is firm enough to roll.

Adjust two racks to divide the oven into thirds and preheat to 375°. Line cookie sheets with parchment or foil, shiny side up.

Work with half of the dough at a time. Place the piece on a lightly floured pastry cloth and turn it over to flour the dough on all sides. With a lightly floured rolling pin, roll the dough until it is a scant ¼ inch thick. Cut cookies with a plain round 3-inch cookie cutter and place them 1 inch apart on the sheets.

Reserve the scraps of dough and roll them all at once in order not to incorporate any more flour than necessary.

Bake for 12 to 14 minutes, until the cookies are lightly colored. Reverse the sheets top to bottom and front to back as necessary to ensure even browning. Do not underbake; these should be crisp.

Let the cookies stand for a few seconds until they can be transferred. With a wide metal spatula transfer the cookies to racks to cool.

These must be stored airtight.

NOTE: Since whole-wheat flour is generally too coarse to be sifted, it should be strained instead. Place a large strainer over a large bowl and, with your fingertips, work the flour through the strainer. Any particles too coarse to go through the strainer should be stirred into the strained flour.

2 cups strained all-purpose whole-wheat flour (see Note)
½ teaspoon baking soda
½ teaspoon salt
1 teaspoon cinnamon
½ teaspoon powdered ginger
4 ounces (1 stick) unsalted butter
2 teaspoons instant coffee
⅔ cup light brown sugar, firmly packed
⅓ cup honey
1 egg

26 LARGE WAFERS

Wild-Honey and Ginger Cookies

This is an old recipe that was originally made with wild honey, which has a very strong flavor. It may be made with any honey. The cookies are large, plain, and gingery. The dough has to be refrigerated 4 to 5 hours or longer.

S ift together the flour, baking soda, salt, and ginger into the large bowl of an electric mixer and set aside. Place the butter and honey in a saucepan over modest heat. Stir occasionally until the butter is melted and the mixture comes to a low boil.

Pour the hot honey and butter all at once over the sifted dry ingredients. On low speed mix until the dry ingredients are all absorbed, and then on high speed mix for about a minute until the dough stiffens slightly.

Tear off a piece of aluminum foil large enough to wrap the dough. Pour a little vegetable oil onto the foil and, with your fingers, spread the oil thoroughly over the foil. The oil is necessary to keep this dough from sticking to the foil.

Place the dough on the foil, wrap, and refrigerate for 4 to 5 hours or overnight.

Adjust two racks to divide the oven into thirds and preheat to 350°. Line cookie sheets with parchment or foil, shiny side up.

Lightly flour a pastry cloth and rolling pin. Unwrap the dough, cut it in half and work with one piece at a time. Place one piece on the pastry cloth and turn the dough to flour all sides. The dough will be quite stiff—pound it firmly with the rolling pin until it softens a bit. Roll out the dough, turning it over occasionally to keep both sides lightly floured. Roll it to ¼-inch thickness.

Cut the cookies with a plain round 3-inch cookie cutter. (Or, using a long, heavy knife or a pastry wheel, cut into large squares.) Reserve the scraps and roll them all together in order not to incorporate any more flour than necessary.

Place the cookies 2 inches apart on the cookie sheets.

Bake about 12 minutes, until the cookies are well colored. Reverse the sheets top to bottom and front to back as necessary to ensure even browning.

With a wide metal spatula transfer the cookies to racks to cool.

These must be stored airtight or they may become soft and limp. But they can be recrisped. Reheat them on foil-lined cookie sheets in a 325° oven for about 5 minutes. Let stand for a few seconds and then, with a wide metal spatula, transfer to racks to cool.

2½ cups sifted all-purpose flour
1½ teaspoons baking soda
¼ teaspoon salt
1 tablespoon powdered ginger
8 ounces (2 sticks) unsalted butter, cut into 1-inch pieces
12 ounces (1 cup) honey

24 LARGE COOKIES

Honey Graham Crackers

These are almost like the store-bought ones—plain, dry, crunchy squares.

Sift together the white flour, baking powder, baking soda, salt, and cinnamon, and set aside. In the large bowl of an electric mixer cream the butter. Add the vanilla, brown sugar, and honey, and beat well. On low speed, add the whole-wheat flour and the sifted ingredients in three additions, alternating with the milk in two additions. Scrape the bowl as necessary with a rubber spatula and beat only until smooth after each addition. If the mixture is not completely smooth, turn it out onto a large board or a smooth surface and knead it briefly with the heel of your hand.

Form the dough into an even, flattened oblong. Wrap it airtight and refrigerate for 2 to 3 hours or longer, overnight if you wish.

Adjust two racks to divide the oven into thirds and preheat to 350°. Line cookie sheets with parchment or foil.

Cut the chilled dough into equal quarters and work with one piece at a time.

On a well-floured pastry cloth, with a floured rolling pin, roll the dough into an even 15 x 5-inch oblong. With a long, sharp knife trim the edges. (The trimmings should be reserved, pressed together, and rerolled all at once in order not to incorporate any more flour than necessary.) Use a ruler as a guide and cut crosswise into six 5 x 2½-inch oblongs. With the back (or dull) side of a knife lightly score across the center of each cracker, dividing it into two halves, each 2½ inches square.

With a wide metal spatula transfer the crackers to the cookie sheets, placing them ½ to 1 inch apart. With a fork, prick the crackers evenly in parallel rows at ½-inch intervals.

Bake for 12 to 14 minutes, reversing the sheets top to bottom and front to back as necessary to ensure even browning. If you bake only one sheet at a time bake it high in the oven. Bake until the crackers are lightly colored.

1 cup sifted all-purpose bleached or unbleached white flour
1 teaspoon baking powder
½ teaspoon baking soda
¼ teaspoon salt
½ teaspoon cinnamon
4 ounces (1 stick) unsalted butter
1 teaspoon vanilla extract
½ cup dark brown sugar, firmly packed
¼ cup honey
2 cups unsifted *all-purpose whole-wheat flour* (stir lightly to aerate before measuring)
½ cup milk

24 TO 30 DOUBLE CRACKERS

Swedish Honey Cookies

These are a Swedish classic; they have a mild and interesting flavor. The dough must be well chilled before rolling.

Sift together the flour, baking soda, salt, and cinnamon. In the large bowl of an electric mixer, cream the butter. Add the coriander seeds and beat well. Gradually beat in the sugar and honey and then the egg. On low speed gradually add the sifted dry ingredients, scraping the bowl with a rubber spatula and beating only until mixed.

Turn the dough out onto a large piece of wax paper or aluminum foil, wrap, and chill for at least several hours (or longer) in the freezer or refrigerator.

Adjust two racks to divide the oven into thirds and preheat to 375°. Line cookie sheets with parchment or foil.

Flour a pastry cloth and a rolling pin. Cut the dough in half and work with one piece at a time, keeping the other piece chilled. Turn the dough over several times on the pastry cloth to flour both sides. If the dough is very firm pound it well with the rolling pin to soften it slightly. Roll out the dough, turning it over occasionally to keep both sides floured. Work quickly before the dough softens, and roll it to ⅛-inch thickness.

Quickly cut the dough with a plain or scalloped round 2½- or 3-inch cookie cutter. These cookies are traditionally scalloped but the scallops must be wide and deep or the design will run together.

With a wide metal spatula place the cookies 1 inch apart on the cookie sheets. Reserve the scraps, press them together, wrap and rechill before rolling them.

Bake for 10 to 12 minutes, reversing the sheets top to bottom and front to back as necessary to ensure even browning. The cookies are done when they are medium brown and semifirm to the touch.

Let stand for a minute or so and then, with a wide metal spatula, transfer the cookies to racks to finish cooling.

These must be stored airtight in order for them to remain crisp.

NOTE: Whole coriander seeds may be ground in a blender or well crushed with a mortar and pestle—they do not have to be powdered or strained.

2 cups sifted all-purpose flour
½ teaspoon baking soda
½ teaspoon salt
½ teaspoon cinnamon
4 ounces (1 stick) unsalted butter
1 teaspoon ground coriander seeds (see Note)
⅔ cup light brown sugar, firmly packed
⅓ cup honey
1 egg

32 TO 42 COOKIES

Swedish Ginger Cookies

Although these do not have to be hung on a Christmas tree, this is a good recipe for making cookies to hang. I am including directions for hanging, but the cookies may be cut with a plain or fancy cookie cutter, and not hung. I have also used this recipe for Christmas-card cookies; using a long knife, cut the dough into oblongs, bake, and then write the greeting on the baked cookies with the following Royal Icing. Once I tripled the recipe and made one huge cookie, as large as my oven would hold. It was made of many different layers that were pasted together with melted chocolate. Although it could have been eaten, it was strictly for show—it won first prize in a professional baking olympics. The design was a large flower. I pasted petals on top of petals and decorated the whole thing with a thin, wiggly line of Royal Icing. If you're artistic and creative and want to design things, use this recipe. Or if you simply want to make plain round or square ginger cookies that are wonderfully good use this recipe.

⅔ cup dark or light molasses
⅔ cup granulated sugar
1 tablespoon ginger
1 tablespoon cinnamon
5⅓ ounces (10⅔ tablespoons) unsalted butter, at room temperature
¾ tablespoon baking soda (see Note)
1 egg
4⅔ cups sifted all-purpose flour

*I*f you are making small cookies, adjust two racks to divide the oven into thirds and preheat to 325°. If you are making something very large and thick on one cookie sheet, adjust a rack to the center of the oven and preheat to 300°. Line cookie sheets with parchment or foil.

In a heavy 2-quart saucepan over moderate heat, bring the molasses, sugar, ginger, and cinnamon just to a low boil, stirring occasionally.

Meanwhile, cut the butter into 1-inch pieces and place them in a large mixing bowl.

When the molasses mixture comes to a boil, add the baking soda and stir until the mixture foams up to the top of the saucepan. Then pour it over the butter and stir to melt the butter.

With a fork, stir the egg lightly just to mix and then stir it into the molasses mixture. Gradually stir in the flour with a rubber spatula or wooden spoon.

Turn the dough out onto a large board or smooth work surface and knead lightly until it is mixed thoroughly.

If you are making thin cookies, work with half of the dough at a time. But for thick cookies work with it all.

Place the dough on a lightly floured pastry cloth, turn it to flour all sides, and form it into a ball. With a lightly floured rolling pin, roll the dough to the desired thickness. If the dough is rolled thick, and if the cookies are not baked until thoroughly dry, they will be similar to gingerbread. But if they are rolled thin and baked dry, they will be like crisp gingersnaps. (I have used this recipe for cookies ranging from a scant ⅛-inch to a generous ½-inch thickness.) Cut the shapes as you wish—

with cookie cutters (which should be floured as necessary if the dough sticks to them); with a long knife, cutting squares or oblongs; or with a small knife, either cutting freehand or tracing around your own pattern. Place the cookies on the cookie sheets. Reserve all scraps. Try not to incorporate any more flour (from the cloth) than necessary. Press scraps together, knead well until smooth, and then reroll them.

If you bake two sheets at a time, reverse the sheets top to bottom and front to back as necessary to ensure even browning. Bake until cookies feel firm to the touch. A rough guide is if the cookies are rolled ⅛ inch thick and baked 13 to 15 minutes they will be very crisp. If the cookies are ¼ inch thick and baked 15 minutes they will be slightly soft. If they are ⅜ inch thick and baked 15 minutes the cookies will be semisoft like gingerbread. This timing will vary depending on the diameter of the cookies—small shapes will take a bit less time, large shapes a bit more. If you make something extremely large and thick, the baking time should be longer. It might take 45 minutes or more at 300°. You will be able to judge by the feel of the cookie.

With a wide metal spatula transfer the cookies to rack to cool. If you are making a very large shape, as large as the cookie sheet, let it cool briefly on the sheet and then use a flat-sided cookie sheet as a spatula to transfer the cookie to the rack to cool.

NOTE: To measure ¾ tablespoon, first measure 1 level tablespoon and then, with a table knife or small metal spatula, mark it into quarters and return one-quarter to the box.

How to Prepare Cookies to be Used as Christmas-Tree Ornaments

Before baking, sew a length of heavy cotton or linen thread through each cookie, sewing from the front of the cookie to the back, about ¼ to ½ inch in from the edge, depending on the size of the cookies. Place the cookies on the foil, carefully arranging the threads so that they do not touch other cookies. After baking and cooling the cookies, tie the threads for hanging.

Another way is to use a small pastry tube (the kind that fits into a decorating bag) to cut a small hole near the edge of the cookie. But, if you do, bake one sample first to make sure that the hole is not so small that it closes during baking. After baking and cooling the cookies, thread string or ribbon through the holes.

A third method is to place a small piece of spaghetti upright, inserting it from the front to the back near the edge of the cookie (do this after the cookies are placed on the sheets). After baking, while the cookies are still warm, push the spaghetti out through the back of the cookie and thread a thin string through the hole.

Royal Icing for Decorating

This makes a generous amount.

Strain the sugar by pressing it with your fingertips through a large strainer set over a large bowl. In the small bowl of an electric mixer beat the egg whites with about half of the sugar at high speed for 5 minutes. Beat in the cream of tartar. Continue to beat while gradually adding more of the sugar, about ½ cup at a time, beating thoroughly after each addition, until the icing reaches the desired consistency. The icing should be thick enough to hold its shape without running or flattening when it is pressed through a pastry bag, but not so thick that it is difficult to press through the bag. Also, if it is too stiff it will not stick to the cookies. It will probably not be necessary to add all of the sugar. If the icing is too stiff, add a bit more egg white or a few drops of water, very little at a time. If it is too soft, add a little more sugar. Keep the icing covered with a damp cloth to prevent a crust from forming.

For fine line decorating or lettering: Use a pastry bag fitted with a tube that has a small round opening. Or use a cone made of a triangle of parchment paper (or baking-pan liner paper). Traditionally the triangle is made by cutting a 15-inch square in half diagonally, but it may be a little smaller than that if you wish. Cut a very small opening in the tip of the cone. First cut off just a tiny bit and try it with some icing. You can always cut away more if necessary.

Practice first on a piece of paper to be sure that the icing is the correct consistency.

(If you wish, the icing may be colored with food coloring—you may divide the icing and make several different colors—but the cookies will be dark and I prefer white icing.)

Just a suggestion: It is fun to use silver dragées. I spread them out on a piece of paper, and to place them where I want them on the icing before it dries, I transfer the dragées with tweezers.

1 pound (3½ cups, packed) confectioners sugar
⅓ cup egg whites (2 to 3 eggs), at room temperature
¼ teaspoon cream of tartar

Viennese Almond Wafers

These are rich and buttery, simple but elegant. The recipe makes a small amount; if you double it, roll only half at a time.

Adjust two racks to divide the oven into thirds and preheat to 350°. Line cookie sheets with parchment or foil. The almonds should be coarsely crushed; this is most easily done if they are frozen. Place them in a plastic bag, freeze them, and then press them in the bag with your fingers to break them into coarse pieces. Set aside.

In the small bowl of an electric mixer cream the butter with the salt and almond extract. Beat in the sugar and then the flour, beating only until mixed.

If the dough is too soft to be rolled, chill it briefly. It may be chilled in the mixing bowl and should be stirred occasionally.

Transfer the dough to a well-floured pastry cloth, turn it over to flour all sides, and form it into a square or an oblong. With a well-floured rolling pin (continue to flour the pin as necessary to keep it from sticking), roll the dough into an even square with straight edges; the square will be about 9 to 10 inches across and the dough will be a scant ⅛ inch thick.

Trim the edges of the dough with a pastry wheel, or use a long, thin sharp knife and wipe the blade after each cut to keep the dough from sticking. Cut the dough into even squares or oblongs.

Beat the egg white until foamy but not at all stiff. With a pastry brush, brush some of the white generously over each cookie. Sprinkle the almonds evenly over the egg white. Press down gently with the palms of both hands to press the nuts slightly into the dough. Carefully brush the remaining egg white over the almonds—it will help to keep them from falling off after the cookies have been baked.

With a wide metal spatula transfer the cookies to the cookie sheets, placing them ½ to 1 inch apart.

Bake about 20 minutes, reversing the position of the cookie sheets top to bottom and front to back as necessary to ensure even browning. If you bake only one sheet at a time, use the higher rack. Bake until the cookies are lightly browned; do not overbake.

With a wide metal spatula transfer the cookies to racks to cool.

3¾ ounces (¾ cup) sliced blanched almonds (see Note), frozen
4 ounces (1 stick) unsalted butter
Scant ⅛ teaspoon salt
¼ teaspoon almond extract
⅓ cup granulated sugar
¾ cup plus 1 tablespoon sifted all-purpose flour
1 egg white

9 LARGE SQUARES OR 24 SMALL OBLONGS

NOTE: "Sliced" almonds are those that have been cut into very thin slices—they are the ones to use for this recipe. The fatter, oblong, julienne-shape pieces are called "slivered" and are too thick for these cookies.

Ischler Cookies

This is a classic and elegant Viennese cookie made of two rich and fragile almond cookies sandwiched together with preserves and partially covered with chocolate glaze. These are made without a mixer.

*I*n a nut grinder, a blender, or a food processor, grind the almonds to a fine powder and place them in a large mixing bowl. Add the flour and sugar and stir to mix. With a pastry blender cut the butter into the dry ingredients until the mixture resembles a coarse meal.

Turn the dough out onto a large board or smooth work surface, then squeeze it between your hands until it holds together. Form the dough into a ball, flatten it slightly, and then "break" it as follows. Using the heel of your hand start at the far end of the dough and push off small pieces (the size of about 2 tablespoons), smearing it against the work surface and away from you. Continue until all the dough has been pushed off. Re-form the dough and then push it off or "break" it again.

Work with half of the dough at a time. Form it into a ball and place it on a large piece of wax paper. Cover with another large piece of wax paper. With your hand flatten the dough slightly, and then, with a rolling pin, roll over the paper to roll the dough until it is ¼ inch thick. If the wax paper wrinkles, peel it off and then replace it in order to remove the wrinkles. (During rolling check both pieces of wax paper for wrinkles.)

Slide a cookie sheet under the dough (still between the two pieces of wax paper) and transfer to the freezer or refrigerate until the dough is firm and the paper may be pulled off easily.

Repeat with the second half of the dough.

While the dough is chilling, adjust two racks to divide the oven into thirds and preheat to 350°. Line cookie sheets with parchment or foil.

While the dough is firm, peel off one piece of the wax paper just to release it, then replace it. Turn the dough in both pieces of paper over. Then peel off but do not replace the second piece of paper.

With a plain round cookie cutter measuring 2¼ to 2½ inches in diameter, cut out cookies and place them (with the help of a metal spatula if necessary) 1 inch apart on the cookie sheets. The dough must be firm enough for the rounds to hold their shape when they are transferred. Reserve scraps and roll, chill, and cut them. You should have about 48 cookies. (See Notes.)

Bake for 15 to 18 minutes, reversing the sheets top to bottom and front to back as

8 ounces (1⅔ cups) blanched almonds
2¼ cups sifted all-purpose flour
⅔ cup granulated sugar
10 ounces (2½ sticks) cold unsalted butter, cut into ½-inch slices
½ to ¾ cup smooth, thick apricot preserves

24 SANDWICH COOKIES

necessary to ensure even browning. When done, the cookies should be sandy-colored or lightly golden but not brown. Let stand for a few seconds and then, with a wide metal spatula, transfer cookies to racks to cool.

If the cookies are different sizes (because the dough was not all rolled to the same thickness), match them up into pairs of equal size. Place one cookie from each pair upside down.

Then, holding the cookie in your hand (carefully because these are fragile), spread the underside with a thin layer of the apricot preserves, keeping it a bit away from the edges. Cover this with another cookie and press them together very gently.

Prepare the following glaze.

Chocolate Glaze

Place the chocolate and shortening in the top of a small double boiler over warm water on low heat. Cover until partially melted. Then uncover and stir until completely melted and smooth. Transfer the glaze to a small narrow bowl for ease in handling. A soup cup is good.

12 ounces semisweet chocolate cut into pieces
2 tablespoons vegetable shortening (such as Crisco)

Line cookie sheets with wax paper. Hold a cookie sandwich between your fingers so that you are touching the two cookies, not the open ends. Dip it, edge down, into the glaze. Dip it deeply enough so that the glaze covers about half of the sandwich, both top and bottom. Gently wipe the edge of the sandwich against the top of the bowl to remove excess glaze. Place the cookie on the wax-paper-lined cookie sheet, laying it on one of the glazed sides.

Glaze the remaining cookies.

When the cookie sheet is covered with glazed cookies, transfer it to the freezer or refrigerator to chill until the glaze is set and the cookies may be lifted from the paper easily and don't stick. Store airtight.

NOTES: These directions make rather large cookies, which is traditional for this recipe. However, they may be rolled thinner and/or cut smaller if you wish.

If there is any glaze left over it may be saved for some other time, or for some other cookies. Line a small bowl with aluminum foil, pour in the glaze and let stand (or chill) until the glaze is firm. Then remove it—with the foil—from the bowl. Place it in a freezer bag or wrap it in enough foil to protect it. It may stand at room temperature for a few days, or longer. When ready to use, remove it from the foil, chop it coarsely, and melt slowly over hot water.

Viennese Chocolate Cookies

These are crisp-crunchy, bittersweet, and mildly spiced. They are made without a mixer, but you will need a food processor.

To prepare the almonds for topping the cookies, they must be split into halves and lightly toasted. First, in order to soften them for splitting, place them in a small pan, cover with boiling water, and boil over high heat for 2 to 3 minutes. Drain the nuts and then, quickly, while they are still warm, insert the tip of a small, sharp knife into the natural cracks to split them in half, the long way. Now, to dry them, place them in a small, shallow pan in a 350° oven. Bake for about 7 minutes, stirring the nuts or shaking the pan occasionally, until they are barely colored. Set the nuts aside to cool.

Adjust two racks to divide the oven into thirds and preheat to 350°. Line cookie sheets with parchment or foil.

Sift together into a large bowl the flour, salt, cinnamon, cloves, and sugar, and set aside.

On a cutting board, with a long, heavy knife, chop both chocolates coarsely and then place them in a food processor and grind them to a powder. Set the chocolate aside.

Without washing the processor, grind the 5 ounces of blanched almonds to a powder (see To Grind Nuts in a Food Processor, page 11) and set aside.

With a pastry blender cut the butter into the sifted dry ingredients until the particles are fine and the mixture resembles a coarse meal. Stir in the lemon rind, ground chocolates, and ground almonds. Beat in the egg yolks.

The mixture will be uneven. Turn it out onto a large board or a smooth work surface and squeeze it between your hands until it holds together. Now "break" the dough as follows: Form it into a ball. Using the heel of your hand, start at the far end of the dough and push off small pieces (the size of about 2 tablespoons), smearing it against the work surface and away from you. Continue until all the dough has been pushed off. Re-form the dough and push it off or "break" it again. All the ingredients should be completely mixed by now, but if not, break the dough again.

Work with half of the dough at a time. Form it into a ball. Place it on a long piece of wax paper, flatten the dough slightly, and then cover it with another long piece of wax paper. With a rolling pin, roll over the top piece of wax paper until the dough is ⅜ inch thick.

Remove the top piece of wax paper just to loosen it and then replace it. Turn

Ingredients

12 blanched almonds (for topping the cookies)

1¼ cups sifted all-purpose flour

Pinch of salt

½ teaspoon cinnamon

Scant ¼ teaspoon powdered cloves

½ cup plus 2 tablespoons granulated sugar

2 ounces (2 squares) unsweetened chocolate

2 ounces semisweet chocolate

5 ounces (1 cup) blanched almonds

5 ounces (1¼ sticks) cold unsalted butter, cut into ½-inch slices

Finely grated rind of 1 lemon

2 egg yolks

1 egg white (for the topping)

24 LARGE COOKIES

over the dough (still between two pieces of wax paper). Now remove and do not re-place the second piece of wax paper.

Cut the cookies with a plain round cookie cutter 2¼ to 2½ inches in diameter. With a small metal spatula transfer the cookies to the cookie sheets, placing them 1 inch apart. Reroll the scraps and cut again.

Beat the egg white only until it is slightly foamy, and, with a soft brush, brush it over the cookies. Place a prepared almond half on each cookie, flat side down. And then brush some more egg white over the almonds.

Bake the cookies for 15 minutes, reversing the sheets top to bottom and front to back as necessary to ensure even browning. Do not overbake—these burn easily.

With a wide metal spatula transfer the cookies to racks to cool.

Tropical Sour-Cream Cookies

St. Augustine, Florida, is the oldest city in the United States. This recipe is adapted from one of the first cookbooks published in St. Augustine. The cookies are large, plain, and semisoft, with a tropical orange and lemon flavor. Plan to chill the dough overnight before baking.

Sift together the flour, baking soda, and salt, and set aside. In a small cup mix the orange rind, lemon rind, and lemon juice, and set aside. In the large bowl of an electric mixer cream the butter. Add the sugar and beat well. Add the egg and beat to mix well. On low speed gradually beat in half of the sifted dry ingredients, then all of the sour cream, and finally the remaining dry ingredients, scraping the bowl with a rubber spatula and beating only until blended. Remove the bowl from the mixer and stir in the rinds and juice.

The dough will be soft. Turn it out onto a large piece of aluminum foil, wrap it in the foil, and place it in the freezer or refrigerator overnight. Adjust two racks to divide the oven into thirds and preheat to 375°. Line cookie sheets with parchment or foil shiny side up.

The dough will soften quickly and become sticky at room temperature, so work quickly. Work with half of the dough at a time, keeping the remainder chilled.

2 cups sifted all-purpose flour
½ teaspoon baking soda
⅛ teaspoon salt
Finely grated rind of 1 large, deep-colored orange
Finely grated rind of 1 large lemon
1 tablespoon lemon juice
4 ounces (1 stick) unsalted butter
1 cup light brown sugar, firmly packed (see Note)
1 egg
½ cup sour cream
Granulated sugar

20 LARGE COOKIES

Generously flour a pastry cloth and a rolling pin. Turn the dough over on the floured cloth to flour all sides and then form it into a ball and flatten it slightly. With the rolling pin, roll the dough to a generous ¼-inch thickness, turning the dough over occasionally while rolling, and adding additional flour to the cloth or pin if necessary to keep the dough from sticking.

Quickly cut the cookies with a plain round 3- to 3½-inch cookie cutter. And then, quickly transfer the cookies with a wide metal spatula to the lined sheets, placing them about 1 inch apart—these spread only slightly during baking.

Reserve the scraps of dough, press them together, rechill, and roll them all out together in order not to incorporate any more flour than necessary.

Sprinkle the tops of the cookies with granulated sugar.

Bake for about 15 minutes, until the cookies are lightly colored. Reverse the cookie sheets top to bottom and front to back as necessary to ensure even browning.

With a wide metal spatula transfer the cookies to racks to cool.

NOTE: If the brown sugar has any hard lumps it must be strained; place it in a large strainer set over a large bowl and, with your fingertips, press the sugar through the strainer.

Caraway Sour-Cream Cookies

Many old English cookie recipes call for caraway seeds. This recipe comes from New Hampshire and has been handed down through several generations. These are large, thin, and crisp with a mild caraway flavor. It is best to mix the dough a day before baking.

Sift together the flour, salt, and nutmeg, and set aside. In the large bowl of an electric mixer cream the butter. Add the sugar and beat well. Add the egg and beat to mix well. On low speed add half of the sifted dry ingredients, scraping the bowl with a rubber spatula and beating only until they are incorporated. Place the sour cream in a small bowl. Add the baking soda and stir together with a rubber spatula. Then add half the sour cream to the dough, beating only until smooth. Add the remaining sour cream to the dough, beating only until smooth. Add the remaining dry ingredients and the caraway seeds and beat only until smooth.

Transfer the dough to a large piece of wax paper or aluminum foil, wrap well, and place the dough in the freezer for several hours or preferably overnight.

When ready to bake the cookies, adjust two racks to divide the oven into thirds and preheat to 375°. Line cookie sheets with parchment or foil.

Work with half of the dough at a time, keeping the remainder in the freezer. Work quickly as the dough will become soft and sticky at room temperature.

Place the dough on a well-floured pastry cloth. Turn it over to flour all sides. Form it into a ball and flatten slightly. With a well-floured rolling pin, roll the dough to ⅛-inch thickness. While rolling the dough, in order to keep it from sticking, roll it up around the rolling pin occasionally, reflour the pastry cloth, and then unroll the dough bottom side up.

With a floured, plain round 3-inch cookie cutter, cut rounds very close to each other and quickly transfer the rounds with a wide metal spatula to the unbuttered cookie sheets, placing them ½ to 1 inch apart.

Press the scraps together, wrap, and refreeze them before rolling.

Bake for 12 to 15 minutes, reversing the sheets top to bottom and front to back as necessary to ensure even browning. Bake until the cookies are lightly colored—they will be slightly darker around the edges. If they have been rolled thicker than ⅛ inch they will take a little longer to bake. (If you bake only one sheet at a time use the higher rack.)

With a wide metal spatula transfer the cookies to racks to cool.

2 cups sifted all-purpose flour
¼ teaspoon salt
½ teaspoon nutmeg
4 ounces (1 stick) unsalted butter
1 cup granulated sugar
1 egg
½ cup sour cream
½ teaspoon baking soda
½ teaspoon caraway seeds

38 COOKIES

Rum-Raisin Shortbread

These are large and thick, with rum-soaked raisins all through them. The dough is very short; the cookies are rather delicate and quite unusual. The raisins must be prepared several hours ahead of time or the day before.

Raisins

Bring the raisins and the rum to a boil in a small saucepan over moderate heat. Remove from the heat, cover, and let stand for several hours or overnight. When ready to bake the cookies drain the raisins in a strainer set over a small bowl; use any leftover rum for something else.

5 ounces (1 cup) raisins
½ cup dark rum

15 LARGE COOKIES

Cookie Dough

Sift together the flour, baking powder, and salt, and set aside. In the large bowl of an electric mixer cream the butter until it is very soft. Add the sugar and beat well until completely smooth. On low speed gradually add the sifted dry ingredients, scraping the bowl with a rubber spatula and beating until smooth. Stir in the prepared raisins.

2 cups sifted all-purpose flour
¼ teaspoon baking powder
¼ teaspoon salt
8 ounces (2 sticks) unsalted butter
½ cup confectioners sugar

Transfer the dough to a large piece of wax paper or aluminum foil, wrap, flatten slightly, and refrigerate for about 1½ to 2 hours. Do not freeze the dough or it will become too firm to roll.

When ready to bake the cookies adjust two racks to divide the oven into thirds and preheat to 375°. Line cookie sheets with parchment or foil.

Place the dough on a lightly floured pastry cloth and turn it over to flour all sides lightly. With a floured rolling pin roll the dough gently only until it is ½ inch thick, no thinner! Use a plain, round cookie cutter about 2½ inches in diameter. Dip the cutter in flour before cutting each cookie and cut them as close to each other as possible. When cutting a cookie press the cutter very firmly into the dough and rotate it slightly in order to cut through the raisins. Press the scraps together, chill them, and reroll.

Place the cookies 1 to 2 inches apart on cookie sheets.

Bake for 20 minutes, or until cookies are golden brown. Reverse the sheets top to bottom and front to back to ensure even browning.

With a wide metal spatula transfer the cookies to racks to cool.

Since these are fragile I like to wrap them individually in clear cellophane. But however you store them—handle with care.

Hot Butter Wafers

An early Colonial recipe reportedly used by Dolley Madison and served at the White House. These are very plain, thin, crisp, and buttery. They may be served as a plain cookie, or as a cracker with soup or salad.

P lace the flour in the large bowl of an electric mixer. Cut the butter into 1-inch pieces and melt it in a small, heavy saucepan over moderate heat. Pour the hot butter all at once into the flour. Beat at low speed to mix—the mixture will be crumbly. Beat in the sugar and then the eggs, one at a time. Beat only until the last egg is incorporated.

Turn the dough out onto a large floured board or a smooth work surface and knead briefly only until completely smooth.

Wrap the dough in wax paper or aluminum foil and chill it in the freezer for 15 minutes—no longer!

Adjust two racks to divide the oven into thirds and preheat to 350°. Line cookie sheets with parchment or foil

Cut the dough into quarters. Work with one piece at a time, keeping the remainder covered at room temperature.

Turn the dough over several times on a floured pastry cloth to flour all sides lightly. Roll the dough with a floured rolling pin, turning it over frequently to keep both sides floured. Reflour the cloth and pin as necessary but don't use any more flour than you really need. Roll the dough until it is paper thin. (Each quarter of the dough should be rolled until it is 15 inches or more in diameter.)

Cut the cookies with a plain round 4-inch cookie cutter. Or use a long knife or a pastry wheel to trim the edges of the dough, then cut it into 4-inch squares. Prick the cookies all over with a fork at ½-inch intervals.

With a wide metal spatula transfer the cookies to the cookie sheets. These may be placed on the sheets actually touching each other since, instead of spreading, they shrink slightly when baked. Reserve the scraps of dough, knead them together briefly, and roll them together in order not to incorporate any more flour than necessary (see Note).

Bake the cookies for 13 to 18 minutes, reversing the cookie sheets top to bottom and front to back as necessary to ensure even browning. Bake until the cookies are golden brown all over with no white spots remaining. With a wide metal spatula remove the cookies individually as they are done and place them on racks to cool.

NOTE: After the dough has been rolled twice it becomes rubbery and difficult to roll thin enough. So try to end up with as few scraps as possible. In any event, roll it thin.

4 cups sifted all-purpose flour
8 ounces (2 sticks) unsalted butter
½ cup granulated sugar
3 eggs

60 WAFERS

Caraway Hardtack

These are similar to the previous Hot Butter Wafers but they are not so plain—these are sweeter and have the additional flavoring of caraway seeds.

4 cups sifted all-purpose flour
8 ounces (2 sticks) unsalted butter
2 cups granulated sugar
3 eggs
Milk (for brushing over the cookies)
Caraway seeds (for sprinkling on top)

55 COOKIES

Place the flour in the large bowl of an electric mixer. Cut the butter into 1-inch pieces and melt it in a small, heavy saucepan over moderate heat. Pour the hot butter all at once into the flour. Mix at low speed, scraping the bowl with a rubber spatula until the flour is all moistened—the mixture will be crumbly. Beat in the sugar and then the eggs, one at a time, continuing to scrape the bowl with the spatula and beating until the mixture is smooth.

Place the dough, still in the mixing bowl, in the freezer for 10 minutes (no longer) or in the refrigerator for 15 to 20 minutes.

Adjust two racks to divide the oven into thirds and preheat oven to 350°. Line cookie sheets with parchment or foil.

Generously flour a pastry cloth and a rolling pin. Work with one-third of the dough at a time, letting the rest stand at room temperature. (If the dough is too sticky to roll, let it stand at room temperature for 15 to 20 minutes, or longer if necessary.)

Place the dough on the floured cloth and turn it to flour all sides. With the floured rolling pin (reflour it frequently) roll the dough until it is ⅛ inch thick. Cut out cookies with a plain, round 3½-inch cookie cutter.

With a wide metal spatula transfer the cookies to the sheets, placing them ½ inch apart (these do not spread).

Reserve the scraps, press them together, and reroll them.

With a pastry brush, brush the tops of the cookies generously with milk and then, before the milk dries, sprinkle a generous pinch of caraway seeds over the top of each cookie.

Bake the cookies for 15 to 20 minutes, until the cookies are lightly browned. Reverse the sheets top to bottom and front to back as necessary to ensure even browning.

Remove the cookies individually as they are ready, leaving the lighter ones until done. With a wide metal spatula transfer the cookies to racks to cool.

Arrowroot Wafers from Bermuda

Arrowroot is the root of a tropical plant that has been dried and then ground to a powder similar to flour. Since it is a highly nutritive and easily digested form of starch, it is often thought of as food for young children and invalids. But everyone likes these cookies, which are thin, plain, dry, and extremely light. Arrowroot is available in small (3⅛-ounce) jars in the spice section of food stores. One of these jars holds about half a cup.

S ift together the arrowroot, flour, baking powder, and salt, and set aside. In the small bowl of an electric mixer, cream the butter with the vanilla and sugar until smooth. Add the eggs one at a time, beating until thoroughly mixed. On low speed, gradually add the sifted dry ingredients, scraping the bowl with a rubber spatula and beating until smooth.

The dough will be soft and sticky. Transfer it to a small bowl (or leave it in the mixer bowl if you prefer), cover airtight, and place in the freezer for a few hours (see Note).

Adjust two racks to divide the oven into thirds and preheat oven to 350°. Line cookie sheets with parchment or foil.

Generously flour a pastry cloth and rolling pin. Work with half of the dough at a time, keeping the remainder in the freezer. With a heavy spoon, transfer half of the dough to the floured cloth. Turn it over to flour both sides. Work very quickly as the dough will soften and become sticky at room temperature! With the floured rolling pin, roll the dough to a scant ⅛-inch thickness (that's thin), turning it over once or twice to keep both sides floured. Cut quickly with a 2½-inch round cookie cutter, and with a wide metal spatula immediately transfer cookies to the sheets, placing them about ½ inch apart. These may be close to each other, as they do not spread; actually they shrink a little. Replace scraps in the bowl and freeze again until firm enough to reroll.

Bake 10 to 15 minutes, reversing sheets top to bottom and front to back to help them brown evenly. Bake only until lightly colored, very pale—a few spots may remain white. Some cookies will color sooner than others and should be removed individually when done. With a wide metal spatula (or with your fingers if you don't mind the heat) transfer the cookies to racks to cool.

½ cup unsifted arrowroot
1 cup sifted all-purpose flour
¼ teaspoon baking powder
¼ teaspoon salt
2 tablespoons unsalted butter,
    at room temperature
½ teaspoon vanilla extract
⅓ cup granulated sugar
2 eggs

46 COOKIES

NOTE: If the dough has been frozen too long it will be too hard to roll. Place it on a floured pastry cloth and pound it heavily with a floured rolling pin, turning it over a few times, until soft enough to roll. Do not just let it stand at room temperature or it will become sticky.

Uppåkra Cookies

These traditional Swedish cookies are thin and delicate and dainty enough for a tea party.
The batter calls for potato flour, which adds to their light, flaky quality.

In the large bowl of an electric mixer, cream the butter. Add the almond extract and sugar and beat well. On low speed, gradually add the potato flour and then the all-purpose flour, scraping the bowl with a rubber spatula and beating only until the flours are thoroughly incorporated and smooth.

Transfer the dough to a large piece of wax paper or aluminum foil, wrap, and refrigerate for only about 30 minutes. (If the dough is chilled longer it will become too hard to roll. If this happens, let it stand at room temperature until it softens enough to roll.)

While the dough is chilling, adjust two racks to divide the oven into thirds and preheat oven to 350°. Line cookie sheets with parchment or foil.

Work with half of the dough at a time. Unless the kitchen is very warm, the other half may wait, wrapped, at room temperature.

The dough is fragile and must be handled with care. On a lightly floured pastry cloth, with a floured rolling pin, roll the dough to ⅛-inch thickness—that's thin; measure it. While rolling the dough, flour the pin as frequently as necessary to keep it from sticking. With a plain, round cookie cutter about 2½ inches in diameter, cut the cookies, and then, with a small metal spatula, transfer them to a cutting board.

With a sharp knife, cut each cookie into two unequal pieces, one one-third of the cookie, one two-thirds. After all are cut, flip the smaller pieces over on top of the larger pieces, lining up the straight edges together. Repeat with the remaining half of the dough. Reserve all scraps and roll them all at once in order not to incorporate any more flour than necessary.

With a metal spatula, transfer the cookies to the sheets, placing them about ½ inch apart—these don't spread.

8 ounces (2 sticks) unsalted
  butter
½ teaspoon almond extract
⅓ cup granulated sugar
¾ cup sifted potato flour (see
  Notes)
1¾ cups sifted all-purpose
  flour

50 COOKIES

Topping

In a small bowl, beat the egg lightly just to mix and set aside. Stir the almonds and the sugar together.

With a soft pastry brush, brush the egg over the tops of the cookies and then sprinkle with the almond-sugar mixture.

Bake about 20 minutes, reversing the sheets top to bot-

1 egg
⅓ cup blanched almonds,
  finely chopped
3 tablespoons crystal sugar
  (see Notes)

tom and front to back to ensure even browning. Bake only until cookies are lightly browned.

With a wide metal spatula, transfer cookies to racks to cool.

Handle with care—these are fragile.

NOTES: Potato flour, also called potato starch, is generally available in Jewish or Scandinavian grocery stores.

Crystal sugar is commonly used to sprinkle over European cookies and pastries before baking. It is also called "pearl sugar" and in German it is *Hagelzucker*. (See page 5.)

Ginger Shortbread Cookies

This is an unusual brown-sugar spice cookie from Scotland.

Adjust a rack one-third down from the top of the oven and preheat oven to 350°. Line a cookie sheet with parchment or foil.

Place the almonds in a small, shallow pan and bake them, shaking the pan occasionally, for about 10 minutes until they are thoroughly dried and only slightly colored. Set aside to cool completely.

Sift together the flour, salt, ginger, cinnamon, cloves, and mustard, and set aside. In the large bowl of an electric mixer cream the butter together with the instant coffee. Add the brown sugar and beat to mix well. On low speed gradually add the sifted dry ingredients, scraping the bowl with a rubber spatula and beating only until the ingredients are thoroughly mixed and the dough holds together.

Turn the dough out onto a large piece of wax paper and cover it with another large piece of wax paper. Flatten the dough slightly with your hand. Then, with a rolling pin, roll over the top piece of paper until the dough is ⅜ inch thick (no thinner). Slide a cookie sheet under the bottom paper and transfer the dough to the freezer or refrigerator for 5 to 10 minutes until the

26 whole blanched almonds
1½ cups sifted all-purpose flour
⅛ teaspoon salt
1 teaspoon powdered ginger
1 teaspoon cinnamon
¼ teaspoon powdered cloves
¼ teaspoon mustard powder
6 ounces (1½ sticks) unsalted
  butter
¾ teaspoon instant coffee
½ cup dark brown sugar,
  firmly packed
1 egg yolk and 1 teaspoon
  water—for glazing the tops
  of the cookies

26 COOKIES

dough is firm enough to be cut with a cookie cutter and the wax paper can be peeled away cleanly, leaving a smooth surface on the dough.

Remove and then replace the top piece of wax paper just to loosen it. Invert the dough (still between both papers). Then remove and do not replace the second piece of paper.

Cut cookies with a plain, round cookie cutter about 1¾ inches in diameter. Place the cookies 1 inch apart on the cookie sheet.

If the dough is very firm let the cookies stand at room temperature for 2 to 3 minutes to soften slightly.

Meanwhile, you can press together the scraps of dough, reroll, and chill them.

Place a baked, blanched almond on each cookie and press it very gently into the dough. (If, when you press on the almond, the dough is still so cold and firm that it cracks, let it stand a few moments longer. But don't let the unbaked cookies stand any longer than necessary in a warm kitchen or the edges will run unevenly during baking.)

Stir the egg yolk and water together just to mix. With a soft brush, brush lightly over the tops of the cookies and the almonds to give a shiny finish.

Bake for about 15 minutes, until the cookies darken slightly and are barely semi-firm to the touch. Reverse the cookie sheet front to back once to ensure even baking. Do not overbake or the cookies will become too hard.

With a wide metal spatula transfer the cookies to a rack to cool.

NOTE: You will probably bake these cookies only one sheet at a time (almost all of them will fit on one sheet, and the remainder that you reroll from the scraps of dough may have to chill while you are baking the first sheet). However, if you do bake two sheets together, adjust the two racks to divide the oven into thirds. Then, during baking, reverse the sheets top to bottom and front to back once or twice to ensure even baking. Baking two sheets together generally takes a bit more baking time.

Dione Lucas's Sablés

These French almond cookies are similar to shortbread. Sablé is French for "sandy," which describes the texture of these cookies. Dione Lucas, one of the greatest cooks of our time, served these for dessert along with a cold soufflé at a memorable formal dinner party.

Adjust a rack to the top position in the oven and preheat to 350°. Line a cookie sheet with parchment or foil. Grind the ½ cup blanched almonds either in a nut grinder or in a blender—they must be ground to a powder. Set aside.

In the large bowl of an electric mixer cream the butter well. Add the salt and the sugar and beat until smooth. Beat in the rum and then the ground almonds. On lowest speed gradually add the flour, scraping the bowl with a rubber spatula and beating only until smooth.

Turn the dough out onto a large board or a smooth work surface. Work the dough with your hands, first squeezing it between your fingers, and then pushing it away from you, a bit at a time, with the heel of your hand, until very smooth.

Form the dough into a ball and flatten it slightly. Place it on a large piece of wax paper and cover with another large piece of wax paper. With a rolling pin, roll over the top of the paper until the dough is a scant ⅜ inch thick (don't make these too thin) and perfectly level. If the wax paper wrinkles during the rolling, remove and then replace the paper to remove the wrinkles.

Slide a cookie sheet under the bottom wax paper and transfer the dough to the freezer for about 10 minutes, or a little longer in the refrigerator, until the dough is almost firm.

Remove the top piece of wax paper just to release it, then replace it. Turn the dough over, still between the two pieces of paper. Remove the second piece of wax paper and do not replace it.

Cut the cookies with a round 1¾-inch cookie cutter. Place them ½ inch apart on the cookie sheet; these will barely spread at all in baking and may be placed quite close to each other. Press the scraps together. Reroll and chill before cutting.

In a small cup mix the egg yolk with the water. With a soft brush, brush the egg wash over the tops of the cookies. Place a whole blanched almond on top of each cookie and press gently until the almond is slightly imbedded—if the cookies are too firm, let them stand for a few minutes to soften slightly.

Now brush the egg wash over each cookie again, generously covering the top of the cookie and the almond.

Bake for 15 to 17 minutes, reversing the position of the cookie sheet front to back to ensure even browning. Bake only until the cookies are slightly colored; do not overbake.

With a wide metal spatula transfer the cookies to racks to cool.

2½ ounces (½ cup) blanched almonds
6 ounces (1½ sticks) unsalted butter
Pinch of salt
½ cup confectioners sugar
2 tablespoons rum (I use Myer's dark rum)
2 cups sifted all-purpose flour
1 egg yolk
1 teaspoon water
38 whole blanched almonds

36 COOKIES

Cornell Sugar Cookies

I created these cookies, but they were inspired by a health-food formula devised by Dr. Clive M. McCay at Cornell University. The formula was originally planned for a nutritious high-protein bread. The special features that make it "Cornell" are the additions of soy flour, nonfat dry powdered milk, and wheat germ. People do not have to be health-food devotees to like these. They are large and plain old-fashioned.

Sift together the white flour, soy flour, baking powder, baking soda, salt, nutmeg, and allspice, and set aside. In the large bowl of an electric mixer cream the butter. Add the vanilla and sugar and beat well. Add the eggs one at a time. Beat in the wheat germ, powdered milk, and then the milk. Beat until smooth. On low speed gradually add the sifted dry ingredients, scraping the bowl with a rubber spatula and beating only until smooth.

Transfer the dough to wax paper or foil, wrap, and refrigerate overnight.

Adjust two racks to divide the oven into thirds and preheat to 425°. Line cookie sheets with parchment or foil.

Place the dough on a well-floured pastry cloth. If the dough is very hard pound it briefly with a floured rolling pin to soften slightly. Turn the dough over and over and press down on it gently to flour both sides. Work quickly before the dough softens and becomes sticky. Roll it with a floured rolling pin, turning it over once or twice as you roll to keep it from sticking. Roll the dough to a scant ¼-inch thickness. Cut with a plain, round 3½-inch cookie cutter. Or use a long, heavy knife and cut into large squares. Press scraps together and reroll.

Place the cookies 2 inches apart on the cookie sheets.

Bake about 8 to 10 minutes, until cookies are golden-colored. Reverse the sheets top to bottom and front to back to ensure even browning. If you bake only one sheet at a time bake it high in the oven.

With a wide metal spatula transfer cookies to racks to cool.

2¼ cups sifted all-purpose unbleached white flour
¼ cup unsifted soy flour (see Note)
1 teaspoon baking powder
½ teaspoon baking soda
½ teaspoon salt (you may substitute sea salt if you wish; see Note)
½ teaspoon nutmeg
¼ teaspoon allspice
4 ounces (1 stick) unsalted butter
1½ teaspoon vanilla extract
1 cup raw sugar (see Note)
2 eggs
2 tablespoons natural untoasted wheat germ (see Note)
2 tablespoons nonfat dry powdered milk
1 tablespoon milk

16 TO 18 VERY LARGE COOKIES

NOTE: Soy flour, raw sugar, natural untoasted wheat germ, and sea salt are all available in health-food stores.

Plain Old-Fashioned Sugar Cookies

These cookies are traditionally made very large, almost saucer size, but you can make any size or shape you want.

Sift together the flour, baking powder, and salt, and set aside. In the large bowl of an electric mixer cream the butter. Add the vanilla and sugar and beat well. Beat in the eggs one at a time and then add the milk. On low speed gradually add the sifted dry ingredients, scraping the bowl as necessary with a rubber spatula and beating only until thoroughly mixed.

Divide the dough in two and wrap each half separately in wax paper or aluminum foil. Chill the dough in the refrigerator for 3 hours or longer if you wish (chilling the dough in the freezer makes it too hard to roll).

Adjust two racks to divide the oven into thirds and preheat to 400°. Line cookie sheets with parchment or foil.

Place one piece of the dough on a lightly floured pastry cloth. Turn it over to flour all sides and form it into a ball. With a floured rolling pin, roll the dough to the desired thickness: For very large cookies roll to a generous ¼ inch. Cut the cookies as you wish. If you want very large cookies, cut with a plain, round 4-inch cookie cutter.

With a wide metal spatula transfer the cookies to unbuttered cookie sheets. If the cookies are large and thick, place them 1½ to 2 inches apart. They may be closer if they are small and thin.

Sprinkle the tops of the cookies generously with granulated sugar.

Bake until the cookies are lightly browned, reversing the position of the sheets top to bottom and front to back as necessary during baking to ensure even browning. Large, thick cookies will need to bake for 10 to 12 minutes.

With a wide metal spatula transfer the cookies to racks to cool.

3¼ cups sifted all-purpose flour
2½ teaspoons baking powder
Scant ¼ teaspoon salt
6 ounces (1½ sticks) unsalted butter
1½ teaspoons vanilla extract
1½ cups granulated sugar
2 eggs
1 tablespoon milk
Additional granulated sugar (for topping)

20 EXTRA-LARGE COOKIES

Chocolate-Chip Pillows

Chocolate chips are sandwiched between two thin, buttery, brown-sugar cookies and baked together.

Adjust two racks to divide the oven into thirds and preheat to 425°. Line the cookie sheets with parchment or foil.

Sift together the flour, salt, and baking soda, and set aside. In the small bowl of an electric mixer cream the butter. Add the vanilla and both sugars and beat well. Beat in the egg yolk and then, on low speed, gradually add the sifted dry ingredients, scraping the bowl with a rubber spatula and beating until the dough holds together.

Tear off two pieces of wax paper, each about 16 to 18 inches long. Place the dough on one piece of the paper and flatten it slightly. Cover with the other piece of paper and, with a rolling pin, roll over the wax paper until the dough is ⅛ inch thick—it will be about 14 inches long and almost as wide as the paper.

Slide a cookie sheet under the dough and papers and transfer to the freezer or refrigerator very briefly, only until the dough is firm enough to cut and handle. (It will take only a few minutes in the freezer.)

Peel off the top piece of wax paper just to loosen it and then replace it. Turn the dough (still between both papers) over. Peel off the second piece of paper and do not replace it.

Now work quickly before the dough softens. Cut about half of the rolled dough with a plain, round 2-inch cookie cutter. Place the cookies 1½ to 2 inches apart on the cookie sheets, using a small metal spatula if necessary to transfer the cookies. Replace the remaining rolled dough in the freezer or refrigerator to keep it firm until you are ready to use it.

Place 6 chocolate morsels in the center of each round of dough on the cookie sheets. Then remove the reserved chilled dough and, following the above directions, cut it into rounds. Place a round of the dough over each cookie. Reroll and form the scraps of dough the same way, chilling the dough as necessary. Seal the edges of the sandwiched cookies by pressing them with the back of the tines of a fork.

Bake for about 10 minutes, reversing the sheets top to bottom and front to back once to ensure even browning. Bake until the cookies are lightly browned.

With a wide metal spatula transfer the cookies to racks to cool.

1½ cups sifted all-purpose flour
½ teaspoon salt
¼ teaspoon baking soda
4 ounces (1 stick) unsalted butter
½ teaspoon vanilla extract
2 tablespoons granulated sugar
¼ cup dark brown sugar, firmly packed
1 egg yolk
2 ounces (⅓ cup) semisweet chocolate morsels (see Note)

18 COOKIES

NOTE: You may use the midget-size morsels if you wish. Just use as many as you can easily sandwich between the two cookies.

Prune Pillows

These are large, old-fashioned, homey cookies with a tender crust and a thick, baked-in prune-nut filling. It is best to make both the crust and the filling the day before. If not, plan on at least several hours for the crust to chill. You will need two large, plain round cookie cutters, one ½ inch smaller than the other. Mine measure 3¼ inches and 2¾ inches, but you can make these either a little larger or a little smaller.

Crust

Sift together the flour, baking soda, and salt, and set aside. In the large bowl of an electric mixer cream the butter. Add the vanilla and sugar and beat to mix well. Beat in the eggs to mix well. On low speed gradually add the sifted dry ingredients, scraping the bowl with a rubber spatula and beating until thoroughly incorporated.

Transfer the dough to a large piece of wax paper or aluminum foil, wrap well, flatten slightly, and refrigerate overnight or for at least several hours. (The dough may be placed in the freezer until it is very cold and partially firm, but if it is left in the freezer too long it will become too solid to roll out.)

2½ cups sifted all-purpose flour
¼ teaspoon baking soda
Scant ½ teaspoon salt
4 ounces (1 stick) unsalted butter
1 teaspoon vanilla extract
1 cup granulated sugar
2 eggs

24 LARGE COOKIES

Filling

Pit the prunes and place them on a cutting board and with a long, heavy knife chop them rather fine to make 1¼ cups of pulp.

Bring the prune pulp with the sugar and lemon juice to a boil in a medium-size heavy saucepan over moderate heat, stirring almost constantly. Let the mixture boil very slowly for about 8 minutes until it is slightly thickened. Set aside to cool and then stir in the nuts. If you have made the filling a day or more ahead, cover and refrigerate it. If it is to be used within a few hours it may wait at room temperature but it must not be warm when used.

When you are ready to bake the cookies, adjust two racks to divide the oven into thirds and preheat to 400°. Line two 15½ x 12-inch cookie sheets with parchment or foil.

1 25-ounce jar or can of stewed prunes (about 28 medium-size prunes—you may use dried prunes and stew them yourself)
½ cup granulated sugar
3 tablespoons lemon juice
3 ounces (scant 1 cup) walnuts, cut or broken into medium-size pieces
Confectioners sugar for topping

Work with half the dough at a time, keeping the remainder refrigerated. Work quickly before the dough softens. Place the dough on a well-floured pastry cloth and turn it over several times to flour all sides. If the dough is too firm to roll, pound it with a rolling pin to soften it slightly. With a floured rolling pin, roll the dough until it is a scant ⅛ inch thick (make it thin enough), reflouring the cloth and pin as necessary to keep the dough from sticking.

With a plain, round 3¼-inch cookie cutter, cut the first half of the dough into rounds. With a small metal spatula transfer the rounds to a fully-lined cookie sheet—they may be placed less than 1 inch apart in order to fit 12 rounds on each sheet. Reserve the scraps, rechill, and reroll them.

Place a rounded teaspoonful of the filling in the center of each cookie, mounding the filling high in the center and keeping it well away from the edges.

Roll out the other half of the dough, which you had left in the refrigerator, cut it the same way as the first half, and use these rounds for tops. Cover each cookie with a top, and then with floured fingertips press down gently around the edges.

Now, to seal and trim the edges, the cookies should be cut again, with the smaller cutter. Since the dough will have softened and become sticky by now, the smaller cutter must be dipped into flour frequently. Recut the cookies with the 2¾-inch cookie cutter. (Don't worry about any small spots where the rounds of dough are not sealed to each other—or any small cracks in the top rounds of dough.) Remove the excess dough; if it does not have any of the filling mixed in with it, it may be reused.

Bake for about 15 minutes until the cookies are delicately browned. Reverse the cookie sheets top to bottom and front to back as necessary to ensure even browning.

With a wide metal spatula transfer the cookies to racks to cool.

Place the racks of cooled cookies over wax paper. Cover the tops generously with confectioners sugar, pressing it with you fingertips through a fine strainer held over the cookies.

Hamantaschen

The name Hamantaschen is derived from Haman's hat. Haman was a wicked man who wanted to destroy the Jewish people, but Queen Esther did him in first. Haman wore a hat shaped like Napoleon's—triangular—and these cookies are made to resemble that shape. These are traditionally served during Purim, the feast of Esther, which is the most joyous day of the Hebrew year, and traditionally they are filled with prune jam, called lekvar, or with a poppy seed and honey mixture. This version is slightly different. (The pastry must be refrigerated overnight.)

Pastry

Sift together, into a large mixing bowl, the flour, baking powder, salt, and sugar. Cut the butter into ½-inch slices, and with a pastry blender cut it into the dry ingredients until the particles are fine and the mixture resembles coarse meal. Beat the egg lightly just to mix. Stir the egg, orange rind, and juice into the dough. Mix thoroughly and then stir well until the dough is completely moistened and smooth. Wrap in wax paper or plastic wrap, flatten the dough slightly, and refrigerate overnight.

The filling may be made the next day or it may be made ahead of time and kept at room temperature for a day or two or refrigerated for a longer time.

2 cups sifted all-purpose flour
2 teaspoons baking powder
¼ tablespoon salt
¾ cup granulated sugar
¼ pound (1 stick) unsalted
*   butter, cold and firm*
1 egg
Finely grated rind of 1 bright-
*   colored orange*
1½ tablespoons orange juice

Filling

Cut the prunes and apricots into small pieces. Place them in a saucepan with the water. Bring to a boil, cover, and lower the heat so that they just simmer for 10 to 15 minutes until very soft. (Some fruits are drier than others—if the water evaporates before the fruit is soft, add another spoonful or two of water and cook a bit longer.) Add the lemon juice and honey. Cook, stirring almost constantly, for about 5 minutes (it should not get too thick; it will thicken more while cooling). Stir in the nuts and set aside to cool.

When you are ready to bake, adjust two racks to divide the oven into thirds and preheat to 400°. Line cookie sheets with parchment or foil.

Work with half of the pastry at a time; refrigerate the other half. Work quickly or the dough will become sticky. On a floured pastry cloth with a floured rolling pin roll out the dough, turning it over occasionally to keep both sides floured. Roll it to an even ⅛-inch thickness (that is thin but be careful—if you roll the dough too thin it will be hard to handle). With a plain, round 3-inch cookie cutter, cut the dough into rounds. (Reserve the scraps of dough, press them together, and rechill until firm enough to roll.)

Hold one round in your hand. Place a rounded teaspoonful of the filling in the center, mounding it rather high—it will not run out in baking. Fold up two sides of the dough—each side should be a third of the circle—and pinch them together where they meet. Now fold up the third side and pinch together at both sides, form-

12 ounces unsweetened dried
*   pitted prunes (about 2*
*   cups, lightly packed)*
6 ounces unsweetened dried
*   apricots (about 1 cup,*
*   lightly packed)*
1 cup water
1 tablespoon lemon juice
½ cup honey (see Notes)
2½ ounces (¾ cup) walnuts,
*   cut into medium-size pieces*

27 HAMANTASCHEN

ing a triangle and leaving a generous opening at the top. The filling should extend above the top of the pastry. (If the rounds of pastry become soft or sticky before you shape them, transfer them with a wide metal spatula to a tray or cookie sheet and chill briefly in the freezer or refrigerator only until they are firm enough to handle.)

Place the Hamantaschen 1½ to 2 inches apart on the cookie sheets. Bake 12 to 15 minutes, until the cookies are barely colored on the sides, slightly darker on the edges. Reverse the sheets top to bottom and front to back to ensure even browning. If you bake only one sheet at a time bake it high in the oven.

With a wide metal spatula transfer the Hamantaschen to racks to cool, or serve them warm. If anyone is in the kitchen with me when I bake these, very few if any actually have a chance to cool.

NOTES: These are better with a mild clover honey than with a strongly flavored one.

There may be a little filling left over. If so, it makes a wonderful conserve. Serve with crackers, toast, or biscuits, and, if you wish, with butter or cottage cheese. You might like it so much that you decide to make it especially for that purpose. If you do, don't cook it until it gets as dry as for the Hamantaschen. If it becomes too dry from standing, stir in a bit more orange juice, prune juice, or apricot nectar.

Danish Coffeehouse Slices

Delicate orange pastry is wrapped jelly-roll fashion around a raisin-nut filling; the rolls are baked and then sliced. These are more like pastry or coffee cake than typical cookies but they may be served with, or in place of, cookies.

Orange Pastry

Cut a piece of parchment or foil to cover the length of a 14 x 17-inch cookie sheet and place it on the sheet. Or line two smaller sheets with parchment or foil. For one large sheet adjust an oven rack one-third down from the top. For two sheets adjust two racks to divide the oven into thirds. Preheat oven to 350°.

Sift together into a large mixing bowl the flour, baking soda, salt, and sugar. In a small cup mix the orange rind and juice and set aside. Cut the butter into ½-inch slices, then with a pastry blender cut the butter into the dry ingredients until the particles are fine and the mixture resembles coarse meal. In a small bowl, with a fork, stir the egg lightly just to mix. Mix the egg with the orange mixture and stir into the dough until the dry ingredients are completely absorbed.

Turn the dough out onto a floured pastry cloth. Knead the dough lightly until it is smooth, and then with your hands form it into a flattened oblong about 5 x 6 inches. Let the dough stand at room temperature while you prepare the filling.

2 cups unsifted *all-purpose flour*
½ teaspoon baking soda
Pinch of salt
½ cup granulated sugar
Finely grated rind of 1 large, deep-colored orange
¼ cup orange juice
4 ounces (1 stick) unsalted butter, cold and firm
1 egg

30 SLICES

Filling

Stir the preserves to soften them and set aside. Stir together the sugar and cinnamon and set aside. Do not mix the remaining ingredients together.

The dough is delicate—handle it lightly and work quickly. Cut the dough into equal thirds and set aside two pieces; work with one piece at a time. On the floured pastry cloth, turn the piece of dough over and over to flour all sides. With a floured rolling pin roll the dough, turning it over occasionally. Roll it into a 6 x 10-inch oblong. Keep the shape as even as possible but don't worry about trimming the edges.

Use a spoon to spread ¼ cup of the preserves over the dough, leaving a 1-inch border all around. Then sprinkle the preserves with ¼ cup of the currants or raisins and ¼ cup of the walnuts, and then with 4 teaspoons of the sugar-cinnamon mixture.

¾ cup apricot preserves, or any other thick jam, jelly, preserves, or marmalade
3 tablespoons granulated sugar
3 teaspoons cinnamon
3½ ounces (¾ cup) currants or raisins
2½ ounces (¾ cup) walnuts, cut or broken into medium-size pieces
Confectioners sugar for topping

Fold over 1 inch of each short side of the dough and press down on the corners to seal. Then roll the dough jelly-roll fashion, starting at a long side. Now with both hands, quickly and carefully transfer the roll, seam side down, to the cookie sheet. If you are using one large sheet place the rolls across the short way, three on the sheet, leaving 3 inches between the rolls. If you are using two smaller sheets place two rolls lengthwise on one sheet and one on the other. If the rolls are thicker on the ends use your hands to flatten them slightly.

Bake for 30 minutes, reversing the one large sheet front to back, or the two smaller sheets top to bottom and front to back, to ensure even browning. Bake until the rolls are golden brown.

Immediately, using a flat-edge cookie sheet as a spatula, quickly and carefully transfer the rolls to a large cutting board.

Let the rolls stand for about 5 minutes and then while they are still warm cut into diagonal slices ¾ to 1 inch thick. With a wide metal spatula transfer the slices to racks to cool.

Place the slices on the rack over a large piece of wax paper. Sprinkle confectioners sugar through a fine strainer to coat the tops of the slices lightly.

These are best while very fresh. They may be frozen.

NOTE: This is a very fragile pastry and must be handled gently, quickly, and as little as possible. The finished product is worth the extra care it takes. The tops of the rolls might crack and open slightly during baking, but don't worry—if the dough has not been rolled thinner than the directions specify, the cracks will be minor and okay.

Big Newtons

A thick, juicy version of the Fig Newtons you buy at the store.

Pastry

Sift together into a bowl the white flour, baking powder, baking soda, and salt. Add the whole-wheat flour and stir to mix well. Set aside.

In the large bowl of an electric mixer cream the butter. Add the sugar and beat well. Beat in the honey and then the egg. On low speed gradually add the dry ingredients, scraping the bowl with a rubber spatula and beating until completely mixed.

Turn out onto a large piece of wax paper, flatten slightly, and wrap airtight. Refrigerate for several hours or overnight, or freeze for an hour or two, until the dough is firm enough to be rolled.

Meanwhile, prepare the filling. Or the filling may be made days ahead and refrigerated.

1 cup sifted all-purpose white flour
1 teaspoon baking powder
½ teaspoon baking soda
½ teaspoon salt
2 cups unsifted *all-purpose whole-wheat flour*
4 ounces (1 stick) unsalted butter
½ cup light brown sugar, firmly packed
½ cup honey
1 egg

30 LARGE NEWTONS

Filling

Remove the tough stems from the figs. On a large board with a long, heavy chef's knife, chop the figs very fine to make 3 cups of finely chopped figs. Or grind them in a food processor or a meat grinder.

In a large, heavy saucepan mix the figs with the honey, water, lemon juice, and orange juice. Place over moderate heat and cook, stirring almost constantly, for about 10 minutes, until very hot but not boiling. Transfer to a dinner plate or a shallow tray to cool. When cool, refrigerate. The filling must be cold when it is used.

Adjust a rack to the highest position in the oven and preheat to 400°. Line a cookie sheet with parchment or foil.

Work with half of the dough at a time; reserve the other half in the refrigerator. Work on a floured pastry cloth with a floured rolling pin. If the dough is too hard to roll place it on the cloth and pound it with the rolling pin until it softens slightly. Roll the dough into an even oblong 15 inches long, 7 inches wide, and ¼ inch thick. Use a ruler as a guide and trim the edges evenly. If necessary, excess cut-off dough may be used to fill in where needed. Work quickly before the dough becomes sticky.

With two teaspoons, one for picking up and one for pushing off, spoon half of the filling evenly down the middle of the dough, lengthwise, forming a band of filling 1 inch deep and 2 inches wide. Stop it half an inch away from the narrow ends. Smooth it with the back of a spoon but do not flatten it.

Use the pastry cloth to help fold the two long sides of the pastry over the filling. They should overlap each other by ¼ to ½ inch. Press lightly to seal. Use the pastry cloth again to help turn the roll over so that it is now seam side down. Do not worry about any shallow surface cracks.

With both hands, one on each long side of the roll, quickly and carefully transfer the roll to a cookie sheet, placing the roll either lengthwise down the middle, or on an angle from one corner to the opposite corner. With your hands, perfect the shape of the roll so that it is smooth and even. Press down gently on the two narrow open ends to seal the dough.

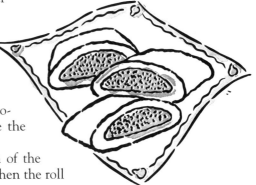

If your cookie sheet is big enough (14 x 17 inches) to fit both rolls, by all means bake them together. Otherwise prepare the second roll while the first is baking.

Bake for 15 minutes, reversing the position of the sheet during baking to ensure even browning. When the roll

1½ pounds dried brown figs (although technically they are "dried," they should be soft and moist; do not use them if they are dry and hard)
¾ cup honey
3 tablespoons water
2 tablespoons lemon juice
2 tablespoons orange juice

is golden brown all over, remove it from the oven and let stand for about 10 minutes, until it is firm enough to be moved. With a long spatula transfer the roll to a rack to finish cooling.

When cool, refrigerate the rolls briefly—the strips are easier to cut when cold.

Use a very sharp knife or a finely serrated one to cut the rolls crossways into 1-inch slices. If necessary, wipe the blade occasionally with a damp cloth.

Hand-Formed Cookies

Kansas Cookies

Margie McGlachlin of Sedgwick, Kansas, won first place in a Kansas State Fair with these very unusual and wonderfully delicious cookies. They are soft, moist, and chewy, and they stay that way. (In a recent poll the results showed that the favorite cookies of most Americans are soft and moist.)

There is a lemon filling similar to lemon cheese (an English spread) mixed with a generous amount of shredded coconut. The cookie dough has molasses and cinnamon; it is all a luscious combination. You will find making these is a bit of a challenge and a lot of fun. The dough and the filling can both be made a day ahead if you wish. This recipe is an adaptation of the original.

Cookie Dough

Sift together the flour, baking soda, salt, and cinnamon, and set aside. In the large bowl of an electric mixer, beat the butter until it is soft. Add the sugar and beat until mixed. Beat in the egg and then the molasses. (The mixture will appear curdled—it is okay.) On low speed, gradually add the sifted dry ingredients and beat, scraping the bowl with a rubber spatula, until the mixture holds together and is smooth. Remove the bowl from the mixer.

Turn the dough out onto a piece of wax paper about 15 inches long. Fold up the long sides of the paper and with your hands form the dough into a fat sausage shape about 12 inches long, and the same thickness all over.

Bring up the sides of the paper to wrap the dough and carefully transfer it to the refrigerator to chill for at least 2 hours or longer. To save time, it may be placed in the freezer for about 15 minutes and then transferred to the refrigerator for an hour. This will be much easier to work with if it is thoroughly chilled (but not frozen); at room temperature it is too soft.

Meanwhile, make the filling.

2¼ cups sifted all-purpose flour
½ teaspoon baking soda
¼ teaspoon salt
1 teaspoon cinnamon
4 ounces (1 stick) unsalted butter
1 cup granulated sugar
1 egg
¼ cup light molasses

40 COOKIES

Lemon Coconut Filling

Place the eggs in the top of a small double boiler off the heat and beat them with a small wire whisk until thoroughly mixed. Gradually beat in the sugar and then the salt, the lemon rind, and lemon juice.

Place over shallow hot water on moderate heat and stir and scrape the sides constantly with a rubber spatula for 7 to 8 minutes, until the mixture thickens to the consistency of soft mayonnaise.

Remove the top of the double boiler and mix in the coconut. Set aside to cool. (The dough must be cold when you use it, but the filling can be cold or at room temperature.)

To shape and bake the cookies: Adjust a rack to the middle of the oven and preheat oven to 350°. Have ready several unbuttered cookie sheets.

Cut the dough crossways into equal quarters.

Lightly flour a large work surface and transfer one piece of the cold dough to the floured surface. Return the remaining pieces of dough to the refrigerator. With your hands elongate the cold dough's sausage shape. Then roll it back and forth under your fingers on the floured surface into a very thin sausage shape, 15 inches long. Roll it toward you a few inches in order to reflour the surface under the dough. Then roll it back onto the floured surface. With your fingers, carefully press down on the dough to flatten it a bit. Or roll over it with a rolling pin until it is 3 inches wide and still 15 inches long. The edges should not be thicker than the rest, but they do not have to be perfectly straight.

You have a generous cupful of the filling. Therefore, you will use a slightly generous ¼ cupful of the filling for each piece of dough. Measure it in a graded ¼-measuring cup.

To make a narrow strip of the filling down the length of the rolled-out dough, use a small spoon and spoon out scant ½ teaspoonfuls just barely touching each other down the middle of the dough. If you use too much filling in any one spot you will not be able to close the sides of the dough over the filling, and you will not have enough to go around. It is not necessary to stay away from the narrow ends; the filling does not run very much.

Now, to raise the long sides of the dough and have them meet over the top of the filling, here are a few hints. First, work quickly before the dough becomes too soft to handle. Second, use either a long, narrow spatula or a wide metal pancake turner to help lift the dough. The aim is to get the two sides to meet on the top and overlap about ½ inch. It is not necessary to wet the dough to make it stick to itself. And it is a waste of time to fuss too much to try to make this very neat, because it runs a bit (just enough to camouflage any irregularities) during baking. Don't worry about little cracks in the dough.

With a ruler, score the strip into 1½-inch lengths. With a sharp knife cut the strip at the scored lines and, using a metal pancake turner, transfer the cookies to an unbuttered cookie sheet, placing them topside up or down, about 1½ inches apart.

Bake one sheet at a time for 15 minutes, reversing the sheets top to bottom and back to front once to ensure even browning. When they are done they will just barely begin to darken and the tops will crack a bit. (Everything's under control.)

Use a wide metal spatula to transfer the cookies to a rack to cool.

Shape and bake the remaining dough and filling.

Store airtight.

2 eggs
½ cup granulated sugar
¼ teaspoon salt
Finely grated rind of 2 lemons
¼ cup lemon juice
3½ ounces (1 cup, packed) shredded coconut (may be sweetened or unsweetened)

Bow Ties

These were made in Poland, Rumania, Hungary, Germany, and many other Middle-European countries. When so many people from those countries emigrated to America and brought their recipes for Bow Ties, they became a standard item at almost all Jewish-American bakeries. They are very popular, but somehow I think that very few people, if any, make them at home. Why? They are as simple as can be, fun to make, quick and easy. They are plain, airy, crisp, and wonderful with tea, coffee, or wine.

This recipe calls for powdered ammonium carbonate, a leavening agent that gives the cookies an especially light and unusual texture. For the last few years it has become more and more difficult to buy. But you can buy it from the House-On-The-Hill in Villa Park, IL, (603) 969-2624. They also sell beautiful cookie molds. Don't be concerned by the ammonia odor, especially during baking; it will not affect the cookies. You will need parchment paper.

Coarsely crush the anise seeds with a mortar and pestle, or whirl them for just a few seconds in a blender (a processor does not do anything to them). Set aside.

Sift together the flour, salt, ammonium carbonate, and the 2 tablespoons of sugar, and set aside.

Open 4 of the eggs into a 1-cup glass measuring cup. Separate the remaining egg, add the yolk to the measuring cup, and add a bit of the white if necessary for the eggs to reach the 1-cup line. (You will not need the remaining egg white for this recipe.)

Place the eggs in the small bowl of an electric mixer, beat to mix, add the oil and vanilla and almond extracts, and beat again to mix.

Gradually, on low speed, mix in about half of the sifted dry ingredients. Beat at high speed for about 5 minutes; the mixture will crawl up on the beaters—adjust the speed as necessary. Then stir in the remaining dry ingredients—the mixture will be thick, sticky, and gooey.

Spread a generous layer of additional flour on a rather large piece of aluminum foil, turn the dough out onto the flour, sift a bit of flour lightly over the top, and let stand, uncovered, for 30 minutes.

Meanwhile, adjust two racks to divide the oven into thirds and preheat oven to 350°. Line two large cookie sheets with parchment paper and set aside.

Now spread a thick layer of the additional granulated sugar on a large board or on a pastry cloth. The dough will still be sticky; pick it up with your fingers (with only the flour that clings to it—no more) and transfer it to the sugared surface. Sprinkle sugar over the top of the dough too.

1 teaspoon whole anise seeds
2½ cups sifted all-purpose flour
½ teaspoon salt
1 teaspoon powdered ammonium carbonate
2 tablespoons granulated sugar
5 eggs
½ cup vegetable oil
½ teaspoon vanilla extract
¼ teaspoon almond extract
Additional flour
Additional granulated sugar

34 LARGE COOKIES

With a rolling pin, roll out the dough, into an oblong about 12 x 6 inches, ½ inch thick, sugaring it more as necessary.

With a long, sharp knife cut the dough into strips 6 inches long and ¾ inch wide. If the knife sticks to the dough, turn the blade in the sugar to coat it. Next, cut the strips into 3-inch lengths, cutting them a few at a time with one cut.

Pick up a strip by its ends and twist the ends once in opposite directions, then place the cookies about 1 inch apart on the prepared cookie sheets. Continue to cut and shape all of the cookies.

Bake for 25 to 30 minutes, reversing the sheets top to bottom and front to back as necessary to ensure even browning. Bake only until the cookies are a pale golden color.

With a wide metal spatula transfer the cookies to a rack to cool.

Store airtight.

Fudge Mallows

Semisoft chocolate cookies with a pecan hidden underneath, a marshmallow on top, and then a thick chocolate icing.

Adjust two racks to divide the oven into thirds and preheat to 350°. Line cookie sheets with parchment or foil. Sift together the flour, baking soda, salt, and cocoa, and set aside. In the large bowl of an electric mixer, cream the butter. Add the vanilla and the sugar and beat to mix well. Add the eggs one at a time and beat until smooth. On low speed, gradually add the sifted dry ingredients, scraping the bowl with a rubber spatula and beating only until thoroughly mixed.

Place a large piece of wax paper on the work surface. Use a heaping teaspoonful of dough for each cookie—place them on the wax paper, making about 28 mounds.

Wet your hands under cold running water and shake off excess water—your hands should be damp but not too wet. Pick up a mound of dough and roll it between your hands into a round ball. Press a pecan half into the ball of dough, placing the curved side (top) of the nut into the dough. Do not enclose it completely.

1¾ cups sifted all-purpose flour
1 teaspoon baking soda
¼ teaspoon salt
½ cup unsweetened cocoa powder (preferably Dutch-process), strained or sifted
4 ounces (1 stick) unsalted butter
1 teaspoon vanilla extract
1 cup granulated sugar
2 eggs
28 large pecan halves (see Notes)
14 large marshmallows (see Notes)

28 COOKIES

Place the cookie on the sheet so that the flat side of the pecan is on the bottom of the cookie. Continue to wet your hands as necessary while you shape the remaining cookies, placing them 2 inches apart on the sheets.

Bake 16 to 18 minutes, reversing sheets top to bottom and front to back once to ensure even baking. Bake until cookies are barely done—not quite firm to the touch. Do not overbake.

While cookies are baking, cut the marshmallows in half crosswise. (Easier done with scissors.)

Remove the cookie sheets from the oven. Quickly place a marshmallow half, cut side down, on each cookie. Return to the oven for 1 to 1½ minutes. Watch the clock! If the marshmallows bake any longer they will melt and run off the sides of the cookies—they should not melt and they should stay on top. These should not actually melt at all—only soften very slightly—and not get soft enough to change shape.

Let the cookies stand for a few seconds until they are firm enough to be moved and then, with a wide metal spatula, transfer to racks to cool.

Prepare the following icing.

Chocolate Icing

Place the cocoa, salt, and sugar in the small bowl of an electric mixer. Melt the butter and pour the hot butter and 3 tablespoons of boiling water into the bowl. Beat until completely smooth. The icing should be a thick, semifluid mixture. It should not be so thin that it will run off the cookies. It might be necessary to add a little more hot water, but add it very gradually—only a few drops at a time. (If the sugar has not been strained or sifted before measuring, you might need as much as 2 or 3 additional teaspoons of water.) If you add too much water and the icing becomes too thin, thicken it with additional sugar. If the icing thickens too much while you are icing the cookies, thin it carefully with a few drops of water. Transfer the icing to a small bowl for ease in handling.

½ cup unsweetened cocoa powder (preferably Dutch-process)
Pinch of salt
1½ cups confectioners sugar
2⅔ ounces (5⅓ tablespoons) unsalted butter
About 3 tablespoons boiling water

Lift a cookie and hold it while you partially frost it with a generous teaspoonful of the icing. Allow some of the marshmallow to show through—preferably one side of the marshmallow—the contrast of black and white is what you want. Also, don't try to cover the entire top of the cookie itself or you will not have enough for all the cookies. Replace cookie on rack. Ice all the cookies and then let them stand for a few hours to set.

NOTES: If you do not have large pecan halves you may use several small pieces—just put them on the bottom of the cookies any which way.

If you use your own homemade marshmallows (page 293) they will be smaller than the regular-size commercial ones. Don't cut them in half; use them whole.

Chocolate Pepper Pretzels

Pretzel superstitions go back to the time of the Romans. People wore pretzels made of flour and water around their necks to ward off evil sprits. They hung them on fruit trees in the belief that the pretzels would cause the trees to have a prolific yield. And they believed that if you broke a pretzel with someone else (like breaking a wishbone) and if you made a wish at the same time, your wish would come true. (Imagine all that and chocolate too.)

All of these reasons have made it a popular custom to hang pretzels on Christmas trees. And also, it is so easy to thread a ribbon through a pretzel. These particular pretzel cookies are best when they are not too fresh—another reason to make them for the Christmas tree.

But Christmas aside, these are delicious and adorable. But they aren't as sweet as cookies usually are. They are peppery, but not sharp or harsh. The wonderful dough handles like ceramicist's clay and is just as much fun, if not more, because you get to eat these. A lovely and unusual way to serve these is with wine.

P lace the cocoa and coffee in a small bowl; add the water and stir to dissolve. Set aside to cool slightly. In the large bowl of an electric mixer, cream the butter. Add the vanilla, salt, allspice, ginger, pepper, and the sugar, and beat to mix well. Beat in the egg, then the chocolate mixture, and then, on low speed, gradually add the flour and beat until smooth.

Turn the mixture out onto a large board or work surface and shape it into a thick cylinder 6 inches long. Wrap it in plastic wrap and refrigerate for at least half an hour or for as long as a few days.

Before baking, adjust two racks to divide the oven into thirds and preheat oven to 350°. Line cookie sheets with parchment.

With a sharp and heavy knife, cut the dough into six 1-inch slices. Then cut each slice into equal quarters, making 24 pieces. (You can cut the six slices but do not separate them; then quarter the whole cylinder.)

To shape pretzels: Roll a piece of the dough on a board or work surface (do not flour the work surface) under the fingers of both hands. Spread your fingers slightly, move them back and forth and gradually out toward the ends of the roll. Each time you do this the roll will increase in length and become thinner. Continue until you have shaped a thin snake 10 inches long.

Form it into a pretzel shape (see illustration) and place the pretzels on a cookie sheet.

¼ cup unsweetened cocoa powder (preferably Dutch-process)
1 teaspoon instant coffee
3 tablespoons boiling water
4 ounces (1 stick) unsalted butter
1 teaspoon vanilla extract
½ teaspoon salt
⅛ teaspoon allspice
¼ teaspoon powdered ginger
1 teaspoon finely ground black pepper
¼ cup granulated sugar
1 egg
2 cups unsifted all-purpose flour

24 PRETZEL COOKIES

Glaze and Topping

Beat the yolk and water lightly just to mix, strain the mixture, and with a small, soft brush (I use an artist's watercolor brush), brush the glaze over about four pretzels at a time. Be careful not to allow the glaze to run down on the sheet or the cookies will stick. (If just a very little runs down it is okay.)

1 egg yolk
1 teaspoon water
Crystal sugar (see page 5)
  or granulated sugar

Using your thumb and forefinger, carefully and slowly sprinkle the crystal or granulated sugar generously over the pretzels.

Bake for about 25 minutes, reversing the sheets top to bottom and front to back once during baking to ensure even baking. Bake until the cookies are thoroughly dry. Do not underbake. If you are not sure, break one to see.

With a wide metal spatula transfer the cookies to racks to cool.

Store airtight. Let stand for at least a day or two before serving.

Chocolate Aggies

These are dense, chocolatey, rather thick, and semisoft. They are mixed in a saucepan, and are rolled in confectioners sugar before baking.

S ift together the flour, baking powder, and salt, and set aside. In a heavy 3-quart saucepan over low heat melt the butter and the chocolate. Stir occasionally until smooth and then remove from the heat. With a heavy wooden spoon stir the granulated sugar into the warm chocolate mixture. Then stir in the eggs one at a time. Add the sifted dry ingredients and stir until smooth. Stir in the nuts.

It will be a soft dough and it must be refrigerated. It may be left in the saucepan or transferred to a bowl. Either way, cover and refrigerate, preferably for 1½ hours (but the dough may be refrigerated longer or overnight if you wish).

Adjust two racks to divide the oven into thirds and preheat to 300°. Line cookie sheets with parchment or foil.

Press the confectioners sugar through a strainer and spread it out on a large piece of wax paper. Sugar the palms of your hands with some of the confectioners sugar. Roll the dough into 1- to 1¼-inch balls, using a heaping teaspoonful of dough for each cookie. Roll the balls around in the confectioners sugar and place them 2 inches apart on the cookie sheets. (If the dough was refrigerated overnight and if the cookies are not baked immediately after being shaped, the confectioners sugar will become wet. If this happens, the cookies should be rolled around in the sugar again and then rolled between your hands again—the cookies will be more attractive if the confectioners sugar coats them heavily.)

Bake the cookies for 20 to 22 minutes, until the tops of the cookies are barely semifirm to the touch. Reverse the position of the sheets top to bottom and front to back once during baking to ensure even baking. Do not overbake—these should be slightly soft in the centers. (If you bake only one sheet at a time bake it high in the oven.)

With a wide metal spatula transfer the cookies to racks to cool.

2 cups sifted all-purpose flour
2 teaspoons baking powder
¼ teaspoon salt
2 ounces (4 tablespoons) unsalted butter
4 ounces (4 squares) unsweetened chocolate
2 cups granulated sugar
4 extra-large or jumbo eggs
2 ounces (generous ½ cup) walnuts, cut medium fine (see page 11)
About 1 cup confectioners sugar; you might need a bit more (to be used when cookies are shaped)

40 TO 45 COOKIES

Chocolate Oatmeal Crispies

These are large, flat cookies that are crisp-crunchy and have a dry, meringue-like texture.

Adjust two racks to divide the oven into thirds and preheat to 350°. Line cookie sheets with parchment or foil.

Melt the chocolate in the top of a small double boiler over hot water on moderate heat. Set aside to cool for a few minutes.

Meanwhile, sift together the flour, baking soda, and salt, and set aside. In the small bowl of an electric mixer cream the butter. Add the vanilla and the almond extracts and the sugar, and beat until blended. Beat in the egg and the melted chocolate. On low speed gradually add the sifted dry ingredients, scraping the bowl with a rubber spatula and beating only until incorporated. Mix in the oatmeal and the coconut.

To divide the dough evenly: On a long piece of wax paper or aluminum foil place the dough by rounded tablespoonfuls in 28 to 30 equal mounds. Roll each mound between your hands to form a ball and place the balls on the cookie sheets at least 2 to 2½ inches apart, no closer.

Press the tops of the cookies with the back of the tines of a fork to flatten them to ½-inch thickness. First press all in one direction and then in the opposite direction.

Bake for about 15 minutes, reversing the sheets top to bottom and front to back once to ensure even browning. When done, the cookies will feel crusty on the tops but semisoft in the centers—they will harden as they cool.

With a wide metal spatula transfer the cookies to racks to cool.

6 ounces semisweet chocolate cut into pieces
1 cup sifted all-purpose flour
½ teaspoon baking soda
¼ teaspoon salt
4 ounces (1 stick) unsalted butter
1 teaspoon vanilla extract
½ teaspoon almond extract
1 cup granulated sugar
1 egg
1 cup old-fashioned or quick-cooking (not instant) oatmeal
3½ ounces (1 cup, firmly packed) shredded coconut

28 TO 30 COOKIES

Chocolate and Peanut-Butter Crescents

These are small, candylike cookies that take time and patience. They have a crisp chocolate dough wrapped around a peanut-butter filling and are formed into crescent shapes.

Cookie Dough

Sift together the flour, cocoa, and salt, and set aside. In the large bowl of an electric mixer cream the butter. Beat in the vanilla and sugar. Add the egg and beat until thoroughly mixed. On low speed gradually add the sifted dry ingredients, scraping the bowl with a rubber spatula and beating until thoroughly mixed. Transfer the dough to a small bowl for ease in handling and set aside at room temperature. Prepare the following filling.

2 cups sifted all-purpose flour
⅓ cup unsweetened cocoa powder (preferably Dutch-process)
¼ teaspoon salt
4 ounces (1 stick) unsalted butter
1 teaspoon vanilla extract
¾ cup granulated sugar
1 egg

66 COOKIES

Filling

In a small bowl thoroughly mix the peanut butter and the sugar.

Adjust a rack to the center of the oven and preheat to 325°. Line cookie sheets with parchment or foil.

To shape the cookies: On a large piece of wax paper or aluminum foil place the cookie dough in mounds, using a slightly rounded teaspoonful (no more) of the dough for each mound—in order not to make them too large it is best to measure with a measuring spoon. Instead of doing all at once you may prefer to measure only a fourth or a half of the dough at one time.

Then do the same with the filling, using a level ½ measuring teaspoon for each mound. Roll them between your hands into small balls. Place these on other pieces of wax paper or foil.

Pick up one mound of the dough, roll it between your hands into a ball, and flatten it between your palms until it is very thin. Then place one ball of the filling in the center of the flattened dough. With your fingers bring the dough around the filling and pinch the edges to seal. Roll the filled dough between your hands into a

¾ cup smooth (not chunky) peanut butter
½ cup strained or sifted confectioners sugar

cylindrical shape about 2 inches long with very slightly tapered ends. Place the cookie on a cookie sheet and as you do, turn the ends down slightly to form a short, fat crescent.

Continue shaping the cookies and placing them ½ to 1 inch apart—these do not spread.

Bake for 13 to 15 minutes, or until the cookies are firm to the touch. Reverse the cookie sheet front to back once to ensure even baking.

OPTIONAL TOPPING: Confectioners sugar or vanilla sugar (see Note). While the cookies are baking spread out a large piece of wax paper or aluminum foil and sift or strain 1 to 2 cups of the sugar onto the paper or foil, forming a mound of sugar.

As soon as the cookies are done, immediately transfer them with a wide metal spatula to the mound of sugar and roll the cookies around to coat them thoroughly with the sugar.

Then place the cookies on another piece of paper or foil to cool. When the cookies are cool, roll them again in the sugar.

NOTE: How to make vanilla sugar: This must be prepared ahead but can be kept for a long time (and can be used for topping all kinds of cakes and cookies). You will need a whole vanilla bean (available in specialty food stores). Place the bean on a board and with a sharp knife split it the long way. Fill a 1-quart jar that has a tight cover with confectioners sugar and bury the bean in the sugar. Cover tightly and let stand for at least several days or a week before using—the sugar will have absorbed the flavor of the bean. Sift or strain the sugar immediately before using, as it will absorb some moisture from the bean and become lumpy—it will have to be strained again even if it was done beforehand. As the sugar is used it may be replaced. If you replace the sugar often, the bean itself should be replaced after a month or two.

Señoritas

These are crisp, crunchy, and chewy with toasted chopped almonds and a butterscotch flavor.

Adjust two racks to divide the oven into thirds and preheat to 400°. Line cookie sheets with parchment or foil. Place the almonds in a small, shallow pan and toast them in the preheated oven, shaking the pan frequently, for about 8 minutes until they are golden brown. Set aside to cool.

Sift together the flour, baking soda, cream of tartar, and salt, and set aside. In the large bowl of an electric mixer cream the butter. Add the vanilla and almond extracts, and then gradually add both sugars and beat well. Add the eggs and beat well. On low speed gradually add the sifted dry ingredients, scraping the bowl with a rubber spatula and beating only until thoroughly mixed. With a wooden spoon stir in the cooled toasted almonds.

Place a large piece of wax paper in front of you. Use a heaping teaspoonful of the dough for each cookie, placing the mounds on the wax paper and forming 48 mounds.

Roll the mounds of dough between your hands, forming them into balls and placing them at least 2 inches apart (no closer) on the cookie sheets.

It is very important to time the baking of these cookies exactly. Bake for 10 minutes (no longer), reversing the position of the sheets top to bottom and front to back once to ensure even baking. When the 10 minutes are up the cookies will still feel soft, but they will harden as they cool and if they are baked any longer they will become too hard—they should remain slightly soft and chewy in the centers.

With a wide metal spatula transfer the cookies to racks to cool.

5 ounces (1 cup) blanched almonds, coarsely chopped or diced (they must not be fine)
3 cups sifted all-purpose flour
1 teaspoon baking soda
½ teaspoon cream of tartar
½ teaspoon salt
6 ounces (1½ sticks) unsalted butter
½ teaspoon vanilla extract
Scant ½ teaspoon almond extract
1 cup granulated sugar
1 cup dark brown sugar, firmly packed
2 eggs

48 COOKIES

Carrot and Honey Oatmeal Cookies

These are large, thick, chewy, satisfying, not-very-sweet health-food cookies. They taste as though they are related to bran muffins, although they have no bran. They keep wonderfully. They may be mailed. A few of these and a glass of milk make a delicious quick meal; they are marvelous for a lunch box or a picnic.

Adjust two racks to divide the oven into thirds and preheat oven to 325°. Line cookie sheets with parchment or foil shiny side up. Wash the carrots (it is not necessary to peel them) and grate them on the coarse side of a four-sided grater (they should not be finer than that), or they may be shredded with the coarse shredder blade of a food processor. You should have 2 generous cups, firmly packed. Set aside.

Pour enough boiling water over the raisins to cover them. Let stand for 2 to 3 minutes, then pour through a strainer to drain, and let stand.

Sift together both of the flours, the baking powder, baking soda, salt, and cinnamon, and set aside.

In the large bowl of a mixer, beat the butter until soft and smooth. Add the honey and sugar and beat until smooth. Add the eggs and beat well until smooth.

Remove from the mixer. With a large wooden spoon, stir in the dry ingredients in the following order: carrots, oatmeal, nuts, and raisins.

To shape the cookies, work near the sink or have a bowl of water near you so you will be able to wet your hands easily as necessary. Spread out a long piece of aluminum foil. Use a heaping tablespoonful of the dough for each cookie (make these large). Place them in mounds any which way on the foil. Wet your hands with cold water, shake the water off, but do not dry your hands. Lift up one of the mounds (if necessary use a metal spatula to lift with) and between your wet hands roll the dough into a ball, flatten it to a generous ½-inch thickness, and place it on a lined sheet. Continue to shape the cookies and place them about 1 inch apart (these spread barely, if at all).

Bake two sheets at a time, reversing the sheets top to bottom and front to back once during baking to ensure even baking. Bake for 25 to 30 minutes until the cookies are lightly colored.

With a wide metal spatula transfer the cookies to racks to cool.

Store airtight in a freezer box with wax paper between the layers. Or, better yet, wrap the cookies individually in clear cellophane or in wax paper or aluminum foil.

NOTE: For these cookies I use Shiloh Farms rolled oats (from Sulphur Springs, Arkansas). I buy them in health-food stores.

6 medium-size carrots (about 1½ pounds)
5 ounces (1 cup) raisins
Boiling water
1 cup sifted all-purpose white flour
1 cup sifted all-purpose whole-wheat flour
2 teaspoons baking powder
½ teaspoon baking soda
½ teaspoon salt
1 tablespoon cinnamon
4 ounces (1 stick) unsalted butter
1 cup honey
½ cup light brown sugar
2 eggs
2 cups quick-cooking (not instant) rolled oats (see Note)
8 ounces (generous 2 cups) walnuts, cut or broken into medium-size or large pieces

36 VERY LARGE COOKIES

Whole-Wheat Cinnamon-Nutmeg Cookies

These delicious, plain, old-fashioned cookies are easy and fun to make. They keep well, they travel well; make them to keep in a cookie jar, or make them for a tea or coffee party. A gentleman friend always has a jar of these on his huge, shiny desk in his sleek, modern, impressive, mirror-and-chrome office—his young daughter makes them for him and he could not be more proud.

Adjust two racks to divide the oven into thirds and preheat oven to 375°. Line two cookie sheets with parchment or foil shiny side up. Through a large strainer set over a bowl, strain the flour (see Note), baking powder, salt, baking soda, cinnamon, and nutmeg, and set aside.

In the large bowl of an electric mixer, cream the butter. Add the vanilla and then the sugar and beat to mix. Then beat in the egg, milk, and lemon rind. On low speed gradually add the strained dry ingredients and beat only until mixed.

Lightly flour a large board or work surface. Turn the dough out, knead it slightly, form it into a ball, and cut it in half. Work with one-half at a time. On the lightly floured surface roll it into a long and thin roll, 18 inches long and 1 inch in diameter. Cut it into 18 1-inch lengths. Repeat with the other half.

Pick up a piece of dough, roll it between your hands into a ball, flatten it slightly between your hands, and place it on a lined sheet. Repeat with the remaining pieces of dough, placing them about 1½ inches apart.

Press the cookies with the back of the tines of a fork, forming ridges in one direction only and flattening the cookies slightly.

2 cups unsifted *all-purpose whole-wheat flour*
1 teaspoon baking powder
Scant ½ teaspoon salt
1 teaspoon baking soda
1 teaspoon cinnamon
½ teaspoon nutmeg
4 ounces (1 stick) unsalted butter
1 teaspoon vanilla extract
1 cup dark or light brown sugar, firmly packed
1 egg
2 tablespoons milk
Finely grated rind of 1 large lemon

36 COOKIES

Topping

In a small cup, mix together the sugar and cinnamon. With a spoon, sprinkle the mixture generously over the tops of the cookies.

Bake for 10 to 12 minutes, reversing the sheets top to bottom and front to back once during baking to ensure even browning. Bake only until the cookies are lightly colored and feel semifirm when gently pressed with a fingertip. Do not overbake.

With a wide metal spatula transfer the cookies to a rack to cool.

If you bake only one sheet at a time, bake it on the higher rack, and it will take a bit less time than when there are two sheets in the oven at once.

NOTE: Some of the whole-wheat flour will be too coarse to go through the strainer; it should be stirred into the part that did go through.

French Filbert Macaroons

These are traditional Christmas holiday cookies in France. They are made extra soft and chewy with chopped cherries and a bit of jam. You will not need an electric mixer.

Adjust a rack to the center of the oven and preheat to 325°. Line cookie sheets with parchment. Grind the nuts to a fine powder in a nut grinder, a blender, or a food processor. (See To Grind Nuts in a Food Processor, page 11.) Place them in a bowl with the sugar and salt and stir to mix thoroughly. Add the jam or preserves and the egg whites. Stir, and then in order to mix the dough thoroughly, squeeze it between your hands until it is smooth. The mixture should be slightly moist but not wet—if it is crumbly and too dry to hold together easily, add a few drops of additional egg white as necessary. Then add the cherries and work the dough again with your hands until they are evenly distributed.

Spread out a large piece of wax paper. Use a slightly rounded measuring tablespoonful of dough for each cookie, making 24 mounds of dough, and placing them on the wax paper.

If necessary, powder your hands lightly with confec-

1 tablespoon granulated sugar
½ teaspoon cinnamon

8 ounces (1⅔ cups) blanched or unblanched filberts (hazelnuts) (see Notes)
1 cup granulated sugar
Pinch of salt
1 tablespoon smooth jam or preserves (see Notes)
About ¼ cup egg whites (1½ to 2 eggs, depending on size)
12 glacéed cherries, finely chopped
Confectioners sugar (for powdering your hands and sprinkling over the baked cookies)

24 MACAROONS

tioners sugar and roll each mound of dough into a smooth, round ball. Place them 1 inch apart on the cookie sheets.

Bake for 20 minutes, reversing the position of the sheets top to bottom and front to back once to ensure even baking. Do not overbake—these should remain chewy-soft in the centers.

Let the macaroons stand for 5 to 10 minutes. Then, with a wide metal spatula, carefully transfer them to a rack to finish cooling.

When cool, place the rack over wax paper. Sprinkle the tops generously with confectioners sugar, pressing the sugar with your fingers through a strainer held over the macaroons.

NOTES: Using unblanched nuts (nuts from which the skins have not been removed) will only affect the color, not the taste.

Any jam or preserves may be used (I like black raspberry) but it must be smooth. If it is chunky, strain it.

If the macaroons have baked too long and are hard or dry instead of moist and chewy, place them (before sugaring the tops) in an airtight container with a slice of bread, a lemon, an orange, or half an apple (placed cut side up on top of the macaroons). Let stand for a day or two until they soften and then remove the bread or fruit.

Danish Butter Sandwiches

These are crisp, brown-sugar butter cookies sandwiched together with a browned-butter filling.

Adjust two racks to divide the oven into thirds and preheat to 325°. Line cookie sheets with parchment or foil. In the large mixing bowl of an electric mixer cream the butter. Add the sugar and beat to mix. Add the egg yolk and beat to mix. On low speed gradually add the flour, scraping the bowl with a rubber spatula and beating until the mixture holds together.

8 ounces (2 sticks) unsalted butter
¾ cup light brown sugar, firmly packed
1 egg yolk
2¼ cups sifted all-purpose flour

24 SANDWICH COOKIES

Place a long piece of wax paper in front of you. Use a slightly rounded teaspoonful of the dough for each cookie, and place the mounds of dough on the wax paper, making 48 mounds.

Roll the mounds between your hands into round balls, and place them 1½ to 2 inches apart on cookie sheets.

With the heel of your hand, or with your fingertips, flatten each mound into a round cookie about ¼ inch thick.

Have a little extra flour in a cup or on a piece of wax paper. Dip a fork into the flour and then press the back of the tines firmly onto the top of a cookie, forming deep indentations, in one direction only. Reflour the fork each time you use it, and make the indentations on all of the cookies.

Bake for 15 to 20 minutes (depending on the thickness of the cookies), reversing the cookie sheets top to bottom and front to back once to ensure even baking. Do not allow the cookies to brown—when done they should be a pale golden color.

With a wide metal spatula transfer the cookies to racks to cool.

Since these cookies are shaped by hand, they will not all be exactly the same size. They should be matched into even pairs before they are filled.

After matching them, place each pair, open, flat side up, on a long piece of wax paper. Prepare the following filling.

Browned-Butter Filling

Melt the butter in a small saucepan over moderate heat. Bring it to a boil and let boil until it browns slightly, shaking the pan gently during the last part of heating to prevent the sediment from burning. Remove from the heat when the butter has a rich golden color, and immediately add the sugar, vanilla, and 5 teaspoons of the cream.

Stir until completely smooth. If necessary, add another teaspoon or so of the cream to make a thick filling.

Transfer the filling to a small custard cup or bowl for
ease in handling.

Place a scant teaspoonful of the filling in the center of a
cookie. Repeat with 4 or 5 cookies. Cover each cookie with its
matching cookie and, as you do so, press the cookies gently together to spread the filling just to the edges of the sandwich. It
is best to hold the cookies in your hands while you do this, and
turn the cookies around so that you can see just where the filling is going.

Repeat, filling the remaining cookies, doing about 4 or 5 at a time. While working with the filling you will find it will thicken and will need to have a few drops of
additional cream stirred in. Add only a few drops at a time in order not to make the
filling too thin.

Let the sandwiches stand for a few hours for the filling to set.

NOTE: Without the filling these are delicious plain butter cookies.

2 tablespoons unsalted butter
*1¼ cups strained or sifted
    confectioners sugar*
½ teaspoon vanilla extract
*About 5 to 6 teaspoons heavy
    cream*

Coconut Washboards

*Years ago when we lived on a dairy farm in Brookfield Center, Connecticut, the local
general store sold these by the pound from a large wooden barrel. They are extra-large,
plain, semisoft, and nostalgic. The dough must be well chilled before the cookies are baked.*

Sift together the flour, baking powder, baking soda, and salt, and set aside. In
the large bowl of an electric mixer cream the butter. Beat in the
vanilla. Add the brown sugar and beat to mix. Add the egg
and the water and beat to mix well (the mixture will appear
curdled—it's okay). On low speed gradually add the sifted dry
ingredients, scraping the bowl with a rubber spatula and beating
only until incorporated. Stir in the coconut.

Cut a piece of wax paper to fit a cookie sheet. Use a heaping
teaspoonful of the dough for each cookie (remember these are
large). Place them close to each other on the wax paper, forming 24
mounds.

Slide a cookie sheet under the wax paper and transfer the mounds of dough to the freezer or refrigerator to chill until they are firm enough to be handled. (If they are in the freezer, watch them carefully—they should not be frozen solid.)

In the meantime, adjust two racks to divide the oven into thirds and preheat to 375°. Line cookie sheets with parchment or foil. Have some flour handy for flouring your hands, and a fork.

Flour your hands. Pick up a mound of the dough and roll it between your palms into a sausage shape about 3 inches long. Place it on a cookie sheet. Continue shaping the remaining mounds and placing them 3 inches apart (no closer).

Flour the fingertips of one hand and, with your fingertips, flatten each sausage-shaped roll of dough until it is only ¼ inch thick, 3½ inches long, and 2 inches wide.

Now, to form the traditional ridges that give these cookies their name, dip a fork into the flour and press the back of the tines onto the cookies, forming deep indentations. Since the cookies are so large, it will be necessary to press the fork onto each cookie four times, once for each quarter of the cookie surface. The ridges should be parallel and should go lengthwise with the shape of the cookie.

Bake the cookies for about 12 minutes, reversing the sheets top to bottom and front to back once to ensure even browning. Bake until the cookies are golden brown all over—do not underbake. If you bake only one sheet at a time, use the higher rack.

Let the cookies stand for a few seconds and then, with a wide metal spatula, transfer them to racks to cool.

2 cups sifted all-purpose flour
¾ teaspoon baking powder
¼ teaspoon baking soda
⅛ teaspoon salt
4 ounces (1 stick) unsalted butter
½ teaspoon vanilla extract
1 cup light brown sugar, firmly packed
1 egg
2 tablespoons water
3½ ounces (1 cup, firmly packed) shredded coconut

24 EXTRA-LARGE COOKIES

Coconut Pennies

These are smaller, richer, crisper, and fancier than the previous Coconut Washboards. This dough too must be well chilled before shaping.

S ift together the flour, baking powder, salt, cinnamon, and nutmeg, and set aside. In the large bowl of an electric mixer, cream the butter. Add the vanilla and almond extracts and the sugar and beat to mix well. Beat in the egg. On low speed, gradually add the sifted dry ingredients, scraping the bowl with a rubber spatula and beating only until incorporated. Mix in the coconut.

Place the dough on a large piece of wax paper or aluminum foil, wrap, flatten slightly, and refrigerate for about 1½ to 2 hours. Do not use the freezer—the dough would become too firm to handle.

Adjust two racks to divide the oven into thirds and preheat to 375°. Line cookie sheets with parchment or foil.

Cut the dough into quarters. Work with one piece at a time. On a floured board, with floured hands, form the dough into a roll 15 inches long. Cut the roll into 1-inch pieces. (Or use a slightly rounded tablespoonful of the dough for each cookie.) Keeping your hands lightly floured, roll each piece into a ball.

Place the balls 2 inches apart on the sheets. With the back of the tines of the floured fork, press each cookie in one direction only to form indentations and flatten the cookie to ⅓-inch thickness.

Bake about 10 minutes, until cookies are lightly colored. Reverse sheets top to bottom and front to back as necessary to ensure even browning. The cookies will be slightly darker at the edges.

With a wide metal spatula transfer the cookies to racks to cool.

2 cups sifted all-purpose flour
¾ teaspoon baking powder
⅛ teaspoon salt
¼ teaspoon cinnamon
¼ teaspoon nutmeg
8 ounces (2 sticks) unsalted butter
1 teaspoon vanilla extract
½ teaspoon almond extract
1 cup dark brown sugar, firmly packed
1 egg
7 ounces (2 cups, packed) shredded coconut

60 COOKIES

Cracker-Barrel Raisin Cookies

These semisoft and chewy old-fashioned cookies are especially good for the cookie jar, for the lunch box, or for mailing.

Sift together the flour, baking soda, salt, and nutmeg, and set aside. Pour boiling water over the raisins to cover and let stand for about 10 minutes. Drain the raisins in a strainer or a colander and then spread them out on several thicknesses of paper towels. (The raisins do not have to be absolutely dry; they add moisture to the cookies.)

In the large bowl of an electric mixer cream the butter. Beat in the vanilla and both sugars. Add the egg and beat well. On low speed mix in half of the sifted dry ingredients, then all of the sour cream, and finally the remaining dry ingredients, scraping the bowl with a rubber spatula and beating only until thoroughly mixed. Remove the bowl from the mixer.

With a heavy wooden spoon stir in the lemon rind and then the raisins.

Now the dough has to be chilled before you roll it into balls (see Note). Spread out three or four large pieces of wax paper, divide the dough—an equal part on each piece of the paper—wrap, and chill in the freezer or the refrigerator until firm enough to handle.

Adjust two racks to divide the oven into thirds and preheat to 375°. Line cookie sheets with parchment or foil.

Work with one portion of the dough at a time, keeping the remainder chilled. Use a well-rounded teaspoonful of dough for each cookie. Flour your hands as necessary to keep the dough from sticking. Roll the dough between your hands into balls and place them 2 to 2½ inches apart on the cookie sheets.

With the back of the tines of a floured fork (reflour the fork as necessary) press the cookies first in one direction and then in the opposite direction to flatten them to ¼- to ½-inch thickness.

Bake the cookies for about 15 minutes, until the cookies are golden brown all over. Reverse the sheets top to bottom and front to back as necessary to ensure even browning.

With a wide metal spatula, transfer the cookies to racks to cool.

4 cups sifted all-purpose flour
1 teaspoon baking soda
1 teaspoon salt
½ teaspoon nutmeg
15 ounces (3 cups) raisins
Boiling water
8 ounces (2 sticks) unsalted butter
1½ teaspoons vanilla extract
¾ cup granulated sugar
¾ cup light brown sugar, firmly packed
1 egg
⅔ cup sour cream
Finely grated rind of 1 large or 2 small lemons

72 COOKIES

NOTE: An easier, time-saving way of shaping these cookies without having to chill the dough is to treat them as drop cookies. The shapes will not be quite as even but since these are very homey, old-fashioned cookies, you might prefer this method.

Adjust the racks, preheat oven, and line the cookie sheets before mixing the dough. After stirring the raisins into the dough, transfer it to a small bowl for ease in handling. Place the dough by well-rounded teaspoonfuls 2 to 2½ inches apart on the sheets. Flatten the cookies as above with a flour fork. Bake, etc., as above.

Austrian Walnut Crescents

These classic Viennese cookies are delicate, fragile, and elegant.

Adjust two racks to divide the oven into thirds and preheat to 325°. Line cookie sheets with parchment or foil. The walnuts must be ground very fine—this may be done in a nut grinder or a food processor. (See To Grind Nuts in a Food Processor, page 11.) Set the ground nuts aside.

In the large bowl of an electric mixer cream the butter. Beat in the vanilla and then the ground nuts and mix well. Add the granulated sugar and beat well. On low speed gradually add the flour, scraping the bowl with a rubber spatula and beating until thoroughly mixed.

Place a large piece of wax paper in front of you. Use a rounded teaspoonful of the dough for each cookie, placing the mounds on the wax paper and forming 56 mounds.

Pick up one mound of dough at a time, rolling it between your hands into a small cigar shape about 4 inches long, with tapered ends and thicker in the middle. Place it on a cookie sheet, curving the ends to form the cookie into a crescent shape. Continue shaping the cookies and placing them about 1 inch apart.

Bake the cookies for 18 to 20 minutes, reversing the position of the sheets top to bottom and front to back as necessary to ensure even baking. Bake only until the cookies are golden-colored on the tips and the bottoms—the center parts of the cookies should remain light. If you bake only one sheet at a time, use the higher rack.

Remove the cookie sheets from the oven but let the cookies stand for a minute or two until they are firm enough to be moved. These are very fragile—handle with care.

5¼ ounces (1½ cups) walnuts
8 ounces (2 sticks) unsalted butter
2 teaspoons vanilla extract
⅔ cup granulated sugar
2½ cups sifted all-purpose flour
Confectioners sugar or vanilla sugar (see pages 5 and 242), for sprinkling over the baked cookies

56 COOKIES

With a wide metal spatula, gently transfer the cookies to racks set over wax paper.

Immediately, while the cookies are still warm, cover them generously with confectioners or vanilla sugar by pushing the sugar through a strainer held over the cookies.

When the cookies are cool, gently and carefully transfer them to a tray or serving dish. Or, if the cookies are to be stored in a box, package them with plastic wrap between the layers.

If necessary, sugar the tops of the cookies again before serving.

Sour Cream and Pecan Dreams

These are rather fancy. They are semisoft brown-sugar cookies with a baked-on sour cream and pecan topping.

Adjust two racks to divide the oven into thirds and preheat to 350°. Line cookie sheets with parchment or foil. Sift together the flour, baking soda, and salt, and set aside. In the large bowl of an electric mixer, cream the butter. Add the vanilla and sugar and beat well. Add the egg and continue to beat for a few minutes, scraping the bowl with a rubber spatula and beating until the mixture lightens in color. On low speed gradually add the sifted dry ingredients, scraping the bowl with the spatula and beating only until the mixture is smooth.

Use a slightly rounded teaspoonful of dough for each cookie—make these a little smaller than average. (To be sure that you are not making the cookies too large, before rolling any of the dough into balls you may divide the dough into 48 equal mounds on wax paper.) Roll the dough between your hands into round balls and place them 2 inches apart—no closer—on the cookie sheets.

With your fingertip or with the handle end of a large wooden spoon make a wide, round depression in the center of each cookie—reaching almost to the edges and leaving a rim.

Prepare the following topping.

2 cups sifted all-purpose flour
½ teaspoon baking soda
¼ teaspoon salt
4 ounces (1 stick) unsalted butter
1 teaspoon vanilla extract
1 cup dark brown sugar, firmly packed
1 egg

48 COOKIES

Sour Cream and Pecan Topping

Place the sugar, cinnamon, and sour cream in a small mixing bowl. With a rubber spatula stir until smooth. Stir in the nuts.

With a demitasse spoon or a small measuring spoon, place some of the topping on each cookie. The topping should be mounded fairly high above the rims of the cookies.

Bake for 13 to 15 minutes, reversing the cookie sheets top to bottom and front to back once to ensure even baking. If you bake only one sheet at a time use the higher rack.

With a wide metal spatula transfer the cookies to racks to cool.

½ cup dark brown sugar,
  firmly packed
½ teaspoon cinnamon
¼ cup sour cream
4 ounces (generous 1 cup)
  pecans, finely chopped
  (these should not be ground
  or chopped so fine that they
  are powdery)

Charlie Brown's Peanut Cookies

These are coated with chopped peanuts and have a baked-on topping of peanut butter and chocolate morsels. They are fancy and take a little longer to make than many other cookies, but they are worth the time and fun to make.

Sift together the flour, baking powder, and cinnamon, and set aside. In the large bowl of an electric mixer cream the butter. Add the sugar and beat to mix. Beat in 1 whole egg and 1 egg yolk (reserve the second white). On low speed gradually add the sifted dry ingredients, scraping the bowl with a rubber spatula and beating only until thoroughly mixed.

Place one long piece of wax paper on the work surface. Divide the dough into 36 equal mounds on the wax paper. Use a heaping teaspoonful for each mound. Flour your hands and roll each mound into a round ball, continuing to flour your hands before rolling each ball. As you roll the balls, replace them on the wax paper.

Adjust two racks to divide the oven into thirds and preheat to 375°. Line cookie sheets with parchment or foil.

In a small, shallow bowl beat the reserved egg white with the water, beating only until mixed and barely foamy.

Place the chopped peanuts on a long piece of aluminum foil or wax paper.

Pick up a cookie and use your fingers to roll it around in the egg white and then place it on the chopped nuts. Next, roll it around in the nuts to coat the cookie thoroughly. Coat 4 or 5 cookies at a time. Place the nut-covered cookies 2 inches apart on the cookie sheets. Continue to prepare all of the cookies the same way.

Now, form a depression in the top of each cookie. Either do it with the handle end of a large wooden spoon or with your thumb to keep the dough from sticking. Make the depression rather deep and wide but not so deep that you make the bottom of the cookie too thin.

With a small, demitasse spoon or a ½-teaspoon-size measuring spoon, place a generous ½ teaspoonful of the peanut butter into each indentation.

Place about 5 or 6 chocolate morsels on the top of each cookie, pressing them slightly into the peanut butter.

Bake the cookies for 12 to 13 minutes, reversing the sheets top to bottom and front to back once to ensure even browning.

Let the cookies cool for a minute or two before removing them with a wide metal spatula to racks to cool.

When the cookies have reached room temperature place them in the refrigerator very briefly—only long enough to set the chocolate morsels.

2 cups sifted all-purpose flour
1 teaspoon baking powder
½ teaspoon cinnamon
8 ounces (2 sticks) unsalted butter
1 cup dark brown sugar, firmly packed
2 eggs (leave 1 egg whole and separate the other)
1 teaspoon water
10 ounces (2¼ cups) salted peanuts (preferably dry-roasted), chopped medium fine (see page 11)
Scant ¾ cup smooth (not chunky) peanut butter (it is not necessary to measure this; you may use it right from the jar)
4 ounces (⅔ cup) semisweet chocolate morsels (see Notes)

36 COOKIES

NOTES: In place of the semisweet chocolate morsels you may, if you wish, use butterscotch morsels. Or use chocolate on half of the cookies and butterscotch on the others. Or you may use the midget-size morsels, in which case use as many as it takes to cover the peanut butter.

Don't worry about placing the morsels exactly in position because as the cookies spread in baking, the morsels will slide out over the tops and won't stay where you put them anyhow.

English Gingersnaps #1

This is a classic recipe for large, dark semisoft gingersnaps.

Sift together the flour, baking soda, salt, cinnamon, ginger, cloves, allspice, and black pepper, and set aside. In the large bowl of an electric mixer cream the butter. Add the brown sugar and beat well. Add the egg and the molasses and beat for a few minutes until the mixture is light in color. On low speed gradually add the sifted dry ingredients, scraping the bowl with a rubber spatula and beating only until incorporated.

Refrigerate the dough briefly (in the mixing bowl if you wish) until it can be handled; 10 to 15 minutes might be enough.

Adjust two racks to divide the oven into thirds and preheat to 375°. Line cookie sheets with parchment or foil.

Spread some granulated sugar on a large piece of wax paper. Use a rounded tablespoonful of dough for each cookie. Roll it into a ball between your hands, then roll it around in the granulated sugar, and place the balls 2½ to 3 inches apart on the cookie sheets.

Bake the cookies for about 13 minutes, reversing the sheets top to bottom and front to back once to ensure even browning. The cookies are done when they feel semifirm to the touch.

With a wide metal spatula transfer the cookies to racks to cool.

2¼ cups sifted all-purpose flour
2 teaspoons baking soda
½ teaspoon salt
1 teaspoon cinnamon
1 teaspoon powdered ginger
½ teaspoon powdered cloves
¼ teaspoon allspice
¼ teaspoon finely ground black pepper
6 ounces (1½ sticks) unsalted butter
1 cup dark brown sugar, firmly packed
1 egg
¼ cup molasses
Granulated sugar (to roll the cookies in)

22 LARGE COOKIES

English Gingersnaps #2

This is a variation of the previous recipe. These are made smaller, and are more crisp and gingery.

Follow the recipe for English Gingersnaps #1 with the following changes: Use only 2 cups plus 2 table-spoons flour, increase the ginger to 2 teaspoons, use light brown sugar instead of dark brown, and stir in the finely grated rind of 1 small lemon and 1 orange.

70 TO 80 COOKIES

Because of the slightly smaller amount of flour in this recipe, the dough will need a bit more chilling time, and then it is best to work with one-fourth of the dough at a time and keep the remainder refrigerated.

Use one very slightly rounded teaspoonful of dough for each cookie, roll into balls, roll in sugar as above, and place the cookies about 1½ inches apart.

Bake for 10 to 12 minutes.

Italian Sesame Sticks

These are dry, light, crisp-crunchy, and plain. The recipe comes from a trattoria on Mulberry Street in New York's Little Italy. I had them with espresso as I watched the regulars dunk one after another in red wine.

Adjust the racks to divide the oven into thirds and preheat oven to 350°. Line cookie sheets with parchment or foil. In the large bowl of an electric mixer cream the butter. Add the vanilla and sugar and beat very well. Add the eggs one at a time, scraping the bowl with a rubber spatula and beating until thoroughly incorporated after each addition. The mixture will look curdled at this point—it's okay. On low speed gradually add the sifted dry ingredients, continuing to scrape the bowl and beating only until smooth.

Remove from the mixer and place the bowl of dough in the refrigerator, stirring occasionally for about 15 minutes only until the dough can be handled.

Meanwhile, pour some milk to a depth of approximately 1 inch in a small bowl.

Also, spread the sesame seeds on a large piece of wax paper near you. And lightly flour a large cutting board.

Work with ½ cup of the dough at a time. Place it on the floured board. With lightly floured hands, roll the dough into a long, thin roll—it should be rolled until it is 20 inches long and about ¾ inch in diameter.

The dough is delicate; handle it gently. Cut the roll into pieces 2½ inches long. With one hand, transfer several of the pieces at a time to the milk. Then, with the other hand (see Notes), lift them out and place them on the seeds, rolling them to coat thoroughly. Finally place the cookies at least 1 inch apart on the cookie sheets. Repeat with remaining dough.

Bake for 20 minutes or until the sticks are golden brown—do not overbake. Reverse the sheets top to bottom and front to back once to ensure even browning. If you bake one sheet at a time, use the upper rack.

With a wide metal spatula transfer the cookies to racks to cool.

4 cups sifted all-purpose flour
1 tablespoon plus 1 teaspoon baking powder
½ teaspoon salt
8 ounces (2 sticks) unsalted butter
1 teaspoon vanilla extract
1 cup granulated sugar
3 eggs
Milk
About 10 ounces (2 cups) sesame seeds (use the seeds that are labeled "hulled" and are white in color)

66 COOKIES

NOTES: The directions for using one hand for dipping the cookies in milk and the other for rolling them in the seeds are a trick I learned from a restaurant chef. For any breading procedure, if you use one hand for wet and the other for dry, you will find it much more efficient than using both hands for both steps. It takes a bit of practice to get used to it, but then you will not have to stop and wash your hands every few minutes. And, in this case, if you don't do it this way, you will waste a lot of the seeds in the milk.

Any seeds that are left over on the wax paper, even if they are wet from the milk, should not be thrown away. Place them in a small shallow pan in a moderate oven, shake them occasionally, and bake until they are dry and golden brown. Reserve them to use for other cookies that call for toasted sesame seeds (or sprinkle them over salads or vegetables).

And More

Craig Claiborne's Chocolate Macaroons

Hip-hip-hooray and three cheers for Craig for creating these sensational macaroons—they are moist, soft, dark, bittersweet, and very elegant. You will need a pastry bag fitted with a large star-shaped tube.

Adjust a rack to the center of the oven and preheat to 400°. Line cookie sheets with parchment or foil.

Grind the almonds to a powder (they must be fine) in a nut grinder or a food processor. (See To Grind Nuts in a Food Processor, page 11.) Place the ground almonds in a large, heavy frying pan. Now grind the chocolate; the whole squares may be ground in a nut grinder, or the chocolate may be chopped coarsely and then ground in a food processor. Add the ground chocolate to the almonds. Or grind the chopped chocolate with the almonds in a food processor. Add the sugar and the egg whites. Stir to mix—it will be a thick mixture.

Place the frying pan over medium heat and, with a wooden spoon or rubber spatula, stir constantly, scraping the bottom and sides. The heat will melt the chocolate and sugar, which will cause the mixture to become a little thinner. Then, as the egg whites start to cook, the mixture will begin to thicken. Do not let the mixture boil, and be careful that it does not burn. The mixture should cook, being stirred constantly, until it starts to thicken to the consistency of soft mashed potatoes—it should take about 5 minutes altogether.

Remove from the heat and transfer to a bowl in order to stop the cooking. Add the almond extract, and stir occasionally for about 10 minutes until the mixture is tepid.

It is best to use a pastry bag about 12 inches long (although you may use a larger one). And it is best to use a #8 star-shaped tube (although you may use a slightly smaller one if necessary). Insert the tube in the bag. Fold down a deep cuff on the outside of the bag. Place the bag in a tall, narrow glass or jar in order to hold it upright. Transfer the dough to the bag. Unfold the cuff and twist the top of the bag closed.

Hold the bag over the lined cookie sheet. Press from the top of the bag to press out rosettes of dough about 1 inch in diameter, shaping them moderately high and placing them ½ to 1 inch apart. (If the mixture was cooked long enough in the frying pan, these will not spread in baking. If it was cooked too long, the dough will be stiff

5 ounces (1 cup) almonds, blanched or unblanched
2 ounces (2 squares) unsweetened chocolate
¾ cup granulated sugar
5 liquid ounces egg whites (3 to 5 eggs, depending on the size)
½ teaspoon almond extract
12 glacéed cherries, cut into halves

24 MACAROONS

and difficult to press through the pastry bag.)

Place half of a glacéed cherry, cut side down, on each macaroon.

Bake for 12 to 13 minutes, reversing the cookie sheet top to bottom and front to back once to ensure even browning. The macaroons will feel dry to the touch but they will be soft and flexible. Do not overbake—these must remain soft and moist inside.

Let stand for 5 to 10 minutes. Then, with a wide metal spatula, remove the macaroons and transfer them to racks to finish cooling.

Almond Macaroons

These are classic French macaroons—soft and chewy. They are formed with a pastry bag and a large star-shaped tube. They may be made without an electric mixer.

Adjust two racks to divide the oven into thirds and preheat oven to 350°. Line two cookie sheets with aluminum foil shiny side up and set aside.

The almonds must be ground to a very fine powder. They may be ground in a nut grinder or a food processor (see To Grind Nuts in a Food Processor, page 11).

Place the ground nuts and the sugar in a medium-size mixing bowl and stir them together until they are thoroughly mixed.

Beat the egg whites until they hold a firm shape and are stiff, but not dry; add the almond extract toward the end of the beating. Fold the whites into the ground almond-and-sugar mixture.

Fit a 12-inch pastry bag with a #8 star-shaped tube. Fold down a deep cuff on the outside of the bag. Support the bag by placing it in a tall narrow glass or jar. Place the macaroon mixture in the bag and, quickly, before the mixture runs out through the tube, unfold the cuff, twist the top of the bag closed, and turn the bag tube end up.

Then hold the bag at a right angle tube-end down to a foil-lined sheet. Press from the top of the bag to press out rosettes of dough, 1½ to 1¾ inches in diameter, placing them 1 inch apart.

8 ounces (1⅔ cups) blanched almonds
⅔ cup granulated sugar
½ cup egg whites (3 to 4 eggs, depending on size)
½ teaspoon almond extract
14 glacéed cherries, cut into halves, or about 3 tablespoons slivered (julienne-shape) blanched almonds

28 MACAROONS

Top each macaroon with a glacéed cherry half or a few pieces of slivered almond.

Bake for about 20 minutes, until the macaroons are lightly colored. Reverse the sheets top to bottom and front to back as necessary to ensure even browning. These are more attractive if they are not too pale, but do not overbake. They should be a golden color on the ridges and the edges, but they may still be pale between the ridges.

Let stand for about 5 minutes. Then peel the foil away from the backs of the macaroons and transfer them to racks to finish cooling.

Fudge Délices

A fancy French recipe, these are buttery shells filled with dark baked-in fudge. It is necessary to have small French tartlet pans for these. The recipe is written for 23 cookies (see Note) made in plain, round pans measuring 2¼ inches across the top and ⅜ inch in depth. These are generally available at specialty kitchen-equipment stores. You will also need a plain, round 2¾-inch cookie cutter.

Pastry

Into a mixing bowl sift together the flour, baking powder, and salt. Then, with a pastry blender, cut the butter into the dry ingredients until the particles are fine and the mixture resembles coarse meal.

In a small bowl beat the egg lightly just to mix, and stir it into the flour mixture. Turn the dough out onto a large board or smooth work surface. Flour your hands. Form the dough into a ball. (The dough will be sticky—use a dough scraper or a wide metal spatula as necessary to remove it from the work surface.) With the heel of your hand, break off small amounts of the dough (about 2 tablespoonfuls at a time), pushing it away from you against the work surface. Re-form the dough in a ball and, if it is not completely smooth and well blended, push it off again. Re-form the dough and flatten it slightly.

Place the dough on a floured pastry cloth and turn it over to flour both sides.

1 cup sifted all-purpose flour
¼ teaspoon baking powder
¼ teaspoon salt
2⅔ ounces (5⅓ tablespoons) cold unsalted butter, cut into ½- to 1-inch slices
1 extra-large or jumbo egg

23 COOKIES

With a floured rolling pin, roll the dough until it is ¹⁄₁₆ inch thick—that's very thin. While rolling, occasionally roll the dough up on the pin and then unroll it with the other side down in order to keep both sides floured. (Reflour the cloth as necessary, but lightly.)

With a plain, round 2¾-inch cookie cutter, cut 23 rounds (see Note).

Put the pastry rounds into the tartlet pans and press them gently into place. Arrange the lined pans on a jelly-roll pan or a large cookie sheet.

Adjust a rack one-third up from the bottom of the oven and preheat oven to 350°.

Prepare the following filling.

Filling

Place the chocolate in the top of a small double boiler, over hot water on moderate heat. Stir until the chocolate is melted and smooth. Add the sugar, butter, milk, and vanilla. Stir until the butter is melted and then remove the top of the double boiler from the heat.

In a small bowl beat the egg just to mix and, very gradually, stir it into the chocolate mixture.

Place a slightly rounded teaspoonful of the filling in each pastry shell. They will be only about ⅓ to ½ full, but the filling will rise during baking.

Place a pecan half on the top of each tartlet.

Bake for 22 to 25 minutes, reversing the sheets top to bottom and front to back once to ensure even browning. Bake until the pastry is barely colored. Do not over-bake—the filling should remain slightly chewy.

Cool the tartlets in the pans for about 10 minutes, and then, with your fingers, remove them from the pans and place them on racks to finish cooling.

6 ounces semisweet chocolate
 cut into pieces
⅓ cup granulated sugar
1 tablespoon unsalted butter
1 tablespoon milk
1 teaspoon vanilla extract
1 extra-large or jumbo egg
23 pecan halves

NOTE: Twenty-three is a strange number of cookies to make, but I like the filling to be generous. If you make 24, the filling is a little too shallow—and if you make 22, it's a little too deep. But 23 is just right.

Chocolate Meringue Ladyfingers

Dry, crisp meringue in the shape of ladyfingers. This is a classic French recipe. You will need a candy thermometer, a 15-inch pastry bag fitted with a plain, round ½-inch tube, and an electric mixer with both a large and a small bowl.

Adjust two racks to divide the oven into thirds and preheat to 275°. Line two 12 x 15½-inch cookie sheets with parchment or foil shiny side up.

Sift together the confectioners sugar and cocoa and set aside.

Place the water and the granulated sugar in a 3-cup saucepan (that's a very small one and it should preferably be narrow and deep instead of shallow and wide, or the thermometer will not register accurately because it might not be deep enough in the syrup). With a small wooden spoon stir over high heat until the granulated sugar is dissolved and the mixture comes to a full boil. Place a candy thermometer in the saucepan and let the mixture boil, without stirring, over high heat until the thermometer registers 240° (the soft-ball stage).

Meanwhile, place the egg whites and the salt in the small bowl of an electric mixer. When the sugar syrup is almost ready, start to beat the whites at high speed and beat until they are very stiff.

When the sugar syrup is ready, and with the beater still going at high speed, very gradually add the syrup to the whites. The syrup must be added in a thin, slow stream. After all the syrup has been added, beat in the vanilla and continue to beat for a few minutes more.

Then transfer the mixture to the large bowl of the electric mixer and continue to beat for several minutes until the mixture is cool and stiff. On lowest speed gradually add the sifted dry ingredients, scraping the bowl with a rubber spatula and beating as little as possible, only until incorporated. Do not overbeat or you will lose the air that has been beaten into the egg whites.

Place a plain tube with ½-inch opening into a 15-inch pastry bag. Fold down about 4 inches of the top of the bag to form a deep cuff on the outside. Support the bag by placing it in a tall narrow glass or an empty jar so that it stands upright while you fill it. Use a rubber spatula to transfer all of the meringue to the bag. Lift up the cuff and twist the top closed.

1¼ cups sifted or strained confectioners sugar
⅓ cup unsweetened cocoa powder (preferably Dutch-process)
⅓ cup water
1 cup granulated sugar
½ cup egg whites (3 to 4 eggs, depending on size)
Pinch of salt
1 teaspoon vanilla extract

36 COOKIES

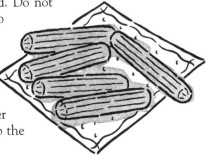

Pressing from the top, force the batter through the bag to form the ladyfingers on the lined sheets. Make the cookies 3 to 3½ inches long and ¾ inch wide.

Bake 30 to 35 minutes, reversing the sheets top to bottom and front to back once to ensure even browning. Turn off the oven heat, open the oven door slightly (if necessary insert something to hold the door open 2 to 3 inches), and let the meringues stand until they are completely cool. Then transfer.

When you bite into one of these your will find it slightly hollow in the center— that's correct.

Chocolate Tartlets

These are tiny cookie cups with a baked-in chewy chocolate filling. To make these dainty French cookies it is necessary to use very small, shallow individual tartlet molds; they may be plain or fluted. Mine are French; they are assorted shapes and they vary in diameter from about 1 to 2 inches. There are Scandinavian ones, generally a little larger, made for Sandbakelser cookies—they may be used for these tartlets. Or you may use plain, round, shallow French tartlet pans about 2 to 2½ inches in diameter and ½ inch deep. These little pans should be washed with only hot soapy water; anything rougher would cause the cookies to stick. Don't make these if you are in a hurry; they take time.

Filling

In a food processor, grind together the almonds and the chocolate (see To Grind Nuts in a Food Processor, page 11). Set aside.

In the small bowl of an electric mixer at high speed beat the eggs for about 5 minutes until very thick and pale in color. On low speed mix in the coffee, almond extract, and sugar, and then gradually beat in the ground almond-and-chocolate mixture. Transfer to a small, shallow bowl for ease in handling and set aside at room temperature.

4 ounces (generous ¾ cup) blanched almonds
6 ounces semisweet chocolate cut into pieces
2 eggs
1 teaspoon instant coffee
¼ teaspoon almond extract
½ cup granulated sugar

60 TO 75 TINY TARTLETS

Pastry

In the large bowl of an electric mixer (with clean beaters) cream the butter. Mix in the salt, vanilla, and sugar, and then gradually add the flour, scraping the bowl as necessary with a rubber spatula. The mixture will be crumbly. Turn it out onto a board or smooth work surface. Squeeze it between your hands until it holds together. Then, with the heel of your hand, break off small pieces of dough (about 2 tablespoonfuls at a time), pushing it away from you on the work surface. Form the dough into a ball. If it is not completely smooth break it again.

6 ounces (1½ sticks) unsalted
  butter
Scant ¼ teaspoon salt
1 teaspoon vanilla extract
½ cup granulated sugar
2 cups sifted all-purpose flour

Adjust a rack one-third up from the bottom of the oven and preheat to 350°.

With your fingertips press a small amount of the dough into each tartlet mold (the molds do not have to be buttered). The pastry shell should be ¼ inch thick or a little less, and it should be level with the rim of the mold—use your fingertip to remove excess dough above the rim.

Place the molds on a cookie sheet or a jelly-roll pan. With a demitasse spoon or a small measuring spoon, place some of the filling in each shell. The filling may be mounded a bit above the edges but only a very little bit or it will run over. It is not necessary to smooth the filling, as it will run slightly and smooth itself as it bakes.

Bake for 20 minutes until the pastry is barely colored. Reverse the sheets top to bottom and front to back once to ensure even browning. Do not overbake these or the filling will be dry instead of chewy.

Remove from the oven and let stand until just cool enough to handle. Then invert each mold into the palm of your hand and, with a fingernail of the other hand, gently release and remove the mold.

NOTE: If you do not have enough molds to bake these all at once, the remaining pastry and filling may wait at room temperature.

Almond Tartlets

These fancy petit-four-type cookies are similar to Chocolate Tartlets, but these have an almond filling instead of chocolate and a different pastry. These are made in the same tartlet pans (see introduction to Chocolate Tartlets, page 267).

Filling

In a food processor (see To Grind Nuts in a Food Processor, page 11), grind the almonds. Set aside.

In the small bowl of an electric mixer beat the eggs until foamy. Add the almond extract and then gradually add the sugar. Beat at high speed for about 7 minutes, until the mixture is almost white and forms ribbons when the beaters are raised. On low speed stir in the ground almonds. Set aside at room temperature.

5 ounces (1 cup) blanched almonds
2 eggs
½ teaspoon almond extract
½ cup granulated sugar

60 TO 70 TINY TARTLETS

Pastry

In the large bowl of an electric mixer cream the butter. Add the salt, vanilla, and sugar, and beat well. Beat in the egg. On low speed add the flour, scraping the bowl with a rubber spatula and beating until the mixture is smooth and holds together.

Adjust a rack one-third up from the bottom of the oven and preheat oven to 350°.

To line the molds with the dough (do not butter them), use a demitasse spoon or a small measuring spoon to place some of the dough in a mold. With the back of the spoon or with your fingertips spread the dough to make a layer ¼ to ⅓ inch thick. Don't worry about making the thickness exactly even, but do make the top edge level with the top of the mold. Line all of the molds and place them on a cookie sheet or a jelly-roll pan.

Now, with a small spoon, put the filling into the lined molds, mounding it slightly higher than the rims. If the almonds in the filling have sunk to the bottom, stir lightly to mix before spooning into mold.

Bake for 20 to 25 minutes, until the crust is golden and the filling is well browned. Carefully reverse the position of the pan front to back once to ensure even browning.

8 ounces (2 sticks) unsalted butter
⅛ teaspoon salt
1 teaspoon vanilla extract
½ cup granulated sugar
1 egg
2 cups sifted all-purpose flour

Remove from the oven and let stand for 5 minutes. Then, with your fingertips, carefully remove the cookies from the molds and place them on racks to finish cooling.

NOTE: If you do not have enough molds to bake these all at once, the remaining pastry and filling may wait at room temperature. The molds do not have to be washed and dried if they are to be re-used right away, but they must be cool.

VARIATIONS: Coarsely chop about ⅓ cup glazed orange peel or pineapple and place a few pieces in each pastry-lined form before adding the filling. Or try pieces of candied ginger.

Place the racks of baked cookies over a large piece of wax paper. With your fingertips press confectioners sugar through a fine strainer held over the cookies to coat them generously.

Connecticut Date Slices

A prize-winning old New England recipe. These are moist, fruity, and sharply spiced.

Adjust two racks to divide the oven into thirds and preheat oven to 350°. Line two 12 x 15½-inch cookie sheets with parchment or aluminum foil. Dissolve the instant coffee in the boiling water and set aside.

Sift together the flour, baking soda, salt, cloves, cinnamon, and mustard, and set aside. In the large bowl of an electric mixer cream the butter. Add the sugar and beat well. Beat in the molasses and then the egg and beat until smooth. Beat in the dates and raisins, then on lowest speed add the sifted dry ingredients in three additions with the prepared coffee in two additions, scraping the bowl as necessary with a rubber spatula and beating only until smooth after each addition.

Form two strips of the dough lengthwise on each cookie sheet as follows: Use one-fourth of the dough, or about 1¼ cups, for each strip. Place heaping teaspoonfuls of

1 tablespoon instant coffee
½ cup boiling water
3 cups sifted all-purpose flour
1 teaspoon baking soda
½ teaspoon salt
1 teaspoon ground cloves
1 teaspoon cinnamon
½ teaspoon mustard powder
4 ounces (1 stick) unsalted butter
1 cup granulated sugar
½ cup molasses
1 egg
8 ounces (1 cup) pitted dates, coarsely cut
3 ounces (⅔ cup) raisins

44 SLICES

the dough touching each other to form an even strip 14 inches long, 2 inches wide, and 1 inch deep. Leave 3 to 4 inches of space between the two strips. With a small metal spatula or a table knife smooth the strips slightly on the sides and top—they will flatten and spread a bit during baking.

Bake for 25 to 30 minutes, until the tops spring back when lightly pressed with a fingertip. Reverse the cookie sheets top to bottom and front to back once to ensure even browning.

While the cakes are baking prepare the following glaze.

Glaze

Mix all of the ingredients in a small bowl until completely smooth. The glaze should have the consistency of a medium-thick cream sauce; if necessary, adjust it with a bit more milk or sugar. Cover the glaze airtight until you are ready to use it.

½ cup plus 2 tablespoons confectioners sugar
2 teaspoons soft unsalted butter
¼ teaspoon vanilla extract
2 tablespoons milk

When the cakes are done let them stand for only a minute or so until they can be transferred (do not let them cool). Then, using a flat-sided cookie sheet as a spatula, transfer the cakes to large racks. Using a pastry brush, immediately brush the glaze over the hot cakes.

If the cooking racks are not raised far enough from the work surface, steam will form and cause the bottom of the cakes to be wet. Raise the racks by placing them over right-side-up cake pans or mixing bowls in order to leave room for air to circulate underneath. Let the cakes cool completely.

Transfer the cooled cakes to a cutting board. With a very sharp, thin knife cut the cakes at an angle into 1- to 1¼-inch slices.

Connecticut Strippers

These are soft, moist fruit-and-nut strips, traditionally a Christmas treat.

Sift together the flour, baking soda, salt, cinnamon, and nutmeg, and set aside. In the large bowl of an electric mixer cream the butter. Add the vanilla and sugar and beat to mix well. Add the whole egg and the egg yolk and beat until smooth. On low speed add the sifted dry ingredients, scraping the bowl with a rubber spatula and beating only until incorporated. Mix in the nuts and currants.

Place the bowl of dough in the refrigerator for about half an hour or until it is firm enough to handle.

Adjust two racks to divide the oven into thirds and preheat to 400°. Line two 12 x 15½-inch cookie sheets with parchment or foil.

Generously flour a large board or smooth work surface. Divide the dough into quarters and work with one piece at a time. Flour your hands, form the piece of dough into a ball, and turn it over several times on the board to flour it on all sides. Then, with your hands, form the dough into a roll 13 inches long and place it lengthwise on one of the lined cookie sheets. Repeat with the remaining pieces of dough, placing two rolls on each sheet about 4 inches apart.

With floured fingertips press each roll of dough to flatten it to ½ to ¾ inch depth.

Prepare the topping.

2 cups sifted all-purpose flour
½ teaspoon baking soda
½ teaspoon salt
1½ teaspoons cinnamon
½ teaspoon nutmeg
5⅓ ounces (10⅔ tablespoons) unsalted butter
1 teaspoon vanilla extract
1 cup dark or light brown sugar, firmly packed
1 egg plus 1 egg yolk (reserve the white for the topping)
3½ ounces (1 cup) walnuts, cut into medium-size pieces
7½ ounces (1½ cups) currants

40 TO 48 STRIPS

Topping

Stir the sugar and cinnamon together to mix thoroughly. Stir in the nuts. In a small bowl beat the egg white until it is foamy, not stiff. Use a pastry brush to brush some of the beaten white generously over one strip of the dough. Sprinkle with one-fourth of the topping. Repeat the process with the remaining three strips of dough.

Bake for 12 to 15 minutes, reversing the sheets top to bottom and front to back once to ensure even browning. Bake until the tops of the strips spring back when lightly pressed with a fingertip.

1 tablespoon granulated sugar
½ teaspoon cinnamon
⅓ cup walnuts, finely chopped (see page 11)
1 egg white (reserved from dough)

Slide the parchment or foil off the cookie sheets and let the strips stand for about 10 minutes. Then, with a wide metal spatula, release but do not remove the strips. Let them stand until completely cool. Then use a flat-sided cookie sheet as a spatula to transfer the strips to a large cutting board.

With a sharp knife cut the strips at an angle into 1- to 1¼-inch slices.

French Sugar Fans

These wafers may be served as plain sugar cookies, or place two of them, points down, at angles into a portion of ice cream. The dough must chill for at least an hour before baking.

Sift together the flour, baking powder, and salt, and set aside. In the large bowl of an electric mixer cream the butter. Beat in the vanilla and sugar. Add the egg and then the milk and lemon rind and beat well. On low speed gradually add the sifted dry ingredients, scraping the bowl with a rubber spatula and beating until the dough holds together.

Tear off four pieces of wax paper. Place one-fourth of the dough on each piece of paper. Wrap the dough and flatten it slightly. Refrigerate (do not chill in the freezer) for at least one hour.

Adjust two racks to divide the oven into thirds and preheat to 375°. Line cookie sheets with parchment or foil.

Flour a pastry cloth and rolling pin very well. Work with one piece of the dough at a time, keeping the rest refrigerated. Work quickly before the dough softens. Place it on the floured cloth and turn it over several times to flour both sides. With the floured rolling pin, roll the dough into a circle ⅛ inch thick and slightly larger than 8 inches in diameter (reflour the pin as necessary).

Now you will need something as a pattern for cutting an 8-inch circle of dough; use a flan ring, a canister cover, or a cake pan turned upside down. Place the pattern on the dough and cut around it with a plain or fluted pastry wheel (the fluted wheel will give a rippled, fanlike appearance). Or, in place of the pastry wheel, a small, sharp knife may be used to cut a plain edge.

2 cups sifted all-purpose flour
1½ teaspoons baking powder
¼ teaspoon salt
5⅓ ounces (10⅔ tablespoons) unsalted butter
½ teaspoon vanilla extract
¾ cup granulated sugar
1 egg
4 teaspoons milk
Finely grated rind of 1 lemon
Additional granulated sugar for sprinkling over the cookies

36 FANS

With a long knife cut the circle into eight pie-shaped wedges. If the blade sticks to the dough, flour it as necessary.

With the back (dull side) of a knife or the edge of a metal spatula, mark each cookie with five or six lines that radiate from the point to the outside curve—the lines should be deep but not deep enough to cut through the dough. Flour the knife or spatula as necessary to keep it from sticking.

With a wide metal spatula transfer the fans to the cookie sheets, placing them 1 inch apart. Sprinkle the fans with granulated sugar. Slide a cookie sheet under the foil.

Bake for 7 to 10 minutes (depending on the thickness of the dough), reversing the sheets top to bottom and front to back as necessary to ensure even cooking. The fans should bake only until they are slightly colored. They should not be brown, but if they are underbaked they will be too soft.

With a wide metal spatula transfer the fans to racks to cool.

Swedish Fried Twists

Most European countries have their own version of these sweet crackers. And in China a similar recipe is called Twisted Generals (in honor of a famous general who was crippled). In Poland they are called Favorki and are traditionally made around Eastertime. In America they are known as Bow Ties, Knots, Christmas Crullers, etc. They are light, dry, airy, and extremely plain. These are generally served with coffee or wine, more probably between meals than as an after-dinner sweet. You will need a deep-frying thermometer and a pastry wheel.

*Y*ou will need a wide saucepan or a large, deep frying pan. Heat at least 2 inches of the oil in the pan over moderate heat. Insert a deep-frying thermometer and slowly bring the temperature to 365°.

Meanwhile, prepare the dough. In the small bowl of an electric mixer beat the egg yolks with the sugar, cardamom, and salt at high speed for 4 or 5 minutes until the mixture is very thick and light lemon-colored. On low speed gradually add the cream and cognac, brandy, or whiskey, scraping the bowl with a rubber spatula and beating only until mixed.

Beat the egg white until it holds a firm shape and is stiff but not dry. On low speed add the beaten white to the yolk mixture. Then, on low speed, gradually add most of the flour, scraping the bowl with the spatula. When you have added enough flour to make a very thick mixture, remove the bowl from the mixer.

Spread the remaining flour out on a large board. Turn the dough out onto the flour. Using only as much flour as necessary to make a dough that is firm enough to knead, knead it on the floured board until it is very smooth and not sticky.

Cover the dough lightly with plastic wrap or with a kitchen towel and let stand for 15 minutes.

Then cut the dough in half. Work with one piece at a time. Set the other piece aside and cover it lightly.

On the floured board (using no more flour than necessary), with a lightly floured rolling pin, roll the dough into an oblong ⅛ inch thick.

Using a ruler, and a plain or zigzag pastry wheel, cut the dough into strips 2 inches wide. Then cut across all the strips at once, so that each piece of dough is about 5 inches long, or a little less (see Note). Don't worry about any different-size pieces on the corners or ends—use them as they are.

Now, with the pastry wheel, cut a slit about 3 or 4 inches long lengthwise down the middle of each piece of dough. Slip one end of the dough through the slit. (You may prepare them all before frying, or you may pull the end through each one just before you fry it.)

Adjust the heat as necessary to maintain the oil at 365°. Fry only a few twists at a time; the number depends on the size of the pan—don't crowd them. Place a few of the twists in the oil, fry until golden brown on the bottoms, then with two flat wire whisks or slotted spoons or spatulas, turn them and fry until the cookies are golden brown on both sides. Drain on heavy brown paper.

When the twists are cool sprinkle the tops generously with confectioners sugar, pressing it with you fingertips through a strainer held over the twist.

Transfer them to a large platter or a deep bowl for serving.

Vegetable oil (for deep frying)
4 egg yolks (reserve 1 white to use later)
⅓ cup confectioners sugar
1 teaspoon ground cardamom
Pinch of salt
¼ cup plus 1 tablespoon heavy cream
2 tablespoons cognac, brandy, or whiskey
1 egg white
About 2¼ cups sifted all-purpose flour
Additional confectioners sugar (for sprinkling over the Fried Twists)

30 VERY LARGE TWISTS

NOTE: These directions are for very large twists. I do it that way because it is fun—and they look wild. But they may be made smaller, ¾ inch x 3 inches if you wish.

Basler Brunsli

This is a classic Swiss recipe for unusual, mildly spiced macaroon-meringue bars. The cookies are baked about 5 hours after the meringue is mixed.

Line two 12 x 15½-inch cookie sheets with parchment or foil and set aside. The almonds and chocolate must both be ground very fine. It is best to use a food processor (see To Grind Nuts in a Food Processor, page 11) and grind them together.

Set aside in a large mixing bowl.

In the small bowl of an electric mixer at moderate speed beat the egg whites with the salt until they become foamy and white. Beat in the sugar 1 tablespoon at a time, then the cinnamon and cloves. Increase the speed to high and beat for 2 to 3 minutes until the mixture is stiff but not dry.

Remove the meringue from the mixer and fold in the kirsch. Then fold this into the almond mixture.

Spread about ⅓ cup of the additional sugar on a large board. It should cover a surface about 9 x 10 inches.

Place the meringue on the sugared surface. Sprinkle about 2 tablespoons of sugar over the top. With your fingertips pat the dough into an 8 x 9-inch rectangle ½ to ¾ inch thick. Use additional sugar if necessary to keep the dough from sticking to your fingers. Make the edges as even as possible. Let stand, uncovered, at room temperature for about an hour.

In order to cut neatly, mark the meringue with the tip of a small knife. Mark the 8-inch side into four 2-inch lengths and the 9-inch side into nine 1-inch lengths. Then use a long, thin, sharp knife to cut the meringue into 1 x 2-inch bars. If the meringue is sticky hold the knife under cold running water before making each cut— or coat the blade with sugar. Try both methods and see which works better for you.

With a wide metal spatula transfer the cookies to the prepared cookie sheets, placing the bars 1 inch apart. You may have to sugar or wet the spatula as you did the knife above.

Let the bars stand uncovered at room temperature for about 4 hours to dry out.

Adjust two racks to divide the oven into equal thirds and preheat oven to 350°. Bake the cookies for 6 to 7 minutes, reversing the sheets top to bottom and front to back once to ensure even baking. Do not overbake—there should be a thin top and bottom crust but the middle must be soft. If you overbake the cookies they will lose their shape—the soft middle will run out on the sides.

8 ounces (1⅔ cups) blanched almonds
1½ ounces (1½ squares) unsweetened chocolate, cut into medium pieces
⅓ cup egg whites (2 to 3 eggs, depending on size)
Pinch of salt
1 cup granulated sugar
1 teaspoon cinnamon
¼ teaspoon powdered cloves
1 tablespoon kirsch
Additional granulated sugar for shaping the cookies

36 BARS

With a wide metal spatula transfer the meringues to a rack to cool. When cool, these will be light colored and crisp on the outside—dark, moist, and chewy on the inside.

Store airtight.

Hazelnut Rusks

This is an old German recipe. The rusks are hard, plain, dry, and crunchy.

Adjust two racks to divide the oven into thirds and preheat to 350°. Line two cookie sheets with parchment or foil.

Sift together the flour, baking powder, and salt, and set aside. In the small bowl of an electric mixer beat the eggs with the sugar at high speed for 12 to 15 minutes, until the mixture is almost white and forms a ribbon when beaters are lifted. Beat in the almond extract.

Transfer the mixture to the large bowl of the electric mixer. On low speed add the dry ingredients, scraping the bowl with a rubber spatula and beating only until smooth. Remove the bowl from the mixer. Fold in the nuts.

The dough will now be placed on the sheets to form three strips, two on one sheet and one on the other. Place tablespoonfuls of the dough touching each other lengthwise on the sheet. The strips should be 13 inches long, 2 to 3 inches wide, and about 1½ inches thick. The two strips that are both on one sheet should be about 3 inches apart. Place the dough carefully to make the strips rather even in shape but do not smooth over the tops or sides—they will run a bit in baking and will level themselves enough.

Bake the strips for 25 to 30 minutes, reversing them top to bottom and front to back once to ensure even browning. Bake until the strips are firm to the touch—they will remain pale in color. Remove the strips from the oven but do not turn off the heat.

With a large metal spatula or a flat-sided cookie sheet transfer the strips to a cutting board. Let stand for a few minutes.

While strips are still slightly warm cut them with a finely serrated knife or long,

3 cups sifted all-purpose flour
1 teaspoon baking powder
¼ teaspoon salt
3 eggs
1¼ cups granulated sugar
½ teaspoon almond extract
12 ounces (2 generous cups) blanched hazelnuts (filberts), coarsely cut (see Note)

ABOUT 78 RUSKS

thin, very sharp slicing knife. Cut crosswise into ½-inch slices. These are best if they are no thicker.

Transfer the slices to the cookie sheets and place them upright with a bit of space between them.

Bake again at 350° for about 8 minutes to dry the cookies. They will feel soft while hot but will become crisp when cool. If they are not crisp they should be baked longer—if they are thicker than ½ inch they will become too hard and dry.

When removed from the oven they may be left on the cookie sheets to cool.

NOTE: If blanched hazelnuts are not available buy the ones that have brown skins and blanch them yourself. To blanch hazelnuts: Spread the nuts in a single layer in a shallow pan. Bake at 350° on the center rack for about 15 minutes or until the skins parch and begin to flake off. Then, working with a few at a time, place them on a coarse towel. Fold the towel over the nuts and rub vigorously. Most of the skin will come off. If a few little bits of skin remain on the nuts just leave them; it's okay. Pick out the nuts and discard the skins.

Blanched almonds may be substituted for the hazelnuts but do try these sometime with hazelnuts—they're so good.

The nuts should be coarsely cut. For this recipe I find that chopping them on a board or in a bowl causes too many fine, small pieces. I prefer to cut them individually with a small paring knife, cutting each nut into halves or thirds.

Black-and-White Rusks

This is German mandelbrot *or "almond bread," although it is not bread and there are no almonds in the recipe. The rusks are hard, plain, and dry.*

Adjust two racks to divide the oven into thirds and preheat to 350°. Line two cookie sheets with parchment or aluminum foil.

Sift together the flour, baking powder, baking soda, and salt, and set aside. Melt the chocolate either in the top of a small double boiler or in a small, heat-proof cup set in shallow hot water over moderate heat, and then set the melted chocolate aside to cool.

In the large bowl of an electric mixer beat the eggs at high speed until foamy. Gradually add the sugar and continue to beat at high speed for a few minutes until pale in color. Beat in the vanilla and almond extracts. On low speed mix in one-third of the dry ingredients, then all of the oil, and a second third of the dry ingredients. The mixture will be stiff; remove it from the mixer and use a wooden spoon to stir in the orange rind and the remaining third of the dry ingredients. Stir until thoroughly mixed.

Transfer ⅔ cup of the mixture to a mixing bowl and, with a wooden spoon, stir in the melted chocolate.

On a board, form the chocolate mixture with your hands into a thick roll 8 inches long. Cut the roll into quarters. On the board (it does not have to be floured), with your fingers, form each quarter into a thin roll 12 inches long. Set the chocolate rolls aside.

Now flour the board lightly (the white dough is a little sticky). Work with one-quarter of the white dough at a time. Flour your hands lightly and form the dough with your fingers into a roll 12 inches long. Then, on the floured board, using your fingers and the palms of your hands, flatten the dough until it is 2½ inches wide. Place one of the chocolate rolls lengthwise in the center of the white dough. With your fingers bring up both sides of the white dough to enclose the chocolate. Pinch the edges of the white dough together to seal.

Place the roll, seam down, lengthwise, on one of the lined cookie sheets, allowing for two rolls on each sheet. Continue making the rolls, four altogether. With your hands, straighten them and shape them evenly.

Bake for 20 to 25 minutes, until lightly browned. Reverse the sheets top to bottom and front to back once to ensure even browning. Don't worry about the tops of the rolls cracking—that's okay.

3 cups sifted all-purpose flour
2 teaspoons baking powder
⅛ teaspoon baking soda (see Note)
¼ teaspoon salt
1 ounce (1 square) unsweetened chocolate
2 eggs
1 cup granulated sugar
1 teaspoon vanilla extract
¾ teaspoon almond extract
½ cup vegetable oil (not olive oil)
Finely grated rind of 1 large, deep-colored orange

75 TO 80 RUSKS

With a wide metal spatula transfer the baked rolls to a large cutting board. Do not turn off the oven.

Do not wait for the rolls to cool—slice the hot rolls at a sharp angle into ½-inch slices. (Try different knives to see which works best; I use a finely serrated knife.)

Return the slices, cut side down, to the sheets. Then return the sheets to the 350° oven to bake the rusks until they are dry. Reverse the positions of the cookie sheets occasionally so that the cookies will dry evenly. Bake for about 10 minutes or until the rusks are only lightly colored—do not allow them to brown too much. They will become crisp as they cool.

Transfer the rusks to racks to cool.

NOTE: To measure ⅛ teaspoon, first measure ¼ teaspoon and then, with a small metal spatula or a table knife, cut away half and return to box.

Macadamia and Milk Chocolate Biscotti

This recipe is a new one that has not been published before. These are very large and divinely and deliciously crisp/crunchy. They are loaded with whole, voluptuous macadamias and extra-large chunks of creamy and dreamy milk chocolate. The flavor has a hint of toasted almonds. They involve a little more work—and a little more expense—than most other biscotti. And they are worth it all. Fantabulous! Get the best milk chocolate you can find.

First toast the almonds in a shallow pan in a 350° oven for about 15 minutes, shaking the pan a few times, until the nuts are lightly colored and have a delicious smell of toasted almonds when you open the oven door. Set aside to cool.

Adjust a rack to the middle of the oven and preheat the oven to 375°. Line a large, flat cookie sheet (preferably 17 x 14 inches) with heavy-duty aluminum foil. Set the sheet aside.

To cut the chocolate into chunks I use an ice pick. However you do it, cut the chocolate into uneven pieces no more than about ½ inch in any direction. Set aside.

Sift together into a large bowl (preferably one with flared rather than straight sides) the flour, baking powder, baking soda, salt, and sugar.

Place about ⅓ cup of these dry ingredients in the bowl of a food processor fitted with the metal chopping blade. Add the toasted almonds. Process for about 45 seconds, until the nuts are very fine and powdery.

Add the processed mixture to the sifted ingredients in the large bowl.

Add the macadamia nuts and the cut-up chocolate. Stir to mix.

In a small bowl beat the eggs, vanilla and almond extracts, and the whiskey or brandy, beating until well mixed.

Add the egg mixture to the dry ingredients and stir—and stir—until the dry ingredients are all moistened (I stir with a large rubber spatula—and a lot of patience). You will think there are not enough liquids; just keep on stirring. (Actually, stir and then turn the ingredients over and over and press down on them firmly with the spatula until the dry ingredients are incorporated.)

Generously spray the lined cookie sheet with Pam or some other nonstick spray.

Turn the dough out onto the sheet. Wet your hands with cold water—do not dry them—and with your wet hands press the dough together to form a mound. Then shape it into an oval and flatten it a bit. With a dough scraper or with a large, metal spatula cut the dough lengthwise into equal halves. Continue to wet your hands and shape into two strips, each one about 12 inches long, about 3 inches wide, and about 1 inch thick, with rounded ends. There should be 2 or 3 inches of space between the two strips, and the strips should be pressed firmly so that they are compact.

Bake for 28 minutes, reversing the sheet front to back once during baking.

Remove the sheet from the oven and slide the foil off the sheet onto a large cutting board and let stand for 20 minutes.

Reduce the oven temperature to 275° and adjust two racks to divide the oven into thirds.

With a wide, metal spatula transfer the baked strips to the cutting board.

Now, to cut these into biscotti, you must be careful. Use a serrated bread knife and cut with a sawing motion. (Actually, I find it is best to cut through the top crust with a serrated knife, and then finish the cut with a very sharp, straight-bladed knife. Or, you might use only one knife—try different knives.) Cut on an angle; the sharper the angle, the larger the biscotti will be. Unless you want very large biscotti, do not cut on too sharp an angle. Cut the biscotti about a scant ¾ inch wide.

At this stage, the biscotti are very fragile; use a large metal spatula or pancake turner to carefully transfer them to two unlined cookie sheets, placing them cut side

1½ ounces (⅓ cup) blanched almonds
12 ounces milk chocolate
2 cups sifted unbleached flour
½ teaspoon baking powder
½ teaspoon baking soda
¼ teaspoon salt
1 cup granulated sugar
7 ounces (1½ cups) roasted and salted whole macadamia nuts (I use Mauna Loa brand—they come in a 7-ounce jar)
2 eggs
1 teaspoon vanilla extract
¼ teaspoon almond extract
2 tablespoons whiskey or brandy

ABOUT 24 LARGE BISCOTTI

down. Bake the two sheets for 35 minutes. Once during baking, turn the slices upside down and reverse the sheets top to bottom and front to back.

When finished, turn the oven off, open the oven door, and let the biscotti cool in the oven.

When they are cool, the chunks of chocolate might still be soft. If so, let the biscotti stand for about an hour, and then store them airtight.

Crackers and Extras

Crackers

The next six recipes are not cookies but I cannot resist including them. They are crackers, to serve with a meal, or with cheese, or just to nibble on, plain, with tea or coffee or wine. They are unusual (some of the directions are strange) and delicious (I don't know of anything that I make that people rave about more than they rave about Corn Melba) and fun to make and I love them.

Corn Melba

About 40 years ago the dining room of the Hampshire House in New York City always had a basket of these on each table. They were unbelievable! They were surely the thinnest (as though they had been made by a special machine—not by a person), the crispest, flakiest, most buttery, most exciting . . . the flavor was bland and mild and simply buttery and simply delicious and I simply had to have the recipe. The hotel would not give it to me. That was the beginning of a hunt that lasted for many years and involved almost everyone I knew from coast to coast. I was getting nowhere.

Sometime before I started my Corn Melba hunt, I had sent 25¢ for a small pamphlet called Menus and Recipes of Famous Hostesses, published by Vogue magazine. I made a few things from it and put it away in a desk drawer and forgot about it. Years later I came across it, and as soon as I opened it I saw Corn Melba; it even had the same name. I don't remember the name of the famous hostess (I wish I did) who contributed it, but I think she lived on Long Island, and I think her menu included broiled fish, and I think it was for a luncheon.

Serve Corn Melba any time, any place, with or without anything.

Making these is a most unusual experience, different from any other baking I have done. And fun all the way.

Corn Melba keeps well for a week or more. What I mean is, it does not spoil. But it is hard to keep it.

This is baked in jelly-roll pans. The recipe

makes six panfuls. If you have only one pan, and therefore bake only one pan at a time, be prepared to spend several hours near the oven. But if you bake three or four pans of it at one time, it can all be completed in about 1½ hours.

This is made in jelly-roll pans that measure 10½ x 15½ x 1 inch. The crackers will be cut into squares in the pans, therefore you should not use pans that have a nonstick finish or you will cut through the finish. You can bake six pans at a time if you have that many pans and oven racks, or you can bake only one or more at a time (the remaining batter should stand at room temperature). Adjust oven racks for as many pans as you have, or adjust a rack to the center for only one pan. Preheat oven to 375°. Butter the pans (see Note).

Sift together the flour, baking powder, and salt, and set aside.

In the large bowl of an electric mixer, beat the butter until it is soft. Beat in the sugar and then the eggs, one at a time. On low speed add the sifted dry ingredients in three additions, alternating with the milk and water in two additions, scraping the bowl with a rubber spatula and beating until well mixed after each addition. Add the cornmeal last and beat only until mixed. The mixture will look curdled during the mixing and might still be lumpy after the mixing. Strain it through a coarse strainer set over a bowl to remove any lumps. It will be a thin mixture.

You will have 4 cups of batter with which to make 6 panfuls of Melba. As closely as I can figure it, that means that for each panful you should use ⅔ cup of batter. Measure it in a glass measuring cup.

Pour the measured amount along one long side of the buttered pan, scraping out the cup with a rubber spatula. Tilt the pan as necessary for the batter to run into a thin, thin layer completely covering the bottom of the pan. Hold the pan almost vertically, turn it one way and then another, and have patience—the batter might run slowly. If, after a reasonable length of time, you see that you simply cannot get the batter to cover the pan, use an extra spoonful or so as necessary.

2 cups double- or triple-sifted all-purpose flour (if your sifter has only one screen, resift the flour before measuring; if it is sifted only once, you will be using a little more flour, and the mixture will be a little too thick)

2 teaspoons baking powder

½ teaspoon salt

4 ounces (1 stick) unsalted butter, at room temperature

2 tablespoons granulated sugar

2 eggs

1 cup milk, at room temperature

1 cup water, at room temperature

½ cup cornmeal (the cornmeal may be white or yellow—I have used both many times—but I think that the Melba is slightly thinner and crisper with white water-ground cornmeal)

96 CRACKERS

Bake one or more pans at a time—you can put a second pan in after the first one has started baking. After about 5 to 7 minutes the batter should be firm enough to be cut; remove it from the oven and, with a small, sharp knife, cut the long way to make 4 strips, and then cut crossways to make 16 rectangles.

Return the pan to the oven and continue to bake for about 25 minutes more, until the Melba is crisp all over—part of it might be golden brown or even darker, and part of it may be lighter (although it is best when it is all an even golden color). During baking reverse the pan top to bottom and front to back as necessary to ensure even browning. The crackers will shrink as they bake, and some of the crackers may still look wet and buttery in places but they will dry and crisp as they cool if they have been baked enough.

The crackers will not all be done at the same time; some may be done in 20 to 25 minutes, others might take as long as 45 minutes. Remove them from the oven as they are done.

With a wide metal spatula, transfer the baked crackers to a paper towel to cool. When you run out of room it is all right to place some of them on top of others.

Wash, dry, and butter the pans each time you use them.

Corn Melba is fragile—handle with care. (Before I knew how to make this, we ordered it by mail from New York; when it arrived in Florida it was pretty well broken up—but we were happy to have it anyway.) Store it airtight but don't worry about this getting limp—it stays crisp. It may be frozen if you want to keep it for many weeks or months.

NOTE: When a friend of mine had trouble with this recipe we talked long distance for hours. We finally found the trouble. She was buttering the pans with melted butter and a pastry brush, and was using much more butter than you use when you spread the butter (not melted) with crumpled wax paper. The excess butter prevented the crackers from baking as they should. The pans should be buttered normally, not extra heavy and not extra thin.

Ralph's Corn Melba

For many years my husband asked me to add some cayenne pepper to this recipe. I don't know why it took me years to do it. I finally did, and Ralph loved it. If you want to try it, add ¼ teaspoon of cayenne to ⅔ cup of the batter and make one panful.

Cheese Pennies

This is not a cookie—it is a cheese cracker to serve with cocktails, or at the table with soup or salad. They are thin, light, and crisp, and I make them quite sharp with cayenne. The procedure is the same as for making icebox cookies—the dough must be refrigerated for several hours or longer.

Sift together the flour, salt, and cayenne pepper, and set aside. Grate the cheese as fine as possible. In the large bowl of an electric mixer cream the butter. Add the grated cheese and beat until thoroughly blended. On low speed gradually add the sifted dry ingredients and beat, scraping the bowl with a rubber spatula, until thoroughly incorporated.

Spread a bit of flour lightly on a board and turn the dough out onto the floured board. Flour your hands lightly. With your hands shape the dough as for icebox cookies into a round or square shape about 8 inches long and 1¾ inches in diameter.

Wrap the roll in plastic wrap or wax paper and place it in the refrigerator (not the freezer—if the dough is frozen it will be difficult to slice).

Let stand in the refrigerator for at least several hours, or several days if you wish.

Any time before baking the crackers, toast the sesame seeds as follows: Spread them in a small, shallow pan and place the pan in the middle of a preheated 350° oven. Shake the pan occasionally until the seeds have turned golden brown—it will take 15 to 20 minutes. Set aside to cool. (Toasting brings out the flavor of the seeds.)

When ready to bake the crackers, adjust two racks to divide the oven into thirds and preheat oven to 350°.

Unwrap the roll of dough and place it on a cutting board. With a very thin, sharp knife cut slices ⅛ to ¼ inch thick (I like these thin) and place them 1½ to 2 inches apart on unbuttered cookie sheets.

Sprinkle the tops of the slices generously with the toasted sesame seeds.

Bake for 12 to 15 minutes, until the pennies are lightly colored. Reverse the sheets top to bottom and front to back as necessary to ensure even browning. They must bake long enough to be very crisp, but overbaking will burn the cheese and spoil the flavor.

1 cup sifted all-purpose flour
½ teaspoon salt
⅛ to ½ teaspoon cayenne pepper (see Notes)
½ pound extra-sharp cheddar cheese
4 ounces (1 stick) unsalted butter
3 tablespoons sesame seeds (see Notes)

55 TO 60 CRACKERS

These crackers must be removed from the sheets as soon as they are taken out of the oven. Use a wide metal spatula to loosen all the crackers from the sheet quickly and then transfer them to racks to cool.

Store airtight.

NOTES: I like these crackers sharp and spicy—I use ½ teaspoon cayenne. With ⅛ teaspoon they will have a good flavor but will be mild, ¼ teaspoon will make them warm, ½ teaspoon will make them hot, but for hot-hot, you may want to use even more. Be your own judge about how much to use.

There are white sesame seeds (hulled) and grayish-tan ones (unhulled)—use the white ones.

Swedish Hardtack

This is the name that came with this recipe when I got it from a lady in Michigan. But they are not what I think of when I hear that name; they are rich and buttery and flaky and so delicious you will eat them plain with soup, salad, cocktails, tea or coffee, or nothing. Once, at a large cocktail party, I served a huge bowl of these along with a variety of hors d'oeuvres. These went first, and I had to promise the recipe to all the guests.

You will need a regular rolling pin and also a special type of corrugated rolling pin with deep ridges about ¼ inch apart in the wood going around the pin like bracelets and making the dough look like matzohs. I was told that it is made for cutting spaghetti—or use it to decorate shortbread-type cookies.

These crackers keep perfectly in an airtight container for weeks.

Do not make these if you are in a hurry; they take a great deal of time and patience. (This is the original Swedish recipe divided by 8—it took me 2 days to make the full amount.) This amount will be enough to serve to 6 people with lunch or cocktails.

The prepared dough must be chilled in the freezer for an hour or two before you use it. While you are making these you can stop in the middle and let the dough wait in the freezer or the refrigerator for days or weeks.

P lace the butter in a small pan (or in a custard cup placed in a little water in a small pan) over low heat to melt slowly. Remove from the heat and set aside to cool slightly.

Meanwhile, sift together into a mixing bowl the flour, baking soda, and salt. Stir in the sugar. Add the buttermilk and the melted butter all at once and stir until smooth.

Wrap the dough in plastic wrap and place it in the freezer for about 1 or 2 hours. (It will become too hard to roll if it is frozen too long. If this happens, let it stand in the refrigerator or at room temperature briefly until you can roll it.)

When you are ready to bake, adjust two racks to divide the oven into thirds and preheat oven to 350°.

Generously flour a pastry cloth and a plain rolling pin. (Both the cloth and the pin will have to be refloured often to keep the dough from sticking.)

Work with 1 rounded tablespoonful of the dough at a time, keeping the rest in the freezer or the refrigerator. (The dough becomes too sticky to handle at room temperature.) Place the dough on the floured cloth and turn it over to flour all sides. With the floured rolling pin, roll the dough gently until it is about ¼ inch thick—the shape does not matter. The rolled-out dough can be turned over as often as necessary to keep both sides floured, but work quickly.

Sprinkle the top generously with sesame seeds, use more than you think are enough, and then add a few more. Roll over the seeds lightly with the rolling pin to press the seeds into the dough and to roll the dough very thin; it should be as thin as you can make it.

Next, flour the corrugated rolling pin (it is best to do this with a pastry brush) and, very gently, roll over the dough, rolling in one direction only until the dough has ridges all over like matzohs. If you press too hard while you are doing this, the dough will stick to the pin (and be a pain). It is best to press only gently; you can repeat this several times, rerolling as you wish. The outside shape of the dough does not make any difference. And it does not matter if the ridges actually cut through the dough in places.

Now, with a pizza cutter, pastry wheel, or long knife, cut the rolled-out dough into halves or quarters. With a wide metal spatula transfer the pieces to unbuttered and unlined cookie sheets, placing them any which way and very close together.

Repeat rolling and cutting the crackers to fill the cookie sheets. (It gets easier and they get thinner and better as you make more.)

Bake for 10 to 15 minutes until the crackers are golden brown, reversing the sheets top to bottom and back to front to ensure even browning. The crackers will be darker on the edges or wherever the dough is thinner, and they will be barely sandy, or not actually colored at all in other areas. (Some of the flour that was used for rolling will remain white and floury on the crackers; it is okay, but if there is really a lot it can be brushed off with a pastry brush after the crackers are baked.) The baking time will vary depending on the thickness/thinness of crackers. Do not underbake.

With a wide metal spatula transfer the crackers to a piece of paper towel as they are done.

1 ounce (¼ stick) unsalted butter

1 cup plus 1 tablespoon unsifted *all-purpose flour*

¼ teaspoon baking soda

¼ teaspoon salt

2 tablespoons granulated sugar

½ cup buttermilk

Sesame seeds (I use the white, or bleached seeds, although either those or the natural ones can be used)

16 TO 20 CRACKERS

WARNING! This dough is sticky and difficult to work with. I think it is worth the hassle. Watchpoints: The dough must be as cold as possible without being frozen when you roll it. It is easier to roll a small piece than a large one. Do not be afraid to keep it well-enough floured (within reason) on both sides to keep it from sticking. Mainly, work quickly!

NOTE: To make a generous number of these crackers, the amounts noted here to the right (four times the recipe) will keep you in the kitchen for most of a day. (It is the amount I like to make.)

4 ounces (1 stick) unsalted
 butter
4¼ cups unsifted all-purpose
 flour
1 teaspoon baking soda
1 teaspoon salt
½ cup granulated sugar
2 cups buttermilk
Sesame seeds

Knäckbröd

This is a rather bland, plain, crisp, paper-thin, whole-wheat Scandinavian cracker 12 inches in diameter. Aside from its unusual dramatic looks, it is extra delicious and fun to make and fun to serve. Serve it with cheese (preferably a semisoft cheese like Brie) or as a table bread. Or just have it around for a nibble. Or make it for a sensational house gift if you are going to friends' for dinner. A basket of this is gorgeous on a buffet table.

easure out the whole-wheat flour and set aside ½ cup. Place the remaining 1½ cups of whole-wheat flour in a large mixing bowl. Add the salt, baking soda, buttermilk, and the melted butter, and stir with a rubber spatula or wooden spoon to make a smooth dough. Add the reserved ½ cup whole-wheat flour and the ¼ cup white flour. Stir to mix.

Flour a large board or work surface and turn the dough out onto it. Knead for a few seconds, adding additional white or whole-wheat flour if necessary. You should add just enough flour to keep the dough from sticking but no more.

Form the dough into a thick cylinder 6 inches long. Cut it into 6 even slices. Each slice will be a Knäckbröd.

Adjust one rack to the center of the oven for baking one Knäckbröd at a time, or adjust two racks to divide the oven into thirds for baking two Knäckbröd at a time. Pre-

2 cups unsifted all-purpose
 whole-wheat flour
1 teaspoon salt
1 teaspoon baking soda
1 cup buttermilk
2 ounces (½ stick) unsalted
 butter, melted
¼ cup unsifted all-purpose
 white flour
Additional white or whole-
 wheat flour
Sesame seeds and/or caraway
 seeds

6 LARGE KNÄCKBRÖD

heat oven to 350°. Generously butter one or two cookie sheets (or more if you wish; you will bake 6 separate breads or crackers, each on a buttered sheet—you can bake just one at a time and roll out the second one while the first one is baking).

Now, you can roll out each piece of dough either on a large board or pastry cloth. Flour the board or cloth and a rolling pin. Roll one piece of the dough into a 12-inch circle; it should be paper thin. While rolling, turn the dough over occasionally to keep both sides floured.

Drape the rolled-out dough over the rolling pin and unroll it onto the buttered sheet. Prick it all over, at ½- to 1-inch intervals, with a fork. Then, with the dull side of the blade of a long knife, press down on the dough to score it (without cutting through the dough) into 12 pie-shaped wedges.

Sprinkle the top generously with sesame seeds or caraway seeds. Roll over the seeds with a rolling pin, pressing firmly enough so the seeds will not fall off. Or sprinkle three Knäckbröd with sesame seeds and three with caraway seeds.

Bake for 12 to 15 minutes. If you bake two sheets at a time, reverse them top to bottom and front to back once during baking to ensure even baking. If you bake only one sheet at a time, reverse it front to back. They should be golden brown all over, but don't let them burn anywhere.

They can cool on the sheet or on a rack or on paper.

To store, place the Knäckbröd in a large plastic bag and fasten the top airtight. Store at room temperature or in the freezer.

To serve, they can be broken into pie-shaped wedges in the kitchen, but it is a shame—they look so great before they are broken. Just place them in a shallow basket or on a large, round board or tray and let people break off their own.

Black Pepper Crackers

Delicate, tender, delicious, thin, and crisp, all-purpose crackers to serve with soup, salad, or with cheese. I use a conservative amount of pepper—just enough to taste—but it may be increased or omitted. Or you can substitute chili powder, or caraway or sesame seeds. Or garlic or onion powder. Or whatever.

Adjust two racks to divide the oven into thirds and preheat oven to 425°. You will use unbuttered and unlined cookie sheets, which may be plain or non-stick.

This may be put together in a food processor or in a bowl with a pastry blender. To do it in a processor (fitted with the steel blade), sift together the flour, sugar, salt, and baking powder, and place them in the bowl of the processor. Add the butter and process very briefly with quick on-and-off "pulses" for about 10 seconds or less, only until the mixture resembles coarse meal. Then, through the feed tube, quickly add the milk or cream and process only until the mixture barely holds together.

To do it without a processor, sift together into a large bowl the flour, sugar, salt, and baking powder. Add the butter and with a pastry blender cut in the butter until the mixture resembles coarse meal. Add the milk or cream and stir with a fork to make a stiff dough.

Work with half of the dough at a time. Press it into a square shape, place it on a floured pastry cloth, and roll it with a floured rolling pin. Keep the shape squarish and roll the dough until it is very, very thin, or as thin as you can make it. (The crackers will be good if the dough is not that thin, but they will be better if it is.)

With a pizza cutter, a pastry cutter, or a long, sharp knife, trim the edges square. With a fork, prick the dough all over at ½-inch intervals. Then brush it all lightly with milk or cream. Now grind the black pepper over the dough. Or sprinkle with whatever topping or combination you wish. I use black pepper, and I use enough so you can really taste it (it is delicious) but not enough to make it really harsh. But it is up to you. (It is a good idea to bake one as a sample; it is too bad to bake them all and then say, "They should have had more pepper.")

Now, with the cutter or knife, cut the entire piece of dough into even squares or oblongs. (I make them about the rectangular size of bought graham crackers. And with the edge of a wide metal spatula, I lightly score each cracker through the middle into halves like graham crackers.)

Place the cracker on unbuttered, unlined cookie sheets. Bake for about 18 to 20 minutes, reversing the sheets top to bottom and front to back as necessary to ensure even browning, until the crackers are golden colored. Be sure to bake them long enough for them to be crisp.

Cool on a rack and then store airtight.

2 cups sifted all-purpose flour
1 tablespoon granulated sugar
¾ teaspoon salt
¼ teaspoon baking powder
2 ounces (½ stick) unsalted butter, cold and firm, cut into ¼-inch pieces (it is best to cut it ahead of time and refrigerate)
½ cup milk or light cream
Additional milk or light cream
Black pepper (preferably use whole peppercorns and a mill, or use ground pepper)

ABOUT 24 CRACKERS

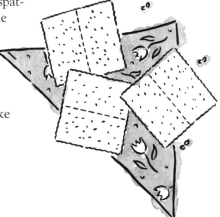

Marshmallows

These are candy—not cookies. But homemade marshmallows are so very popular and such fun to make that I want to share the recipe with you. You will need a candy thermometer and an electric mixer. And the cooked marshmallow mixture must stand for 8 to 12 hours (or a little longer if it is more convenient) before it is cut into individual pieces.

Prepare a 9 x 13 x 2-inch pan as follows. Invert the pan. Cut a piece of aluminum foil long enough to cover the bottom and sides of the pan. Place the foil shiny side down over the inverted pan and fold down the sides and corners just to shape. Remove the foil and turn the pan right side up. Place the foil in the pan and press it gently into place. With a pastry brush or crumpled wax paper coat the foil thoroughly but lightly with vegetable shortening. Set aside.

Place half of the cold water (reserve remaining ½ cup) in the large bowl of an electric mixer. Sprinkle the gelatin over the surface of the water and set aside.

Place the sugar, corn syrup, salt, and reserved ½ cup water in a heavy 1½- to 2-quart saucepan over moderately low heat. Stir until the sugar is dissolved and the mixture comes to a boil. Cover for 3 minutes to allow any sugar crystals on the sides of the saucepan to dissolve. Uncover, raise the heat to high, insert a candy thermometer, and let the syrup boil without stirring until temperature reaches 240°. Do not overcook. Remove from heat.

Vegetable shortening (such as Crisco), for preparing the pan
1 cup cold water
3 tablespoons (3 envelopes) unflavored gelatin
2 cups granulated sugar
¾ cup light corn syrup
¼ teaspoon salt
1½ teaspoons vanilla extract
Confectioners sugar (for coating the marshmallows)

1 POUND, 10 OUNCES OF MARSHMALLOWS

Beating constantly at medium speed, pour the syrup slowly into the gelatin mixture. After all the syrup has been added, increase the speed to high and beat for 15 minutes until the mixture is lukewarm, snowy white, and the consistency of whipped marshmallow, adding the vanilla a few minutes before the end of the beating. (During the beating, occasionally scrape the bowl with a rubber spatula. The marshmallow will thicken and become sticky—if the mixture crawls up on the beaters as it thickens, carefully wipe it down with a rubber spatula.)

Pour the slightly warm and thick marshmallow mixture into the prepared pan and, with your forefinger, scrape all the mixture off the beaters. Smooth the top of the marshmallow. Let stand uncovered at room temperature for 8 to 12 hours or a little longer if it is more convenient.

Then, sift or strain confectioners sugar generously onto a large cutting board to cover a surface larger than the 9 x 13-inch pan. Invert the marshmallow over the sugared surface. Remove the pan and peel off the foil. Strain confectioners sugar generously over the top of the marshmallow.

To cut the marshmallow into even 1-inch strips, use a ruler and toothpicks to mark it every 1 inch. Prepare a long, heavy, sharp knife by brushing the blade lightly with vegetable shortening. Cutting down firmly with the full length of the blade, cut the marshmallow into 1-inch strips. (After cutting the first slice, just keep the blade sugared to keep it from sticking.)

Dip the cut sides of each strip into confectioners sugar to coat them thoroughly—you should have enough excess sugar on the board to do this.

Now cut each strip into 1-inch squares. (You may place three strips together and cut through them all at once.) Roll the marshmallows in the sugar to coat the remaining cut sides. Shake off excess sugar.

Store in a plastic box or any air tight container—or in a plastic bag like the commercial marshmallows.

NOTE: An interesting little aside about marshmallows. I gave this recipe to a friend who is a high school home-economics teacher. She was ecstatic about it and taught it in all of her classes. She started each class by asking her students to write down the ingredients they thought were in marshmallows. No one knew. The guesses included egg whites, milk, cream, flour, cornstarch, and some said "marsh" or "mallow," which they thought was a natural substance that grows on trees.

But they soon found out, and my friend tells me that it is the single most popular recipe she has ever taught, and that now there are hundreds of girls in Miami Beach who make marshmallows regularly.

Everybody's Favorite Fudge

My chocolate book has a fudge recipe; it is the classic, traditional fudge which, frankly, is temperamental and tricky to make. Since the publication of that book, I continue to receive other fudge recipes from readers, recipes that are foolproof. They are all variations on a theme that includes evaporated milk, marshmallow, and chocolate morsels. This is the one that seems to be everybody's favorite. This is never too soft to eat or too hard to handle or too sugary; always smooth and creamy.

Line an 8-inch square pan with aluminum foil as follows: turn the pan upside down, center a 12-inch square of foil shiny side down over the pan, press down the sides and corners of the foil to shape it to the pan, remove the foil, turn the pan right side up, place the shaped foil in the pan and gently press the foil (with a potholder if you wish) into place in the pan. Set aside the lined pan.

Pick over the optional nuts carefully (sometimes they include a piece of shell), and remove and reserve about ½ cup of the best-looking halves or pieces to decorate the fudge. Set the nuts aside.

Pour the evaporated milk into a heavy 2½- to 3-quart saucepan. Add the marshmallow cream, butter, sugar, and salt. Place over low to medium-low heat and stir constantly with a wooden spoon until the mixture comes to a boil. This mixture wants to burn; adjust the heat as necessary, and scrape the bottom of the pan occasionally with a rubber spatula to be sure it is not burning.

As soon as the mixture comes to a full boil, start timing it; let it boil and continue to stir for 5 minutes. (After the 5 minutes are up, the mixture will have caramelized slightly. It is not necessary to test the mixture with a thermometer—just time it—the temperature will be 226° to 228° when the boiling time is up.)

Remove the saucepan from the heat and add the morsels, stir until melted and smooth—a strong wire whisk is a big help—stir in the vanilla, and then 1½ cups of nuts. Quickly pour into the lined pan, smooth the top, and place the reserved ½ cup of nuts onto the top of the fudge, spacing them evenly and pressing down on them enough so they will not fall off.

Let stand until cool. Then chill until firm. Remove the fudge and foil from the pan by lifting the corners of the foil. Or, cover the pan with wax paper and a cookie sheet, turn the pan and sheet over, remove the pan and foil, cover the fudge with a cookie sheet or a cutting board, and turn it over again, leaving the fudge right side up.

With a long, sharp knife carefully cut the fudge into pieces. Wrap them individually in clear cellophane, wax paper, or aluminum foil. Or place the fudge in an airtight freezer box. If you want to store for more than a few days, freeze it.

Optional: 7 ounces (2 cups) pecans, toasted (see To Toast Pecans, page 4), or walnuts, halves or pieces

5 or 5 ⅓ ounces (about ⅔ cup) evaporated milk

1 7-ounce jar marshmallow cream

2 ounces (½ stick) unsalted butter

1½ cups granulated sugar

¼ teaspoon salt

12 ounces (2 cups) semisweet chocolate morsels

1 teaspoon vanilla extract

A BIT MORE THAN 2½ POUNDS—24 LARGE PIECES

Fantastic Vanilla Ice Cream

Rich, luxurious, extravagant, delicious, de luxe, smo-o-oth; the best! This fabulous ice cream will not freeze too hard to serve easily—it will remain creamy and heavenly and perfect—even after days in the freezer.

P lace 1 cup of the cream (reserve the remaining 1 cup) in the top of a double boiler over hot water on moderate heat. Let stand, uncovered, until a slightly wrinkled skin forms on the top of the cream.

Meanwhile, in the small bowl of an electric mixer, beat the yolks for a few minutes until they are pale and thick. On low speed gradually add the sugar. Then beat on high speed again for 2 or 3 minutes more.

When the cream is scalded, on low speed, very gradually add about half of it to the beaten-yolks-and-sugar mixture. Scrape the bowl well with a rubber spatula. Then add the yolk mixture to the remaining cream. Mix well, and place over hot water again, on moderate heat.

Cook, scraping the bottom and sides frequently with a rubber spatula, until the mixture thickens to a soft custard consistency. It will register 178° to 180° on a candy thermometer. (When the mixture starts to thicken, scrape the bottom and sides constantly with the rubber spatula.)

Remove from the hot water, transfer to a larger bowl, stir occasionally until cool, and mix in the vanilla and the reserved 1 cup of heavy cream.

It is best to chill this mixture for an hour or more before freezing it. Freeze in an ice cream maker, following the manufacturer's directions.

2 cups heavy cream
4 egg yolks
½ cup granulated sugar
1 teaspoon vanilla extract

1½ PINTS

Devil's Food Chocolate Sauce

Elegant; rich and buttery, dark and delicious chocolate. Serve warm or at room temperature; it may be reheated. Or serve it cold (it is great refrigerated—it becomes very thick when it is cold) over coffee ice cream.

This wants desperately to burn on the bottom of the pan while you are making it; use an enameled cast-iron pan (Le Creuset or any other equally heavy pan).

*I*n a 1- to 2-quart saucepan over low heat, melt the butter and chocolate, stirring occasionally. Add the sugar, cocoa, and cream. Stir with a wire whisk until thoroughly incorporated. Increase the heat a bit to medium-low. Stir with a wire whisk occasionally and also scrape the bottom with a rubber spatula occasionally, until the mixture comes to a low boil. (If you are impatient and if you use medium heat, scrape the bottom constantly with a rubber spatula.) Watch carefully for burning and adjust the heat as necessary.

When the mixture comes to a low boil, remove the pan from the heat and stir or whisk in the vanilla.

Serve hot or cooled. Reheat carefully to prevent burning (a double boiler is the safest way). Refrigerate up to two weeks if you wish.

4 ounces (1 stick) unsalted butter
1 ounce unsweetened chocolate
⅔ cup granulated sugar
¼ cup unsweetened cocoa powder (preferably Dutch-process)
½ cup heavy whipping cream
1 teaspoon vanilla extract

1⅔ CUPS

NOTE: I like to double the recipe and have an extra jar for our guests to take home.

Index

A

Alcohol (as ingredient)
  Chocolate Icing, 131
  Denver Brownies, 121–22
  Dione Lucas's Sablés, 218–20
  Rum-Raisin Shortbread, 212–13
  Toasted Pine-Nut Cookies, 81
Alfred A. Knopf Peanut Butter
  Candy, 305
All-American Brownies, 120
Almond Macaroons, 263–64
Almond paste, leftover, 36
Almond Spicebox Cookies, 181
Almond Sugar Cookies, 192–93
Almond Tartlets, 269–70
Almonds (as ingredients)
  Almond Filling, 157
  Almond Macaroons, 263–64
  Almond Spicebox Cookies, 181
  Almond Sugar Cookies, 192–93
  Almond Tartlets, 269–70
  Cardamom Cookies from Copen-
    hagen, 183
  Cinnamon Almond Cookies,
    145–46
  Dione Lucas's Sablés, 218–20
  Ischler Cookies, 206–7
  Les Petites, 194–95
  Maxines, 167–68
  Viennese Almond Wafers, 205
  Viennese Chocolate Cookies,
    208–9
Aluminum foil, 2
Anise Icebox Cookies, 182
Anise seed, 107
Anise Seed Cookies, 106–7
  Bow Ties, 234
Apple Cookies
  Chocolate Apple Saucers, 43
  Johnny Appleseed Squares,
    115–16
Apricot and Date Rocky Road,
  300–302
Apricot Filling, 155–56
Arrowroot Wafers from Bermuda,
  215
Aspen Date-Nut Fingers, 153
Aspen Oatmeal Bars, 151
Austrian Walnut Crescents, 253–54

B

Banana Cookies
  Banana Rocks, 88
  Chocolate Banana Cookies, 42
Banana Rocks, 88–89
Bar Cookies, 100–158
  All-American Brownies, 120
  Anise Seed Cookies, 106–7
  Aspen Date-Nut Fingers, 153
  Aspen Oatmeal Bars, 151
  Brittle Peanut Bars, 141
  Butterscotch Brownies, 135
  Butterscotch Walnut Bars,
    144–45
  California Fruit Bars, 110–12
  Charleston Cheesecake Bars,
    109–10
  Chocolate Mint Sticks, 126–27
  Christmas Brownies, 118–19
  Christmas Fruitcake Bars, 139
  Cinnamon Almond Cookies,
    145–46
  Cream-Cheese Brownies, 124–25
  Dark Rocky Roads, 132–33
  Denver Brownies, 121–22
  Dutch Chocolate Bars, 128
  Fig Bars, 102–3
  Florida Cream-Cheese Squares,
    136
  Florida Lemon Squares, 137
  Fudge Brownies, 125–26
  Georgia Pecan Bars, 147–48
  Greenwich Village Brownies,
    123
  Hermit Bars, 139–40
  Honey Date-Nut Bars, 152
  Hungarian Walnut Bars, 141–43
  Johnny Appleseed Squares,
    115–16
  Lebkuchen, 104–5
  Light Rocky Roads, 134
  Palm Beach Brownies, 117
  Palm Beach Pineapple Squares,
    138
  Pecan Chews, 149
  Pecan Festival Bars, 148–49
  Pecan Square's Americana,
    100–102
  Pennsylvania Squares, 107–8
  Petites Trianons, 119–20
  Polish Wedding Cakes, 155–56

Sour Lemon Squares, 113–14
  Supremes, 129–30
  Texas Cowboy Bars, 150–51
  Viennese Chocolate-Walnut
    Bars, 130–31
  Viennese Linzer Cookies, 154–55
  Viennese Marzipan Bars, 157–58
  World War II Raisin Squares,
    112–13
Bar Cookies (Chocolate)
  All-American Brownies, 120
  Chocolate Mint Sticks, 126–27
  Christmas Brownies, 118–19
  Cream-Cheese Brownies, 124–25
  Dark Rocky Roads, 132–33
  Denver Brownies, 121–22
  Dutch Chocolate Bars, 128
  Fudge Brownies, 125–26
  Greenwich Village Brownies,
    123
  Light Rocky Roads, 134
  Palm Beach Pineapple Squares,
    138
  Pennsylvania Squares, 107–8
  Petites Trianons, 119–20
  Supremes, 129–30
  Viennese Chocolate-Walnut
    Bars, 130–31
  See also Brownies
Basler Brunsli, 276–77
Big Newtons, 228–30
Big Old-Fashioned Chocolate
  Cookies, 40
Big Sur Chocolate-Chip Cookies,
  20–21
Billy Goats. See Date-Nut Rocks
Biscotti
  Macadamia and Milk Chocolate,
    280
Bitter-Chocolate Glaze, 127
Black-and-White Coconut Slices,
  164–65
Black-and-White Rusks, 279–80
Black Pepper Crackers, 291–92
Blind Date Cookies, 89–90
Blossoms. See Cookie Kisses
Bow Ties, 234
  Swedish Fried Twists, 274–75
Brandy. See under Alcohol
Brittle Peanut Bars, 141
Brown sugar, straining, 12, 210

Browned-Butter Filling, 248–49
Brownie Drops. See "Chocolate
    Street" Cookies
Brownie Cookies, 27–28
Brownies
    All-American Brownies, 120
    Brownie Cookies, 27–28
    Butterscotch Brownies, 135
    Christmas Brownies, 118–19
    Cream-Cheese Brownies, 124–25
    Denver Brownies, 121–22
    Fudge Brownies, 125–26
    Greenwich Village Brownies,
    123
    Palm Beach Brownies, 116–17
    See also Squares
Burned edges, 117
Butter, 8
Butterscotch
    Butterscotch Brownies, 135
    Butterscotch Molasses Cookies,
    97
    Butterscotch Thins, 173
    Butterscotch Walnut Bars,
    144–45
    Butterscotch Walnut Topping,
    144–45
    Pecan Butterscotch Icebox
    Cookies, 174
Butterscotch Brownies, 135
Butterscotch Molasses Cookies, 97
Butterscotch Thins, 173
Butterscotch Walnut Bars, 144–45
Butterscotch Walnut Topping,
    144–45

C
California Fruit Bars, 110–12
Candied fruit, 119
Candy Cookies, 31
Caraway (as ingredient)
    Caraway Crisps, 180
    Caraway Hardtack, 214
    Caraway Sour-Cream Cookies,
    210–11
Caraway Crisps, 180
Caraway Hardtack, 214
Caraway Sour-Cream Cookies,
    210–11
Cardamom Cookies from Copen-
    hagen, 183
Carrot and Honey Oatmeal Cookies,
    243–44
Carrots, using, 84
Cellophane, 2–3
Chapman, John (Johnny Apple-
    seed), 115
Charleston Cheesecake Bars, 109–10

Charlie Brown's Peanut Cookies,
    255–56
Charlie's Cookies. See Chocolate
    Whoppers
Cheese Pennies, 287–88
Child, Julia, 121
Chocolate
    Basler Brunsli, 276–77
    Bitter-Chocolate Glaze, 127
    Black-and-White Rusks, 279–80
    Chocolate Filling, 129–30
    Chocolate Glaze, 40
    Chocolate Meringue Ladyfingers,
    266–67
    Chocolate Tartlets, 267–68
    Chocolate Walnut Filling, 130
    Craig Claiborne's Chocolate
    Macaroons, 262–63
    Devil's Food Chocolate Sauce,
    297
    Everybody's Favorite Fudge,
    302–3
    Fudge Délices, 264–65
    Hershey's Milk Chocolate Kisses,
    28
    Judy's and Joan's Chocolate
    Truffles, 295–97
    Macadmia and Milk Chocolate
    Biscotti, 280
    Texas Truffles, 297–98
Chocolate Aggies, 239
Chocolate and Peanut-Butter Cres-
    cents, 241–42
Chocolate and Peanut-Butter
    Ripples, 47–48
Chocolate Applesaucers, 43
Chocolate Banana Cookies, 42
Chocolate Bar Cookies
    All-American Brownies, 120
    Chocolate Mint Sticks, 126–27
    Christmas Brownies, 118–19
    Cream-Cheese Brownies, 124–25
    Dark Rocky Roads, 132–33
    Denver Brownies, 121–22
    Dutch Chocolate Bars, 128
    Fudge Brownies, 125–26
    Greenwich Village Brownies,
    123
    Light Rocky Roads, 134
    Palm Beach Pineapple Squares,
    138
    Pennsylvania Squares, 107–8
    Petites Trianons, 119–20
    Supremes, 129–30
    Viennese Chocolate-Walnut
    Bars, 130–31
    See also Brownies
Chocolate-Chip Pillows, 222

Chocolate Chocolate-Chip Cookies,
    37
Chocolate Drop Cookies, 16–47
    Big Old-Fashioned Chocolate
    Cookies, 40
    Big Sur Chocolate-Chip
    Cookies, 20–21
    Brownie Cookies, 27–28
    Candy Cookies, 31
    Chocolate and Peanut-Butter
    Ripples, 47–48
    Chocolate Apple Saucers, 43
    Chocolate Banana Cookies, 42
    Chocolate Chocolate-Chip
    Cookies, 37
    Chocolate-Chip Chocolate
    Oatmeal Cookies, 33–34
    Chocolate Fudge Candy
    Cookies, 36–37
    Chocolate Gingersnaps, 23–24
    Chocolate Hermits, 19
    Chocolate Miracles, 32–33
    Chocolate Peanut Butter
    Cookies, 30
    Chocolate Peanut Cookies, 48
    Chocolate Raisin Cookies, 46
    "Chocolate Street" Cookies, 39
    Chocolate Whoppers, 16–17
    Cookie Kisses, 28–29
    David's Cookies, 24–25
    Down East Chocolate Cookies,
    35–36
    Extra-Bittersweet Chocolate
    Chunk Monster Cookies,
    26–27
    Key West Chocolate Treasures,
    41
    Marjorie Kinnan Rawlings's
    Chocolate Cookies, 17–18
    Santa Fe Chocolate Wafers, 38
    Savannah Chocolate Chewies,
    22–23
Chocolate Fudge-Candy Cookies,
    36–37
Chocolate Fudge Cookies. See
    Chocolate Miracles
Chocolate Glaze, 49
    for Ischler Cookies, 207
    for Viennese Marzipan Bar, 158
Chocolate Gingersnaps, 23–24
Chocolate Hand-Formed Cookies
    Chocolate Aggies, 238–39
    Chocolate and Peanut Butter
    Crescents, 241–42
    Chocolate Oatmeal Crispies, 240
    Chocolate Pepper Pretzels,
    237–38
    Fudge Mallows, 235–36
Chocolate Hermits, 19

Chocolate Icebox Cookies
  Black-and-White Coconut
    Slices, 164–65
  8-Layer Cookies, 161–62
  Maxines, 167–68
  Neapolitans, 170–71
  New Mexican Chocolate Icebox
    Cookies, 163–64
  Pinwheels, 184–95
  Wienerstube Cookies, 166
Chocolate Icing, 41–42, 43–44
  for Denver Brownies, 122
  for Fudge Mallows, 236
  for Viennese Chocolate-Walnut
    Bars, 130–31
Chocolate Meringue Ladyfingers,
  266–67
Chocolate Mint Sticks, 126–27
Chocolate Miracles, 32–33
Chocolate Oatmeal Crispies, 240
Chocolate Peanut Butter Cookies,
  30
Chocolate Peanut Cookies, 48
Chocolate Pepper Pretzels, 237–38
Chocolate Raisin Cookies, 46
Chocolate Rolled Cookies
  Chocolate-Chip Pillows, 222
  Les Petites, 194–95
  Viennese Chocolate Cookies,
    208–9
Chocolate semisweet morsels, substi-
  tuting, 17, 256
"Chocolate Street" Cookies, 39
Chocolate Tartlets, 267–68
Chocolate Whoppers, 16–17
Chocolate-Chip Chocolate Oatmeal
  Cookies, 33–34
Chopping, sizes for, 11
Christmas Brownies, 118–19
Christmas Cookies, 202–3
  Christmas Brownies, 118–19
  Christmas Fruitcake Bars, 139
  Connecticut Strippers, 272–73
  Swedish Ginger Cookies, 202–4
Christmas Fruitcake Bars, 139
Cinnamon Almond Cookies,
  145–46
Cinnamon Sugar, 64
Cobblestones, 168–69
Coconut Cookies
  Black-and-White Coconut
    Slices, 164–65
  Chocolate Oatmeal Crispies, 240
  Coconut Cookies, 191–92
  Coconut Grove Cookies, 44–45
  Coconut Oatmeal Cookies,
    56–57
  Coconut Pennies, 251
  Coconut Washboards, 249–50

Lemon Coconut Filling, 232–33
  Mrs. L.B.J.'s Moonrocks, 52
  Sunflower Coconut Cookies, 75
Coconut Oatmeal Cookies, 56–57
Coconut Pennies, 251
Coconut Washboards, 249–50
Coffee (as ingredient)
  Chocolate Applesaucers, 43
  Chocolate Banana Cookies, 42
  Chocolate-Chip Chocolate
    Oatmeal Cookies, 33–34
  Chocolate Hermits, 19
  Chocolate Icing, 131
  Chocolate Whoppers, 16–17
  Coconut Grove Cookies, 44–45
  Denver Brownies, 121–22
  Giant Ginger Cookies, 71–72
  Ginger Shortbread Cookies,
    217–18
  Key West Chocolate Treasures,
    41
  Palm Beach Brownies, 117
  Pecan Chews, 149
  Pinwheels, 184–95
  Tijuana Fiesta Cookies, 96–97
  Whole-Wheat Honey Wafers,
    198
  World War II Raisin Squares,
    112–13
Confectioners sugar, straining, 12,
  146
Connecticut Date Slices, 270–71
Connecticut Nutmeg Hermits, 71
Connecticut Strippers, 272–73
Cookie cutters, 3
Cookie Kisses, 28–29
Cookie racks, 3
Cookie sheets, 3
Cookies
  dipping, 259
  slicing, 171
  storing, 13
Coriander seeds, crushing, 97, 201
Corn Melba, 286
  Ralph's Corn Melba, 286
Cornell Sugar Cookies, 220
Corrugated rolling pins, 288
Cracker-Barrel Raisin Cookies,
  252–53
Crackers, 284–92
  Black Pepper Crackers, 291–92
  Cheese Pennies, 287–88
  Corn Melba, 284–86
  Knäckbröd, 290–91
  Ralph's Corn Melba, 284–86
  Swedish Hardtack, 288–90
Craig Claiborne's Chocolate Maca-
  roons, 262–63

Cream cheese
  Charleston Cheesecake Bars,
    109–10
  Cream-Cheese Brownies, 124–25
  Florida Cream-Cheese Squares,
    136
  Rugelach (Walnut Horns),
    188–89
Cream-Cheese Brownies, 124–25
Crescents
  Austrian Walnut Crescents,
    253–54
  Chocolate and Peanut Butter
    Crescents, 241–42
Crisp Oatmeal Wafers, 55–56
Crisps
  Caraway Crisps, 180
  Savannah Crisps, 65–66
Cross Creek Cookery, 17
Currants
  Connecticut Strippers, 272–73
  Danish Coffeehouse Slices,
    226–28
  Giant Ginger Cookies, 71–72
  Raisin Oatmeal Cookies, 93
  Rugelach (Walnut Horns),
    188–89
  softening, 72
Cutting, sizes for, 11

D

Danish Butter Sandwiches, 248–49
Danish Coffeehouse Slices, 226–28
Dark Rocky Roads, 132–33
Date Cookies
  Aspen Date-Nut Fingers, 153
  Blind Date Cookies, 89–90
  Connecticut Date Slices, 270–71
  Date-Nut Rocks, 87
  Date-Nut Wafers, 76
  Honey Date-Nut Bars, 152
  Mrs. L.B.J.'s Moonrocks, 52
  Whole-Wheat and Honey
    Hermits, 70
Date-Nut Rocks, 87
Date-Nut Wafers, 76
Dates
  Apricot and Date Rocky Road,
    300–302
  cutting, 89
David's Cookies, 24–25
Denver Brownies, 121–22
Devil's Food Chocolate Sauce, 297
Dione Lucas's Sablés, 218–20
Double broiler, 3–4
Down East Chocolate Cookies,
  35–36
Drop Cookies, 52–98
  Banana Rocks, 88–89

Blind Date Cookies, 89–90
Butterscotch Molasses Cookies, 97
Coconut Oatmeal Cookies, 56–57
Connecticut Nutmeg Hermits, 71
Crisp Oatmeal Wafers, 55–56
Date-Nut Rocks, 87
Date-Nut Wafers, 76
Farmer's Wife's Pecan Cookies, The, 81–82
Giant Ginger Cookies, 71–72
German Oatmeal Cookies, 94
Grand Oatmeal Spice Cookies, 54–55
Granny's Old-fashioned Sugar Cookies, 63–64
Half-Moon-Shaped Cookies, 64–65
Hawaiian Pineapple Cookies, 85
Indian Figlets, 84–85
Lemon Walnut Wafers, 78
Mountain Honey Ginger Snaps, 73
Mrs. L.B.J.'s Moonrocks, 52
My Mother's Gingersnaps, 60–61
Norman Rockwell's Oatmeal Wafers, 90–91
Nut-Free Walnut Jumbles, 82–83
Oatmeal Molasses Cookies, 92–93
Oatmeal Snickerdoodles, 91–92
Old-Fashioned Jumbo Lemon Wafers, 79–80
Old-Fashioned Spiced Pecan Cookies, 53–54
100-Percent Whole-Wheat Ginger Cookies, 61–63
Poppy-Seed Wafers (Mohn Cookies), 95
Praline Wafers, 77
Pumpkin Rocks, 86
Raisin-Nut Cookies, 57–58
Raisin Oatmeal Cookies, 93
Raisin Pillows, 68–69
Route 7 Raisin-Nut Cookies, 81
Savannah Crisps, 65–66
Sour-Cream Ginger Cookies, 74
Sunflower Coconut Cookies, 75
Sycamore Cookies, 67
Tea Cakes, 58–60
Tijuana Fiesta Cookies, 96–97
Toasted Pine-Nut Cookies, 81
24 Karat Cookies, 83–84
Vanilla Butter Wafers, 98
Whole-Wheat and Honey Hermits, 70

Drop Cookies (Chocolate), 16–47
Big Old-Fashioned Chocolate Cookies, 40
Big Sur Chocolate Chip Cookies, 20–21
Brownie Cookies, 27–28
Candy Cookies, 31
Chocolate and Peanut-Butter Ripples, 47–48
Chocolate Applesaucers, 43
Chocolate Banana Cookies, 42
Chocolate Chocolate-Chip Cookies, 37
Chocolate Fudge Candy Cookies, 36–37
Chocolate Gingersnaps, 23–24
Chocolate Hermits, 19
Chocolate Miracles, 32–33
Chocolate Peanut Butter Cookies, 30
Chocolate Peanut Cookies, 48
Chocolate Raisin Cookies, 46
"Chocolate Street" Cookies, 39
Chocolate Whoppers, 16–17
Chocolate-Chip Chocolate Oatmeal Cookies, 33–34
Cookie Kisses, 28–29
David's Cookies, 24–25
Down East Chocolate Cookies, 35–36
Extra-Bittersweet Chocolate Chunk Monster Cookies, 26–27
German Oatmeal Cookies, 94
Key West Chocolate Treasures, 41
Marjorie Kinnan Rawlings's Chocolate Cookies, 17–18
Santa Fe Chocolate Wafers, 38
Savannah Chocolate Chewies, 22–23
Dutch Chocolate Bars, 128

E
E. Shaver bookstore, 22
Eggs, 8–9
    freezing, 8
    size, 8
    whites, 8
    yolks, 8
8-Layer Cookies, 161–62
El Molino Old-Fashioned Hull-less Rolled Oats, 153
Electric mixer, 4
English Gingersnaps #1, 257
English Gingersnaps #2, 258
Equipment, 2–7
    aluminum foil, 2
    cellophane, 2–3
    cookie cutters, 3

cookie racks, 3
cookie sheets, 3
double broiler, 3–4
electric mixer, 4
flour sifter, 4
grater, 4
measuring cups, 4–5
measuring spoons, 5
nutmeg grater, 5
pastry bag, 5
pastry brush, 5
pasty cloth, 5–6
rolling pin, 6
rolling pin, stockinette cover for, 6
rubber spatulas, 6
ruler, 6
thermometer, 6–7
Everybody's Favorite Fudge, 294–95
Extra-Bittersweet Chocolate Chunk Monster Cookies, 26–27

F
Fantastic Vanilla Ice Cream, 296
Farmer's Wife's Pecan Cookies, The, 81–82
Fig Bars, 102–3
Fig Cookies
    Big Newtons, 228–30
    Fig Bars, 102–3
    Indian Figlets, 84–85
Fillings
    Almond Filling, 157
    Apricot Filling, 155–56
    Browned-Butter Filling, 248–49
    Chocolate Filling, 129–30
    Chocolate Walnut Filling, 130
    Lemon Coconut Filling, 232–33
    Walnut Filling, 143
Fingers
    Aspen Date-Nut Fingers, 153
    Sesame Fingers, 179
Flavorings, 9
Florida Cream-Cheese Squares, 136
Florida Lemon Squares, 137
Flour, 9
    potato flour, 217
    soy flour, 220
    too coarse to sift, 63
Flour sifter, 4
French Sugar Fans, 273–74
Fruit, 9
Fruit Bars
    California Fruit Bars, 110–12
    Christmas Brownies, 118–19
    Christmas Fruitcake Bars, 139
Fruit Cookies
    Chocolate Applesaucers, 43
    Fruitcake Icebox Cookies, 172

Hawaiian Pineapple Cookies, 85
Johnny Appleseed Squares,
115–16
Palm Beach Pineapple Squares,
138
Prune Pillows, 223–24
Fruitcake Icebox Cookies, 172
Fudge
Chocolate Fudge Candy
Cookies, 36–37
Chocolate Miracles, 32–33
Everybody's Favorite Fudge,
294–95
Fudge Brownies, 125–26
Fudge Délices, 264–65
Fudge Mallows, 235–36
Fudge Brownies, 125–26
Fudge Délices, 264–65
Fudge Mallows, 235–36

G

General Mills, 33
Georgia Pecan Bars, 147–48
German Oatmeal Cookies, 94
Giant Ginger Cookies, 71–72
Ginger Cookies
Giant Ginger Cookies, 71–72
Ginger Shortbread Cookies,
217–18
Mountain Honey Ginger Snaps,
73
100-Percent Whole-Wheat
Ginger Cookies, 61–63
Sour-Cream Ginger Cookies, 74
Swedish Ginger Cookies, 202–4
Wild-Honey and Ginger
Cookies, 199
Ginger Shortbread Cookies, 217–18
Gingersnaps
Chocolate Gingersnaps, 23–24
English Gingersnaps #1, 257
English Gingersnaps #2, 258
My Mother's Gingersnaps, 60–61
Glaze
for Banana Rocks, 88–89
for Big Old-Fashioned Chocolate
Cookies, 40
Bitter-Chocolate Glaze, 127
for Blind Date Cookies, 90
Chocolate Glaze for Viennese
Marzipan Bar, 157–58
for Chocolate Hermits, 20
for Chocolate Peanut Cookies,
49
for Cinnamon Almond Cookies,
146
for Dark Rocky Roads, 132–33
for Hermit Bars, 140
for Lebkuchen, 105

for Pumpkin Rocks, 86
White Glaze for Sour-Cream
Ginger Cookies, 74
Gottlieb, Isser, 22
Gottlieb's bakery, 22, 23
Grand Oatmeal Spice Cookies,
54–55
Granny's Old-fashioned Sugar
Cookies, 63–64
Graters, 4
Greenwich Village Brownies, 123

H

Half-Moon-Shaped Cookies, 64–65
Hamantaschen, 224–26
Hand-Formed Cookies, 232–58
Austrian Walnut Crescents,
253–54
Bow Ties, 234
Carrot and Honey Oatmeal
Cookies, 243–44
Charlie Brown's Peanut Cookies,
255–56
Chocolate Aggies, 238–39
Chocolate and Peanut Butter
Crescents, 241–42
Chocolate Oatmeal Crispies, 240
Chocolate Pepper Pretzels,
237–38
Coconut Pennies, 250–51
Coconut Washboards, 249–50
Cracker-Barrel Raisin Cookies,
251–52
Danish Butter Sandwiches,
248–49
English Gingersnaps #1, 257
English Gingersnaps #2, 258
Fudge Mallows, 235–36
Italian Sesame Sticks, 258–59
Kansas Cookies, 232–33
Señoritas, 242–43
Sour Cream and Pecan Dreams,
254–55
Whole-Wheat Cinnamon-
Nutmeg Cookies, 245–46
Hardtack
Caraway Hardtack, 214
Swedish Hardtack, 288–90
Hawaiian Pineapple Cookies, 85
Hazelnut Rusks, 277–78
Hazelnuts
blanching, 278
Hazelnut Rusks, 277–78
Les Petites, 194–95
Hermit Bars, 139–40
Hermits
Chocolate Hermits, 19
Connecticut Nutmeg Hermits,
71

Whole-Wheat and Honey
Hermits, 70
Hershey's Milk Chocolate Kisses.
See Cookie Kisses
Honey (as ingredient)
Carrot and Honey Oatmeal
Cookies, 243–44
Honey Date-Nut Bars, 152
Honey Graham Crackers, 200
Mountain Honey Ginger Snaps,
73
Swedish Honey Cookies, 201
Whole-Wheat Honey Wafers,
198
Wild-Honey and Ginger
Cookies, 199
Honey Date-Nut Bars, 152
Honey Graham Crackers, 200
Hot Butter Wafers, 213
Hot Peppered Pecans, 304
House-On-The-Hill, 234
Hungarian Walnut Bars, 141–43

I

Ice Cream
Fantastic Vanilla Ice Cream, 296
Icebox Cookies, 161–85
Almond Spicebox Cookies, 181
Anise Icebox Cookies, 182
Black-and-White Coconut
Slices, 164–65
Butterscotch Thins, 173
Caraway Crisps, 180
Cardamom Cookies from Copen-
hagen, 183
Cobblestones, 168–69
8-Layer Cookies, 161–62
Fruitcake Icebox Cookies, 172
Icebox Nut Cookies, 178
Maxines, 167–68
Neapolitans, 170–71
New Mexican Chocolate Icebox
Cookies, 163–64
Oatmeal Icebox Cookies, 175
Peanut Butter Icebox Cookies,
160
Peanut-Butter Pillows, 176
Pecan Butterscotch Icebox
Cookies, 174
Pinwheels, 184–95
Sesame Fingers, 179
Whole-Wheat Peanut-Butter
Cookies, 177
Wienerstube Cookies, 166
Icebox Cookies (Chocolate)
Black-and-White Coconut
Slices, 164–65
8-Layer Cookies, 161–62
Maxines, 167–68

Neapolitans, 170–71
New Mexican Chocolate Icebox
    Cookies, 163–64
Pinwheels, 184–95
Wienerstube Cookies, 166
Icebox Nut Cookies, 178
Icing
    Chocolate Icing for Denver
        Brownies, 122
    Key West Chocolate Icing,
        41–42
    Mint Icing, 127
    Royal Icing for Swedish Ginger
        Cookies, 202–4
    for Tijuana Fiesta Cookies,
        96–97
    White Icing for Denver
        Brownies, 122
India Tree, 10
Indian Figlets, 84–85
Ingredients, 8–10
    butter, 8
    eggs, 8–9
    flavorings, 9
    flour, 9
    fruit, 9
    nuts, 9
    oatmeal, 9
    spices, 10
    sugar, 10
Ischler Cookies, 206–7
Italian Sesame Sticks, 258–59

J
Joe Froggers, 189–91
Johnny Appleseed Squares, 115–16
Johnson, Lady Bird, 52
Jumbles
    Nut-Free Walnut Jumbles, 82–83

K
Kansas Cookies, 232–33
Key West Chocolate Treasures, 41
Kisses. See Cookie Kisses
Knäckbröd, 290–91

L
Ladyfingers
    Chocolate Meringue Ladyfingers,
        266–67
Latimer, Nicholas, 305
Leand, Barbara, 32
Lebkuchen, 104–5
Lemon (as ingredient)
    Florida Lemon Squares, 137
    Lemon Walnut Wafers, 78
    Old-Fashioned Jumbo Lemon
        Wafers, 79–80

Sour Lemon Squares, 113–14
Lemon Coconut Filling for Kansas
    Cookies, 232–33
Lemon Walnut Wafers, 78
Les Petites, 194–95
Light Rocky Roads, 134
Lindt Excellence, 17
Linzertote. See Viennese Linzer
    Cookies
Lucas, Dione, 218

M
Macadamia and Milk Chocolate
    Biscotti, 280
Macaroons
    Almond Macaroons, 263–64
    Craig Claiborne's Chocolate
        Macaroons, 262–63
McCay, Clive M., 220
McGlachlin, Margie, 232
Madison, Dolley, 213
Marjorie Kinnan Rawlings's Choco-
    late Cookies, 17–18
Marshmallows, 293–94
Marzipan Bar (Viennese), 157–58
Maxines, 167–68
Measuring cups, 4–5
Measuring spoons, 5
Meringue Topping for Coconut
    Grove Cookies, 45
Mint Icing, 127
Mohn Cookies (Poppy-Seed
    Wafers), 95
Mountain Honey Ginger Snaps, 73
Mrs. L.B.J.'s Moonrocks, 52
My Mother's Gingersnaps, 60–61

N
Neapolitans, 170–71
New Mexican Chocolate Icebox
    Cookies, 163–64
Nicholas, Nancy, 254, 305
Norman Rockwell's Oatmeal Wafers,
    90–91
Nut Cookies
    Almond Sugar Cookies, 192–93
    Aspen Date-Nut Fingers, 153
    Banana Rocks, 88
    Black-and-White Coconut
        Slices, 164–65
    Brittle Peanut Bars, 141
    Butterscotch Walnut Bars,
        144–45
    Cardamom Cookies from Copen-
        hagen, 183
    Charleston Cheesecake Bars,
        109–10
    Chocolate Applesaucers, 43

Chocolate Banana Cookies, 42
Chocolate Chocolate-Chip
    Cookies, 37
Chocolate Peanut Cookies, 49
"Chocolate Street" Cookies, 39
Christmas Brownies, 118–19
Cobblestones, 168–69
Connecticut Nutmeg Hermits,
    71
Dark Rocky Roads, 132–33
Date-Nut Rocks, 87
Date-Nut Wafers, 76
Dione Lucas's Sablés, 218–20
Extra-Bittersweet Chocolate
    Chunk Monster Cookies,
    26–27
Farmer's Wife's Pecan Cookies,
    The, 81–82
Fig Bars, 102–3
Fruitcake Icebox Cookies, 172
Georgia Pecan Bars, 147–48
German Oatmeal Cookies, 94
Honey Date-Nut Bars, 152
Hungarian Walnut Bars, 141–43
Icebox Nut Cookies, 178
Ischler Cookies, 206–7
Lemon Walnut Wafers, 78
Les Petites, 194–95
Light Rocky Roads, 134
Maxines, 167–68
Mrs. L.B.J.'s Moonrocks, 52
Neapolitans, 170–71
Norman Rockwell's Oatmeal
    Wafers, 90–91
Nut-Free Walnut Jumbles, 82–83
Oatmeal Icebox Cookies, 175
Oatmeal Molasses Cookies,
    92–93
Old-Fashioned Spiced Pecan
    Cookies, 53–54
Palm Beach Brownies, 116–17
Pecan Chews, 149
Pecan Butterscotch Icebox
    Cookies, 174
Pecan Festival Bars, 148–49
Pecan Squares Americana,
    100–102
Pinwheels, 184–95
Praline Wafers, 77
Pumpkin Rocks, 86
Raisin-Nut Cookies, 57–58
Route 7 Raisin-Nut Cookies, 81
Rugelach (Walnut Horns),
    188–89
Sycamore Cookies, 67
Texas Cowboy Bars, 150–51
Toasted Pine-Nut Cookies, 81
24 Karat Cookies, 83–84
Viennese Almond Wafers, 205

Viennese Chocolate Cookies,
208–9
Viennese Chocolate-Walnut
Bars, 130–31
Whole-Wheat and Honey
Hermits, 70
See also Almonds; Brownies;
Hazelnuts; Peanut Butter
Cookies; Pecans; Walnuts
Nut-Free Walnut Jumbles, 82–83
Nutmeg grater, 5
Nuts, 9
Chocolate Walnut Filling, 130
Cinnamon Almond Cookies,
145–46
Hot Peppered Pecans, 304
Pecan Topping, 101–2
Spiced Pecans, 303–4
substitution, 164
using unbleached, 247

O
Oatmeal, 9
El Molino Old-Fashioned Hull-
less Rolled Oats, 153
Shiloh Farms rolled oats, 244
Oatmeal Cookies
Aspen Oatmeal Bars, 151
Banana Rocks, 88
Carrot and Honey Oatmeal
Cookies, 243–44
Charleston Cheesecake Bars,
109–10
Chocolate Oatmeal Crispies, 240
Chocolate-Chip Chocolate
Oatmeal Cookies, 33–34
Coconut Oatmeal Cookies,
56–57
Crisp Oatmeal Wafers, 55–56
Florida Lemon Squares, 137
German Oatmeal Cookies, 94
Giant Oatmeal Spice Cookies,
54–55
Norman Rockwell's Oatmeal
Wafers, 90–91
Oatmeal Icebox Cookies, 175
Oatmeal Molasses Cookies,
92–93
Oatmeal Snickerdoodles, 91–92
Raisin Oatmeal Cookies, 93
Texas Cowboy Bars, 150–51
Oatmeal Icebox Cookies, 175
Oatmeal Molasses Cookies, 92–93
Oatmeal Snickerdoodles, 91–92
Old-Fashioned Jumbo Lemon
Wafers, 79–80
Old-Fashioned Spiced Pecan
Cookies, 53–54
100-Percent Whole-Wheat Ginger
Cookies, 61–63

P
Palm Beach Brownies, 116–17
Palm Beach Pineapple Squares, 138
Parchment paper, 33
Party Bazaar, 2
Pastry bag, 5
Pastry brush, 5
Pastry cloth, 5–6
preparing, 11
Peanut Bars (Brittle), 141
Peanut Butter Cookies
Charlie Brown's Peanut Cookies,
255–56
Chocolate and Peanut Butter
Crescents, 241–42
Chocolate and Peanut-Butter
Ripples, 47–48
Chocolate Peanut Butter
Cookies, 30
Peanut-Butter Pillows, 176
Whole-Wheat Peanut-Butter
Cookies, 177
See also Nut Cookies
Peanut Butter Icebox Cookies, 160
Peanut-Butter Pillows, 176
Pearl sugar, 217
Pecan Butterscotch Icebox Cookies,
174
Pecan Chews, 149
Pecan Festival Bars, 148–49
Pecan Squares Americana, 100–102
Pecan Topping, 101–2
Pecans (as ingredient)
Black-and-White Coconut
Slices, 164–65
Charleston Cheesecake Bars,
109–10
Chocolate Chocolate-Chip
Cookies, 37
Dark Rocky Roads, 132–33
Dutch Chocolate Bars, 128
Farmer's Wife's Pecan Cookies,
The, 81–82
Fruitcake Icebox Cookies, 172
Fudge Délices, 264–65
Georgia Pecan Bars, 147–48
German Oatmeal Cookies, 94
Greenwich Village Brownies,
123
Hot Peppered Pecans, 304
Icebox Nut Cookies, 178
Johnny Appleseed Squares,
115–16
Old-Fashioned Spiced Pecan
Cookies, 53–54
Pecan Butterscotch Icebox
Cookies, 174
Pecan Chews, 149
Pecan Festival Bars, 148–49

Pecan Squares Americana,
100–102
Pecan Topping, 101–2
Pinwheels, 184–95
Praline Wafers, 77
Raisin-Nut Cookies, 57–58
Rocky Road Topping, 134
Sour Cream and Pecan Dreams,
254–55
Spiced Pecans, 303–4
See also Brownies
Pennsylvania Squares, 107–8
Perfect Pan, 288–90
Petites Trianons, 119–20
Pillows
Chocolate-Chip Pillows, 222
Peanut-Butter Pillows, 176
Prune Pillows, 223–24
Raisin Pillows, 68–69
Pineapple Cookies
Fruitcake Icebox Cookies, 172
Hawaiian Pineapple Cookies, 85
Palm Beach Pineapple Squares,
138
Pinwheels, 184–95
Plain Old-Fashioned Sugar Cookies,
221
Polish Wedding Cakes, 155–56
Poppy-Seed Wafers (Mohn
Cookies), 95
Poppy seeds, 95
Post and Courier newspaper, 109
Potato flour, 217
Praline Wafers, 77
Pretzels
Chocolate Pepper Pretzels,
237–38
Procedures
pastry cloth, preparing, 11
sizes for chopping and cutting, 11
stockinette cover, preparing, 11
storing cookies, 13
straining sugar, 12
timing, 13
Prune Pillows, 223–24
Prunes (as ingredient)
Banana Rocks, 88
cutting, 89
Hamantaschen, 224–26
Prune Pillows, 223–24
Pumpkin Rocks, 86

R
Raisin Cookies
Chocolate Raisin Cookies, 46
Cobblestones, 168–69
Connecticut Nutmeg Hermits,
71
Cracker-Barrel Raisin Cookies,
252–53

Mrs. L.B.J.'s Moonrocks, 52
Raisin-Nut Cookies, 57–58
Raisin Oatmeal Cookies, 93
Raisin Pillows, 68–69
Route 7 Raisin-Nut Cookies, 81
Rum-Raisin Shortbread, 212–13
Sunflower Coconut Cookies, 75
World War II Raisin Squares,
    112–13
Raisin-Nut Cookies, 57–58
Raisin Oatmeal Cookies, 93
Raisin Pillows, 68–69
Ralph's Corn Melba, 286
Raspberry preserves
    Viennese Linzer Cookies, 154–55
Rawlings, Marjorie Kinnan, 17
Rocks
    Banana Rocks, 88–89
    Date-Nut Rocks, 87
    Pumpkin Rocks, 86
Rocky Roads
    Apricot and Date Rocky Road,
        300–302
    dark, 132–33
    light, 134
Rolled Cookies, 188–230
    Almond Sugar Cookies, 192–93
    Arrowroot Wafers from
        Bermuda, 215
    Big Newtons, 228–30
    Caraway Hardtack, 214
    Caraway Sour-Cream Cookies,
        210–11
    Chocolate-Chip Pillows, 222
    Coconut Cookies, 191–92
    Cornell Sugar Cookies, 220
    Danish Coffeehouse Slices,
        226–28
    Dione Lucas's Sablés, 218–20
    Ginger Shortbread Cookies,
        217–18
    Hamantaschen, 224–26
    Honey Graham Crackers, 200
    Hot Butter Wafers, 213
    Ischler Cookies, 206–7
    Joe Froggers, 189–91
    Les Petites, 194–95
    Plain Old-Fashioned Sugar
        Cookies, 221
    Prune Pillows, 223–24
    Rugelach (Walnut Horns),
        188–89
    Rum-Raisin Shortbread, 212–13
    Swedish Ginger Cookies, 202–4
    Swedish Honey Cookies, 201
    Swedish Rye Wafers, 195–96
    Tropical Sour-Cream Cookies,
        209–10
    Uppåkra Cookies, 216–17

Viennese Almond Wafers, 205
Viennese Chocolate Cookies,
    208–9
Whole-Wheat Honey Wafers,
    198
Whole-Wheat Squares, 196–97
Wild Honey and Ginger
    Cookies, 199
Rolled Cookies (Chocolate)
    Chocolate-Chip Pillows, 222
    Les Petites, 194–95
    Viennese Chocolate Cookies,
        208–9
Rolling pin, 6
    corrugated rolling pins, 288
    stockinette cover for, 6
Route 7 Raisin-Nut Cookies, 81
Rubber spatulas, 6
Rugelach (Walnut Horns), 188–89
Ruler, 6
Rum. See under Alcohol
Rum-Raisin Shortbread, 212
Rusks
    Black-and-White Rusks, 279–80
    Hazelnut Rusks, 277–78

S
Santa Fe Chocolate Wafers, 38
Sauce
    Devil's Food Chocolate Sauce,
        297
Savannah Chocolate Chewies,
    22–23
Savannah Crisps, 65–66
Sea salt, 220
Semisweet morsels, substituting, 17,
    256
Señoritas, 242–43
Sesame Fingers, 179
Sesame Seeds (as ingredients), 179
    Italian Sesame Sticks, 258–59
    Sesame Fingers, 179
Shiloh Farms rolled oats, 244
Silver Tipped Blossoms. See Cookie
    Kisses
Shaping cookies, 64–65
Shortbread
    Ginger Shortbread Cookies,
        217–18
    Rum-Raisin Shortbread, 212–13
Soho Charcuterie, 16
Sombreros. See Cookie Kisses
Sonrisa bakery, 16
Sour Cream and Pecan Dreams,
    254–55
Sour Cream and Pecan Topping, 255
Sour-Cream Cookies
    Blind Date Cookies, 89–90

Caraway Sour-Cream Cookies,
    210–11
Chocolate Raisin Cookies, 46
Cobblestones, 168–69
Cracker-Barrel Raisin Cookies,
    252–53
New Mexican Chocolate Icebox
    Cookies, 163–64
Nut-Free Walnut Jumbles, 82–83
Sour Cream and Pecan Dreams,
    254–55
Sour-Cream Ginger Cookies, 74
Tropical Sour-Cream Cookies,
    209–10
Sour-Cream Ginger Cookies, 74
Sour Lemon Squares, 113–14
Soy flour, 220
Spatulas, 6
Spiced Pecans, 303–4
Spices, 10
Squares
    Florida Cream-Cheese Squares,
        136
    Florida Lemon Squares, 137
    Johnny Appleseed Squares,
        115–16
    Palm Beach Pineapple Squares,
        138
    Pecan Squares Americana,
        100–102
    Pennsylvania Squares, 107–8
    Sour Lemon Squares, 113–14
    Whole-Wheat Squares, 196–97
    World War II Raisin Squares,
        112–13
    See also Brownies
Stimpson, Charles, 16
Stockinette cover for rolling pins, 6
    preparing, 11
Storing cookies, 13
Sugar, 10
    brown sugar, 12
    cinnamon sugar, 64
    confectioners sugar, 12
    pearl sugar, 217
    vanilla sugar, 242
Sugar (straining)
    brown sugar, 12, 210
    confectioners sugar, 12, 146
Sugar Cookies
    Almond Sugar Cookies, 192–93
    Cornell Sugar Cookies, 220
    Granny's Old-Fashioned Sugar
        Cookies, 63–64
    Plain Old-Fashioned Sugar
        Cookies, 221
Sunflower Coconut Cookies, 75
Supremes, 129–30
Swedish Fried Twists, 274–75

Swedish Ginger Cookies, 202–4
Swedish Hardtack, 288–90
Swedish Honey Cookies, 201
Swedish Rye Wafers, 195–96
Sweet Celebrations, 10
Sycamore Cookies, 67

T

Tartlets
    Almond Tartlets, 269–70
    Chocolate Tartlets, 267–68
Tea Cakes, 58–60
Texas Cowboy Bars, 150–51
Thermometer, 6–7
Thins
    Butterscotch Thins, 173
Tijuana Fiesta Cookies, 96–97
Timing, 13
Toasted Pine-Nut Cookies, 81
Tobler Tradition, 17
Toppings
    for Butterscotch Walnut Bars,
        144–45
    for Dark Rocky Roads, 132–33
    for Georgia Pecan Bars, 147–48
    for Light Rocky Roads, 134
    Meringue Topping for Coconut
        Grove Cookies, 45
    for Oatmeal Snickerdoodles, 92
    for 100-Percent Whole-Wheat
        Ginger Cookies, 62–63
    Pecan Topping, 101–2
    Sour Cream and Pecan Topping,
        254–55
Tropical Sour-Cream Cookies,
    209–10
Twists
    Swedish Fried Twists, 274–75
24 Karat Cookies, 83–84

U

Uppåkra Cookies, 216–17

V

Vanilla Butter Wafers, 98
Vanilla ice cream, 296
Vanilla sugar, 242
Viennese Almond Wafers, 205
Viennese Chocolate Cookies, 208–9
Viennese Chocolate-Walnut Bars,
    130–31
Viennese Linzer Cookies, 154–55
Viennese Marzipan Bars, 157–58

W

Wafers
    Arrowroot Wafers from
        Bermuda, 215
    Caraway Hardtack, 214
    Crisp Oatmeal Wafers, 55–56
    Date-Nut Wafers, 76
    Hot Butter Wafers, 213
    Lemon Walnut Wafers, 78
    Norman Rockwell's Oatmeal
        Wafers, 90–91
    Old-Fashioned Jumbo Lemon
        Wafers, 79–80
    Poppy-Seed Wafers (Mohn
        Cookies), 95
    Praline Wafers, 77
    Santa Fe Chocolate Wafers, 38
    Swedish Rye Wafers, 195–96
    Vanilla Butter Wafers, 98
    Viennese Almond Wafers, 205
    Whole-Wheat Honey Wafers,
        198
Walnut Filling, 143
Walnut Horns (Rugelach), 188–89
Walnuts
    cutting, 143
Walnuts (as ingredients)
    Austrian Walnut Crescents,
        253–54
    Banana Rocks, 88
    Blind Date Cookies, 89–90
    Butterscotch Walnut Bars,
        144–45
    Butterscotch Walnut Topping,
        144–45
    California Fruit Bars, 110–12
    Chocolate Aggies, 238–39
    Chocolate Applesaucers, 43
    Chocolate Banana Cookies, 42
    "Chocolate Street" Cookies, 39
    Chocolate Walnut Filling, 130
    Cobblestones, 168–69
    Connecticut Nutmeg Hermits,
        71
    Danish Coffeehouse Slices,
        226–28
    Date-Nut Rocks, 87
    Date-Nut Wafers, 76
    Extra-Bittersweet Chocolate
        Chunk Monster Cookies,
        26–27
    Fig Bars, 102–3
    Hamantaschen, 224–26
    Honey Date-Nut Bars, 152
    Hungarian Walnut Bars, 141–43
    Icebox Nut Cookies, 178
    Lemon Walnut Wafers, 78
    Mrs. L.B.J.'s Moonrocks, 52

Norman Rockwell's Oatmeal
    Wafers, 90–91
Nut-Free Walnut Jumbles, 82–83
Oatmeal Icebox Cookies, 175
Palm Beach Brownies, 117
Palm Beach Pineapple Squares,
    138
Prune Pillows, 223–24
Pumpkin Rocks, 86
Raisin-Nut Cookies, 57–58
Route 7 Raisin-Nut Cookies, 81
Rugelach (Walnut Horns),
    188–89
24 Karat Cookies, 83–84
Viennese Chocolate-Walnut
    Bars, 130–31
Walnut Filling, 143
Whole-Wheat and Honey
    Hermits, 70
See also Brownies
Wheat germ, 153, 220
White Glaze for Sour-Cream Ginger
    Cookies, 74
White Icing for Denver Brownies,
    122
Whole-wheat, shifting, 198
Whole-Wheat and Honey Hermits,
    70
Whole-Wheat Cinnamon-Nutmeg
    Cookies, 245–46
Whole-Wheat Cookies
    100-Percent Whole-Wheat
        Ginger Cookies, 61–63
    Whole-Wheat and Honey
        Hermits, 70
    Whole-Wheat Cinnamon-
        Nutmeg Cookies, 245–46
    Whole-Wheat Honey Wafers,
        198
    Whole-Wheat Peanut-Butter
        Cookies, 177
    Whole-Wheat Squares, 196–97
Whole-Wheat Honey Wafers, 198
Whole-Wheat Peanut-Butter
    Cookies, 177
Whole-Wheat Squares, 196–97
Wienerstube Cookies, 166
Wild Honey and Ginger Cookies,
    199
World War II Raisin Squares,
    112–13

Y

Yogurt (as ingredient)
    Savannah Crisps, 65–66

Metric Conversion Chart

Common Measurement Equivalents

1 teaspoon (tsp)	=	5 ml				
1 tablespoon (tbsp)	=	3 tsp	=	15 ml		
2 tbsp	=	⅛ cup	=	1 fluid ounce	=	30 ml
5 tbsp plus 1 tsp	=	⅓ cup	=	80 ml		
12 tbsp	=	¾ cup	=	180 ml		
1 cup	=	½ pint	=	8 fluid ounces	=	240 ml
1 pint	=	2 cups	=	16 fluid ounces		
1 quart	=	4 cups	=	32 fluid ounces	=	950 ml

Conversions of Ounces to Grams*

Ounces	Grams	Ounces	Grams	Ounces	Grams	Ounces	Grams
1 oz	30 g	6 oz	180 g	11 oz	310 g	16 oz	450 g
2 oz	60 g	7 oz	200 g	12 oz	340 g	20 oz	570 g
3 oz	85 g	8 oz	225 g	13 oz	370 g	24 oz	680 g
4 oz	115 g	9 oz	255 g	14 oz	400 g	28 oz	790 g
5 oz	140 g	10 oz	285 g	15 oz	425 g	32 oz	910 g

Approximate. To convert ounces to grams, multiply number of ounces by 28.35.

Conversions of Pounds to Grams and Kilograms*

Pounds	Grams/Kilograms	Pounds	Grams/Kilograms
1 lb	450 g	5 lb	2¼ kg
1¼ lb	565 g	5½ lb	2½ kg
1½ lb	680 g	6 lb	2¾ kg
1¾ lb	800 g	6½ lb	3 kg
2 lb	910 g	7 lb	3¼ kg
2½ lb	1,135 g; 1⅛ kg	7½ lb	3½ kg
3 lb	1,350 g	8 lb	3¾ kg
3½ lb	1,600 g; 1½ kg	9 lb	4 kg
4 lb	1,800 g	10 lb	4½ kg
4½ lb	2 kg		

Approximate. To convert pounds into kilograms, multiply number of pounds by 453.6.

Conversions of Inches to Centimeters *

Inches	Centimeters	Inches	Centimeters	Inches	Centimeters	Inches	Centimeters
1/16 in	1/4 cm	4½ in	11½ cm	10 in	25 cm	21 in	53½ cm
1/8 in	½ cm	5 in	13 cm	11 in	28 cm	22 in	56 cm
½ in	1¼ cm	5½ in	14 cm	12 in	30½ cm	23 in	58½ cm
¾ in	2 cm	6 in	15 cm	13 in	33 cm	24 in	61 cm
1 in	2½ cm	6½ in	16½ cm	14 in	35½ cm	25 in	63½ cm
1½ in	4 cm	7 in	18 cm	15 in	38 cm	30 in	76 cm
2 in	5 cm	7½ in	19 cm	16 in	40½ cm	35 in	89 cm
2½ in	6½ cm	8 in	20 cm	17 in	43 cm	40 in	102 cm
3 in	7¾ cm	8½ in	21½ cm	18 in	46 cm	45 in	114 cm
3½ in	9 cm	9 in	23 cm	19 in	48 cm	50 in	127 cm
4 in	10 cm	9½ in	24 cm	20 in	51 cm		

*Approximate. To convert inches to centimeters, multiply number of inches by 2.54.

Conversions of Fahrenheit to Celsius *

Fahrenheit	Celsius	Fahrenheit	Celsius	Fahrenheit	Celsius
170°F	77°C	300°F	150°C	450°F	230°C
180°F	82°C	325°F	165°C	475°F	245°C
190°F	88°C	350°F	180°C	500°F	260°C
200°F	95°C	375°F	190°C	525°F	275°C
225°F	110°C	400°F	205°C	550°F	290°C
250°F	120°C	425°F	220°C		

*Approximate. To convert Fahrenheit to Celsius, subtract 32, multiply by 5, then divide by 9.

Conversions of Quarts to Liters *

Quarts	Liters	Quarts	Liters
1 qt	1 L	5 qt	4¾ L
1½ qt	1½ L	6 qt	5¾ L
2 qt	2 L	7 qt	6½ L
2½ qt	2⅜ L	8 qt	7½ L
3 qt	2¾ L	9 qt	8½ L
4 qt	3¾ L	10 qt	9½ L

*Approximate. To convert quarts to liters, multiply number of quarts by 0.95.